Our Children's Burden

Also by Raymond W. Mack

Transforming America

Our Children's Burden

*Studies of Desegregation
in Nine American Communities*

Edited and
with an Introduction by
Raymond W. Mack

Vintage Books
A Division of Random House
New York

Vintage Books Edition, July 1968

© Copyright, 1968, by Raymond W. Mack

All rights reserved under International and Pan-American Copyright
Conventions. Published simultaneously in Canada by Random House of
Canada Limited, Toronto.

Manufactured in the United States of America

Vintage books are published by
Alfred A. Knopf, Inc. and *Random House, Inc.*

For

Julie, Meg, and Meredith

and the other kids
who inherit the burden—
and the opportunity

Our responsibility is not discharged
by the announcement of virtuous ends.

John F. Kennedy

Introduction

Less than a year ago I set out to select some American communities which would constitute a cross section of what is happening in the desegregation of education in the United States. From the wondrously varying universe of American communities, these represent a small and irreverent sample. Different economic bases, varying political structures, separate historical traditions, many religions and other national backgrounds are woven into the fabric of American society. How should one choose communities to characterize this rich diversity?

When a social scientist selects a set of sites for case studies, he wants them to vary not only on the factor he is studying—in this case, desegregation—but on the characteristics he suspects may influence that factor. We wanted, then, communities which would differ in their histories of educational segregation, differ in the kinds and amounts of segregation they currently practice, and differ in the process of desegregation. Two gross social characteristics seemed likely to assure a good deal of variation in these factors: the size and locations of the communities.

I decided to choose a few huge metropolitan areas, some small towns, and several medium-sized cities, at least one of each (small, medium, and large) in the South, with coverage of the Northeast, the Midwest, and the Southwest as well. Even these decisions leave a considerable amount of latitude in the choice of specific communities, until the final consideration emerges—I had to select scholars capable of doing the job.

If one is going to try in a matter of a few months to achieve some understanding of how a total community is structured, he must seize every available tool to accomplish the task. He must read, he must observe, he must listen to what people say and how they say it, he must listen for what they don't say. He must be alert, sensitive, and shamelessly opportunistic in data gathering. I am fortunate in counting among my friends a number of social scientists and social-science-trained writers who have worked at cultivating the skills necessary for community research. I set out to impose upon them and recruit them to join me in this project.

I chose field workers acquainted with communities of different sizes in the various regions of the country, and asked each field worker to do his observing and interviewing in the community he already knew best. To make our work as comparable as possible, I wrote a set of field research instructions and drafted an outline of what should be reported in each chapter. What I tried to do was recruit the best possible research people, specify enough about data and outline to guarantee some comparability among the community studies, and leave the instructions open-ended enough so that we would not lose interesting and meaningful data from overspecification of content or research approach.

The writers of the chapters bring various experiences and perspectives to the task. Nine of us are social scientists; two are writers—we all hope the occupations are not mutually exclusive. Three are women, two are Negroes, two white Southerners. Nine are teachers. All of us believe that racial segregation flaws the democratic and Judaeo-Christian ideals of America, and that success in desegregating our schools will test whether we can create and maintain an open system, encouraging each and all to achieve to the limit of his capacities.

This report is truly a joint one. It is a shared product to an extent unusual even in what is sometimes called team research in social science. We participated in planning each other's work and criticizing each other's manuscripts. Before going into the field, the researchers met at my home to discuss and modify the research instructions and the chapter outlines. When the field work was completed, we met again to compare notes, exchange findings, and evaluate alternative interpretations; each writer then went home to finish his manuscript. I have edited each chapter, but given the joint nature of the enterprise, have tried to keep the editing to a minimum.

Our cross-country tour of segregation and desegregation

in American schools begins in Riverside, California, in a freshly desegregated school system. We then move eastward to the Mississippi Delta: two studies, one of a small town and one of a medium-sized city, are combined in Chapter II. Our trip eastward through the South terminates with an analysis of desegregation in Savannah.

We then swing northward to the border town of Newark, Delaware, and continue to Long Island for a view of the suburban school system of Hempstead, New York.

Turning westward, we explore desegregation in Kalamazoo, Michigan, and then listen to the voices of teachers in Chicago, whose public schools are more segregated now than they were two years ago. We end our trip where we started, in Southern California, with an examination of the East Los Angeles Mexican-American ghetto.

This book is a summary and interpretation of what we found when we observed American citizens, black and white, in nine American communities, grappling with their most trying domestic social issue. One methodological note may be of interest. This research was initiated under the auspices of the U. S. Office of Education, in response to Section 402 of the Civil Rights Act of 1964. These case studies were undertaken to supplement the massive statistical survey designed and administered by James S. Coleman and Ernest Q. Campbell. Professor Coleman, Professor Campbell and I hoped that we might put flesh on the bones of the survey data by learning something from observation and unscheduled interviews about definitions of situations and the interactional contexts of the data sought by survey methods.

In evaluating the reliability of the conclusions reached from the two separate but related studies, it is appropriate to raise the question of independence of analyses and interpretations of the two sets of data. I went ahead and edited the eight field reports and wrote the summary and conclusions before seeing the outcome of the survey—indeed before analysis of the survey data had been completed. A comparison of the results from the two research projects perhaps justifies a kind word for those delicate and difficult techniques of data collection often described in our profession as "soft methods."

In no instance do the survey data and the observational data lead us to contradictory conclusions. On several important points, such as the amount of segregation in American public education, and the trends in desegregation, the separate studies independently arrive at parallel conclusions. In several critical cases, the data from one of the studies allow an informed interpretation of some data gathered in the other study.

For instance, we found that much of the pressure for desegregation stems from the Negroes' definition of the situation which equates desegregated education with improved education. The survey data suggest that the Negro parents' definition of the situation is factually accurate.

> . . . the earlier tables show that the principal way in which the school environments of Negroes and whites differ is in the composition of the student bodies, and it turns out that the composition of the student bodies has a strong relationship to the achievement of Negro and other minority pupils . . .

> The responses of pupils to questions in the survey show that minority pupils, except for Orientals, have far less conviction than whites that they can affect their own environments and futures. When they do, however, their achievement is higher than that of whites who lack that conviction.

> Furthermore, while this characteristic shows little relationship to most school factors, it is related, for Negroes, to the proportion of whites in the schools. Those Negroes in schools with a higher proportion of whites have a great sense of control. Thus such attitudes, which are largely a consequence of a person's experience in the larger society, are not independent of his experience in school.*

Since our two studies evidence a high degree of reliability where their focus is overlapping but were primarily addressed to somewhat different questions, we shall not allude to the survey until our final chapter of summary and conclusions. In that last chapter we shall summarize what we learned from our nine case studies and try to suggest general trends in education desegregation under five substantive headings:

1. Small towns and medium-sized cities, North and South, are desegregating their schools, at least to a token extent.

---

* James S. Coleman *et al., Equality of Educational Opportunity,* Washington, D.C.: U. S. Government Printing Office 908–869, July 2, 1966, p. 29.

2. Huge metropolitan areas, North and South, are resegregating their schools; the trend is toward more rather than less segregated educational facilities.

3. Negro parents have defined equal-educational opportunities as the route to the achievement of a better life for their children; Negroes equate desegregated education with improved education, and see both as providing access to the American dream of economic prosperity coupled with respect for one's personal worth.

4. Social organization is a critical variable for understanding the amount of desegregation in a community; protest pays.

5. Americans are asking their children to bear the brunt of the difficult social process of desegregation.

Raymond W. Mack

Evanston, Illinois

Contents

I

Violence and Civic Responsibility: Combinations of "Fear" and "Right"

Troy Duster

This report will differ from most of the others in this volume in two important ways. First of all, I was directly involved in the immediate school desegregation issue in Riverside, California, as a partisan. For example, I met in an advisory session with a four-man committee and the superintendent of schools during the six-week planning period for the Master Plan for Desegregation. My position was in favor of complete desegregation at the earliest possible time. In the final open hearings of the board of education, I delivered an argument from the vantage point of my academic discipline. And for a period of almost three years I had been somewhat active as a partisan in local civil rights matters. I knew personally several of my informants, either as friends or as adversaries—this is not the usual recipe for objectivity.

Second, I was asked to write this report just days after the school board's decision was reached. Desegregation was very fresh in Riverside, and the memories of the people I interviewed reflected this. Note with particular interest, therefore, the divergencies that exist in recall of the same event.

These two factors, in combination, make this report unique. I have tried to focus the study in such a way as to take advantage of these properties, rather than to allow them to act as stumbling blocks. In any event, I doubt that I can lay any claim to being the detached observer. The best that I can hope for is that my training as a sociologist has allowed me to "take the role of the other" and portray it.

The Watts revolt had just ended. Watts and Greater Los Angeles were still simmering in early September of 1965, and the whole of Southern California was on edge when "they" put a match to one of Riverside's three minority elementary schools and burned it down. It was done late at night and no one was physically harmed by the Lowell School fire, but its effect on the community of Riverside was wide-ranging and significant.

Within a few weeks little Negro and Mexican-American children were being transported by bus into previously all-white schools across the beautiful arroyo that had served for decades as a racial barrier, as a symbol to certain middle-class whites of having "made it." And for many of these whites the sight of little dark-skinned children crossing that arroyo signaled the end of the world.

Riverside, California, is a sprawling town of 130,000 people, located 60 miles east of Los Angeles. It is the tranquil twin of San Bernardino, ten miles to the north, population 100,000. Together they comprise a central urban complex of what natives like to call the Inland Empire. San Bernardino is a pulsating, vibrant town, predominantly working-class in flavor, while Riverside has all the appearances of a sleepy middle-American suburb spotted with gas stations and shopping plazas. The few members of the lower classes in Riverside tend to be the racial and ethnic minorities. It is certainly not unusual for minorities to be at the bottom of the occupational and social ladder, but the extremely small proportion of middle-class ethnics in Riverside provides a striking contrast with other cities in the United States.

The nature and quality of life are partially captured in the attitude of the San Bernardino law enforcement authorities toward Riverside. The San Bernardino police are disgruntled, they say, because juvenile delinquents from Riverside come over to San Bernardino to engage in vandalism, theft, and fighting, then get in their cars and go back to Riverside for the night.

It is a relatively quiet town, and if life has any richness and vitality, it must be found in the private sector. There is no public arena in which it is observable. Despite the fact that the city is host to a University of California campus, there is not a single bookstore which carries even a moderately reasonable supply of current books or paperbacks; there is not a single movie theater which presents the film as an art form; and there is no established off-campus meeting place for the students or faculty. The university has had few visible exchanges with or influences upon the character of the city.

The Scene Is Set

After the burning of the Lowell School the question of what to do with the displaced children who were to begin their fall semester in a matter of days evoked a response in the Negro community. There was a fear that either nearby Irving School, also predominantly Negro, would be used to handle the surplus, or the unburnt section of Lowell would be a triple-shift school with poor instruction. This issue awakened an otherwise indifferent Negro citizenry to a level of participation in civic matters unheard of up to that time. A school boycott was called. Freedom Schools were established under private auspices, staffed primarily by sympathetic community people, some students, faculty, and faculty wives from the nearby branch of the University of California. Negro and Mexican-American parents agreed to send their children to these makeshift classes, and they achieved an effective one-day boycott of the public schools.

It was during this period that the board of education began considering various possibilities, conducting informal inquiries on the problem, and most especially, listening to the sentiments of articulate members of both the minority community and the university. Arthur Littleworth, chairman of the board of education, said later in an interview that he was ". . . surprised and at first a bit resentful" at the Negroes' hostility and mistrust of him. The afternoon of the day the school burned down he discussed the relocation problem with a group of Negroes, but he was not prepared to offer permanent and thoughtful solutions. He reported later in an interview that he suggested a period of deliberation and assessment, a course which he believed anyone would regard as reasonable. "I was shocked at the response. They no sooner heard me say that we would have to think it over than they began to accuse me of stalling tactics, insincerity, and duplicity. It was not until much later that I learned how the mistrust of any white official is perhaps engendered by the kinds of contacts Negroes have with the social and political system of the city."

Because of the publicity of the Lowell fire, the recency of Watts, and the boycott, the school board decided to hold open hearings on the subject and to discuss with all interested members of the community at large the problem of segregation vs. integration of the schools. Riverside, like other middle-class American towns its size, has a history of segregated schooling that is not entirely based upon patterns of segregation in housing. True, there are always Negro ghettos in cities where the Negro population is large enough to be noticed as a minority group. Schools are usually built in or around these ghettos, and after a time the school becomes predominantly if not totally occupied by Negroes. According to the minorities, the city fathers engaged in a bit of gerrymandering in order to preserve the segregated schools. The "Longfellow Corridor," which will be discussed, was as conspicuous as an angry sore for knowledgeable Negroes in the town. It symbolized for them a statement of public policy: even the city officials were willing to admit to something undesirable in attending the minority schools.

In this setting the school board began to consider what to do with the Lowell schoolchildren. This was the official reason for the hearings, but the issue was clearly the larger one of what should be done about the problem of integration vs. segregation of schoolchildren in Riverside.

During heated public hearings petitions with two thousand signatures were presented to the board which were negative toward a busing plan. The chairman of the board estimated that approximately half of these signatures were on moderate petitions, requesting that more time and thought be given to the proposal before it was made permanent. The remainder were strongly against the plan for reasons that included everything from racist sentiment to the desire to preserve the standards of the curriculum, to "concern for the children" being bused. Most of the signatories were from the districts which wished to preserve the school system along residential lines.

The large issue which loomed before the school board was captured in a woman's angry question at the last hearing: "Are you in the business of social reform, or are you in the business of educating children on how to read and write?" The question came directly after an argument in favor of planned integration of the schools. The basis of this argument was that integrating the schools was the one last hope of salvaging contact between the races, and thereby helping to eradicate bigotry and prejudice in the community. The woman therefore put a question to the board and to the community which clearly stated the ideological issues under consideration: Is education tied up with the question of racial integration, or can it and should it be a separate issue?

One loud and clear strain from the community was that the quality of education was the solitary concern for a school board. Many white parents and some white schoolteachers and administrators said that they wanted the children to have the best possible education. If this was compromised by integrating the schools, then the integration of the schools, for them, was wrong:

> The school board has only one function, and that is to make sure that schoolchildren learn the school curriculum in the best way possible. Anything which goes against this primary goal they should cast aside. . . .

The speaker is a schoolteacher in one of the schools that was previously all-white, but which was the recipient of some of the transported minority children. An official of the Parent-Teacher Association of that school had this to say:

> I don't care what color the children are in this school. My only concern is that the schoolrooms not be overcrowded, and that the standards are kept high. The Negro and Mexican-American children are behind. It is clear from the record. It is just not fair to the children in this school that they be dragged behind by slow learners. That is the issue, and it has nothing to do with whether or not I am in favor of integration or segregation of the races.

As far as can be judged from the kind of study and review made of the community, this was the rhetoric of most who were opposed to the busing plan. There was a general reluctance openly to oppose integration of the schools because one was against integration. Rather, the strategy was to oppose the consequences of integration which were incompatible with high educational standards. As far as the anti-integrationists were concerned, the important consequences of integration are incompatible with high educational standards.

On the other side was a vocal and articulate minority. At one moment they could speak of the justice and justness of pursuing the "right" course, namely, integration for its own sake, and in the next could hint with only slightly veiled threats of more fires and another Watts if things were not righted. No other issue had served to arouse the Negroes of Riverside to such a level of community participation. Just five months earlier, when Negro political leaders had tried to get a Negro elected to the city council, Negro voters had been apathetic, despite the relevance of the election to minority problems, and few turned out to vote for the Negro candidate. More significantly, there was little grass-roots political activity by Negroes in the fight on Proposition 14, which had appeared on the ballot the preceding November. Proposition 14 revoked legislation which made discrimination in housing against Negroes illegal in selected cases. So, there had been a history, even within the last year, of dramatic instances in which Negroes might well have been aroused, but in which apathy had reigned. What was it about the school issue and the fire at Lowell that stirred the passions of these same people sufficiently to get them out at night, into community meetings, hot and angry, hurling bitter charges at the city administration, and more than anything else, setting up their own Freedom Schools? The answer to this question is complex, and the partial answer suggested here should be treated as one important contributing factor in an intricate matrix.

Almost two decades ago Ely Chinoy, a sociologist, published a study on automobile workers in the Detroit factories, and discussed their hopes and aspirations—and their resignations. Chinoy wanted to know if these men still held on to the American Dream that success and moving up in the social and economic levels of society comes from hard work, perseverance, and thrift. He wanted to know if Americans in such working-class occupations as factory piecework retained the hope that they would succeed in these terms.

He found that very young adults still talked about their own eventual social movement, but that by the time factory workers reach their late thirties they are more or less resigned to their continued existence in that social, economic, and occupational status. Interestingly, however, they have not abandoned the American Dream in a larger sense. These men transfer their own early hopes for success to their children, and firmly believe that the American class system is open to those who work hard and take advantage of the opportunities. The automobile workers felt strongly that their children could realize a better life, and invested themselves completely in this possibility. In a very similar fashion, many American Negroes cling to the American Dream. Like the auto workers, elderly or middle-aged Negroes are often resigned to their own stagnant positions, but cherish the idea that someday their children will make a great success. *The pathway that they see is education:*

> I didn't get a good education. That's why I have to work with my back. If I had known then what I know now, I would have stayed in school and worked hard at that. Now my child has got to understand that education and schooling is the way. You can't get anything in this world from the white man until you get enough education to outsmart him.

It is easy for this parent to understand why he can become involved directly in issues of public education, and yet ignore local elections and even Proposition 14. It is the one area where there is immediate and direct contact with the possibilities of achievement; and if Negro parents believe that their children are not being given the best opportunity for a good education, they can become aroused to action as in no other sphere of community life.

As has been suggested, many whites say that educational standards are primary, thereby equating high educational standards with the absence of Negroes. In that Negroes assume that white city administrators will give preferential treatment to white schools, they equate high educational standards with integration into these schools. Thus, the scene for battle is set.

———•———

Background and Context for the Problem

Riverside is best described as "one hour away from. . . ." Many residents regard as its unique blessing, others as its greatest curse, the fact that it is sixty minutes from the mountains and good skiing, sixty minutes from the beaches of Southern California, and sixty minutes from Los Angeles and night-life and culture. This fact greatly influences life in the city—the political, social, and recreational life in particular. For these reasons the city contains many people who came because they wanted to be "only an hour away." In this sense, it is different from cities of comparable size located five hundred miles from action. Many Riversiders are displaced urbanites who really want to be *around* a city, while many others are displaced rural types who want to be *near* the mountains and farms. On both ends they are people only one hour away from what they want and who they are. Their suspension is translated into the suspension of activity: "Why develop culture in Riverside when Los Angeles is only an hour away?" "Why develop night-life when . . . ?" Indeed, why develop when X is only an hour away?

Towns like Eugene, Oregon, must try to achieve something of their own as towns because they are ten hours from San Francisco. However, men come to Eugene because there is a certainty about the choice of life-style, of hunting and fishing with only a smattering of the "other." Political life in Eugene can absorb men as it cannot in Riverside, because the Riversider is continually reminded that he is "only an hour" from where the *real* political action is. This, at least, has been the case historically. The tale of racial segregation and racial integration of the schools brought a poignant reality to the community of Riverside that made its residents forget they had to drive an hour to get to an engaging public arena.

In the early 1830s, the Spanish and Mexicans displaced some of the Indians in the territory and settled the area. There was a very slow growth around an agricultural base of livestock and fruit until the early 1890s, when the area was incorporated. Gross population figures (Table 1) reflect a growth pattern that would be remarkable for any area except Southern California. Indeed, despite these figures, Riverside County has not grown as fast as the rest of Southern California.

Table 1: Gross Population Figures, City of Riverside*

YEAR	SIZE
1910	15,000†
1930	30,000†
1940	35,000
1950	47,000
1960	84,000
1965	133,000

* From *Riverside County*, A Report to the Riverside County Board of Trade by Industrial Survey Associates, San Francisco, September 1952.
† Figures for these two years are taken from *A Social Survey of Riverside, California*, Report to the Riverside Chamber of Commerce, October 4, 1930.

Using Colin Clark's now classic distinction between levels of economic activity, Riverside has clearly progressed to the "tertiary stage," with trade and service occupations predominating. Agriculture provides for less than 1,300 jobs in a labor market of more than 35,000, while trade and services provide more than half, with 18,000. A close second is industrial work, with manufacturing contributing little more than a third of the total jobs. The aircraft industry and kitchenware manufacturing are the most important of this group.

The population has grown very rapidly in the last twenty years, partly from migration but largely through the incorporation of adjacent areas within the last three years. The 1960 census lists only 84,000 for Riverside, but by 1965 its size was 133,000. Recency of arrival of the Negro population is revealed by the fact that some 60 per cent of the Negroes in the city have parents who were born in the South.

In 1953 Riverside adopted a city manager and city council form of government. Originally, the council was composed of seven residents of the city elected at-large. However, in 1963 there was a change to the ward system, with seven wards sending one councilman to city government. This system assured geographic representation, and resulted in the election of one minority member, a Mexican-American from the ghetto area.

The city manager is the chief administrative officer of the city, appointed by the council and responsible to it. The council establishes various departments of city government, and the manager appoints the department heads. The mayor is chiefly a ceremonial figure, whose task is to advise the council and inform the people of the activities of the government.

The city and county boards of education are separate units of government, not responsible to or controlled by local governmental authorities. The members of the city board are elected officials who make policy for all primary and secondary schools. The Riverside Unified School District Board is composed of five members elected to four-year terms. The superintendent of schools is appointed by the board, and he is responsible to it. The political organization should be kept in mind when we return to the discussion of the decision to integrate the public schools.

Riverside's Mexican-American population has been a significant, indigenous minority for a large part of the city's history. Reliable records on the subject do not antedate the late 1920s, but there is sufficient evidence for this period to make legitimate certain speculation about the ethnic composition before that time. Table 2, taken from a project report for the Riverside Chamber of Commerce, is interesting in that it gives a good indication of the proportion of minority members in the city, but the commentary in the report immediately following the table is perhaps more revealing as a glimpse at a history of an attitude toward a minority.

The document goes on to cite the ethnic distribution of minors in Riverside. According to the "Registration of Minors" report for 1927, the following represent percentages of various groups of children: "American" 81 per cent, "Mexican" 15 per cent, with Negro and Japanese 2 per cent each.

A California state law authorized and sanctioned separate schools for Mexican-Americans; it was repealed in 1946, but a long-established tradition is difficult to break, unless there is systematic effort to reverse the tradition. Until the middle 1960s there was no such effort in Riverside, and the effective segregation of the races into separate schools was a fact. Until about 1910 there was no minority "problem" in the schools. This was simply because so few Negro or Mexican-American children attended school in Riverside until this period.

Table 2: Births, City of Riverside,
1927–1929, by Ethnicity

	1927	1928	1929	(1927–1929) TOTAL	PER CENT
White	381	463	438	1282	70.3
Mexican	102	176	189	467	25.0
Negro	11	12	13	36	2.6
Japanese	10	14	4	28	1.5
Other	6	1	4	11	.6
					100.0

It will be noticed that a brisk increase in Mexican births has occurred in recent years and that the percentage of the total is more than 25. In other words, one-fourth of the births occur among Mexicans—a fact which from the standpoint of Americanization is of serious portent. Births among Negroes and Japanese are relatively few. These groups, therefore, do not constitute [a] serious . . . problem.

Although Negroes did not constitute a sizable minority until the 1930s, as early as 1910 they were very visible and more of a "problem" to city administrators than the above report would indicate.

Just before the First World War, Negro and Mexican-American families in noticeable numbers moved into the eastern portion of the city. They sent their children to the Irving Elementary School, and an immediate development was the construction in 1912 of the Lowell School just three blocks away. White children from the Irving School transferred to Lowell to avoid integration with minority children. An elderly Negro who has lived in Riverside for sixty years described the resentment his parents felt when seeing whites walk past Irving into the new school:

The only difference between now and then is that they were obvious about it then. Now, they're ashamed to admit what

they're doing. They build new schools for whites whenever
Negroes crowd over into an area and integrate a school. Then
all the whites run out of the integrated school into the new segregated school. It's a pattern in this town that's been going on
for fifty years.

The reference to the contemporary scene relates to the fact
that the Lowell School itself became slowly integrated during the
Second World War. The minority ghetto was expanding due to a
large migration of Negro industrial workers, and selected minority children were admitted to Lowell after a series of changes in
district boundaries. By the middle 1950s Lowell had a sizable
minority population. There developed at this time a need for a
new school. The Emerson, built just east of Lowell, received
whites into what was to be for a time a new segregated situation.
Not only did many whites who formerly attended Lowell go to
Emerson, but whites from other parts of the city were transported by bus into the new school. The inevitable happened at
Lowell: by 1961 it was half minority; by 1965 it was 95 per
cent minority. It was the Lowell School that "they" burned
down in September 1965.

There has been a long history in Riverside of maintaining
and reinforcing the segregation of schools by transporting schoolchildren by bus, henceforth to be called "busing." Quite contrary
to the present situation, all of the previous busing was of white
children. As far back as the period before the First World War,
white children were bused several miles across town, past minority schools, such as the Mexican-American school of Casa
Blanca, into white schools.

The school administration administers several batteries of
tests to pupils in the grade schools at various points in their
careers; the sixth grade is a critical point at which such tests are
given. In analyzing quantitative test materials for the sixth grade
of all the schools in the system, some interesting results could be
obtained that bear great relevance to the issue of segregated
schools. In 1961 a school that was predominantly white ranked
second among twenty-one schools in the "School and College
Ability" tests. During the next three years there was an influx of
Negroes into the area. By 1965 the same school had fallen to
tenth place among twenty-seven on the same test battery for that

grade. More dramatically, this school, which was almost completely white in 1961, ranked eighth among twenty-one that year on the quantitative tests. Just two years later, following the minority succession pattern (that rendered the school about one-third Negro and Mexican-American), that school ranked number twenty among twenty-three.

Economics and the Housing Situation

In the opening section it was noted that Riverside is now a quiet, predominantly middle-class town—that is to say, the whites, who constitute over 85 per cent of the population, are mainly middle-class. The Negroes, who are less than 4 per cent, have the working- and lower-class occupations. Approximately 60 per cent of the whites in the labor force are in white-collar occupations: clerical, sales, professional, or managerial. Of the Negroes who are employed, however, almost 75 per cent have blue-collar jobs, and over half of these are service workers and/or privately employed in households. Nearby March Air Force Base employs minority members in various capacities, and the huge plantation-like orange groves surrounding the area provide sporadic employment for some Mexican-American farm laborers.

Racial segregation can be seen in all facets of everyday life, so much a part of the orderly operation of things that it goes unnoticed and without comment. Citywide dances for teenagers, sponsored by the Park and Recreation Department, draw only whites. Men's fraternal organizations explicitly and formally exclude "non-Caucasians"; of the 130 women's clubs in town with over 10,000 members, a minority member is a rarity. The two ghettos in town have their own parks. Negroes contribute 10 per cent to the arrest rate, and the relationship with the police is a much discussed sore point in the Negro ghetto. Until 1963 the 150-man Riverside police force had only one Negro. A second Negro officer was hired recently, and the police department claims that no other Negro applicants have been able to meet the requirements.

As in the rest of the country, whites typically go to all-white churches, Negroes typically attend all-Negro churches. The Senior Citizens' Club, sponsored by the city, has twenty-one hundred members, but not a single Negro or Mexican-American. Segregation and discrimination are as silent as they are insidious, taken for granted and accepted as the natural course of things. There is no anger about it in the white population, hardly even awareness. Whites can point to nondiscriminatory public accommodations such as hotels and motels and restaurants to prove that their hands are clean. The only resentment they express about race relations is when they feel that Mexican-Americans or Negroes are about to encroach upon their personal lives or private property rights. In this the typical Riversider is a typical American. He voted overwhelmingly in 1964 to outlaw legislation which guaranteed equal housing opportunities to whites and Negroes on the grounds that it violated his rights to private property. He allows the state to tell him what kind of room specifications go inside his house; he allows the state to determine what kinds of business and commerce are allowed on his street; the state determines the kind of minimal education his own child is to get, etc.; but he feels violated by the state when he is told that he cannot practice racial bigotry in the *sale* of his property.

The housing situation in the city is critical to an understanding of the whole complex of issues in race relations, segregation, and education. Negroes remain in substandard ghetto housing through the combined efforts and practices of the real estate salesmen and the private citizens who own apartment buildings and houses. Most realtors in the town flatly and explicitly refuse to show houses to Negroes who want to leave the ghetto. Such Negro professionals as physicians and dentists who have the money to purchase property run into rigid barriers from realtors. A Negro college professor was told repeatedly by realtors in the city that they "did not handle Negroes":

I was shocked by the blatant character of the bigotry of the real estate people. I am not inexperienced in these matters. I have tried to obtain housing in larger cities. The same problems exist there, but the language used in refusing to deal with me was mild and somewhat apologetic. In Riverside there was no attempt to conceal the fact that I was affronting them by having the nerve to ask to see a house outside of the Negro area. It was as though there were a law, inviolable.

The speaker, a member of the staff of one of the colleges, continued to recount his experiences in seeking accommodations through private means and through contacts through the newspaper advertisements:

It is remarkable that there is not complete and total segregation. There is a tight caste-like system very similar to the situation in India. The major difference is that Americans think of themselves as equalitarian and individualistic. They seem unaware that since they all individually act the same way with respect to renting and selling housing to Negroes, they come up with a caste system just as powerful as the one in India. I don't know how many times I had property owners tell me that "It's not me, it's the neighbors." After months and months of this, most Negroes just give up and go to the ghetto. Some continue until they find one white property owner who has both (1) the integrity to pursue his convictions and (2) is not bigoted; and that takes quite a hunt.

The ecological and economic situation for ethnics in Riverside is therefore roughly similar to what it is in larger cities in the rest of the country. Of the 4,000 Negroes in the city, over 95 per cent live in the ghettos. Only 150 reside in predominantly white areas. The median family income for the total population in 1962 was almost $7,000, while for Negroes the median family income was only $4,000. The systematic character of discrimination is revealed by the fact that Negroes have a much higher educational achievement level than do Mexican-Americans in the community, but the median family income for Mexican-Americans is $5,000, a full 25 per cent more. It is even more remarkable that in the adult population over twenty-five years of age, 50 per cent of the Negroes were at least high school graduates, while only 18 per cent of the Mexican-Americans had completed a high school education.

However, it is easy to become distracted from the quality and consequences of discrimination by focusing upon differences between the minorities. The most striking and significant differences exist between the whites and the minority populations. In early 1960 an extensive household survey of Riverside was completed which used an index of socioeconomic status composed of a number of factors. The index divided economic levels into ten strata. Fewer than one in five whites fell in the bottom two socioeconomic categories, compared to two-thirds of the Negroes and Mexican-Americans in the same bottom two categories. More than one-third of the whites were in the top four levels, while fewer than one in ten minority members made it into the top levels. The occupational distribution figures are even more striking—44 per cent of the white "heads of household" were either professional or managerial in job status; but only one Negro in ten and an even smaller percentage of Mexican-Americans were in these occupations.

Thus it is that when we turn to education and hear teachers express a preference for children from upper-middle-class homes in Riverside, this preference tends to coincide with ethnic and racial boundaries. The chances are very good that a Negro child is *not* from a middle-class social and economic background. As we shall see momentarily, this is one of the most significant factors in the teaching of schoolchildren. The middle-class schoolteacher is convinced that the child from the upper-middle-class home is the "most tractable" learner in our present school system. The schoolteacher is, almost by definition, middle-class. It also turns out that almost by definition, she is right.

The Career and Career Mobility of the Schoolteacher

As far as the administrative officers of the school system are concerned, there is no such thing as career mobility in the schools. The chairman of the board of education says that while the various schools have different characters and atmospheres, there is no differential ranking. The director of personnel also indicated that in placing and transferring teachers in the school system, many different criteria are used, but rank is not one of them. That is, teachers who are judged good by some criteria are not sent to one school any more than to any other school. According to the personnel office:

> What few requests that we do receive for transfers from one school to another are never in terms of bettering the position. Instead, reasons are usually such personal ones as the desire to teach at a place closer to where one lives, or the request for a change of environment, and so forth.

A Riverside schoolteacher for five years and former president of the Riverside Teachers' Union had a quite different picture of the situation. First of all, he said, male teachers do not go into elementary school teaching as a career. Rather, if a man takes a teaching position in a grade school, it is usually as a stepping stone to an administrative job. (To this point we will return later, but it is more important here to focus upon the far more numerous female elementary teachers.) For females, he said, there is a definite pecking order of schools:

> The "good" schools are those which are predominantly servicing upper-middle-class families, and which have few if any minority children. In the late 1950s, the teachers felt that the best school in the town was Victoria. It is just across from the country club, and takes children from the old, stable, and well-to-do part of town.

This preference for the Victoria School and others like it is almost never expressed in terms of wanting to elevate one's own status by teaching there. Instead, the language is that "those children are the most tractable." A white schoolteacher who compared students from the schools in which she had taught said:

> Children from the Victoria area are just easier to teach. They come to school interested in learning. Their parents give them the motivation at home, and for those who do not, the parents are always hovering over them, checking up on their progress in class, and generally doing what *teachers* in the Irving and Lowell schools have to do before they can begin to teach. I suppose the best way to express it is to say that the Victoria kids sort of teach themselves. The teacher just presents the material. But at Lowell, you have to spend so much time getting past the *attitude* that teaching is extremely difficult.

There is movement from the less desirable schools to those where the women want to teach. The criteria for granting the moves are ambiguous, though principals of the schools have a large say in the proceedings. The predominantly minority schools have occasionally attracted a large share of idealistic young teachers who wanted to work with "problem" areas. The personnel office offered this information but also inadvertently admitted to a ranking system of good and bad schools. In response to a question about the relative quality of academic and administrative personnel in the minority schools, a personnel official said:

> As a matter of fact, we send some of our best, well-trained people into Irving and Lowell [minority schools] precisely because they have to deal with a more taxing kind of situation. When all the furor developed about how competent the teachers were at those two schools, we could point to records which indicated that these teachers were among the best in the school system.

This statement gives more than a hint of the idea that the administrative officials are aware of differential ranking of the schools, not only as it may vary by individual taste, but also in terms that are clear, public, and consensual.

As was indicated earlier, one important kind of career mobility for the schoolteacher is the move into an administrative position. It is very enlightening, therefore, to learn that Riverside has had only one minority group member in an administrative post, and he was only appointed in 1963. This means that in terms of the way in which employees within the school system see career advancement, Negroes do not advance. More important historically, Negro schoolteachers were not given assignments in the white upper-middle-class schools, which are regarded as the best assignments in the city.

> When I went in for my interview with the people at the school district office, I was told that there were not that many openings . . . that I would probably be given an assignment in the Irving School [Negro]. I expected this, since I had talked to other Negro teachers who had similar experiences. Like the rest, I accepted, because I wanted a job. It's best not to get labeled as a troublemaker *before* you get hired. Later on, I met

several other white teachers from other schools who were hired at the same time as I was, or even just afterwards . . . who were given assignments in the white schools.

This person is a Negro schoolteacher who was somewhat active in the civil rights movement in the area. As such, she was more active than most of the others, and was regarded as something of a "troublemaker" even in the school in which she worked because of her vocal criticism of the policy of sending Negro teachers to the ghetto schools.

I went back to the personnel office two years after I was hired, just to bug them. I asked why I had been assigned to Irving, when there were openings elsewhere at the time that I knew about. Their answer was standard, or at least it has become the standard position of that office ever since I can remember. They said that they were primarily concerned with "compatibility" of the schoolteacher and the school in which he is placed. It seems to me that their definition of compatibility comes very close to racial compatibility.

Certainly at one level this description is in concert with the official position of the personnel office. In an interview, the director of personnel indicated that the placement of new teachers is done by his office on the basis of an interview. The key issue, he said, is whether the prospective teacher has the background, training, and interests which make him likely to fit in well in a particular school. A staff member said:

There are many different kinds of schools in this city, each with its own atmosphere and character. For example, take the elementary school up near the university. The parents of the children there are university people, and they are demanding of the kind of education their children get, and rightly so. We just don't send *anyone* up there. We place teachers there who have a strong academic background and interest, and who are not likely to be pushed around or intimidated by professors. The same thing is true in a different way for the minority schools. We are very much concerned here with the problem of teachers trying to impose their values and way of life on others. Some of our teachers come in here with a strong middle-class background. Before we send them to the minority schools, we have to find out if they are the kind of people who are flexible in their views, and tolerant and understanding of differences that may be cultural.

When asked how this malleability was determined, the reply was that it came out during the interview with the applicant. This may explain how some white teachers are chosen to go into the ghetto, but it does not explain to the Negro teachers the small proportion of Negroes historically assigned outside the ghetto. As far as they are concerned, this is an "explanation" which cuts both ways:

> Because we are Negroes, it is "assumed" that we will be happier in the minority schools, and when that assumption doesn't coincide with our wishes, then the personnel office is sure that it knows best about our happiness. The personnel office claims to be able to tell from looking at you and talking to you for a few minutes what school district you "belong" in. Well, I guess they are right about that, only they could dispense with the interview part. . . . They can just look at a Negro and tell that he would not have the "cultural" background that made him "compatible" with the children of upper-middle-class whites, or should I say, incompatible with the wishes of the parents themselves, and the principals of those schools?   .

The following information is taken from an interview with a Negro elementary schoolteacher in Riverside who has been in the system eight years. In her first few years she was a substitute teacher and gained extensive experience in twenty of the then twenty-four elementary schools in the city.

> When I first approached the administrative office of the schools back in 1958, I was told that although I had a degree and many courses in education, I could not qualify to be even a substitute until I went back to school and took some more courses. Well, now it just so happened that I knew independently from some friends that a large proportion of white teachers had been given assignments with what are called "provisional credentials."

A provisional credential is a method of allowing individuals who have not completed all the formal course requirements and examinations and interning to teach in the schools on a temporary or year-to-year basis. Ordinarily, a teacher must have a full teaching credential if he is to receive a regular permanent appointment. The teacher in this interview presently has a full credential in the Riverside schools, but recounts the time when she did not, and was just starting to inquire about the possibility of employment as a substitute:

In addition to this private information, I had the luck of running across newspaper stories in the local press about provisional credentials. I clipped it out and took it to the County Superintendent of Schools. He has no formal control, but he called the City Superintendent of Schools and told him to look into the matter and make sure that there was no racial discrimination, and I was hired.

She went on to say that this issue of the provisional credential is one of the biggest problems that prospective Negro teachers face in getting into the school system. Of the more than forty Negro teachers, all of them have full credentials, she claims. This is in striking contrast to a significant proportion of the approximately two thousand white teachers who have provisional credentials:

> They do a lot of their recruiting in the Midwest, where they go after white students who obviously could not have completed the specific requirements demanded of the California system. Each state has its own policy, and its own sets of credentials that make it virtually impossible for one who is fully credentialled in one state to transfer. So, the Riverside recruiters go out of the state and bring in whites, never Negroes, and give them provisional credentials.

In relating her own experiences as a teacher in predominantly white schools, she said that her biggest problem was not with principals, other teachers, or the administration, but the parents of white children.

> They would actually call me at night to find out what kind of lesson I had planned for the coming week; they would ask that I give special attention to some minor problem which their child was having, or just anything as an excuse to inquire about my teaching. Other Negro teachers have experienced the same thing: as soon as some white parents learn that a Negro is in charge of the class of her little Johnny, she joins the P.T.A., comes to every meeting, comes to talk to the teacher, and for the first time in her life becomes a responsible citizen actively interested in the quality of education in the school system.

With the widespread desegregation of the fall 1965 semester, Negro teachers were scattered relatively evenly throughout the schools. Many of these teachers faced for the first time the kind of situation described above, and expressed to the person interviewed some of their means of adapting. In the elementary schools male Negro teachers confront the most important kinds of restrictions. Several have deep resentment because one among them whom they felt was next in line for the job of principal was passed over for a white outsider who knew nothing about the school. Instead, the person in question was given a "teaching-principalship," which means that he is a much harassed go-between for the real administrative power in the principalship and the other teachers in his school.

For the most part, however, the Negro schoolteachers in Riverside are a quiet lot who are not particularly oriented to problems which do not directly concern them *as teachers*. They are "classroom oriented" in the sense that their jobs as teachers assume paramount interest, and the occasional issues which creep up concerning minority relations in the community evoke little response unless specifically related to teaching.

A Mexican-American resident was very distressed about the lack of sophistication in the adult Mexican-American community about the importance of education:

> It is as though they were from migrant farm labor camps. If the child simply stays in school, that is regarded as success. Whatever minimal scholastic achievement he may have is usually in spite of, not because of, what happens in the home. The study that was done here a few years ago showed that the median level of achievement for Mexican-Americans was only seven years, for adults, whereas for Negroes and whites it is closer to twelve years. Well, these facts are fairly well known in the city now, and do you think it matters to these people? Up until very recently, the answer was *no!*

The respondent could offer no explanation as to why in the past two years the Mexican-Americans seemed to be taking a more active interest in the problems of education. However, he did point to one important fact which substantiates his observation about increasing concern. In the September 14, 1965, boycott of the schools, the Mexican-American community showed surprising solidarity with the Negroes and made the boycott effective. Participants estimate that more than half the Mexican-American parents joined the boycott, a remarkable figure for a community which for decades has had the reputation of being indifferent and apathetic in these matters.

There is considerable evidence that many elements in the Mexican-American community in Riverside, and in Southern California in general, have resented the attention, emphasis, and success of the Negro minority as a result of the latter's more aggressive civil rights activities of the last five years.

A great deal of federal, state, and local money has been channeled into selected Negro areas as a consequence not only of concerted effort and lobbying pressure, but also of the Watts explosion itself. It is widely believed in minority communities in California that several hundred thousand dollars in poverty money was poured into the Negro slum of West Oakland within a few weeks after Watts, precisely because the situation there was so similar, and therefore "ripe" for a repetition. Even before this development prominent members of the Mexican-American community in Los Angeles had expressed their strong disapproval of many favorite programs of the civil rights organizations of California. As an excellent example, the Mexican-American Chamber of Commerce in Los Angeles voted to support Proposition 14, a vote which supported the right to engage in racial discrimination in housing.

The important question, therefore, is why the Mexican-Americans suddenly joined the Negroes in the school boycott. The most plausible of answers to that question concerns the awakening of this community to the political consequences of collective action:

> The Negroes are right. The only way to get equal treatment in the search for jobs, housing, and schooling is to fight for it. Otherwise, you find yourself being closed into tight areas where the jobs are poorest, the schools are inferior, and the condition of housing is a natural consequence. But the Mexicans have always been indifferent to integrating into American life. We have our own traditions, and success in schools has never been one of them, nor has political activism. But the Negroes have begun to show the way. At first, the Mexicans were angry and hostile at being slighted. Now, many are coming around, and they see the way.

To the extent that this appraisal of the situation is accurate, it signals an important development in minority relations in the urban areas of the Southwest. If Negroes and Mexican-Americans begin to act together in these encounters with white administrators, it will be a force of great magnitude that will inevitably feed upon its own successes.

———————•———————

The Longfellow Corridor

The Longfellow Elementary School in Riverside was one of the few schools in the city with a relatively high proportion of Negro students *before* the Lowell fire. Close to one-third of Longfellow was minority in 1964, but it was not always this way. As late as 1959 there were only occasional instances when a Negro or a Mexican-American enrolled. Then, in the early 1960s, Negroes moved into one of the oddly protruding sections of the Longfellow district, the "Longfellow Corridor." Men act on the basis of what they *believe* to be the realities around them, and so an examination of their beliefs is critical to an understanding of their behavior.

The Negro Version of the Longfellow Corridor

According to the Negroes who participated in the school boycott after the Lowell fire, the Longfellow Corridor was a gerrymandered piece of land designed to keep the Longfellow School segregated. There was a thoroughly integrated school (the Emerson) in a nearby district that was "in danger of going Negro" in 1960. This was a consequence of the "invasion" and "succession" pattern of residence that is so typical of American communities. Simply stated, when Negroes begin to move into an area formerly occupied only by whites, the whites rapidly begin to leave. Riverside is no exception. There was a major north-south dividing line, however, which the Negro population did not cross, and this line bordered the Longfellow and Emerson Schools. There were whites who lived along the western border and who ordinarily would have gone to the closer-by integrated Emerson School. There was a sudden redrawing of the Lowell district boundaries to include an unusual protuberance along that western border from the Longfellow district which swallowed up the white residents and placed them in the Longfellow School.

This "corridor" in the Longfellow district enabled the white residents to send their children to the Longfellow School, and not to increasingly Negro Emerson. But invasion and succession patterns do not accede to school district boundaries. Within a few years' time, Negroes had crossed the western boundary line, and had moved into the Longfellow Corridor. Negro children began attending the Longfellow School for the first time, and within a few years Longfellow was one-third Negro. According to the Negroes, the Negro children in Longfellow School received a better education than Negroes in the predominantly Negro schools, and consequently they performed better. They used this argument to insist upon the integration of the schools.

The White Version of the Longfellow Corridor

· In simplest terms, there was no white version of this problem, in that so few whites either knew of or acknowledged the existence of a gerrymandered district. What was for Negroes a blatant administrative policy was to whites nonexistent. The only whites conversant with the existence of the Longfellow Corridor were a group of politically active liberals, mostly associated with the university community. Their view of the situation coincided with that of the Negro activists. However, the director of testing for the schools expressed surprise as to how anyone could have information about the performance level of Negro vs. white children for any school. She indicated that the school administration does not keep records on children by race, and the most that anyone could say about the relative academic performance of Longfellow Negro children vs. Lowell Negro children would be impressionistic.

Behind the Decision to Desegregate
(The Minorities' Version)

The Alcott Elementary School opened in early 1961, drawing a sizable white population from the Lowell School; Lowell became 90 per cent minority, and disgruntled Negro parents complained to the school board about the effective completion of segregation. Nothing happened for two years. However, in 1963 the school board did respond to some of the pressure to try to raise the quality of performance of minority students. A program of "compensatory education" was established. As far as many Negroes were concerned, this was a device to affirm and solidify the pattern of segregation in much the same manner as the South used the "separate but equal" principle prior to 1954. (Southern states poured millions of dollars into construction of new buildings and the renovation of older Negro school facilities between 1946 and 1954, precisely because educational facilities had been so unequal. Southern legislators in the Congress had heard of impending federal investigations of Negro education. Because they were still operating under the aegis of the Supreme Court decision of 1898, they concluded that the best way to head off integration was to meet the challenge by attempting to show that schools were racially separate, but equal in facilities.) A leader of the Riverside group in favor of integration said:

> In 1963, almost ten years *after* the Supreme Court denied the possibility of "separate but equal," the Riverside school board decided to upgrade its minority schools, rather than desegregate them. That was the reason for the compensatory education program. If it succeeded, it was to be used as a justification for a continuation of segregated schools.

In September 1963 an official communication from the school administration acknowledged that children from minority schools had lower academic achievement than children from white schools. Teaching interns from the university were used in special tutorial projects, libraries were installed and expanded in the minority schools, and several other programs were instituted. Negroes saw these things as tokens at best and bribes to keep silent about the segregation problem at worst. They used a report of September 1964 as documentation for their attitude. Whereas a report on the compensatory education problem in February of that year had called for a study of the segregation problem, the September report simply reminded the community of a search for "every means for promoting actual social and educational integration" as a *long-range* goal. The school board had not, by late 1964, achieved any satisfactory realization of the promises of reading therapists, school social workers, expanded adult education programs, Spanish cultural programs in the regular curriculum, or more field trips.

During the summer of 1965 several Negro and Mexican-American parents, concerned about what they regarded as the failure of the compensatory education program, decided to register formal protests. Robert Bland, a director of the school boycott, had this to say:

> Some of the parents were fed up with the compensatory education program at the Lowell School, and they wanted to transfer their children out. They ran into considerable trouble securing transfers, and this was what really led them to want to register collective protest. The first week of September, we circulated a petition among parents of children at the Lowell and Irving Schools, requesting a closing of these two schools, and requesting a program of integration. The petitions were signed *before* the Lowell School fire, because the fire occurred at 3 A.M. on Monday, September 7, and we presented the petition to the school board that same Monday.

During the week of September 1, the mayor was invited to a meeting of approximately thirty-five to forty minority parents from the Lowell and Irving Schools. Said Bland:

> At this meeting, tempers flared because we could not all agree about the procedures for putting pressure on the school board to desegregate the schools. It became very heated at one point, and one Negro, Don Harris, became so angry at the vacillation and disagreement that he got up and said, "If we don't stop postponing and discussing and postponing, people may get so fed up that we'll start to hear things like 'Burn, baby, burn' here in Riverside."

This version of Harris' statement is important to include here, because the mayor's recollection of the incident (to be repeated later) is at some variance, and it captured the mood of much of the white community's response toward what later happened with the Lowell fire.

Schools were scheduled to open on Monday, September 14. The Lowell School was set on fire on September 7. According to the Negroes, the Chairman of the Board of Education, Arthur Littleworth, came to talk to them on the Monday afternoon of the fire. Another Negro leader recounted:

> Even though the Lowell School was almost completely gutted, with only a few classrooms left, Littleworth told us that he was

going to keep the school open, with double shifts. He said he would arrange a nursery on the lawn outside of Lowell. This infuriated us, and more than any other single thing, it led us to the decision to boycott the schools.

The local newspaper, the *Riverside Press-Enterprise,* gave considerable play to the planned school boycott on September 8. The Los Angeles newspapers and radio picked up the story of the fire and the boycott immediately, and gave it primary emphasis, especially in the wake of the Watts riots. The Associated Press and the United Press International both carried the stories across the Western states, and Riverside was suddenly the focus of its most remarkable newscoverage since the speed races. On the following day, Bland says, Mr. Littleworth met with him to discuss the boycott:

> That Wednesday, Littleworth said for the first time that he would bus the children from Lowell into white schools, thinking that this would end the threatened boycott. By this time, however, the Mexican-American and Negro communities were aroused, and the leaders knew that they could not settle for less than a more complete integration of children in the *other* minority schools.

By the week's end the organizers of the boycott were committed to go through with it, and it is very likely that no matter what the school board promised, the boycott would have been attempted. As it was, there was a point on which the minority people felt they could legitimately rest a grievance. They demanded a specific time in the future by which the schools would be integrated, and set the deadline as September 1966. The school board refused to meet this demand, arguing that it would have to make extensive studies of the situation before the members could commit themselves to a time schedule that they might not be able to meet. The people who supported the boycott interpreted this as more hedging, more stalling, and, in general, as obstructionist tactics to delay or thwart integration. They could use as ammunition the integration promises of early 1964 which had not been realized, or even attempted (as far as they could see) in good faith. The boycott was called for the opening day of school, September 14, 1965.

Behind the Decision to Desegregate
(The Dominant Version from Whites)

We realize that children from homes in the minorities' section of town do not perform as well as children outside of that area. However, the key variable is economic status, and not color. White children from lower socioeconomic backgrounds in a certain school in town also consistently perform poorly by comparison with the town average. The variable is not race, but economic status.

The speaker is the director of testing in the Riverside school system. This version of the real problem at issue reflects the dominant view expressed by school administrators. The program of "compensatory education" which began in 1963 was an official recognition of this "class" problem, but it was directed only at the minority schools, and not at a lower-socioeconomic-status district with a school predominantly low- and working-class white. This simple fact indicates that regardless of the pronouncements of the administrators, they *act* in terms of the realities of the *racial* situation and not the socioeconomic elements and factors.

The program of compensatory education was achieving noticeable results, according to the director of testing services. A review of the records of students at the minority schools revealed that they were consistently scoring lower than children at the white segregated schools, and always had. This did not change with the new program, but two things need to be said about that: the whites felt that "compensatory education" had not been given enough time and allowed to develop; secondly, because the minority children remain on the bottom does not mean that they have not been improved. In sum, the chief administrators of the school system, all white, seemed to regard the program of compensatory education as a step which demonstrated their good faith. Further, they regarded it as moderately successful as far as it got. As a final demonstration of good faith on the race relations issue, in 1963 the school district appointed its first and only Negro to an administrative post, one tied into the compensatory education program.

Things were progressing peacefully and successfully, except for occasional disgruntlement from a few angry and militant Negroes, and a handful of parents of Negro children, who requested transfers away from the minority schools. Then, in late August and early September of 1965, these groups got together in a series of meetings, requesting that something be done immediately about *de facto* segregation in Riverside. The mayor, who attended one of these meetings, later recalled that he heard remarkable militancy and threats at this meeting; he remembered that one of the Negroes present had stated that unless Riverside desegregated the schools, it would "Burn, baby, burn," the battle cry of Watts.

The Lowell School did burn. Arthur Littleworth, Chairman of the Board of Education, later recounted his feelings and experiences the afternoon of the fire:

> We went out to look over the situation, to see what some of the alternatives and solutions might be. I felt that the only reasonable course to take was to say that we could not offer final solutions at that time [the afternoon of the fire], but that we would investigate further. I was distressed and a bit angry that this was interpreted by some of the people in that area as stalling tactics and duplicity.

The minority leaders threatened to boycott the schools unless their demands for desegregating the schools were met. In the middle of the week, before the publicity became so widespread, the administration treated the demands as impetuous. More privately, some voiced an opinion that the demands reached into the board's jurisdiction, and that these demands constituted an illegitimate violation of the territory of a legally constituted body:

> The board of education alone has the right to determine the boundaries of school districts. The demands of the boycott people were a clear encroachment of these rights, and the board should not have responded. It set a dangerous precedent that whenever a militant minority gets militant enough, it can have its way.

The great amount of publicity given the Lowell School fire and the threatened boycott was seen as an unfortunate development by many in the administration, in that it gave an immediacy to a problem that they considered long-range and complicated. The minorities' boycott of the schools began on the first day of classes, September 14. By this time a series of meetings between the boycott leaders and administration officials had produced remarkable convergence: all agreed in principle to the need for and desirability of total desegregation. The differences centered around the most effective means, and therefore the most appropriate and possible speed in desegregating. The leaders of the boycott demanded that complete desegregation be effected within one year The administration felt that it could not commit itself without further study.

After the first day of the boycott a compromise was reached. The board of education agreed to set up an immediate study plan for total desegregation, and report on it *within six weeks,* in return for an end to the boycott. There was some internal dissension within the minority population as to what should be done. One group wanted to accept the six-week moratorium. Others pressed for complete and total desegregation *now.* Because they could not agree, they obviously could not have as effective a boycott, and so the boycott ended after only one day. Meanwhile, the busing of minority children from the burned Lowell School began.

During the six weeks between the opening of schools and the October 18 date for a desegregation plan, the community of Riverside was aroused from its typically somnolent, politically apathetic state. Mothers who previously knew nothing about the political structure of the community were suddenly aware of the relationship between the city council and the board of education. The city council refused to take a stand on the desegregation issue, arguing that the school board was independent, and should make independent decisions. The council, however, was one of the only groups with some formal relationship to the issues that did not take a stand. Organizations all the way from the independent California Democratic Clubs to the affiliated California Teachers Association lined up and took sides. Old established clubs took a stand, and new neighborhood associations were formed for the purpose of taking a stand. There is no official way of recording precise organizational support or lack of it, but the impression is strong among people who were active and knowledgeable in the community that while most *organizations* formally stated support for integration of the schools, most *individuals* were ambivalent to negative. Petitions with over two thousand signatures indicated that 90 per cent of the signators were against the integration program.

The school board held two dramatic open hearings in October. At the end of the second hearing, they came to a decision.

The Final Open Hearings and the Vote to Desegregate

On a Tuesday evening in late October 1965 more than five hundred people jammed into an auditorium, standing-room only, to continue and conclude the public hearings on the school board's master plan for desegregation. It was an evening filled with suspense, emotion, and some foreboding, because it was rather well understood that the five-member board of education would vote that very evening on whether to integrate the schools. People on both sides were afraid of an unfavorable outcome. It was often said that the meeting was a mere formality; that the board had already made up its mind how it was going to vote; that the hearings were simply used to simulate responsiveness to public sentiment and expression.

A wide range of social types filled the hall, and their views and manner of articulating them covered the entire spectrum of life-styles in Riverside. There were extremely stylish and sophisticated women from the old established area of town; interested undergraduates from the nearby colleges who came to see local politics in action; grandmothers from the poorest section seated next to well-dressed businessmen and their wives; middle-class Negroes and Mexican-Americans; some angry working-class Negroes and some angry working-class whites, both early adult; representatives from the state and county offices of education; some of the liberal faculty from the university and some of the conservative *nouveaux riches* from an area that was especially threatened; schoolteachers and principals from the schools; and parents of children who had been dropouts. They were all there, and it seemed that all had some passionate interest in the outcome.

The Chairman of the Board of Education, Mr. Littleworth, made some introductory remarks, asked that the audience refrain from emotionalism and listen to each speaker, and then opened the hearings to public discussion. The topic under discussion was the superintendent's "Proposed Master Plan for School Integration." The critical feature of the plan was the superintendent's proposal to close the two predominantly Negro schools and transport these schoolchildren by city bus to what had been predominantly white schools around the city. Of the first ten speakers, six were firmly opposed to the plan, two asked for clarifications, and two spoke in favor of it. After each speaker finished his say of a few minutes' duration, parts of the audience applauded vigorously or remained silent, depending upon the side taken. The largest and the loudest segment of the audience was opposed to the integration of the schools.

The most vocal group of speakers opposed to busing minority children into white schools were parents from an area which was very newly built and very upper-middle-class. The school itself, the Alcott, was only four years old. Many of the homes which sent children to this school had been built only within the past three years. The Alcott School was on the "right" side of the arroyo; to live there, with no Mexicans or Negroes in sight, with Proposition 14 security that none would be in sight, to send your children to a newly built all-white school, was to have achieved a level of conspicuous success:

> What are the Negroes saying about themselves when they want to integrate with the whites? Are they admitting that they are inferior, and the only way that they can overcome it is to associate with whites? The school board seems to be going along with this line of reasoning. They say that the facilities in the Negro schools are just as good, so it must be that they just want to be around us.

This speech got a resounding applause from the audience, but not so much as the woman who said that:

> We have the right to discriminate. We've earned it. This is America, not Red country, where the state tells you what to do and think.

But the audience was made a bit uneasy by blatantly racist language of a young man about thirty years old, who got up and walked menacingly down the aisle toward the front table, and told the board:

> I don't want my children going to school with no Polacks, no Jews, no Mexes, and no Niggers.

Shortly after this speech a well-dressed and articulate middle-aged man rose to say that he wished to "disassociate myself from the racist elements in the audience, but. . . ." His statement set forth a theme that was the dominant plea of the moderate group who asked only for a delay of integration: the Alcott School was already overcrowded, and the school board was sacrificing its primary function to an extraneous goal.

A second important theme in the criticism of the superintendent's plan to desegregate was the complaint about the cost of transporting the children. Many resented the fact that their tax dollars were being spent to bus children. They wouldn't care, they said, if Negro and Mexican-American children came of their own free will and by their own means, but to bus them at public cost was unfair. These people were ignorant (or chose to be ignorant) of a long history of busing white children past the Mexican-American school into white schools. Others argued that busing was a violation of the neighborhood concept of schools, an idea that was vital to maintaining the "integrity" of the community.

There was veiled guilt and justification of 1949 clichés. Several of those against the integration plan rose to relate how "some of my best friends are Negroes." One woman, who presented to the board chairman almost eight hundred names on a petition opposing integration, recounted a long episode in which she once held a Negro baby at a bank window for a woman for a few moments.

Those in favor of the integration of the schools were outnumbered. Their arguments were largely counterstatements to those of the other camp, such as a display that the cost of busing was minimal and insignificant, easily covered by the budget, etc. There was an attempt by this group to raise a larger ideological issue that had not been freely discussed previously. The argument was presented that formal education is very much tied to the "broader" education of the community, and should include such matters as the reduction of racial and ethnic prejudice and discrimination. In this line one speaker favored the integration of the schools solely on the grounds that it would produce contacts between the various groups at a relatively equal level, thereby reducing the degree of intergroup hostility in the community.

This statement evoked a counterargument that also achieved the status of a firm ideological posture:

> The schools are not a social reform agency. They are in the business of teaching children how to read and write, and they are not to allow a zeal for social reform to get in the way of this primary task.

So spoke a white mother who argued that the subsequent overcrowding of the Alcott School (as a consequence of integration) would sacrifice the high educational standards. This, she concluded, was an intolerable violation of the *real* function of a board of education.

The board handled the issue with deftness and incorporated both positions. The chairman of the board said in private session that the board had to serve two functions: not only must they be concerned about imparting skills to the schoolchildren, but they must also be concerned with the broader education of the child. As such, they were committed simultaneously to the broadening of the child's experience through integration and also to the acquisition of his technical education.

The Vote

After several hours of heated discussion Mr. Littleworth summarized the various positions. He concluded that the petitions to delay integration were not justified; that the board had made an exhaustive study of the economic problems in executing the desegregation plan and found it feasible. More than that, he said, he found that it was "right." Each of the other members of the board was asked to comment. There was no dissent in the even, cautious language of committee members who had heard these arguments before. In turn, each of the four members cast his vote in favor of the superintendent's plan for busing minority children into white schools. The battle was over. Men and women and children filed out of the auditorium. Some were elated, some were angry and hostile, but most were simply resigned to the inevitable.

———————•———————

Summary and Prospects

Riverside, California, is one of the three communities in the state which has instituted a systematic plan to integrate its public school system. California is the largest and one of the most progressive states in the country. It is easy to conclude that most other cities have not instituted such programs, and have no intention of doing so.

Riverside integrated its schools primarily because someone set fire to the Lowell Elementary School *in the wake of* Watts. True enough, the school board voted unanimously to integrate the schools because, in their own terms, they had come to believe "that it was the right thing to do." The important point of this analysis, however, is that they were led to come to that conclusion only after a threat of violence hung over the city. They did not come to that conclusion independently, or if they did, they were certainly not going to act upon it without the fire as a catalyst.

The white community voiced a real fear. They argued that to accede to the wishes of the minorities under these conditions was to bow before a threat of violence, and thus to feed the idea that concessions can be gained by violent activity. That would appear to be true, but one of the things that must strike social scientists in the United States with continual awe and amazement is not that there is so much violence from Negroes, but that there is so little. As a tactic, it seems to produce results.

The violence of Watts produced an unclogging of the networks of the poverty program that had been tied up for months and months in local civic squabbles around the nation. The Lowell School fire set Riverside to responsible civic participation and discussion, and, finally, to what was called the "right" action.

Negroes are becoming increasingly militant about civil rights in general, but it also seems clear that they are beginning to focus upon the education of the child as an issue of that militancy. If that is true, we can look for the equivalent of more Lowell School fires. The trouble, of course, is that while Riverside is a small enough town with few enough Negroes (four thousand) to transport by bus, a city like Chicago or New York or Los Angeles would run into a critical tactical problem. How could any of those cities effectively bus a quarter of a million children for miles and miles outside of the ghettos of Harlem, the Near South Side, or the East Side without serious problems?

Certain features of this report are already dated. In the two short years that have elapsed since this paper was written, Newark and Detroit have exploded, and there have been such significant changes in the mood of blacks and whites concerning integration that it seems more like two decades. As a small example of changes in the atmosphere, if I were to write about a similar development now, I am sure that I would use the word "black" at almost every point where I used "Negro" in 1965. That is because "blacks" have taken over many of the leadership roles in the increasingly militant black revolution. This is an important factor, for there is now much more ambivalence over the question of integration of the schools in the black community. Though the majority probably favor some form of desegregation, blacks are now moving further and further away from integration as a primary strategy. Baldwin's phrase is repeated over and over again—"Who wants to integrate into a burning house?" The trouble that we now see more clearly than ever before is that school integration is insoluble when viewed in isolation from residential segregation. The great resistance of Boston and more recently of San Francisco and Chicago to "busing" has come both from whites and blacks. The still wet print of the President's Commission on Civil Disorders casts a gloomy pall over what appears to be the choice we will make of our last remaining choices, violence or civic responsibility.

II

Tokenism in the Delta:
Two Mississippi Cases*

———•———

Michael Aiken and N. J. Demerath III

* We are indebted to Cora E. Bagley for research assistance and to many others—Southerners and Northerners, academicians and nonacademicians—for critical readings of the manuscript.

THE REAL CHOICE is whether we're going to obey the law with Federal aid or obey the law without Federal aid. . . . If we sit back and say, "Make us, sue us," then we only postpone the inevitable until after school starts. Then we would be faced with real administrative chaos, and I don't feel we should visit that on our schools (*White school board president*).

Those of you who do not want to send your children to school with niggers, get out and vote against these liberals and cheap politicians who would jeopardize your child's future for future gain. . . . Go out of town to buy before trading with integrated merchants. . . . The yen for profit has warped the sound judgment of these business leaders (*Midnight leaflet from "White Voters' League"*).

So far it's been a honest-to-God miracle. There ain't been any real troubles; our kids has been treated pretty well. It can be did, but it's just beginning, and the real trouble ain't even begun yet (*Parent of a Negro child in a white school*).

W̲ith more of a whimper than a bang, school desegregation came to much of Mississippi in the fall of 1965.[1] This is a report on its problems and its prospects as of the winter of 1966. It is a distillation of interviews with many different people in two quite different contexts within the Mississippi Delta: one is a growing city with some forty thousand people and a tradition of cosmopolitan elitism; the second is a rural county with a host

[1] The qualifying phrase "much of" is important here in two senses. First, five Mississippi localities were desegregated by court order for 1964–1965, although in one of these towns no Negro students chose to attend the white schools that were technically available to them. Second, however, there are a number of Mississippi communities which are still segregated in their schooling either because of outright refusal to comply with the federal requirements or because, again, local Negroes have been too intimidated to take advantage of the "free choice" that is legally open to them.

of small towns still encapsulated within the "closed society." Throughout this report we strive for objectivity. But let it be said at the outset that we are two former Southerners who returned to the South with a firm faith in the virtues of equal opportunity and an uncomfortable apprehension concerning Mississippi, the "land of violence." These are our biases, but there are further qualifications that also belong at the beginning.

Although neither of us is a stranger to the South, we spent only eight days in this particular region for this particular study. Like every other report in this volume, this one is impressionistic. There is nothing wrong with impressionism or even impressionistic sociology within limits. However, there are special difficulties with topics that produce anxiety in a climate where candor is suspect. Talk about race relations is not cheap with either Mississippi whites or Mississippi Negroes; it is especially difficult to communicate with both groups on a single visit to a small town. While many of our respondents were surprisingly gracious and forthright, others were frightened or coy. Most of our questions received direct answers, many were either answered too well or not at all. In short, it is always hard to assess conversational data, but particularly in the present case.

Then too, consider the problems of sampling, or, rather, the consequences of a "non-sample." With whom does one talk to learn the pulse of a community or the range of its opinion? Elected officials are often public relations specialists; bureaucrats frequently suffer from both myopia and the pressures of self-preservation; dissidents sometimes bloat their concerns out of perspective; and the mythical average citizen often cares little and knows less. Yet with all their disadvantages, these are one's informants. Moreover, the problem of sampling individuals within communities is reflected in the additional difficulty of sampling communities within a state or states within a region. Mississippi, often stereotyped as a monolithic structure with little variation and still less flexibility, in fact has sufficient heterogeneity to give pause to those who would single out one or two communities as "representative." It is true that we have taken pains to consider two quite different contexts. Still, both are part of the Mississippi Delta, and the Delta itself must be distinguished from the "hill country" to the east and the "Gulf Coast" to the south. In Mississippi geographical distinctions become sociological distinctions, hence, generalization from one area to another is risky.

Without systematic empirical techniques one is left to weave a rug of truth out of dubious threads. If there is any hope at all, it lies in a conceptual loom that allows one to pick and choose according to a broader orientation. But this in itself can be dangerous. Quick conceptualization may be seduced by first impressions and first respondents. Add a manuscript deadline, and there is little opportunity to retreat from early analytic commitments with the wisdom of leisurely hindsight. In sum, our conclusions include a great deal of conjecture and very little certainty. While we are confident that we have isolated important variables in the desegregation process, we are unsure of their relative weights and interrelationships. We have understood more than we expected, but we have no illusions of any grand design or ultimate rigor.

Part of our reservations, however, stem from the subject matter itself. Mississippi's school desegregation has barely begun: even white teachers, administrators, and citizens confess that the present stage is merely token compliance; most expressed fears of what is yet to come. It is true that there have been few serious incidents so far, but all concerned are hesitant about using the present to predict the future. As the proportion of Negroes in white schools increases, as whites begin to attend Negro schools, as faculties become integrated, and as other aspects of the community become more affected, harassment and even violence may emerge. We have taken a single blurred frame out of a film that is just beginning. Its ending holds suspense for the nation as well as for the actors who must play it out.

Just as we have reservations about predicting future school desegregation, we also have reservations about generalizing in other aspects of the larger desegregation process. It is true that the initial step in the schools has been a success as far as it has gone, but it is also true that the schools have certain advantages not afforded the desegregation of jobs, housing, public accommodations, political affairs, and day-to-day social relations. As we shall see, school desegregation has benefited from bureaucratization, a dependence on the federal government, and the fact that it involves children out of the mainstream of daily life rather than adults within it. This is not to say that the schools do not have troubles of their own ahead, but rather that the problems awaiting desegregated education are neither as severe nor as widespread as the problems awaiting other aspects of life.

Finally, the names of places and people have been changed throughout to protect the guilty as well as the innocent. A necessary condition for respondent rapport, this is itself a commentary on the open wounds of the Deep South. Our intention was not to serve as Feds, finks, or pettifoggers. Yet even the results of anonymous research can be harsh.

So much, then, for the introductory qualifications of the study.

A Romance Gone Sour

The Mississippi Delta is a flat half-moon of rich alluvial soil occupying the northwest corner of the state and tucked into the bends of "the River" between Memphis and Natchez. Here the Black Belt is blackest, not only because of the large proportion of Negroes, but also because of the dark earth that lies in sharp contrast to the red clay east and south. The area basks in the romantic imagery of the old plantation society, where cotton was king and the Negroes its vassals.

The Delta was purchased in 1820 from the Choctaw Indians by the U.S. government, and the first settlers arrived several years later. Anxious to escape the influence of incipient abolitionism and eager to amass their fortunes in splendid isolation, they gradually converted a swamp forest into one of the richest farming regions in the world. Yet these were no frontiersmen. One long-time resident recalled them this way in a publication of a local county historical society:

> The pioneers . . . were not the rough-and-ready type so often associated with the winning of the American West, clad in Conestoga boots and buckskins. A great many of the men and women . . . were from families of wealth and culture in the older South. . . .

Certainly the pioneers made a quick leap to the status of aristocrats, a leap over the toiling backs of over the 85 per cent of the population who were Negro slaves. Labor, land, and levees seemed to insure continued prosperity. But then the war. It is difficult to rely on local histories for accounts of the "great Southern tragedy" and its bitter aftermath. These are "white" histories, which combine sentimentalism with righteous indignation. But certainly there was suffering, and not only from the privations of war and political control by the Negro Radical Republicans and the carpetbaggers' Freedmen's Bureau. In 1878 a yellow fever epidemic cost River City a third of its citizens, including the mayor and all but one of the city councilmen. But the Delta recovered, and by 1890 the planters were back in control and the Negroes were back in harness, both politically and economically.

The biggest single impetus to renewed prosperity was the railroad. In 1884 the Yazoo-Mississippi Valley Railroad completed its trunk line through the Delta, linking Memphis to New Orleans. Further east-west spur lines provided a transportation network that opened the area for the exportation of both timber and cotton. Small towns began to dot the railroad tracks. The population grew quickly. As the rural areas thrived agriculturally, River City became a financial and distribution center. By the turn of the century it had become a city rather than a mere steamboat landing.

The Delta's prosperity continued through the first two decades of the twentieth century. But as early as 1920 the area began to undergo ominous changes. During the twenties came the first evidence that King Cotton could be brought to his knees. Even Delta Negroes began to leave for the North and the world of industrial employment prior to the Depression. Since then, the Delta as a whole has seen a gradual population decline, although River City has absorbed rural refugees and continued its own growth as an urban haven.

Since World War II, changes in the Delta have been even more dramatic. A number of interrelated factors have gone far to transform the old way of life and to effect a change of mood from the romance of prosperity to the drama of impoverishment. First, the traditional cotton economy has been the victim of a variety of technological innovations, including mechanization (tractors, cotton pickers, etc.), improved seeds and fertilizers, and highly efficient chemicals to control the growth of weeds and grass. Such innovations have greatly increased the per acre yield of cotton. In the pursuit of market equilibrium there has been a steady stream of Federal controls limiting the number of acres to be planted each year. Indeed, the relation between federal reductions in acreage allotment and the planters' efforts to exploit the available acreage has produced a cycle with additional technological innovations and still more restrictions. The situation can be seen statistically on a national basis. In 1953 there were 28 million acres in cotton in the U.S. This decreased to 16 million by 1965 with another reduction of 35 per cent in the offing for 1966.

The consequences have been a Southern analogy to the nineteenth-century Industrial Revolution of Western Europe. The small farmer, whether white or Negro, has been squeezed out and the Southern sharecropper system has been virtually eliminated. According to the figures of the Mississippi Employment Security Commission, some 6,500 of the 26,000 Negro tractor drivers employed in 1965 in the Delta would lose their jobs in 1966. The 25,900 cotton choppers and pickers of 1965 will be cut by half in 1966. While it is true that tractor drivers earn only six to eight dollars a day and the choppers and pickers only three dollars for a twelve-to-fourteen-hour shift, there is little employment and less money to be had elsewhere. Mississippi's average weekly welfare payment was $10.72 per case, and this includes only the blind, the disabled, and the aged, as well as those on public assistance and A.D.C. children. Thus, the average yearly income for such cases was only $514.44 (using the same June 1966 date), a figure that is well below any accepted poverty level and one that places Mississippi fiftieth among the nation's states. Perhaps predictably, the local administration of surplus food has been the object of considerable grievance by Negroes in general and by striking plantation workers in particular. The forty-nine Negro residents of the fabled Tent City in the heart of the Delta have no illusions of eliciting concessions from the mechanized plantations. But they do hope to attain a life and land of their own, and tactics such as the "live-in" at a nearby deserted air base are meant to win national support for federal programs that have been impeded by local administrators. One woman was quoted recently on her lot, referring to white plantation owners simply as "The Man."

> The Man didn't want me. Once the acreage got cut, he didn't need me. There wasn't nothing for me to do. I really need somebody's help 'cause I ain't got nothin' but a husband and three kids. [A remarkably small family at that.]

One possible answer is, of course, to leave. Great numbers of displaced agricultural laborers—both white and Negro—have emigrated to cities in the South as well as the North. In 1950 the Delta's eleven-county area had a population of 409,732. Between 1950 and 1960 there was a net out-migration of 137,426 persons, and the fertility of those who remained was unable to prevent a decline of more than 10 per cent in the area's population. These figures reflect the situation of the state as a whole: over 1.2 million of those currently alive and born in Mississippi have moved out of the state, and this in a state whose current population is just over two million. Illinois has the highest proportion of those now living elsewhere—nearly one-fifth. The proportion of Negroes in the Delta has steadily declined over the years, from over 85 per cent in 1860 to 73 per cent in 1940, and finally to 65 per cent in 1960. These figures reflect the Negro's tendency to quit the South altogether and trade rural poverty for the urban poverty of places like Chicago.

But the census reveals more than out-migration. The economic transformation is also manifest in the shifting base of the labor force. Over 70 per cent of the employed workers in the Delta were in agriculture in 1940, but only 40 per cent were in 1960. Industry apparently abhors a vacuum, since it has moved in to fill the void left by a retrenching cotton economy. The state has encouraged industry ever since the Depression, when it established a program to Balance Agriculture With Industry (BAWI) in 1936. After World War II, and especially in the last decade, industry has responded increasingly to the call of a tax break and cheap, non-unionized labor. This is particularly the case in River City. In 1960 almost 20 per cent of its labor force was involved in actual manufacturing. Since then several additional plants have moved into the city and the figure has probably risen to almost 25 per cent, a proportion that is above the average of the South if slightly below the national rate. But the city, like the region, has yet to sever the tie with cotton. Industry has not been able to absorb a great many agricultural workers who are unskilled, perhaps untrainable, and who continue to live in plantation shacks with dwindling plantation wages. The Delta partakes of the nation's irony; there is a crisis of unemployment but a shortage of workers, and the lack of skilled labor is a prime impediment in attracting more industry.

The economic crisis of the South provides a backdrop for still another drama, which has played to a more attentive audience—Freedom Now! Clearly there is a relationship between the economic situation and the awakening of Negro demands for equality. The dismantling of the old economic order, with its paternalistic system of credit and sharecropping, has loosened white control by lessening the potential for white recriminations. As one displaced Negro laborer commented on Northern civil rights volunteers:

> These people are down here to help folks like me. I ain't got nothin' at all to lose by joinin'.

We have already seen ample statistical support for his conclusion. To make the point in another way, in 1960 almost two-thirds of the families in the Delta had annual incomes below the accepted poverty standard of $3,000. Needless to say, the vast majority of these families were Negro. Or consider the matter of schooling: in 1960 over half of the adult Negroes in the area had less than five years of education (compared with less than 15 per cent of the whites), and less than 5 per cent of the Negroes had completed high school (compared to 45 per cent of the whites). Not only do many older Negroes have little to lose, but they have little hope of gaining anything in the future. Here is still another pernicious circle in which poor schooling contributes to low occupational skills, which means a high unemployment rate, and in turn, a need to pull one's children out of school to support the family in whatever fashion possible. The problem is perpetuated across generations. But the civil rights movement offers a ray of hope in a dismal climate. As we shall see later, the movement has had its triumphs as well as its defeats. Certainly it has renewed many Negro aspirations and contributed to a new romanticism which is doing battle with the old.

This, then, is the Delta. But earlier we suggested that even within the Delta itself there are differences between the urban and rural areas; we have already alluded to some of these. Here it is appropriate to present a more pointed comparison between River City and its rural contrast, Bayou County.

The essential differences between River City and Bayou County concern time and tone. River City and its immediate area have always been roughly a decade and a half ahead of Bayou County. Thus, the county surrounding River City was settled and thriving before Bayou County was a gleam in the eyes of its planting paternalists. Then too, River City was quicker to throw off the yoke of the Civil War and its aftermath, in spite of a yellow fever epidemic. By 1880 River City whites had regained complete political control from the Negroes, but it wasn't until 1895 that Bayou County was able to do the same. Finally, River City and its immediate area were quicker to adapt to the decline of cotton after the Depression. As an urban center it was able to attract industry. With a sophisticated upper class it avoided alienating "Yankee" interests and was able to communicate with their representatives. Bayou County remains much more agricultural and much more dependent on its crumbling cotton system. Few firms have entered the area, and those that have are small. Compared to River City and its own county, Bayou is less urbanized, less industrialized, and more agricultural. It is also host to a higher proportion of Negroes (60 per cent compared to 55 per cent), and has more families living on less than $3,000 per year (70 per cent vs. 50 per cent).

Many of these differences in time are reflected in differences of tone. River City has long been a cultural oasis in the Mississippi desert, with a literary and even racially moderate tradition. The line between its white elite and its low-status white "peckerwoods" or "rednecks" is an important class distinction even alongside the more rigid caste difference between white and black. This is not so in Bayou County, where there is little sense of an aristocracy and the "rednecks" exert more influence. River City has never had an effective Ku Klux Klan; Bayou County historians lionize the Klan for its role in ridding the area of the Negro Reconstruction leadership—*The Birth of a Nation* writ small. Bayou's white residents cling to an image of the past that smacks loudly of the D. W. Griffith scenario. While the Klan has not been a factor in the recent history of Bayou County, the White Citizens' Council has been an active agent of resistance ever since 1954. Scorned in River City, the Council has had a stranglehold on the white leadership of Bayou County and has stifled scorn as well as desegregation.

Finally, a word about the schools in these two contexts. Before the Civil War, it was illegal in Mississippi to educate Negro slaves, and prior to 1870, white education was virtually restricted to private schooling. River City was one of the first communities in the state to opt for public schooling after the war's end. In 1869 it established one public school for whites and one for Negroes; by 1886 there were four "brick buildings for white schools" and "three frame buildings for Negro schools," as well as one or two private schools. As a local River City educational historian wrote in 1912:

> The River City [public] schools are second to none in the state and the graduates are admitted without examination into the universities of the different states.

Of course, the reference was to the white schools. But at that time River City and its county had ninety-three Negro schools with "over a hundred teachers." It was not until 1917, during Bilbo's reign as governor, that school attendance became compulsory in Mississippi. While the law was rarely enforced and was revoked shortly after the 1954 Supreme Court decision, River City's schools continue to grow. At the moment, the schools have a staff and budget that loom large in the local economy. The city still prides itself on the quality of its schools, a strategic factor to be discussed later.

Bayou County offers a consistent contrast. Its public school system was not established until 1886, and then only haphazardly. Until 1916 public schools arose on a random basis in various small towns. A general move toward countrywide supervision and control was not culminated until 1957, when a state statute ushered in consolidation by law. In all of this the Negroes were largely neglected. There is evidence of private Negro schools as early as 1900, but the county's Negro public schools developed long after River City's. Once again Bayou County has lagged behind its more urban counterpart.

So much for a general view of the study's context. Four

major sections follow. First, we shall describe what actually happened in the school desegregation of River City. Second, we will give a similar description for Bayou County, concentrating on two small towns. Third, we will try to probe several variables in the two settings that have both facilitated and impeded the process to different degrees. Finally, we shall offer a summary and some conjectural predictions for a future that is hazy but hardly rosy.

---•---

Compliance in River City

> The time has come for foot-dragging public school boards to move with celerity toward desegregation. . . . The rule has become: The later the start, the shorter the time allowed for transition.
>
> *(Judge J. Minor Wisdom*
> *U.S. Court of Appeals for the Fifth Circuit*
> *June 30, 1965, Jackson, Mississippi)*

There is no doubt that legal intervention has been crucial for the token desegregation that has occurred in Mississippi so far. However, the state's school districts have taken two quite different positions with respect to the educational provisions of the 1964 Civil Rights Act. One position involves waiting for an actual court order, whether out of defiance, inertia, or fear of local white reprisals. Needless to say, this position has been the most common in Mississippi: some school systems are still waiting; others, like Bayou County, have fallen victim to the courts, unprepared and at a late date. But a second position is quite different: a few school systems decided to act out of anticipation rather than forced reaction; River City was one of these.

As early as February 1965 the River City school board made it known that it was voluntarily preparing a desegregation plan to submit to the U.S. Office of Education. A school board member explained the decision this way:

> Sure we could have postponed desegregation for a while. But it wouldn't have been for long, and besides, this would have

meant cutting ourselves off from federal funds. These funds can make the difference between a poor school system and a good one. We have a long-standing commitment to good schools that we were not about to back down on.

There was, of course, disgruntlement with the decision. But there was also support. Not only did the town's daily newspaper back the decision, so did the student newspaper of the local white high school:

> [This decision] was a significant step forward in better race relations. . . . The test of the maturity of River City High School's student body will come when and if the school is integrated. We must show the general public that River City will not submit to disorder and chaos but will set the example for the rest of Mississippi.

Yet it was one thing to decide to submit a plan and quite another to prepare the plan itself. The details were subject to extensive debate among the school board members as well as within the community at large. Four Negroes who were asked to meet with the board argued that total integration would be just as easily accomplished as any more gradual process, including a grade-a-year plan. The board found the logic elusive. Ultimately, in May, it submitted a plan that fell short of the Office of Education requirement that four grades be desegregated in the fall. The board hoped that desegregating only the first and second grades would suffice for the first year; it set a target of five years for the full desegregation of all twelve grades. The reasoning was that the racial situation in Mississippi constituted circumstances so extenuating that precipitous action might produce violence and wholesale disruption. The reasoning was applauded by the local newspaper, which argued in an editorial that the proposal was wisely cautious but represented a courageous move forward:

> This is no time for the faint of heart to sit on a Deep Southern school board. Nor is it time for those who still believe that a shrill bellow of defiance from this section of the nation is sufficient to bring the federal walls tumbling down.

"Shrill bellows" may seem unconventional, but diehard Southerners have long since abandoned the more orthodox forms of protest.

In any event, the board went ahead to implement the proposal before the Office of Education made its decision. The mechanism for first- and second-grade desegregation was to be "freedom-of-choice." That is, every first- and second-grade student in the city was allowed his choice of any elementary school in the city—whether formerly all-white or all-Negro. Two days were set aside for registration during the last of May. The school officials held their breaths. Would the registration itself provoke racial incidents? Would there be an avalanche of Negro applications to white schools, thus provoking white recriminations? Would the new distribution of students—both white and Negro—upset planning for the forthcoming year in terms of budget, teacher placement, and equipment allocation? The answer was "no" to all three anxieties.

The registration went "smoothly" and "efficiently," according to all concerned. A local Negro leader reported several phone calls from whites, who warned of trouble if the Negroes should completely abandon their former schools, but no more was heard and the scene itself was without incident. This was partly because a chief of police restricted the area to parents, pupils, and officials. It was partly because Negro applications to white schools were far fewer than many had expected—the feared avalanche was at most a trickle. River City's first hesitant but voluntary step in the direction of desegregation was gratifying to its white leadership. The absence of trouble in May augured well for the following September.

But this three-month interval was hardly uneventful. Feedback was far from reassuring concerning federal acceptance of the two-grade plan already in effect. Warnings were given teeth in late June. Then a decision of the U.S. Court of Appeals for the Fifth Circuit ordered the Jackson, Mississippi, schools to conform to the full letter of the Office of Education's requirements for 1965–1966—namely, to desegregate four grades by the fall of 1965 and to complete full desegregation in all twelve grades by the fall of 1967.[2] This was far less deliberate speed

2 The background of this court order is important. We have already mentioned that five school districts had been ordered to desegregate for the 1964–1965 school year. This desegregation applied only to the first grade, but it was extended to include the second grade as well for 1965–1966, after a hearing in March 1965. Now the position of the Office of Education is that it will abide by any federal court decision that carries through to ultimate, full desegregation, no matter how long the process may take or how "ultimate" it may be. Thus, Mississippi schools were originally encouraged about the prospects of a grade-

than River City's voluntary plan had intended. Nevertheless, under Title IV of the Civil Rights Act, it was clear that the Court's decision could be quickly extended to River City on the initiative of the Justice Department. Delaying tactics were no longer feasible. As the president of the school board pointed out:

> The crucial clause of the Civil Rights Act had nothing to do with Title VI and eligibility for federal funds. Instead it was Title IV under which the Attorney General himself could initiate legal action in a hurry, to force compliance. The precedent established in Jackson was bound to reach us in a matter of months. It would be foolish for us to ignore the handwriting on the wall. Why not read it, and accept the federal funds to be had in the bargain? . . . The real choice is whether we're going to obey the law with federal aid or obey the law without federal aid.

At this point the school board withdrew its earlier proposal and submitted an extended version that was in full agreement with the requirements of both the Office of Education and the court decision. In addition to the first and second grades of the elementary school, desegregation was extended to the seventh and twelfth grades—one grade each in the junior and senior high schools.

Why these particular grades? River City's superintendent of schools explained it this way:

> As long as we were going to desegregate, we felt that we should do it right. It seemed only fair to give the Negro twelfth-graders a chance at desegregation during their last year in the system. It also seemed fair to expose the junior high schooler to desegregation, because they're going to find out about it sooner or later, and it might as well be sooner. We stuck with the desegregation of the first and second grade because we had already registered them back in the spring. Besides, what do the little kids know about white and black? We have thought all along that the elementary school would be the easiest.

---

a-year plan; after the March decision, many felt that two grades per year would be the very most expected of them. The full significance of the June 30 decision was its unequivocal statement that the Office of Education's own requirements must be followed from now on. This meant that school districts could no longer hope to get clearance for more gradual plans from the courts. Mississippi's schools were put firmly within the control of the Office of Education itself.

It is certainly true that the school administration avoided the strategy of grouping the "undesirables" in one or two grades or schools where they could be isolated from the white remainder and ruled with an especially heavy hand; it is even true that seating within classrooms was done alphabetically or in some other manner to prevent racial clustering. On the other hand, in all of this the local school officials may claim too much credit for merely complying with the Office of Education's requirements. Thus:

> Desegregation will be extended to at least four grades for the 1965–66 school year; the grades covered must include the first and any other lower grade, the first and last high school grades, and the lowest grade of junior high, where schools are so organized. . . .

With only one exception, River City's desegregation conformed to these unequivocal demands. The desegregation of grades one, seven, and twelve is clearly stipulated. Since River City has no public kindergarten, it was not obliged to integrate "any other lower grade" below the first. Note, however, that River City did not desegregate the tenth grade (or first year of high school), but chose instead the second, largely because it had already conducted freedom-of-choice registration for the second grade, and thus was committed. Here is one of several instances in which River City took advantage of a later clause in the Office of Education guidelines, indicating that a different pattern of desegregation would be acceptable in "exceptional cases." In the concluding section we shall indicate other chinks in the compliance, and speculate on the prospects and consequences of eliminating them.

Meanwhile, the choice of grades one, two, seven, and twelve seemed reasonable enough to River City's Negroes. A second registration period was held in late August; freedom-of-choice was offered once more to first- and second-graders, and to seventh- and twelfth-graders for the first time. Again there were no incidents. The process went smoothly except for the school administrators, who were frantically trying to keep abreast with the late changes in student distribution over some sixteen separate schools. Yet just as in May, the number of Negroes choosing to attend white schools was small. By the end of this second registration period, fewer than 1 in 10, or only 147 of some

1,500 eligible first-, second-, seventh-, and twelfth-grade Negroes had opted for desegregation. Moreover, of the 147 Negroes originally registered, only 135 actually attended white schools on the first day of classes; of these only 120 remained by January.

There are two distinct issues here. The first concerns the low turnout of Negroes in the white schools generally, something we shall comment on at length in the section concerning resistance in Bayou County. The second concerns the attrition over time of almost one-tenth of the original Negro students entering the white schools. It is plausible to imagine that the school board was responsible for both the low turnout and the high attrition, but this was not the case. Negro parents and leaders had no complaints about the registration periods themselves; they were adequately advertised and neither the white school board nor the white administrators placed obstacles in the path of free choice. What is more, the school officials did not take advantage of the opportunity to shuttle Negro students back to the Negro schools once the term had begun. The superintendent of schools himself put it this way:

> At the beginning of the year several Negro students wanted to change their registration and switch back into the Negro schools. Imagine what would have happened if we had allowed some six thousand students this privilege! It would have meant in effect still another registration period, and neither my office nor my staff were up to it. We just put our foot down and said, "Brother, you chose to go to a white school, and now you're going whether you say you want to now or not." I don't care what color a student's skin is—white, black, purple, or orange—I'm not going to run an educational cafeteria on a short-order basis.

But why else the attrition of such a substantial proportion of the entering Negroes? Part of it is attributable to geographic mobility in a region from which Negro families are leaving at a rapid rate.[3] But another part has to do with the simple problem

---

[3] This statement should be tempered. A common pattern of out-migration involves young Negro adults who leave their school-age children behind to reside with distant kin or neighbors, since the children are a problem and an economic liability to people who must be flexible in the pursuit of employment. The continued presence of these children helps to account for a disproportionate rise in Negro school enrollment compared to the overall decline in Negro population. Indeed, during the past year Mississippi legislators sought to counter the process. Arguing that Negro school attendance was unsupported by

of adjustment. Many Negro students were intimidated by potential academic and/or social barriers; some of these simply dropped out of the school system altogether. Recall that Mississippi revoked its compulsory education law soon after the 1954 Supreme Court decision. The state superintendent of education now estimates that as many as twenty-two thousand of Mississippi's school-age children shun the education available to them. Deplorable as this may be, it probably does serve as a facilitating mechanism for desegregation itself. Many of the potential "troublemakers" who are alienated from the schools in the first place are allowed to cool themselves out of the system altogether.

For whatever reason, there has been little trouble so far. This is the consensus of a wide variety of respondents—not only school administrators and teachers, but also militant civil rights leaders, Negro parents, white citizens, and the reputed leader of the local United Klans of America chapter. All confess astonishment at the lack of difficulty. All indicate satisfaction with the behavior of their opposite numbers—whether white or Negro.

This is not to say that incidents have not occurred. Three of some proportion are reported below, one at each of three levels—elementary, junior high, and senior high:

(1) The president of the school board reported with a grin that at one of the elementary schools, a first-grade white girl reported to her teacher that she had been kissed by her hallmate, a first-grade Negro boy. The little girl mentioned the incident without rancor; the teacher quickly dismissed it with no more than a general de-emphasizing comment. However, the matter reached both white and Negro parents through the children involved. The white parents went to the teacher and inquired soberly of the event; they were reassured and made no more of it. The Negro parents went to the teacher, and out of ob-

parental taxes, the legislators passed a law requiring tuition fees in the public schools for those whose parents or legal guardians lived outside the state. Similar laws occur in other states, such as New York, for example. But here the statute was clearly designed to force Negro students out of the schools at a time when there is no compulsory school attendance. Note, however, that the law has been challenged and is now in legal limbo with little chance of ever becoming effective. Interestingly enough, the white president of the River City school board was among the first to declaim against the law on moral and constitutional grounds. A white city official of Bayou City also had some qualms, since, until this year, he would have been forced to pay tuition for his own grandchildren. The migration pattern is not unique to Negroes.

vious embarrassment, wanted to withdraw their child from the school. At this point the superintendent of schools entered the matter. He refused to allow them to withdraw the child, commenting, "You certainly wouldn't think of it if the kissing involved two white first graders. Little kids will do that sort of thing, and we've all got to get used to it and take it in stride." In all of this, the only complicating factor concerned the relatively ineffective local KKK and the press. The incident was mentioned in an anonymous leaflet concerning an alleged rape of a white woman by a Negro teen-ager. A Memphis reporter called the superintendent of schools to probe the issue further. The superintendent reports that he was able to persuade the reporter that the first-grade incident was merely "kidstuff." He also threatened the reporter with lack of cooperation in the future if the story were featured. It was in fact given a soft touch and buried deep in a page of supermarket ads.

(2) The principal of the junior high school reported his only major incident as follows: A group of white boys, led by a "troublemaker and a liar," confronted a Negro boy on the stairs between classes. The white leader said, "Hey, Nigger, we're gonna gang you." The Negro boy drew a pocket knife and replied, "You ain't gonna gang me; you gonna gang this knife." Teachers interrupted the confrontation at this point. The principal reported that he expelled the white leader and temporarily suspended the Negro boy for not reporting where he had obtained the knife. The boy's parents later related that the boy ultimately confessed that he had borrowed it from a "non-integrated" friend. The boy was reinstated on the condition that he realize that no one was going to have a knife in the school, whether he was black or white. The Negro parents supported the principal, claiming that he had handled the situation fairly.

(3) At a River City High School football game, two of its new Negro girls provoked a near-scuffle by allegedly cursing several white students sitting behind them and then the white police officers who sought to settle the affair. The two girls explained that the white students had been throwing cigarette butts at them, and our Negro respondents felt that the provocation had justified the reaction. Predictably enough, white respondents had a different view. From their perspective the provocation was no more than the normal routine of popcorn throwing; they

regarded the Negro girls as "looking for trouble." It came as no surprise that the position of the white municipal judge was closer to that of his fellow white citizens. He found the girls "guilty of disorderly conduct by using obscene and profane language." He delivered a brief lecture and fined them fifteen dollars apiece. The girls were not expelled from the high school, however, and there have been no subsequent repetitions or repercussions.

These, then, have been the major incidents. The first two were dispatched quickly and to the satisfaction of all concerned; the third left a trace of bitterness that has since subsided. While it is true that these three stories were known to most of our respondents, these were the only three that had attained public status. For example, two further matters came to light only after our own probing, and are not generally known to either the community's whites or Negroes.

The Negroes are proud of two recent instances in the River City High School: in one, two Negro boys were selected captains of their respective basketball teams during a physical education class; in the other, a Negro boy was nominated for the vice-presidency of the Dramatics Club. But note that the stories have been distorted in the telling: the two captains were not elected but appointed by the physical education teacher to ward off the embarrassment of white boys having to choose Negroes for their own teams; the Dramatics Club nomination was rescinded on the order of the school principal who explained to us—inconsistently and at embarrassing length—that it was done to protect the Negro boy from the mockery that may have been intended by his clubmates. We learned later that the boy was the most popular Negro student in the school; it was just possible that the election may have been genuine within a Dramatics Club, which is unlikely to appeal to lower-class students and arch segregationists. The point is that discrimination and exceptional procedures were invoked in both cases. But many local Negroes still perceive the two as rare instances of real acceptance.

Of course, acceptance and true "integration" are a far cry from desegregation, and for the most part, the cry has yet to be answered. Negro children are still pushed, shoved, and elbowed more than necessary in the crowded school hallways, and "nigger" is frequently muttered audibly under white breaths. Yet the

Negro parents do not regard these as major problems, for they expected far worse, and even these difficulties have declined. Moreover, there are heartening stories of the opposite hue.

The few positive instances occur largely among the youngest students. One white girl made a delighted report to her mother after the first day of school because she was even allowed to hold a Negro girl's hand as part of the buddy system in the halls. Another girl answered her father's instructions to treat the Negroes with respect and courtesy by asking if she could bring a Negro friend home with her after school: "No, darling, not yet." Finally, a Negro parent reported that her young son spent a great deal of time on the telephone with a white classmate, discussing the evening television fare. But these moments appear to be virtually nonexistent at the high school level, where the Negro students are treated decently but distantly. While one boy has captured the fancy of his classmates, he has paid the traditional price of a shuffling step and an ingenuous grin. In general, the Negro students eat together, talk together, and change classes together, however "desegregated" their formal classes may be.

Through all of this there is an understated theme: not only has the school superintendent's office performed creditably, according to the Negroes, but so have the white teachers and principals. In some cases both teachers and principals have been slow to "come around," but for the most part the situation had eased by the end of the fall. The following remarks are from different Negro civil rights leaders and parents:

> The principal at one of the junior high schools was at first frightened by the potential problems. He was initially afraid to consult with Negro parents and tried to use me as a mediator. Finally he got to the point where he would handle the problem directly. Given the amount of potential conflict, there has been little disturbance, and he has handled the situation well (*Militant Negro leader*).

> From my first-hand knowledge, it is going smoothly. Teachers teach my children the same as white children. There were problems at first, and we had to convert a few people to make them accept it emotionally. But now the Negro kids are given every consideration and are happy. Oh, my kids complained about one teacher, but they said that she's mean to everyone (*Negro parent and civil rights leader*).

There was a little pickin' at the beginning, but the teacher made both the white boys and the colored boys stay after school, and it's better now (*Negro parent of a seventh-grader*).

I remember once the principal whipped a Negro child who was fighting, but not the white child. But we saw him and settled the issue, and there ain't been no trouble since (*Negro parent of a second-grader*).

One night my son showed me what he thought was a mistake in his arithmetic grade. I knew it was a mistake, but I told him I wasn't sure and to ask the teacher. He did the next day, and when he came home, he said: "Daddy, I told her, and she changed my grade right away" (*Negro parent of a seventh-grader*).

Not only have the white teachers been approachable to the Negro parents but the Negro parents have actually approached them. At first this was done by a Negro grievance committee selected by the larger group of "desegregated" Negro parents, a group that holds poorly attended, but nevertheless periodic meetings. Now the parents of individual children tend increasingly to go directly to the teacher or principal. Moreover, Negro parents have attended P.T.A. meetings. One woman commented that some white parents went out of their way to introduce themselves, and she mentioned that her husband, who was very sensitive to subtle racial slurs, felt well received. Note that River City's P.T.A. is thus doubly unique. The P.T.A. has been formally disbanded in many desegregated communities to avoid interracial contact between parents. In those communities that have retained the organization, it is generally an exclusive white preserve. A River City assistant superintendent explained the local situation this way:

We are going to do what we have to do. We're not going to disband the P.T.A. . . . It's been useful in the past and should be useful right now. While it's true that middle-class Negro parents come more often than your lower-class Negroes, there is one school where the parents of all ten Negro children have come to every meeting.

Some school officials hope that the P.T.A. will serve as their bridge with the white parents as well as the Negro parents. The organization may function as either a safety valve or a source of myth-breaking and social adjustment. Clearly, the white parents are a source of difficulty. While only one school administrator was able to report even a single late-night phone call from a disgruntled segregationist, another commented:

> The major problem we have is with parents, not with students. That is, the problem is not to get students to accept Negroes but to get their parents to allow them to.

Here, however, one must caution against an undue inference. If the major source of hostility lies with the parents, one might predict a pattern of recriminations against the Negro families whose children are in the white schools. Once again River City is distinctive. There was one unsubstantiated story of a man who lost his job, but this may be because of participation in a picket line rather than sending his children to a white school. While it was rumored that one bank in town, led by a once active member of the White Citizens' Council, had tightened up on loans to the parents of "desegregated Negroes," none of our Negro respondents were sure of this. In the main the Negro parents and leaders were pleased. No cuts in welfare payments, no sudden mortgage foreclosures or interest increments, and no housing evictions came to our attention.[4] As we shall see later, such things do occur elsewhere.

Perhaps it is significant that a discussion of Mississippi school desegregation should wait so long before mentioning academic performance. Scholarship is rarely salient where violence is a possibility. And yet the question remains crucial: How well have the Negroes in white schools performed? The answer, of course, depends upon a number of factors. Certainly it depends upon whether one is discussing the children of middle-class or lower-class Negroes. It also relates to sex differences, since

---

[4] There was, however, one complaint from the civil rights workers concerning discriminatory administration of free lunch funds among the schoolchildren. The workers had no definite information, but asked us to inquire about the matter. We did, and discovered that there was also concern on the part of a River City assistant superintendent. While he was reluctant to accuse the welfare agency of discrimination, he did admit that the agency was "overworked" and that it was quite possible that many children were not getting the lunches to which they were entitled. The administrator then showed us a proposal to Washington which will put the free lunch program into the orbit of the school officials themselves for next year, with more money and more extensive coverage. In all of this, it is important to underline the difficulty of tracking down incidents that have occurred during desegregation. Many problems exist of which we are no doubt unaware. Communication is far from free or perfect even within the Negro community itself. The point is that only incidents of magnitude become common knowledge, and there were few of these.

Negro girls generally fare better than Negro boys. But most importantly, the answer depends upon the grade level at issue.

In general, Negro first- and second-graders perform more comparably with their white classmates than do either the seventh- or twelfth-graders. This at least is the testimony of the teachers and administrators. Part of the explanation is that the first and second grades put less of a premium on competitive performances which reveal differences in family background. Another factor is that first- and second-grade classes reach the student early enough to counteract the disadvantages of an educationally inert home. And yet the most important explanation in the relative success of the younger Negroes in the white schools is that they have had less exposure to the handicaps of the Negro schools. They have not had the "opportunity" to fall behind or to learn incorrectly. They are able to start at a point where differences of social-class background are not compounded by the racial differences within the school system itself.

Note that two years ago any assertions of the inferiority of the Negro schools would have met considerable resistance from white school administrators. The shibboleth of "separate but equal" has long been a guilt-allaying mechanism.[5] Recently, however, there has been a re-examination of the Negro schools in anticipation of more extensive desegregation. A member of the school board commented accordingly:

5 The statistics of "separate but equal" are fascinating in themselves. For example, one wonders whether the state board of education prepares its summaries to please the Northern liberals or the Southern conservatives. The heralded gap between white and Negro education expenditures may not be as large as the statistics suggest. Thus, per-pupil expenditures are *allocated* on the basis of average daily school attendance, but they are evidently *reported* on the basis of school enrollment. Since Negroes have a lower ratio of attendance to enrollment, they seem to be getting less money than they actually are, compared with whites. Note, too, that the difference between white and Negro expenditures is also an artifact of teachers' salaries. Quite apart from direct salary discrimination, white teachers are more likely to have advanced degrees and thus more likely to qualify for higher steps on the salary scale. This also inflates the gap or at least provides a hint of justification for it, though it is true enough that Negro teachers have fewer opportunities to obtain more advanced credentials. Finally, the state has for some time engaged in a policy designed to make "separate but equal" a fact rather than a slogan. Since the late 1950's, Mississippi has allocated more money for Negro school construction than for white. Needless to say, this has not been adequate to the task, and it leaves the problems *within* these schools untouched. At the same time, it has had the effect of easing the ultimate day when whites will have to attend formerly all-Negro schools that are now only second-rate instead of third-, fourth-, or fifth-rate by the whites' own standards concerning physical plants.

I think we always knew that the Negro schools were starting far behind the whites, when the state reacted to the 1954 Supreme Court decision by allocating them even more money than the white schools to build them up. Since then, many people were confident that they were being built up and that the new construction of the exteriors reflected new quality inside. But in the past couple of years we have been taking some close looks and have found that it just wasn't so. Sure, there are a few good Negro teachers—one or two as good as our best white teachers. But for the most part the teachers, the materials, and facilities are shocking!

Clearly, the longer a student is dependent on such schools, the more difficult is his adjustment to the white schools. This is apparent among the seventh-graders in the junior high school.

Fisher Junior High has the largest proportion of Negroes in the city—some 47 out of 307 seventh-graders. The principal and the teachers concur that the students are generally doing poorly; statistics bear them out. While the school has no single overall average for each student, it does keep performance records for English, reading, arithmetic, and social studies. The following table presents the results at four points during the first semester by noting the proportion of Negroes' marks in these courses that were A and B, and D and F. Thus, 16 per cent of the Negroes'

Cumulative-Performance Record of Negro Seventh-Graders in River City

	PER CENT As AND Bs	PER CENT Ds AND Fs
First six weeks:	16	49
Second six weeks:	21	44
Third six weeks:	21	41
First semester average (including final exam grade):	14	51

marks were As and Bs after the first six weeks; this rose to 21 per cent during the next two periods but dropped to a low of 14 per cent after the semester's final examinations. The figures for Ds and Fs reflect the same tendency but are alarming in their proportions. At the end of the semester further data indicate that some 49 of 307 seventh-grade students had failed at least one subject, and that 20 of these were Negroes. Put another way, Negroes account for 15 per cent of the students but 41 per cent of the failing students. But consider the performance over time. This table indicates that the Negroes improved academically through the first three grading periods, only to drop by the semester's end to a point lower than where they had begun. Why the sudden reversal? Of course, one possibility is discriminatory grading, yet the parents of the Negro children had no grievances here, even under prodding. A more plausible answer revolves about the final examinations themselves. Not only did the examinations demand skills and speed that had been untapped in the students' previous experiences in the Negro schools, but the exams also were a first major form of structured competition with the whites, and were all the more intimidating for this reason. This was a factor with which both parents and teachers concurred; it also confirms a general axiom among those who administer personality and intelligence tests to disadvantaged groups on a wider scale.

Clearly, then, the Negro students in the junior high school are performing below the white level. And yet there are a few Negro students, largely from middle-class homes, who are doing well. It is comforting to suppose that these students provide an example of excellence for their less successful Negro classmates. But, alas, it appears that a stratification system persists among the forty-seven Negroes themselves which reflects distinctions of performance as well as distinctions of background. Simply put, the successful "middle-class" Negro students will have little to do with the unsuccessful from the lower classes.

Finally, let us turn to the senior high school and the Negro twelfth-graders. We have already mentioned that the older the Negro student, the longer his exposure to low-quality Negro schools. If this was a factor in the seventh grade, it should be even more important in the twelfth. But note, too, that River City has long been proud of its white high school and has taken advantage of a state in which poor students are not obliged to attend by making the high school a fairly rigorous preparation for college. Of last June's graduating class, some 76 per cent actually enrolled in the fall at such colleges as Harvard, Princeton, Duke, and Vanderbilt, as well as the state schools. In short, competition among whites alone is intense. It should come as no surprise that the Negro students have done poorly.

The consequences have extended to the curriculum itself. Consider the plight of the school's prize history teacher, a man who was honored as one of the nation's outstanding teachers several years ago and who takes enormous pride in a seminar for advanced students. Mr. Bernstein was one of the few teachers who had no qualms about desegregation. He had earlier experiences with integrated classes elsewhere and had "already adjusted to technicolor." In fact, he had adjusted so well that he was willing to lower his seminar standards in order to admit a Negro girl rather than fall prey to charges of discrimination. He now wonders about the future of his own work and of the advanced classes generally at River City High School. He may well have to make a choice between seeming discrimination and a long-term lowering of standards.

To summarize, River City's token desegregation has been without incident but with academic difficulty. Despite an abortive start at voluntary compliance, the schools ultimately satisfied somewhat relaxed federal standards and without the severe consequences that were predicted. The local Cassandras—both white and Negro—found their predictions largely unconfirmed. Before seeking more elaborate explanation of what has happened in River City, let us go on to consider the somewhat different events of Bayou County.

Resistance in Bayou County

> I don't know many school people who are really hostile toward the plan, but the fact is, we just weren't ready (*County superintendent of schools*).

> If we didn't have to do it overnight, it might be easier. If I was on the other side of the fence, I'd understand how they [the Negroes] feel. We had a hundred years to do something for them, and we didn't (*White high school principal*).

If River City was distinctive in trying to anticipate desegregation, Bayou County was more typical in seeking to postpone it. Without any last-ditch show of organized defiance or legal maneuvering, school officials buried their heads in tradition and hoped that the crisis would pass. Frightened leaders crossed nervous fingers on the chance that the courts would bypass their sanctuary, leaving them untouched and uncomplying. Certainly, there was little preparation for what was to come. And it came hardly a week before school began.

On August 24 the U.S. District Judge ordered Bayou County to desegregate at least four grades through "freedom-of-choice" by the time school opened for the 1956–1966 school year. The county's school systems differed in the particular four grades to be opened. In a nearby county one school system went so far as to desegregate all twelve grades, whether out of guilt come home to roost or, more likely, out of a defeated resignation akin to a dam bursting. The more common pattern was to open grades one, ten, eleven, and twelve. The first was required; ten, eleven, and twelve were calculated to minimize Negro attendance for reasons we shall see later. Note that Bayou County was not obliged to comply with Office of Education requirements in the choice of grades. The court order allowed the county latitude, and the Office of Education recognized compliance with the court as satisfactory in itself.

Obviously the county's whites were unhappy. But many leaders saw no choice other than compliance, and the Bayou City Chamber of Commerce passed a resolution to this effect. Violence and its implications had little appeal. Most whites seemed to agree with the sentiments expressed by one citizen as follows:

> Sure, I have reservations about the Civil Rights Act that has brought this integration about. I'd be lying if I said I didn't. But it's the law of the land. We've got to obey it because we have no choice.

Lacking any choice, freedom-of-choice registration was staged a few days after the court directive. County authorities were apprehensive. Twenty policemen were assigned to special duty during the registration period. There were no incidents but very few Negroes. Although Negroes comprise almost 75 per cent of some sixteen thousand children in the Bayou County schools, only forty-eight Negro children registered for white schools, and only thirty-nine of these were still in attendance by

January. Thus, approximately 2 per cent of the eligible Negroes in Bayou County opted for desegregation, compared to some 10 per cent in River City.

One reason so few Negroes registered was the screening procedure. Negro students qualified in spite of strong pressures for disqualification. As one small-town school official remarked:

> There were fifteen Negroes who qualified and registered. I know they qualified because there was enormous political pressure put on the school board to have them disqualified. I certainly wouldn't have checked fifteen white students so thoroughly.

But many Negroes were afraid to send their children to register in the first place. Bayou County is more intimidating than River City. The possibilities of white recriminations were greater, and the presence of *white* policemen and *white* school officials was hardly calculated to woo a substantial Negro response. And yet the Negroes might have responded in greater numbers had they had more time to prepare. One Negro leader indicated that the court decision came so late in the summer that the Negro community had little time for mobilizing students to take advantage of it. He suggested guardedly that the decision may have been purposely late for precisely this reason. He also noted that if the decision had occurred a year before, things might have been different:

> If the court order had come in the summer of 1964, there would have been hundreds of Negro kids in the white schools, but by 1965 everything had cooled off. People were afraid, and the movement had lost some of its momentum.

Yet timing was not the only complaint of the Bayou County Negroes who had initiated the court action. Their original suit had demanded desegregation in more than four grades and faculty integration as well. In their view an elephant had labored to produce a mouse and the August decision had actually protected the county's lily-white school system. It was certainly true that a number of white schools in the country "escaped" Negroes altogether. Whether because of timing, overly rigid qualifications, or Negro fear, some schools still have no Negro students despite their legal right to attend.

But consider the white schools that did have Negroes on

the first day. Indeed, consider the first day itself. One white high school principal recalls his reaction to the Negro students who attended:

> I have tried to bend over backward to make sure that they are treated fairly. When they came to school, they were scared, but we've tried to treat them all the same. . . . The day the Negroes reported to school I took the seven girls and had a private talk with them. I told them that if they would act right, they would earn the respect of the white students and parents. If not, we'll have to dismiss you. I told them about Jackie Robinson and how he had helped his people by being the right sort of person in the world of baseball, and I suggested that they had the responsibility and opportunity to do the same thing for their race.

He continued by describing his anxieties:

> You don't know how I sat here on pins and needles the first month of school, fearing that some white child was going to get into trouble with some Negro child and I'd have to expel them both. . . . I wasn't worried about the Negro children, how they would act, but about some white children, especially those from more deprived homes. I was afraid of these groups fighting it out.

Despite these concerns, Bayou County school officials and citizens are unanimous in indicating that things have gone more smoothly than they expected. One commented with a sigh, "We've gone a long way." Another remarked as follows:

> We were surprised that things went so well. We haven't had trouble between the races in this area. Our leaders of the Negro people have controlled this thing.

Note the suggestion here that if trouble is to be averted, it is the Negroes who must be controlled. Another citizen explained the lack of trouble in a somewhat different fashion:

> We've had so little integration that we have had no problems. The major feeling in the community is fear of the unknown.

This last statement portends difficulty for the future as integration occurs on a more extensive scale. Further pessimism comes from the teachers themselves. It is true that most teachers, like most administrators, have sought to comply with the law. It is especially true that experienced teachers have developed habituated techniques that brook no alteration even with the influx of Negro students. Still, teacher acceptance has been reluctant. As one school official remarked:

> Teachers are uncomfortable with the Negro students. When I go to classes and see those Negro children, it startles me, too.

Bayou County school administrators are generally fearful that some teachers may resign if large numbers of Negroes choose to attend white schools. Several would have resigned this year had the late court decision not left them so little time. And the resignation of a white teacher in Mississippi is not an idle matter —white recruits are hard to come by at the state's startlingly low salary level. This may be the beginning of forced faculty integration as Negro teachers provide the only pool of replacements.

Turning to the reaction of white students and the white community outside of the schools, there are three major variables at work. First, tolerance is inversely related to grade level, so that racial interaction is more positive among first-graders than among twelfth-graders. Second, Negro girls are apt to provoke fewer incidents than Negro boys. Third, the smaller the town or the more rural the setting, the less tolerant the atmosphere. Let us consider the variables in order.

While no one would argue that first-graders are totally unaware of the racial issue, it is nevertheless true that the only meaningful extracurricular interaction among Negroes and whites occurs at this level. Consider an elementary school of Bayou City, the county seat. Here Negro and white first-graders sit side by side in the classroom, eat together in the cafeteria, and talk with little apparent stigma. Although the four Negro girls keep to themselves on the playground, the one Negro boy frequently plays with his white classmates. However, his teacher commented, he was "a bit rough" for them. And the principal reported that the play often revolves about a game that is innocently symbolic of Mississippi's larger racial crisis. Thus:

> Little Henry's favorite sport is to play gorilla with the white boys. It's a sort of tag game, where Henry pretends to be the gorilla and the white boys run away and escape on the jungle jim. I've seen it happen a number of times. And you know, Henry has all the sounds and gestures down pat; he's pretty convincing.

But the symbolism in not the only ominous factor here. Another school administrator commented that even his first-graders' interaction had decreased somewhat since the start of the year:

> The little children, around six years old, accept the Negro children readily, but this is declining because of pressures put on by parents.

By high school, of course, when parental influence has been largely absorbed, interaction drops precipitously. It is true that a few white students in one school were friendly with the Negro students at the beginning of the year. Later, however, these whites were teased into compliance with a collective cold shoulder. A superintendent of another system remarked with a mixture of concern and satisfaction:

> At our high school they get the "deep freeze" treatment. Not one white student has spoken to them. It's been 100 per cent. . . .

And yet the "deep freeze" is given different interpretations. Some school officials and teachers claim that the Negroes have segregated themselves. One administrator compared the Negro students to the sprinkling of Chinese students that have been in his schools for more than a decade: "Both groups have a tendency to clique by themselves." Of course, the Negroes tell a different tale. They reply that insofar as they do keep together, it is only because of their fear of what would happen otherwise in the Bayou County high schools.

Turning now to sex differences as a factor governing incidents and friction, there are several reasons why Negro girls should outnumber Negro boys in attending white high schools in particular. For one, Southern Negro girls are more likely than boys to complete their high school education, hence, there is a greater proportion of girls who are eligible to attend. For another, the Negro boys who do persist in high school are often oriented to college and to achieving either academic or athletic scholarships. Since their academic records would likely suffer in the white schools and since the white high schools have made no provision for integrating varsity athletics, the boys are seldom tempted to make the jump. But there is still another factor: young Negro males are traditionally viewed as troublemakers in Mississippi society. Whether because of their mythical threat to white virginity or a greater disinclination to accept segregation passively, they are held at arms' length. One district superintendent commented:

> The students are predominantly girls. It works much better that way. The little harassment there has been was directed at the one boy of the eleven Negro children who actually attend.

A Negro leader in the same town put the issue more strongly:

> They don't like Negro boys in their schools, and the one boy in Raeford has had more trouble than all the girls put together. He was accused of cursing a white girl and an affidavit was sworn out for his arrest.

Clearly, it makes a difference whether one is discussing girls or boys.

But still another variable, the size of the town, is more important. Bayou City is the largest town in Bayou County and has witnessed relatively few incidents of major proportion. To be sure, it has had its share of name-calling and jostling, both within the halls and on the school buses, though this has declined since the beginning of the year. One teacher reported that lower-class white students had picked on a Negro student in her class, but the teacher went on to mention that she had seated several middle-class whites around the girl to provide a shield of status and that the problems have subsided. Another Negro girl was asked if she attended any school events in the evening and she answered, "No, I live out in the country and I'm afraid to come in town at night." One Negro girl was summarily dismissed for "cursing white students," an allegation that was difficult to assess. White officials reported it matter-of-factly; Negro students denied that the girl's behavior was out of line, and felt that the expulsion was unjustified.

But there is a different sort of incident that plagues the Delta Negroes. It concerns recriminations against the parents who send their children to white schools. In Bayou City we uncovered two instances of this. One man, whose daughter attended the white schools, found his working time and, therefore, his wages reduced in his job with a local construction company. Another mother was fired from her job as a domestic. According to the white principal the firing occurred not solely because she had a child in the first grade, but rather because the child was in the same classroom with the daughter of her employer. While these were the only two recriminations that have occurred in Bayou City, most of the Negro parents are not vulnerable to this kind of pressure. Some are in independent businesses; others have left town altogether, leaving their children behind with aged grandparents. On balance, Bayou City has had more than its share of problems compared to the larger River City, but it has had fewer and less severe incidents than some of the still smaller towns and rural areas in Bayou County itself.

Consider one small town in particular—Raeford, Mississippi. With a population of less than two thousand people, Raeford has been a hot spot of civil rights activity and countermeasures since 1964. School desegregation has been a sustained struggle between civil rights militants and segregationist community officials. Thus, it was only through the efforts of the civil rights groups that some fifteen Negroes were willing to register for the white school. The registration itself was done in the face of scarcely concealed threats of reprisals. The tone of the community's whites is best represented by the following sentiments expressed by a local school official: "We don't have many Negroes in Raeford; most of ours are niggers." The official made it clear that he was pointing to his perception of the Negro's economic and moral impoverishment. At the same time, this was the first time that we had heard any term other than a carefully pronounced "Negro" used by white school authorities to refer to the "opposition." Even "nigra" had been dropped from the rhetoric of our other respondents, although the concluding vowel sometimes had an awkward sound about it, and the pronunciation of "Negro" may have been a performance for our benefit rather than a newly acquired habit fired in the forge of brotherhood. We certainly should not imply that the terms "nigra" or even "nigger" have been wholly purged from the white vocabulary. Indeed, it would probably take a purge in the strict sense to render them extinct.

In Raeford incidents between students have been numerous —too numerous, in fact, to list in detail. Yet one of the most distinctive forms of Negro complaint indicts the teachers themselves. Unlike both River City and Bayou City, the Raeford teachers are alleged to discriminate in their grading. Negro parents report that their children appear to do well enough in classwork and in exams only to get unsatisfactory marks at the end of a grading period. One Negro child had been an all-A student at the Negro high school, but failed consistently in the white school. The sudden discrepancy brought on a reported nervous breakdown, and the girl had to be taken out of school altogether.

Raeford is also a more severe atmosphere for the parents of the Negro children attending white schools. Wage cuts, job firings, housing evictions, and sudden increases in loan interest are all mentioned as reprisals in the area. In this respect Raeford resembles a number of small towns in the Delta, including one in which the NAACP recently brought suit against six plantation owners who had fired and evicted thirty Negroes whose children had been sent to white schools. One leader of the Mississippi Freedom Democratic Party was quoted as saying:

> As soon as you register your child for a white school or register to vote, everyone knows about it and they tell you they don't need you any more.

A Raeford school principal admitted that these sorts of pressures existed, "But there's been no violence or knifings or that sort of thing." Plainly, anything less than outright violence is seen as only a "moderate" reprisal in the Raeford context.

But note that Raeford is distinctive in other ways as well. One of these concerns the P.T.A. The logic of integrated schools implies the integration of parents and teachers in the P.T.A. In a community with a history of moderate race relations such as River City, the P.T.A. continues on an integrated basis, with no untoward consequences. The Bayou County response has been twofold. In Bayou City none of the parents of the ten children still attending the formerly white schools have chosen to attend the meetings, and the problem has been avoided. In Raeford, as in some other communities, the strategy was simply to disband the P.T.A. itself. This is hardly out of character in view of the more antagonistic racial climate of Raeford. Yet the reaction of Freedom Democratic Party was quoted as saying:

> Our P.T.A. isn't functioning this year. As far as I'm concerned, it never really functioned. It was run by extremists—with John Birch Society types dominating it. So we haven't lost anything. Had it been a good P.T.A., we would be suffering now.

Thus, even a "bad" P.T.A. is added to the victims of racism.

Finally, Raeford is one of several Mississippi communities

with citizens who have withdrawn their children from the public schools to educate them in "private" schools. The term "private" here is actually a misnomer, since the state legislature has abetted the strategy by providing tuition of $185 for each white student choosing to attend. Since schools costs are considerably more than this, however, only the more affluent families can afford the extra fees required. We asked the Raeford elementary school principal for his reaction to the private schools:

> I think the state's support of private schools is legally and morally wrong, though I feel the same way about the Civil Rights Act, too. There is a market for the private schools, however. Remember that this is an area in which hatred of Negroes crosscuts all social lines—the banker as well as the "peckerwood."

Apart from morality, the principal may also be concerned about the threat to his job in the public schools. In any event, Raeford's private school is further evidence of its contrast to River City.

Last in this section, let us consider the Negroes' academic performances in the white schools of Bayou County. The matter can be stated bluntly: the Negroes have done poorly here just as in River City. Of course, a plausible explanation for this in a town like Raeford is discriminatory grading. But in Bayou City none of the Negro high school students complained of this, yet all of them were performing below average, and most were failing at least one subject by the end of the term. This was true despite one important difference between River City and Bayou City. In the former the Negroes were all allowed to enter the college preparatory curriculum; in the latter they were all girls in a dominantly vocational program built around home economics. It is true that this smacks of a segregated track system, but on the other hand, the vocational program is less difficult than the college preparatory track, and still the girls have suffered by comparison with most of their white classmates.

Actually, Bayou County and River City share a common characteristic that may help to explain such common low performance. In both areas the "best" Negro students chose to remain in the Negro schools, especially at the high school level. Later we will explore the reasons for this in some detail. Suffice it to say here that there was no disagreement over the facts themselves; indeed, white school officials in Bayou City and Raeford went out of their way to mention this and to add that the attraction of desegregation for their Negro high school students was more civil rights than education. One school administrator asserted:

> All of the Negro students in the white schools come from hard-core, militant families. If there are any superior students, they're still over at the Negro high school.

An actual majority of the girls who originally registered at the white Bayou City High School had been arrested at civil rights demonstrations in Jackson during the preceding summer. And the white school officials were supported in their views by the principal of the local Negro high school:

> Those students don't represent our better students. They represent people in the civil rights movement! Most are average to below average in their abilities.

In all of this, the undertone of white school sentiment was best expressed by a white elementary school principal:

> Everybody around here thinks that the Negro parents are being paid to send their children to the white schools. I doubt it, but it might be. I do know that the parents are the raunchiest you've ever seen. They have no sense of responsibility or co-operation.

Neither the principal nor anyone else—white or Negro—indicated evidence of payment. But the principal did relate several stories of unkempt Negro homes and poorly disciplined Negro children. He then showed us the following handwritten letter from a Negro mother requesting a consultation with her daughter's teacher, a consultation that was never held:

10–21–1965
19 arrow ST
BayoucityMiss

hello Mrs Cheek

 Reason I amm Writting you to let you no Can I make a pearmont With you and the principal monday about 5 minuute tree o clock I want to talk to you about my Daughter Linda

From Lind Mother
Luva Lloyd Minor

The letter may be unconvincing evidence of "raunchiness," lack of "responsibility," or lack of "cooperation," but it certainly is evidence of Bayou County's past educational failures and future educational challenges.

———•———

On Making the Omelet: Ingredients of Success and Failure

Throughout this whole desegregation thing a lot of us white school people haven't been able to go as far or as quick as maybe we'd like to. On the basis of what has happened so far, I think it probably would have been easier to do it all at once and get it over with. But just try convincing the school board of that (*White Bayou County high school principal*).

The analogy between successful desegregation and a well-turned omelet has a number of facets: both require delicacy in the midst of heat; both depend upon the breaking of "eggs"; and both run the risk of ultimate disaster as the ingredients separate. This chapter explores a number of factors that seem to make the difference between the relative success of River City and the relative failure of Bayou County. One fashionable mode of explanation involves value differences or the distinction between the morally sensitive and the brutishly immoral. These differences are undeniably discernible within Mississippi. But the rhetoric of values, morality, and ideology yields explanations which are too crude and too superficial. There are people with the "best" of intentions who are unable to translate them into action; there are people who are forced to act "nobly" despite their predilections. Clearly, more structural factors are at work; we shall examine them under three major rubrics: Delta politics, the schools as bureaucracies, and the role of the civil rights movement within the local Negro communities.

The Politics of School Desegregation in the Delta

Mississippi could never be accused of leading the nation in political innovation. Its fabled reverence for "States' rights" finds a parallel in "county rights" within the state itself. The state government has always been a reluctant finger in the local pies, especially in education. Before 1957 local school systems had exercised their autonomy to create a hodgepodge of political and administrative forms. In 1957 the state took tentative hold of the situation and delimited three types of school politics. The first is simply a unified county school system under a single school administration without regard to the borders between towns or villages within the county. The second scheme is one of consolidation, in which a county school board and a county superintendent oversee finances and transportation, but there are also district boards and superintendents who have the effective power over their own sub-domains within the county. Finally, a third model is designed to allow larger urban areas to operate their own systems without heed to their county contexts. Bayou County chose the second, or consolidated arrangement; River City opted predictably for urban autonomy.

The distinction is far from idle. It is axiomatic in Mississippi that hard-core segregationist sympathy lies in the rural areas, the havens of the "rednecks." Bayou County schools are largely controlled by a rural population. Even the county seat in Bayou County—a town of more than ten thousand with moderating tendencies—is constrained by the wider county influence as represented by the county school board and the more powerful county board of supervisors. The supervisors control their districts like satraps. Responsible only to their districts for election, they have little sense of countywide responsibility, to say nothing of the state as a whole. More importantly, because these men are tied to a constituency that patrols them closely, they have little opportunity to resist the sentiments of their electorates. Much the same can be said of the elected members of the county and district school boards. And here there is even greater constituency pressure since the constituency is commonly a mere handful of prominent citizens who vote in an election announced by a controlled murmur rather than a public proclamation. In fact, the leading Negro civil rights activist of one Bayou County town had no idea how the elections were run, let alone when. This from a man who *is* a registered voter.

River City offers a contrasting case. Here the school board supports the schools instead of constraining them. This is only partly because the River City school system is distinct from the county system and removed from a rural population base. It is also because River City is one of the few cities in the state in which the school board is *appointed* rather than elected. Thus, the board is afforded a certain protection from the mood of the city as a whole. It can act more independently (*viz.* more "moderately") since it is not directly responsible to a capricious electorate, and it is only on this basis that it could have attempted any voluntary desegregation at all.

And yet it is true that even an appointed and autonomous school board in Bayou County would be far different from the River City's. It plainly matters *who* is appointed and what kinds of people are available. The earlier brief history of River City notes its distinctive tradition of cosmopolitan elitism. The wonder is not only that an elite exists, but also that it has eschewed withdrawal to take an active role in the city's affairs, not the least of which are its schools. To be sure school board appointments are made by the mayor and the city council. Yet both are responsive to the local aristocracy that controls the River City economy and its political purse strings. Appointments are much more likely to reflect the elite than the electorate, and the elite is willing to serve as well as counsel.

If one asks about the network of power in River City, one finds a ready response. Its members are not the Northern managers of imported industry, but indigenous planters, lawyers, and newspapermen. It does not include the members of the city council, the mayor,[6] or the respected chief of police, but rather persons who operate behind the façade of elected office. The actual leaders are economically autonomous because of independent wealth, a much demanded professional practice, or a

---

[6] But the mayor is an interesting figure in his own right. He seems to be cultivating a power base with the new middle class. While he pays obvious heed to the opinions of the old elite, he was elected over their opposition and apparently intends to build a political following of his own which will obviate the need for their support. This day has not arrived, however, and the mayor is currently biding his time compliantly.

monopoly on a community service. They are people who see each other frequently and provide mutual reinforcement. In all of this, River City is similar to many American cities. The arresting feature of its elite is not its composition or its operation but the sympathies it puts into play.

The single most influential figure in River City is a lawyer who is a statewide shadow in the seats of power. His relatives include a prominent contemporary novelist as well as literary figures of the past. They also include an uncle who vanquished a local candidate of the Ku Klux Klan in a dramatic confrontation on the courthouse steps in the 1920s. Wilbur Cobb has all of the instruments of power but few of the affectations. His conversational style is chatty, even hip. He luxuriates in candor as much as wealth. That Cobb is "in but not of" his community is suggested by the juxtaposition of two remarks:

> You certainly can't account for desegregation here by the conscience of the local citizens. Most of us acted out of necessity rather than moral principles.

But, on the other hand:

> The biggest sin the whites have committed against the Negroes is not the denial of jobs, of schools, or the vote. All of that is true enough and important, but the big thing is the denial of human dignity. Yeah, that's the mama sin.

In talking with men like Cobb, one infers that consciences have long been sore but that conscience alone is not equal to the task of breaking with tradition. Many seem to be relieved by the compulsory federal legislation. They are now in the position of complying rather than initiating, and Cobb expresses their greatest fear "that Ross Barnett will be re-elected governor" to obstruct the process and create more havoc. Thus, as soon as the Civil Rights Bill of 1964 was passed, a group of some fifteen community leaders began to meet regularly to discuss the mechanisms of orderly change. Known to the local Negro leaders as the "Friday Evening Tea Club," the group gave important support to the school board in its decision to desegregate voluntarily.[7] Nor

[7] Despite this moderating influence, it is not true that all of the members of the Friday Evening Tea Club are moderates as individuals. The effective leader saw the need for including representatives of all factions, and the group's composition included arch segregationists as well as arch liberals. There were several occasions when both groups came close to exiting in disgust. The club

is the influence of these men confined to the schools and school desegregation. In May of 1965 the Chamber of Commerce (the one formally constituted organization that includes virtually all of the city's power figures) issued a manifesto for fair employment. The city government itself was the first to respond. In what seemed a calculated move, the police department hired a Negro woman as a photography technician the next day.

Some members of the River City elite have become infamous in Mississippi for their racial moderation. Lest one think that only vowed civil rights workers risk violence in the state, consider the following incident. One of River City's most outspoken moderates was driving through another Delta community, Ledbetter, when he had a flat tire. He had a local filling station repair the tire, giving them his credit card in advance. The attendant asked if this was *the* Galen Hedgepeth of River City. An affirmative response drew a muttered sign of recognition. Mr. Hedgepeth picked up his car later and drove the 130-odd miles back to River City. The next day his wife noted peculiar noises and vibrations coming from the wheel. A local garage discovered that two lugs had been left off altogether, and the others had been loosened.

While this sort of thing is beyond the pale of River City itself, it would be a mistake to assume that the moderate elite has always been clasped to the city's bosom. Indeed, as late as the spring of 1964 River City's moderates were River City's radicals. As the most liberal members of the community, they were largely denied public influence in local affairs. While their redeeming social status forestalled any outright incidents, they were nevertheless regarded with suspicion. Then came the civil rights workers. In the summer of 1964 the "movement" became a local reality instead of the distant apparition that it had been since 1960. As volunteers with SNCC, COFO, and the Delta Min-

is now in a dormant mood brought on by a heated debate over the decision of its right-wing members to support a white voter registration campaign in opposition to the Negroes. The campaign, known as VERA, has amounted to very little. The club's meetings may resume when the Office of Education hands down its more stringent guidelines for 1966–1967. Finally, there is one more important figure in the River City affairs of the moment, the current chief of police. Chief Watts is highly respected for his foresight, his training, and his iron control of the police department itself. Even the civil rights workers admit that he is cut from a different cloth than the typical Mississippi police officer. He is plainly not the sort of official on whom nonviolent demonstrations thrive and depend. He prefers reason to violence.

istry of the National Council of Churches began to take up local residence and step up local activities, the mantle of radicalism found new shoulders. Now men like Wilbur Cobb were dubbed "reasonable." These were the local men of vision whose moderation was to lead the community out of the wilderness of potential violence and possible federal occupation. Compared to the demands of the civil rights workers, the school board's voluntary compliance seemed a mild compromise indeed. We shall see later that the presence of the civil rights workers served related functions for the River City Negro leaders. Not only did the "movement" force their hand, but it made them also appear "reasonable" by contrast. This opened up new lines of communication with a white elite that needed cooperation from their Negro counterparts.

Clearly, city size is a crucial variable. River City is large enough to provide its leaders with a degree of autonomy and to ward off wholesale polarization in response to the civil rights crisis. Not so in the towns of Bayou County. Lacking both white and Negro elites, these communities have been impaled by the civil rights movement. Here the lines between black and white are sharper now than in the past. Several respondents commented that the once typical residential intermingling of Negroes and "rednecks" had declined now that it carries the name of "integration." As white and black move to more segregated corners, one is reminded of boxers before the bell.

This is not to say, however, that there are no moderate whites in Bayou County. There are several, but they are clearly outflanked. Most are confined to the county's largest town, and they are unable to exert effective leadership even there. Mississippi's small communities employ a conspiracy of silence. The ideology of segregation is as much public display as private conviction. The problem is less the sentiments of individuals as individuals, but more the individual's concern for what other people may think. One can conceive of a situation in which every resident is privately moderate but all are fearful of breaking with what they perceive as the dominant conservative mood. Of course, we are not suggesting that small-town Mississippi meets this model completely. The opposite also applies, since many citizens are more inclined to violence than they are willing to declare. But the crucial matter is that leaders who are privately moderate are reluctant to speak out and provide a public model. This is not simply a failure of nerve or an indication of moral shallowness; it is profoundly related to structural factors that differ between a small town and a good-sized city.

Bureaucratization and the Role of the School Superintendent

A major distinction between River City and Bayou County is that the former allows its school administrators to pursue their professional course while the latter throws up a spate of obstacles. The River City school system enjoys an autonomy with which to follow bureaucratic guidelines established in part by the U.S. Office of Education. Its administrators react more impersonally than emotionally to desegregation. They find their mandates from codes of instructions rather than from current political sentiment. Eying careers at higher levels in larger systems, they are determined not to jeopardize those aspirations by violating bureaucratic principles.

All of this is much less the case in Bayou County. Here the school system is far from an impregnable fortress; it is shot through with ideological calculation and political caprice. The small-town school superintendent has few sources of support. Many of these school officials have long since abandoned aspirations to more important posts; most orient to the community rather than to any professional reference group. Here there is little commitment to quality education. The administrator who pursues it may be more a liability than an asset, since community tradition and stability are considered more important than educational excellence. But let us consider this distinction between River City and Bayou County in more detail.

Like a great many school administrators in Mississippi, River City's superintendent is a former football coach. Coaching involves experience with discipline, and *good* coaching insures community popularity. More important, the state's low teaching salaries discourage men from entering the school system as pure academics. In any event, Superintendent Jones has served a long administrative apprenticeship in addition to his Friday nights on the gridiron. The River City job was a plum won after many thumbthrusts. And since both Jones and his assistant superintendent are new to their posts, they are hypersensitive to bureaucratic procedures and highly responsive to the "moderate" school board that appointed them.

A near universal among bureaucracies is that success can be measured in monetary terms. This is certainly the case within the River City school system. River City prides itself on a commitment to educational excellence, and currently excellence requires federal funds. Negro leaders in the community are keenly aware of the bureaucratic and monetary orientation of the River City school administration, and many of their strategies derive from this knowledge. Said one Negro tactician:

> The reason they complied with that much integration is because of the pressure for money on the part of the school system. They realized that in order to do anything, they would have to have money. This has been a lesson in how we can deal with these school administrators. We convinced Jones that we were going to make him or break him. We would make him if he was willing to comply with the Civil Rights Act in order to get enough federal funds to be a first-rate administrator. We would break him if he did not. Being an ambitious man, he came around. We finally got to him. During the last six months he has undergone a fairly dramatic change for a white Southerner. Since then he has handled the situation fairly well.

At the moment, the superintendent's office resembles a factory for the manufacture of federal grant proposals. The schools are already operating beyond the normal local tax share after a special referendum; they are now seeking to capitalize fully on federal moneys from the Poverty Program and the Elementary-Secondary Education Act. Grant requests for the coming year total more than one million dollars. New proposals are in for special reading laboratories, library supplements, an expanded free-lunch program, increased supervisory staff, teaching the mentally retarded, and even a labor-retraining program as part of an adult education curriculum. In the words of the assistant superintendent:

> We're out to get every dime Washington has to offer, and we're not going to let segregation stand in our way.

Of course, it is precisely this spirit that Washington is seeking to foster. At the same time, the gap between the spirit and the reality can be disturbingly wide. Some school systems plan to support their very expensive dual education for whites and Negroes by using token integration to obtain the kind of federal money that cannot be had from local revenues. A large amount of federal money is restricted to schools serving a high proportion of families making less than $2,000 yearly, and, of course, the only schools that qualify in many Southern areas are all-Negro. This strategy may be operating in River City as well, but we saw no evidence of it. It is precisely this sort of maneuvering that is anathema to this sort of bureaucracy. Indeed, it is more likely to occur in many Northern cities, whose school systems have long since learned to circumvent the spirit of federal legislation through sophisticated cunning, seemingly hopeless entanglements, or political influence. A school system like River City's is still new to the larger federal game, perhaps too new to have learned how to bypass its rules.

But River City is complying out of more than inexperience or the need for money. Compliance "is the law of the land" and small bureaucracies observe the law scrupulously to avoid being caught up short by it. Moreover, River City's school officials begrudge the time and effort required to take advantage of legal loopholes. The superintendent's office has little patience for any pattern that is needlessly demanding. The criterion is one of efficiency rather than ideology. Hence, the remarks of a school official concerning "freedom-of-choice" registration:

> Frankly, as school administrators, we'd just as soon abolish the distinction between white and Negro schools and do the whole thing on a purely neighborhood basis even though this would mean sending white kids to formerly Negro schools and getting some situations where the Negroes amount to anywhere from 60 per cent to 90 per cent of the students. Sure this would cause some friction, but I feel better handling a little friction than I do handling the last-minute headaches and paperwork involved in free choice. The neighborhood system would be a lot simpler from our point of view.

The concluding section will comment on some of the difficulties of the neighborhood plan from the perspective of others. Here the point is the peculiar vision of the administrator. One of the characteristics of bureaucracy is planning ahead in the interests of efficiency. Certainly, something that remains ahead is faculty integration, and yet River City schoolmen have begun to ponder and even act on the problem. The school board has already decided to bring Negro faculty salaries up to the level of the whites' for 1966–1967, and the equalization has been moving gradually toward this closure for the past several years.[8] Moreover, there are now integrated faculty meetings for the first time in the school system's history. This was a condition of Office of Education acceptance of desegregation plans (and at that an informal substitute for the stated requirement of actual faculty integration which was deferred until 1966–1967). But Bayou County officials made no mention of such meetings in all of their attempts to impress us with their liberalism. Nor has Bayou County given any evidence of planning ahead for faculty integration itself. In contrast, the River City school officials have been meeting privately for some time to weigh Negro faculty candidates for the white schools in order to adjust more smoothly to a requirement they feel is inevitable. In the light of this, we asked the River City superintendent a question that had seemed starry-eyed before. The exchange went like this:

INTERVIEWER: Mr. Jones, I wonder what would happen if there were no more federal legislation concerning school desegregation, if there were no more pressures put on River City. Do you think there is any chance that your office might go further anyway?

JONES: To be honest, I don't know. But I can conceive of the possibility. For example, we have a hard time getting first-rate white teachers to stay in the state since every other state around us has much better salaries. It may happen that I'll need a physics teacher and will have to choose between a poorly prepared white and a well-prepared Negro. If that happens, I don't see how I could pass up the Negro even if it means teacher integration.

INTERVIEWER: Then you'd hire the Negro.

JONES: I didn't say *that*. I said I didn't see how I could *not* hire the Negro.

[8] It is deceptive to say that Negro and white teachers' salaries are equalized, however. It will remain true that white teachers continue to qualify for higher positions on the *equalized scale*. Some school systems will even devise means of maintaining salary differentials at the same point on the scale through a bonus system. There is ample statistical evidence that Santa Claus discriminates; Mississippi may add still more if local school officials take unequal advantage of the Christmas season and the Christmas bonus. Finally, it is important to recall that salary equalization is no new charge to Southern schools. It dates back to 1896 and the U.S. Supreme Court decision of Plessy v. Ferguson. Hopefully, compliance will come much quicker for more recent decisions.

The superintendent took a similar view concerning the composition of the school board. There is no current federal requirement for integrated school boards and it follows that the River City board is exclusively white. But while Jones appreciated the presence and backing of these "high-status men of vision," he is also sympathetic with the case for including Negroes:

> Let's face it, when you have as many Negroes involved in the school system as we do here, they have every right to demand representation on the board. Some of the white leaders are already talking about it. I don't know when it will happen but it shouldn't be too long, and the people that make the decisions already have a few possible Negro leaders in mind who are qualified.

Here is another instance of thinking ahead. It is worth noting that the remarks came from a bureaucrat rather than a publicly elected official. For example, we asked the mayor of River City about the issue and his response was tight-lipped, if not close-mouthed.

> That's something I really don't know anything about. I certainly couldn't say who the first Negro might be. The problem is that none of them are really knowledgeable enough to handle the complex problems that the school board faces. There's certainly nothing in the works right now.

Fear of the impolitic is obvious here. In fact, the mayor knows a good deal more than he reports. Other respondents indicate that he is willing to abide by the moderate consensus and appoint a Negro to the school board's next opening. Nor would this be the first Negro in River City's municipal government. More than a year ago a Negro was appointed to the city's Board of Recreation—one of the first such appointments in the state since the Reconstruction era. But let us return to the issue of bureaucracy in the schools and consider a school system and a school official operating in sharp contrast to River City and Mr. Jones.

Earlier we described the particularly hostile climate surrounding desegregation in Raeford, Mississippi, a small town in Bayou County. This was the town described as a "hot spot." It is also the context for the statement, "We don't have many Negroes . . . most of ours are niggers." Sentiments like this are not restricted to Raeford. They occur in River City and even in Northern towns and cities. The point is, however, that Raeford allows such sentiments to penetrate the school administration itself and become a governing force in its day-to-day policy. The school bureaucracy is inadequate to the task of defending its functionaries from community influence and is unable to compel them to pursue a different course. Again, the issue is not so much the ideological convictions of the school administrator but the structural framework within which he must operate.

We asked the local white high school principal how long he had been there and Mr. Sullivan replied quickly, "Too damn long—eleven years." When asked why he has stayed despite his disenchantment, he answered: "Well, you get into a little place and you take the path of least resistance. That means you can never get out."

What is this path of least resistance? In part, Sullivan had his economic situation and his family in mind. He lives comfortably on a salary that he claims is more than adequate, with a free house that is beyond his capacity to utilize fully. His family has grown accustomed to the salary, the perquisites, and indeed the town itself. But Sullivan admitted that this is only a minor part of what his statement intended. A more important factor is that in appeasing Raeford's resident ideologists, he virtually seals himself off from positions in more sophisticated school systems such as River City. He described the appeasement accordingly:

> Occasionally, I have to reassure them by saying, "Down with the niggers." Sometimes I have to give an impression without shouting from the rooftops. I try to avoid hypocrisy. But really, my social philosophy doesn't differ much from the average Mississippian—I have my social snobbery and I'm basically a conservative. But I like to think of myself as more progressive and, besides, as an administrator I have a responsibility to everyone in my district.

The statement, of course, is rife with inconsistencies. These sorts of contradictions were common throughout our interview. They reflect the strong contradictory pressures exerted on Sullivan in the community context. The difficulty was to determine whether he was donning artificial guise for us or whether he contrived to wear wolf's clothing for the sake of the town itself.

Sullivan commented on the social position of the small-town school official: "We are lonely men. I think my position is very similar to the President's. We often walk alone." He went on to indicate that this has been particularly the case since 1964 and the first intimations of school desegregation:

> Because of my position I have learned to stay pretty much to myself—perhaps even more so in the last year. There are some people I can talk to, like the Catholic priest and a few Jews in town. Then, too, I don't think the Methodist minister is as strong a segregationist as he seems, but I guess he can justify it as staying close to his sinners in order to save them.

All of this suggests the plight of a Southern moderate under duress. But there is a contrasting side to Sullivan that may be more revealing. As we saw above, he did not camouflage his segregationist sympathies. Indeed, he lent them the classic intellectual defense:

> I suppose deprivation is a factor in racial differences, but I also think there are inherent racial differences and that genes are important. Heredity even has a bearing on white families—we can see that in our work.

Apparently, Sullivan's defense of genetic differences is more than mere intellectualism. We later learned that he exerts unusually authoritarian control over the local Negro schools and that he is the single most despised white among the Raeford Negro community. Moreover, it is rumored that Sullivan has sought to extend his influence elsewhere in the state.

This is a man for whom the "path of least resistance" has become a superhighway. Sullivan seems to have buckled under the strain, while cultivating the illusion of having resisted it. Unlike school administrators in River City, he is more of an impediment than a lubricant in the school desegregation process; he has created problems rather than controlling them; he fans the local passions instead of dissipating them. Of course, much of this is due to Sullivan's personality. But more important, it is also attributable to structural factors and the absence of organizational protection. Sullivan is subject to a myriad of pressures from local politicians, influential white parents, and on the other hand, federal guidelines and Raeford's civil rights movement. Lacking bureaucratic armor, he stands naked before these forces. In this respect Raeford is far more typical of Mississippi than is River City. River City may point the way to the future, but most Deep Southern communities are firmly mired in the past.

And yet the River City school bureaucracy is not only distinctive when compared to communities like Raeford, it is distinctive when compared to such metropolitan centers as Chicago, New York, and Los Angeles. In many of these latter instances, the bureaucracy is bloated, and its size has led to internal stalemates, which produce inertia rather than innovation. River City has the sort of bureaucracy that is neither too much nor too little, the sort that early sociologists had in mind when discussing bureaucracy as a rational instrument for mobilizing men and channeling effort.

So far, however, we have concentrated solely on the *white* school professionals. It is appropriate to conclude with remarks concerning their Negro counterparts. While it can be argued that the Negro school administrator should await discussion of the Negro community, there are clear reasons for including him here. In a very real sense, the Southern Negro school principal is more bound to the white bureaucracy than to his Negro fellows. Two Negro leaders concurred independently on the point:

> Negro leaders in the schools have been picked because of their deference to whites.

> To a man, the principals have been chosen because they will fall in line with what the white man wants or what they think he wants.

The point, however, is not to denigrate individuals. At the risk of jargon, the individual must be understood in terms of his "role." The Negro school administrator is plainly the prisoner of his position, and this is the case in River City as well as Bayou County. Regardless of what he thinks, he must guard his statements and actions carefully for fear of antagonizing the whites in command. Of all the persons we talked with, the Negro school administrators were the least at ease and the most concerned about closed doors, anonymity, and feedback. Their responses were filtered through a broad smile that may be interpreted as obliging to us or as ironic amusement at themselves.

Their position is precarious for reasons other than white pressures. These are men whose very jobs depend upon dual education. Without all-Negro schools, there would be few Negro administrators in the South; there are certainly very few in the "integrated" North. The Negro principal has a vested interest in defending his school in order to defend his job. It is not surprising that of all our respondents, the Negro school officials were the only persons who equivocated concerning the inferiority of the Negro schools. The equivocation extends to student conferences as well, especially those concerning desegregation. Here, of course, Negro principals, counselors, and teachers are in a two-way bind. To encourage the student to attend the white school is to risk the enmity of the white administrator and risk the loss of one more Negro pupil. To do otherwise is to risk the enmity of the Negro community and risk the respect of one more Negro pupil. The solution, for the most part, has been silence. Negro principals have instructed their counselors to avoid the issue wherever possible. Of course, avoidance is itself a negative influence on desegregation. As one Negro parent in River City commented: "Our big problem is not with the white school system, but with the Negro schools."

As all of this suggests, then, the concept of "dual education" is a partial misnomer. To be sure, there are dual physical plants as well as a double standard of quality. Yet the administration of the dual system is tightly in the hands of the whites themselves. If an efficient white bureaucracy can be an asset in some respects, it is obviously a liability in others.

Fragmentation vs. Polarization: The Negro Community in River City and Bayou County

There is a long-standing tendency to refer to the crisis of segregation as "the Negro problem." However, the first two sections of this chapter suggest that the crisis may be more of a "white problem," since both guilt and the opportunity for redemption fall on uneasy white shoulders. Still, one cannot deny the difficulties that exist within the Negro community itself. Few have leapt to exercise their freedom of choice; few are either willing or able to communicate their grievances to the whites.

Since this is more the case in Bayou County, what is there about the River City Negroes that accounts for the difference?

Perhaps the most striking single attribute of the typical Delta Negro is his stark and overwhelming poverty, a poverty that is growing worse instead of better. Note, however, that poverty's scourge is more universal among the Negroes of Bayou County than it is in River City. The latter, more urban setting fosters a Negro middle class that includes merchants, civil servants, and autonomous professionals. Now the Negro middle class has a long tradition of cultivating its own garden without tending the fields of its lower-class brethren. But while the black bourgeoisie is a well-known lair of the Uncle Tom, stereotypes of this sort can be dangerous. Not all members of the middle class are equally in retreat from civil rights activities. It matters whether they are operating in a metropolitan area, a medium-sized city, or a small town. Age is an important variable. Certainly one must distinguish between the businessman who depends upon lower-class Negro trade vs. one who depends upon white concessions, the civil service employee vs. the employee in a locally owned white firm, the autonomous lawyer or physician vs. the Negro school administrator whose job depends upon white favor, and indeed, the locally autonomous Baptist minister vs. the African Methodist Episcopal clergyman. Finally, one recent factor looms particularly large: the emergence of the civil rights movement on a large scale.

Earlier we mentioned that the presence of the civil rights movement in River City served to make "moderate" whites *and* indigenous Negro leaders seem "reasonable" by comparison. Civil rights workers often create an impression that mystifies and alienates both the local white and Negro community. The workers' public statements are frequently beyond the scope of the public goals they pursue. For example, one militant white volunteer was asked by the police if his organization had right-wing as well as left-wing literature in its office: "Yes, we have a copy of Milton." Or to take another instance, when a Northern volunteer was under legal pressure to make payment on clothes previously purchased on credit, he was quoted in the local papers:

. . . future alienation of Dun and Bradstreet does not bother me greatly as that sort of thing shall not enter into my future and is an integral part of a system I have largely left behind.

. . . Should you continue to send your racist allies to my door daily to dun me about a three-year-old debt that is out of the question, [I'll let my lawyers handle it].

This is hardly a mollifying statement to the whites of River City; it is confusing to the Negroes. But while the outside civil rights worker often cuts himself off from local communication, he has served to bring about increased contact between the white leaders and some of River City's Negroes. Predictably enough, these Negroes are middle-class. But the civil rights movement has insured that these middle-class leaders would not take on the compliant characteristics of the fabled Uncle Tom. The movement has forced their hand. Having ignited a spark, the movement requires that these people feed the civil rights flame or suffer in their occupational and social standing within the Negro community as a whole. River City is simply not large enough to afford an isolated retreat for Negro leaders who would shrink from the struggle. It is true that the local Negroes were not so militant as to satisfy the civil rights workers themselves, and there is an undeniable rift between the indigenous Negro leaders and the local representatives of the Delta ministry and the Freedom Democratic Party. But it is exactly this rift that is important if the voices of the local Negroes are to be heard.

At this point it is important to introduce a major distinction. The local Negroes alone could not have produced school desegregation. The civil rights movement and its outside workers were crucial for putting pressure on River City, on Mississippi, and on the nation itself. Without the movement, there would have been no law, and without the law together with the movement, there would have been no change. But one must distinguish between desegregation as a legal requirement and desegregation as a social process. River City's Negro middle class were inadequate to effect a change of federal, state, or local law, but they have been a major factor in influencing the process of compliance with the law once passed. The Negroes have developed a keen eye for noncompliance and are maintaining a constant vigil. As one River City Negro leader put it:

The school board is going to try gimmicks to slow down integration. Nothing overt, but anything they can do under cover to slow down the pace they'll continue to do until their hand

is called. When it is, they'll act because they don't want unfavorable publicity.

Or, again:

Jones has done a fair job as superintendent. We have to keep
a close watch on him, however.

Of course, close watches entail sophistication and sufficient
communication to find out what is happening. Both of these are
more likely to develop among middle-class Negroes. One commented on his way of getting information:

I don't think anybody on the school board knows how much I
know about what goes on there. But I see most of them from
time to time, and I get little bits of information from this
member and that member that aren't any trouble to piece together. Why, just the other day I ran into Superintendent Jones
on the municipal golf course. This was an occasion, though,
where I wanted to play through and he wanted to talk. I had
to run away from him.

Another advantage supplied by the middle-class Negroes to
the larger process of desegregation is their children. Because
River City is large enough to afford occupational havens from
job reprisals, the Negro middle class is more adventurous in pursuing integration. As another Negro leader stated:

In other areas, it's the poverty-class children who send their
children to the white schools, and the middle class doesn't—
they have too much to lose. But here all classes have sent their
children to the white schools.

There are qualifications that should be added here, however. It is true that middle-class Negro students attend the white
elementary and junior high schools in River City, but not the
white high school. Moreover, as we saw earlier, while the middle-
class Negroes are more successful academically, they also tend to
segregate themselves from the lower-class Negroes and provide
less leadership than they might. Still, the fact that some Negro
children do well and that some are from Negro families with all
the scrubbed characteristics of the white ideal serves to challenge
white stereotypes. The fact that the Negro middle class sends its
children at all helps to contribute several more students to the
small minority who were willing to risk the hazards of desegregation.

This last point suggests a major difficulty not only among River City Negroes but among Southern Negroes generally. As indicated earlier, freedom-of-choice has elicited the few and not the many. In requiring the Negro to take the initiative, it asks him to put aside a century of fear and suspicion. The Negro knows full well that the whites are acting out of forced compliance instead of contrition. It is one thing to open a door willingly and invite a guest to enter; it is quite another to set the door ajar and expect an entrant to brave the menacing scowls of those who stand on guard.

The Negroes' fear has several facets. Not only are they fearful of violence, but they are also frightened of failing academically. Not only are they concerned about economic reprisals, but they are also anxious about leaving the ties that bind them to the Negro schools.

We have already commented that freedom-of-choice has not drawn the best Negro students. This is partly because the best students are more entwined in a network of activities and relationships within the Negro schools. They are more likely to be involved with Negro teachers and administrators who find it against their own interest to urge desegregation; they are more likely to have attained some leadership prominence among their Negro classmates. Moreover, the Negro student is asked to forego certain activities, ranging from music and drama to varsity athletics. Finally, and most important among the high school upperclassmen, the best Negro students jeopardize their chances for college scholarships. Since scholarships are meted out according to the nitty-gritty of a grade-point average and since there is common recognition that the white schools are more difficult, many students defer the immediate gratification of integration to choose the delayed rewards of higher education, albeit Negro higher education.

What is the response of the River City middle-class Negro leadership to all of this? Certainly, by sending some of their own children to the white schools they are doing more than adding to the trickle. Insofar as this occurs, it is an important symbol suggesting to others that risks must be taken even by those who stand to lose the most. Further, the middle-class Negroes have been active in mounting campaigns to insure that freedom of choice will be more widely exercised in the future:

Our philosophy is this: we have 146 children in the white schools. These white schools can't get many more Negroes registered without moving to a double shift. . . . If we can get enough Negroes in the white schools by 1967, then they will have to devise a new system. Then white children will have to go to Negro schools, and the moment that happens they are going to have to bring those Negro schools up to the standards of whites.

This is a firm but not a militant position. The statement overestimates the number of Negroes currently enrolled in the River City white schools (121); it is cast completely within the rules of freedom-of-choice without seeking immediate changes in that system; it points to a future in which the distinction between white and Negro schools persists. Nevertheless, these middle-class leaders are hardly shrinking from the problem.

When asked how many Negroes will exercise their freedom-of-choice in the eight grades to be open in 1966–1967, one replied, "My hope is that there'll be seven hundred Negro children going to the white schools next year."

But a hope is not a firm estimate, and answers to the question vary widely. This is clearly a problem facing the white school administrators in their anxiety to plan ahead. It is also a challenge to the Negro leadership, and a challenge to which they are trying to respond. The parents of the present Negro children in the white schools are planning now to "knock on every Negro door in town when registration opens in May." Of course, the same group tried knocking on doors last year with disappointing results. They hope this year to capitalize on the relative absence of incidents during the first year of desegregation.

Yet there is one more important element in the strategy of the River City Negro leaders. It revolves about Project Headstart, and again the militant civil rights movement is an important ingredient. During the summer of 1965 the only Headstart program in River City was run by an agency from outside the community—the Child Development Group of Mississippi—using civil rights workers. Needless to say, it disturbed the whites to have the local Negro children in the hands of the militants for so long and under such an aegis. Accordingly, the whites decided to counter the move in 1966. Realizing that any Headstart Board of Directors would have to be integrated to appeal to Washington, the board was half Negro in composition and featured one of the most prominent middle-class Negro strategists as president. As of January, the board seemed to be functioning smoothly from the reports of both whites and Negroes. Nor are these Negroes merely shuffling to the tunes of the white pipers. As the president explained it:

> I'm not sure that the white members of the board realize the potential of a Headstart program of this size. First of all, the kids are going to be dominantly Negro and there will be a lot of them. But second, we are going to do our best to use the program to funnel these Negro preschoolers right into the white first grades. Now if you figure that the program will include at least two hundred Negroes, you can imagine what that is going to mean in terms of desegregation for next year.

Again, River City's middle-class Negroes are operating within the system rather than outside of it, but they are operating rather than sitting on their hands. Led by a professional who depends upon Negro clients and whose appetite for desegregation was whetted by a number of years as an army officer, they are not backing off but only approaching the problem in a way different from the militants. Of course, it remains to be seen whether this strategy will be executed or if the leaders themselves will be co-opted by an invitation for one of them to join the school board. Nevertheless, the situation in Bayou County poses a different set of problems and a different set of questions for the future.

If the last several years of the civil rights struggle have served to fragment River City to some advantage, they have polarized Bayou County to considerable disadvantage. Not only does Bayou County have few "moderate" whites who have gained legitimacy by comparison with the demands of the civil rights workers, but it also has few resident Negroes who have achieved new respect and influence without conceding their case altogether. The conflict has shoved a new wedge into the small-town relationships between black and white. It has reduced contact instead of increasing it. As mentioned earlier, there is more contact between Negroes and white leaders in River City than there is in Raeford, although River City is some twenty times larger and would seem to offer more room in which the two elements might avoid each other. Of course, one explanation is that Bayou County has no white elite to compare with River City;

another is that it has no Negro elite. Whereas a Negro professional is the resident spokesman and tactician among the River City Negroes, the job falls to a federal blue-collar employee in Bayou City. But there is more than a difference of class here. Even a Negro lawyer or physician would have difficulty in Bayou City or Raeford. Despite his professional pedigree, he would be suspect among the whites; because of his pedigree, he might be suspect among the Negroes. In River City the middle-class Negro has an accepted niche and a communication link to the community as a whole. In Bayou County the middle-class Negro is more of a man apart with less chance of communication with either Negroes or whites. From the perspective of the Bayou County whites, a Negro is either a militant or a man who can "be had." There is no middle ground and even these two plots offer more quicksand than firm footing.

These considerations point to still another explanation for the difference in school desegregation between River City and Bayou County. In contrast to River City, the Bayou County Negroes have no middle-class leaders who are either aggressive or informed. In Bayou City, for example, two middle-class Negroes who pushed for freedom-of-choice registration apparently chose not to send their own eligible children to the white schools for fear of the consequences. This obviously poses a crisis of leadership, and it is no surprise that freedom-of-choice in Bayou County has elicited only a 2-per-cent response as compared to 10 per cent in River City.

Moreover, there is little shepherding of the students who did elect to go to the Bayou County white schools. Some of these students were counting on transportation from the Negroes who persuaded them to attend in the first place. The students claim that the transportation has now fallen through. Lacking a spearhead and a spokesman, it is understandable that the students' parents should shy away from conferences with white teachers and administrators. It is also predictable that whereas River City Negro parents attend integrated P.T.A. meetings frequently, Bayou County parents are conspicuously absent. And yet the point is not a simple lack of courage or motivation. Certainly, the county's more polarized social setting is far more intimidating than the River City situation. Certainly the threat of violence and reprisal is more commonly realized. The problem again becomes one of structure. The important factor is not the Negroes' failure but the lack of facilitating devices.

This is even true with regard to planning for the future. While the River City Negro leadership has crystallized plans and objectives, one senses little of this in Bayou County. There are, of course, a sprinkling of militants who are intensely dissatisfied and anxious to act. But they are frustrated because of a lack of information on which to base their tactics.

We have already described the importance of Project Headstart in River City. Consider the case of the Community Action Program (CAP) in Bayou County. Here, too, the board of directors has been integrated, but it is an integration of a different sort. A militant Bayou City Negro leader described it as follows:

> The Negroes on the board don't represent us. They were handpicked to represent the whites. Actually I know more about some of the whites on the board than I do the Negroes. Almost all the Negroes come from the same town, belong to the same fraternal association, and most are even related by kin to the same family. It looks like there are a lot of them, but the big question is, who are they?

The quest for information has been consistently stymied. For example, the CAP board and its white president have been touring the county to talk to Negro groups, but they choose their circumstances and their circumlocutions carefully. Most meetings are held within Negro churches whose ministers are selected for their docility. While we were in the area, a meeting scheduled in conjunction with the Bayou City Negro P.T.A. was aborted as the CAP board failed to attend and the P.T.A. members found the school building locked upon their arrival. Clearly, neither the Poverty Program generally nor Project Headstart in particular is apt to exert leverage on future desegregation in Bayou County. For the most part the struggle is just beginning. True, violence has not occurred thus far, but then neither has large-scale desegregation.

———•———

Beyond Tokenism

> We have some people who think this thing is just a bad dream, and that we'll all wake up some morning and the dream will be over (*White Bayou County high school principal*).

Reactions to this report will vary. Some will be relieved at the absence of violence; others will be incensed at the presence of reprisals. Some will be surprised at the degree of compliance; others will be shocked at the undeniable tokenism. Some will argue that federal law and freedom-of-choice have done too little; many Southern and Northern whites alike will argue that the law has gone too far and that even "freedom-of-choice" is an outrageous violation of an autonomous and traditional way of life.

In all of this, two facts should be clear. First, without the Civil Rights Act of 1964, there would be no desegregation at all in Mississippi. Second, if one looks closely at the law, existing desegregation falls short of its spirit if not its letter. River City has gone slightly farther and somewhat more smoothly than Bayou County. But both have far to go and can expect severe crises in the future.

The requirements for school desegregation during 1965–1966 were set forth in a publication of the Office of Education: "General Statement of Policies Under Title VI of the Civil Rights Act of 1964 Respecting Desegregation of Elementary and Secondary Schools." If one compares the formal requirements with reality, there is a gap. The document requires faculty integration as well as the integration of any activities, facilities, or services provided or sponsored by a school system. River City as well as Bayou County are wanting on each count. It is true that River City has held integrated faculty meetings and has begun to plan ahead for integrated staffs; it is also true that Bayou City has one non-college-educated white shop teacher who serves both Negro and white high schools. But all of this is meager compliance indeed, and neither River City nor Bayou County has witnessed extensive integration of activities. There has been no provision for Negroes in varsity athletics; Negroes are discouraged from participating equally in glee clubs or drama groups; the most common pattern is simply to drop the Spring Prom and reschedule it as a private white party without formal school sponsorship.

But the point is not flagrant dereliction or defiance. The Office of Education relaxed some of its standards for 1965–1966, and River City did meet the adjusted requirements sufficiently to gain full federal funds. Moreover, the Office of Education allowed continued federal funds in Bayou County although there was desegregation on an even lesser scale. Bayou County was desegregated by federal court order and did not submit a plan. The Office of Education's implementing guidelines accept compliance with the federal courts as satisfactory, even though the court requirements may fall short of the office's own.

The major question concerns the future. The Office of Education issued stepped-up requirements for 1966–1967. These include the faculty integration that was deferred for 1965–1966. They also restate that eight grades must be desegregated by the fall of 1966. Federal requirements are crucial, and all indications point to an increase rather than a decrease in this pressure. But there are difficulties. We have already commented on the problems of "freedom-of-choice," and there is no sign that the procedure will be changed. Even though the new guidelines stipulate performance standards that must be met by free choice, desegregation will continue to occur at a minimal pace because of the fears and anxieties of Negro students. Moreover, any immediate shift from free choice to geographical attendance areas awaits local initiative instead of occurring at the behest of the federal government itself. Federal regulations have the advantage of being imposed and perchance enforced from "outside." Local decisions are much more vulnerable to local pressures and are much more likely to provoke recriminations. Let us consider the road ahead in more detail.

In Bayou County neither the Negroes nor the school officials were making plans for next year as of January. However, River City Negro leaders were mobilizing for the registration to govern 1966–1967. Here the plan was to knock on every door and use

Project Headstart as a way of putting far more Negroes in the white schools next year. Negro leaders hope to force the hand of the school officials. The Negroes reason that the moment one white child enters a formerly all-Negro school to alleviate over-crowding in the desegregated white schools, the Negroes will begin to obtain improved educational quality. School administrators are even now forced to consider the likelihood of sending white students to Negro schools. From the standpoint of the school professionals, freedom-of-choice is a headache that may become an administrative debacle. Some are willing to shift to a geographical system for administrative reasons alone. If close to one thousand Negro students enter the River City white schools next year with a similar number the year following, a shift will have to occur. The Negro schools should indeed begin to improve and administrative burdens will be eased. But, unhappily, these are not the only possible consequences of a shift to a geographical attendance plan.

There is both a Scylla and a Charybdis confronting such a shift. On the one hand, many towns are so residentially segregated that a shift to geographical attendance means simply a conversion to *de facto* school segregation. Here the gains resulting from an abandonment of freedom-of-choice may be more illusory than real. This is the case with a number of towns in Bayou County, just as it has characterized many Northern cities and the resegregation of Southern metropolitan areas, as reported elsewhere in this volume.

On the other hand, River City represents a contrasting case that is widespread in the South. Here Negro residential areas are less defined by the kind of "natural boundaries or perimeters of compact areas" that are acceptable to the Office of Education. Negroes live in many areas of the older parts of the city, tucked neatly within and between white neighborhoods.[9] This means that the local school officials will have more difficulty in contriving formally acceptable *de facto* segregation. It also means that an increase in friction may be likely.

[9] And yet the residential intermingling of River City whites and Negroes shows signs of changing. Some people estimate that in a few years, it will be possible to use a major highway as a natural border with virtually no Negroes on one side of it and virtually no whites on the other. Here too then there are possibilities for a reversion to segregation on a geographical basis, though the time is still sufficiently distant that many whites are concerned about the interim.

It is no surprise that the residentially integrated Negroes in River City do not live near the middle- or upper-class whites, but rather near the lower-class "rednecks." These are precisely the whites who are least pleased to have their children attend school with Negroes, let alone attend formerly all-Negro schools with a high proportion of Negroes remaining. But these are also the people who cannot afford to move out of the area, especially with the drop in property values that may occur. Even now these people cannot afford to take advantage of the current freedom-of-choice to send their children to white schools in the white middle-class suburbs. More like the Negroes than high-status whites, they can not afford the transportation. All of this means, then, that under a geographical system in a town such as River City, the Negroes will be "integrated," not with whites at random but with lower-class whites, those who are most likely to provoke and carry through incidents. The further consequence is that the Negroes may find their hope of greatly improved educational quality to be futile. Quality differentials may merely begin to occur along the lines of economic *class* rather than racial *caste*.

This leads to a final word on the transition from racial to economic problems in the future of the Delta. One can imagine the day when the South will have achieved the dubious Northern par in its race relations. One can even imagine the time when the question of money will supersede that of skin color. Certainly the problems that are most likely to plague the South disproportionately in 1986 are the problems of a depleted economy. The downfall of cotton and the lack of a skilled work force with which to attract industry hang like a pall over the Delta in particular and the South generally. Manpower-retraining programs are admirable and important, but hardly equal to the task. Unionization is necessary to bring wages up to a meaningful standard, but unionization creates difficulties in attracting industry in the first place. While a moratorium on state and local taxes has served to woo some industry, it is precisely the taxes that are necessary if the region is to benefit from the industry it has seduced.

All of this has implications for the schools. In the short run, it makes the schools more dependent upon federal funds and hence more vulnerable to federal requirements. In the long run, the state will suffer from the inadequacy of its own resources, and this suffering has already begun to take its toll. Not only is it difficult to envision a significant rise of teachers' salaries, but it is also hard to imagine compulsory school attendance that is enforced. Recall that compulsory attendance was rescinded shortly after the Supreme Court decision of 1954. While the move was designed primarily to obviate integration, it was really only a formal statement of what had been the case all along. Mississippi cannot afford to educate all of its young. The law was not enforced when it was on the books. Should it be re-enacted, it will require mammoth sums to enforce it anew.

It is within this framework that school desegregation, and, indeed, desegregation of any sort, must be seen. Talk of equal opportunity in education, employment, and even at the polls seems hollow when addressed to people ensnared by poverty. Equal opportunity increasingly means an opportunity to share in the problems rather than the benefits of the region. Equal schooling will be poor schooling. Equal employment will be equal *un*employment. And equal voting will be an equal chance to make decisions of little impact. There is no doubt that there are immediate problems that can and must be solved quickly. But the effectiveness of federal legislation only points to the necessity of massive federal funds. The tragedies of Mississippi have yet to reach their climax.

———•———

Postscript

The data and observations in this study go back more than two years, but we obtained more recent data on River City and its school integration as of February 1967.

Little has changed in qualitative terms. Although a great deal of flak was raised over the Office of Education guidelines for the 1966–1967 academic year, the pattern of quiet compliance remained as before. Because the number of classes to be integrated through freedom-of-choice doubled, so the number of Negro students attending formerly all-white schools has doubled

—but little more. The system has yet to integrate the teaching staff, but it is not alone in failing to comply in this respect, and it has made a token response by bringing the Negro administrator in charge of the Negro schools into the offices of the white school administration.

But one ironic twist merits special attention. The River City school system was successful in applying for federal free lunch funds for schools with a high proportion of lower-class children, funds provided under the terms of the Elementary and Secondary Education Act. It now happens that these "liberal" monies have unintentionally "conservative" consequences. Only the Negro schools had sufficient proportions of lower-class students to qualify. So if a Negro student moves to a white school he loses his free lunch, sometimes his only decent meal of the day. Here is yet another respect in which integration involves a sacrifice rather than an unmixed blessing. For many, the hunger for food is understandably more salient than the thirst for knowledge. Once again freedom-of-choice in the Delta offers a poor choice at best.

III

The Savannah Story:
Education and Desegregation

Ruth P. Simms

A GRAVE RESPONSIBILITY rests upon the people of this state to keep our schools open. For them to close, even temporarily, would bring economic disaster and, far worse, would do incalculable injury and injustice to our children (*Georgia Grand Jury*).

[We are] unalterably opposed to any form of integration in our schools. . . . (*President of the Savannah–Chatham County States Rights Council*).

If our [Negro] students are going to qualify for jobs that are opening up to them, it is essential that they get the best education, and the best happens to be "white" right now. . . . (*A Negro minister*).

The superintendent doesn't care who Negro principals hire. But when Negro teachers start teaching white children, he will care. . . . (*President of the NAACP*).

Negroes prefer their own schools because they are just as good as white schools. . . . (*Superintendent of Schools*).

A nd so the story goes. This is Savannah, Georgia, a city in the Deep South that "calmly" integrated public schools in 1963. This is a report on the educational practices and ideologies of the system.

The discussion is heavily biased in the direction of the Negro community—how they perceive the situation and practices in their schools. I have tried to present an objective report reflecting the views expressed by informants as well as the factual data that could be secured. Remaining objective, however, has been extremely difficult for me—a Negro product of the Savannah elementary and secondary school system.

The report, first written in the winter of 1966, is divided

into three parts. The first presents a social profile of the community. This is followed by a very broad coverage of education in the community, including the culture of segregation, the process of desegregation, and definitions of the situation by relevant individuals and groups. The final section is an attempt to discuss the future implications for education in Savannah.

———— • ————

Social Profile of Savannah

Savannah, Georgia, is located on the Savannah River, the dividing line between Georgia and South Carolina in the southeastern section of the state. It is situated inland, some 18 miles from the Atlantic Ocean, approximately 83 miles south of Charleston, South Carolina, and 123 miles north of Jacksonville, Florida.

The area within the city limits is 21 square miles. The metropolitan area, considered to be Chatham County, of which Savannah is the county seat, is 441 square miles.

General James Edward Oglethorpe and a band of 120 followers are considered to be the founders of Savannah. They came over from England and pitched their tents in Savannah on February 12, 1733. Before the Europeans, however, there were the Cherokee Indians and their famous chief, Tomo-chi-chi, who settled in the northwestern section of Savannah which is now called "Yamacraw."

Today Savannahians boast their claim as the "mother city of Georgia"; the "heart of the coastal empire"; the "leading naval store port of the world"; the "locale of the world's longest palm drive"; and the "world's largest pulp, paper mill, and bag factory."

The Economy

Savannah's economy combines the advantages of an industrial center and port city. The diversified industries include manufacturing, transportation activities, ocean-borne commerce, trade with surrounding area, tourism, and military and other government installations. Principal products made in Savannah are paperboard, paper bags, refined sugar, processed seafoods, lumber and other planing mill products, and miscellaneous concrete products. Shipbuilding (dredges, barges, and tugboats) and ship repair are other aspects of the manufacturing complex. There is also a chemical industry which includes the production of fertilizers, rosins, aluminum sulfate, paint, and asphalt compounds.

Savannah is one of the leading ports on the South Atlantic seaboard—approximately 114 steamship lines go in and out the port, served by 33 deep-water berths.

The economy of the historic city is also dependent upon military and other government establishments in the vicinity. There is Hunter Army Airfield, five miles south of the downtown area, and there is Fort Steward, a tank-training center, about 40 miles west of Savannah.

Table 1 shows the occupational distribution of workers in Savannah. Of the total male population employed, craftsmen, managers, and proprietors make up over 54 per cent. The distribution changes considerably for Negro males, who are employed first as operatives, then as laborers, followed by service and craft jobs. Also significant is the fact that a higher percentage of Negro females are employed in professional and technical jobs than Negro males. The former constitute 8.9 per cent, the latter 2.6 per cent.

Although the city's economy has expanded over a period of years, Savannah has its share of problems and lags behind its growth potential. One Chamber of Commerce official indicated that

> Savannah has difficulties attracting new industries. On one hand, this is partly attributed to the lack of skilled people. On the other, trade and transportation routes to a number of areas are extremely limited.
> Primary industry for example has a 50-mile radius, secondary trade a 100-mile radius, and tertiary industry a 150-mile radius, serving about one half million people . . . direct airline routes to major cities outside the South is also another limiting factor. . . .

According to the 1960 census data, the median income for families in Savannah is $4,761. The figure for nonwhite resi-

Table 1: Percentage Distribution
of Workers in Occupations, by Sex*

| | TOTAL | | NONWHITE | |
	Male	Female	Male	Female
Employed	31,433	19,186	10,125	7,732
Professional, technical, and kindred workers	7.98	14.04	2.63	8.87
	(2,509)	(2,695)	(267)	(686)
Managers, proprietors including farm	14.31	3.85	2.77	1.59
	(4,501)	(740)	(281)	(123)
Clerical and kindred workers	6.64	24.62	3.83	2.71
	(2,088)	(4,724)	(388)	(210)
Sales workers	7.52	7.29	1.60	0.95
	(2,364)	(1,399)	(162)	(74)
Craftsmen, foremen and kindred workers	18.58	0.71	10.37	0.64
	(5,841)	(138)	(1,050)	(50)
Operatives and kindred workers	21.42	8.91	30.87	10.23
	(6,734)	(1,710)	(3,126)	(791)
Private household workers	0.18	20.06	0.49	47.01
	(59)	(3,849)	(50)	(3,635)
Service workers except household	7.26	15.16	13.88	22.56
	(2,283)	(2,909)	(1,406)	(1,745)
Laborers except mine	12.18	0.86	29.78	1.77
	(3,831)	(165)	(3,016)	(137)
Occupations not reported	3.59	4.46	3.74	3.63
	(1,223)	(857)	(3.79)	(281)

* Source: 1960 Census.

Table 2: Family Income in Savannah*

| | TOTAL POPULATION: 36,693 | | NONWHITE: 11,837 | |
	Number of Families	Per cent	Number of Families	Per cent
Under $1,000	2,253	6.14	1,620	13.68
$1,000–1,999	3,702	10.09	2,418	20.42
$2,000–2,999	4,577	12.47	2,656	22.43
$3,000–3,999	4,601	12.53	1,937	16.36
$4,000–4,999	4,221	11.50	1,404	11.86
$5,000–5,999	4,327	11.79	704	5.94
$6,000–6,999	3,085	8.40	394	3.32
$7,000–7,999	2,571	7.00	267	2.25
$8,000–8,999	1,960	5.34	144	1.21
$9,000–9,999	1,470	4.00	109	0.92
$10,000–14,999	2,856	7.78	184	1.55
$15,000–24,999	816	2.22	——	——
$25,000	254	0.67	——	——

* Source: 1960 Census.

dents is $2,708, a little over half the median. Approximately 29 per cent of the people earn less than $3,000; among nonwhites the percentage is 56.5. Further details of the family income distributions are in Table 2.

Unemployment ranges between 4 and 7 per cent. Educational achievement is low, so that 30 per cent of all adults have received less than eight years of education.

Table 3: Employment Status*

| | WHITE | | NONWHITE | |
	Male	Female	Male	Female
Fourteen years and over	47,380	54,617	15,446	19,535
Labor force	37,913	20,352	11,289	8,341
Per cent of total	80.0	37.3	73.1	42.7
Civilian labor force	33,185	—	10,995	—
Employed	31,433	19,186	10,125	7,732
Unemployed	1,752	1,119	870	—
Per cent civilian labor unemployed	5.3	5.5	7.9	—
Not in labor force	9,467	34,265	4,157	—
Married women in labor force		10,284		3,692

* Source: 1960 Census.

Table 4: Years of Schooling Completed *

| | TOTAL: 77,758 | | NONWHITE: 26,354 | |
	Number of Persons 25 years and over	Per cent	Number of Persons 25 years and over	Per cent
No school years completed	1,996	2.56	1,626	6.16
Elementary:				
1–4 years	8,368	10.76	6,618	25.11
5–7 years	13,383	17.21	6,989	26.51
8 years	7,234	9.30	2,247	8.46
High school:				
1–3 years	15,375	19.77	4,198	15.92
4 years	19,181	24.66	2,778	10.54
College:				
1–3 years	6,865	8.82	949	3.60
4 years	5,356	6.88	949	3.60
Median school years completed	10.5		7.1	

* Source: 1960 Census.

Population Trends

According to the 1960 census, the population of the central city of Savannah was 149,245, and that of the Chatham County metropolitan area was 188,299. Unofficial figures for 1967 estimate the metropolitan population to be well over 209,000. Savannah has shown a substantial population gain during the past two decades. This is largely attributed to immigration from other parts of Georgia and rural counties in South Carolina. A large influx of new residents was particularly noticeable between 1941 and 1945. Defense industries and postwar industrial expansion attracted these people and permitted them to remain. During the fifties continued industrial expansion attracted new workers. This was aided by the reactivation of Hunter Air Force Base, which had been closed after World War II. This brought in large numbers of military personnel. There have been close to 5,000 personnel and their dependents, making a community of over 16,000 people.

As of 1960 whites numbered 95,987 of the total inhabitants of Savannah. Nonwhites numbered 53,258. Those of foreign stock constitute 7,036, or 5 per cent of the total population.

Most of the recent migrants, both white and Negro, originate from adjoining counties in Georgia and South Carolina with a predominantly agricultural economy. The migration from these areas to Savannah increased during the last decade as the demand for farm manpower experienced a considerable decline.

As indicated in Table 5, the proportion of nonwhite residents has shown a significant decline since 1940. This may in part reflect the growing exodus of substantial numbers of Negroes to large urban centers in the South and other parts of the country.

Between 1940 and 1960 there was a 4-per-cent drop of white residents within the city limits, and a 2-per-cent drop for Negro residents. Although the figures are small the trend is significant; white residents are continuing to spread outward from the central city while the Negro population continues to form a central core in the city.

In large part this may be attributed to three urban renewal

Table 5: Savannah and Chatham County,
by Race 1940–1960*

	CITY OF SAVANNAH	REST OF COUNTY	METROPOLITAN TOTAL	PER CENT IN CITY
White:				
1940	52,700	12,327	65,027	81.0
1950	71,288	21,646	92,934	76.7
1960	95,987	28,129	124,116	77.3
Colored:				
1940	43,296	9,647	52,943	81.8
1950	48,350	10,197	58,547	82.6
1960	53,258	10,925	64,183	82.9
Total:				
1940	95,996	21,974	117,970	81.4
1950	119,638	31,843	151,481	79.0
1960	149,245	39,054	188,299	79.3
Per cent Colored:				
1940	45.1	43.9	44.9	
1950	40.4	32.0	38.7	
1960	35.7	28.0	34.1	

* Based on U. S. Census data, this table is taken from *Industrial Survey, Savannah, Georgia,* compiled and published by the industrial committee of the Savannah District Authority, October 1, 1963.

projects, which have been in operation on the west side of the city since 1958 and have uprooted low-income Negro and white families. On one hand, Negro families have moved into areas where low-income whites used to reside. The latter have moved into other areas of the city, where they seek homogeneity. On the other hand, the continued movement of low-income Negroes has spread into areas which were once popular Negro middle-class neighborhoods. As a result, middle-class Negroes are beginning to move out from the center, although remaining within the city limits, into homogeneous newly built residential developments. This continuing population shift reflects the delicate intertwine between race and class. Nevertheless, the possible development of a black belt in the central city has a number of implications for the economic and political power of the Negro population.

Historically, Negroes have not been effective participants in the political arena, and even now not one holds a key administrative position in the local city government. During Reconstruction days, however, Negroes in Savannah held key governmental and political jobs: there were congressmen, senators, a municipal court judge, and a customs collector.

Since the beginning of this decade, the bargaining power and political potential of the nonwhite population has changed considerably. In the early months of 1960, sit-in demonstrations started. Subsequently, Negroes under the leadership of the NAACP launched a successful eighteen-month boycott of downtown merchants. Among the demands met by local merchants were the removal of discriminatory practices including segregated lunch counters, and the hiring of Negro personnel in sales and other clerical jobs.

Simultaneously, the Voters Registration League was formed, launching a massive Negro voter-registration drive. This is extremely significant in view of the growing "black belt" in the central city. With these developments white politicians actively campaigned for the Negro vote, which has been the decisive factor in recent city and county elections.

In addition, two Negroes have been appointed to the school board, one to the library board, and several to other local city authorities. The NAACP, under the leadership of W. W. Law, has been instrumental in effecting these changes.

These factors—realization of its economic buying power and the effectiveness of its vote—has put the Negro community in one of the best bargaining positions it has held since Reconstruction days. And the net effect of these changes has had a number of far-reaching ramifications for the structure of education in the community.

Education in Savannah

The Savannah-Chatham County board of education recently completed a $10 million building program, which included 273 new classrooms, and four controlled-environment junior high schools; two additional area trade schools were completed in 1966. A current program of $1.3 million is adding a high school and 22 elementary classrooms. A budget of $12,-744,400.08 was adopted for the 1965–1966 school year.

Table 6: Estimated Number of Schools by Type and Predominant Race

	NEGRO	WHITE	TOTAL
Senior High	3	3	6
Junior High	4	7	11
Elementary	19	24	43
Total	26	34	60

In the 60 public schools there are 1,414 classrooms for approximately 42,000 students.

Table 7: Estimated Pupil Enrollment by Race

	NEGRO		WHITE		
	Number	*Per cent*	*Number*	*Per cent*	TOTAL
Elementary	11,000	40	16,450	60	27,450
Secondary	5,000	35	9,420	65	14,420
Total	16,000	39	25,870	61	41,870

For permanent employment, teachers are required to have a four-year-college professional certificate. There are well over 1,483 full-time teachers (excluding visiting teachers and those in special education), 16 supervisors, 59 supervisory principals, and 14 assistants; the number of full-time employees is 2,567.

In addition to the public schools, educational facilities include sixteen parochial schools (Catholic and Protestant), three private schools, two vocational schools, and one business college.

Table 8: Number of Teachers by Race and Sex

	NEGRO			WHITE			TOTAL		
	Male	*Female*	*Total*	*Male*	*Female*	*Total*	*Male*	*Female*	*Total*
Elementary	15	293	308	15	441	456	30	734	764
Secondary	103	155	258	161	300	461	264	455	719
Total	118	449	566	176	741	917	294	1,189	1,483

The state's first institution of higher learning, the University of Georgia, was founded in Savannah in 1785. Currently there are two four-year colleges. Savannah State College (formerly Georgia State College), a unit of the university system of Georgia, is a predominantly Negro institution with an average enrollment of twelve hundred students. It offers programs in arts and sciences, teacher education, business administration, applied home economics, and engineering technology, leading to the A.B. and B.S. degrees.

Armstrong College, formerly a junior college offering two-year transferable college preparatory programs, as well as two-year terminal programs, is now a four-year institution in the university system. It expects to graduate its first senior class in 1968 on new campus facilities now under construction. As a junior college its enrollment was around nine hundred. The first Negro student enrolled in 1960.

Culture of Segregation

Token integration has come to Savannah. The general level of education is improving for Negroes and whites, particularly the former. Traditionally, a double standard of education has prevailed in Savannah. Policies of separate education produced two different subsystems, Negro and white. Teachers, students, and administrators within the two subsystems have had little to no mutual contact. Until recently, teachers and principals have participated in different organizations.

As in other Southern school systems, there have been disparities between racial groups in the general qualitative and quantitative aspects of education. While figures are not available for Savannah, a 1948 report on Negro education provides historical insight concerning education inequalities in the South.[1]

During the 1943–1944 school year Southern school systems spent an average $84.79 per white pupil, but $36.97 for the Negro pupil; within Georgia the average current expenditures per pupil were, respectively, $73.79 and $23.63. For the entire South the expenditure per pupil for white students was

[1] Caliver, Ambrose; "Education of Negro Leaders," Bulletin No. 3, Federal Security Agency, U.S. Office of Education, 1948.

129 per cent higher than for Negroes; in Georgia the difference was 212 per cent.

Similar differences were found in teacher salaries. The 1943–1944 average for white staff within Georgia was $924, compared with $404 for Negro staff. In 1945–1946 their respective salaries were $1,279 and $651. The salaries for whites were 96.5 per cent higher than for Negroes.[2] Presently there is little if any difference in the pay range.

Up to the early fifties there were fewer than ten elementary schools for Negroes and one major high school. During this period the Negro population constituted over two-fifths of the total population of Chatham County. This is significant since Negroes are now about one-third the total population, and almost twice as many facilities are available.

Separate and unequal conditions have been characteristic of education in Savannah. Although the gap continues to narrow, tradition prevails with separate education for the races still the rule.

Process of Desegregation

In 1956 the Savannah chapter of the NAACP, with assistance from their legal defense fund, presented a petition to the board of education to formulate plans for the desegregation of local schools. The first attempt to remove discriminatory barriers, was ignored by the Board.

The second petition, filed in 1959 by another group of parents, under the guidance of the NAACP, requested school integration by September 1960. The board at that time referred the case to the legal committee, where it was tabled.

Meanwhile, the Georgia Grand Jury formed an investigating committee known as the Sibley School Study Commission. They held meetings in each congressional district of the state to determine the public's attitude toward any compromise with integration. As reported in the Atlanta *Constitution,* March 4, 1960, two choices were put to witnesses regarding the school situation:

[2] *Loc. cit.*

(1) Stand by Georgia's present school closing laws and accept tuition grants in lieu of public schools if federal courts order all public schools desegregated, or
(2) Accept some sort of local option plan that might allow integration in some areas of the State.

In March 1960 Chatham County residents testified before the Sibley Commission. With one or two exceptions, Savannah residents spoke out in favor of a student placement plan rather than close the schools in the face of integration. One exception was the president of the States Rights Council of Chatham County. According to the *Savannah Evening Press,* March 18, 1960, he stated that the organization with about two hundred members is ". . . unalterably opposed to any form of integration in our schools. . . ."

The pro-placement speakers indicated that they represented such groups as the Parent-Teacher Association, the League of Women Voters, church groups, ministerial associations, B'nai B'rith, social workers, and the American Association of University Women.

During this period sit-in demonstrations and voter registration drives were occurring in the Savannah area. Nonetheless, there were no concrete steps taken regarding the local issue. Again in 1962 another group of Negro citizens, headed by Rev. L. L. Stell, chairman of the educational committee of the NAACP, filed a petition with the board. And again, they were given the "runaround."

In March 1963 a motion was filed for a preliminary injunction (*Stell et al. v. Savannah-Chatham County Board of Education*). The case was taken to the Georgia Supreme Court and the local board was requested to come forward with a plan for desegregation by the 1963–1964 academic year.

Following the desegregation court order, white parents, elsewhere referred to as the Intervenors, filed a countersuit. According to one well-informed respondent, the Intervenors are supposedly affiliated with the White Citizens' Council; furthermore, their legal counsel is reputed to be its president. In any case, this countersuit was taken to the United States District Court of Appeals. The presiding judge, the Honorable Frank M. Scarlett, overruled the Georgia Supreme Court and ruled in favor of the Intervenors.

An informant who was present at the hearings commented on the "parade of witnesses" presenting testimony for the Intervenors. Among them was a psychologist, identified as a former professor of Kenneth Clark's, who asserted that Negroes were tested and found to be mentally and psychologically inferior to whites. Another was said to be a Canadian anthropologist who addressed the question of differences in skull makeup and brain size. These men and other witnesses presented the usual "inferiority of the Negro" argument, which has been utilized by racists since the early days of slavery.

In the late summer of 1963, however, the U. S. Court of Appeals reversed the Honorable Judge Scarlett's ruling and requested that the Savannah school board submit a plan for desegregating public schools. The decision of the board was to begin "top downward" integration with the twelfth grade, moving downward a grade a year.

The Event

The first school integration occurred in Savannah in September 1963. Nineteen Negroes entered the twelfth grade in two former white schools—Groves and Savannah High Schools. School integration came to Savannah with little overt public drama. From time to time there were isolated incidents in the two schools, but there were no major crises involving state troopers or jeering crowds. It appears that the most tender spot was at the Groves school. It is located in a rural suburb, bordering on the western fringe of the Savannah city limits. The school caters to students from neighboring communities and townships in Chatham County.

According to one Negro mother:

> Part of the problem was the lack of cooperation on the part of the principals and teachers. A few interested white and Negro parents came together and requested better cooperation from the faculty. Student leaders were called in and agreed to cooperate, and eventually a new principal was assigned to the school.

Another parent pointed out that the first year of integration was extremely difficult for the first nineteen students.

They had a number of social and psychological pressures working against them and it showed up in their work. Not one made the honor roll that first year. Psychologically it was difficult because they switched schools their senior year. . . . Their sense of [in]security, loss of friends, and teachers heightened their displacement.

Aside from the individual problems in various schools, the public accepted school integration calmly to the extent that the usual moblike drama characteristic of the Deep South was avoided. Several factors contributed to this outward manifestation of calmness. First, while the desegregation court order was impending, the board was shopping around for a new superintendent, one who would be capable of handling school integration when it came. They hired the incumbent superintendent who was formerly the assistant superintendent of schools in a Florida community which had experienced desegregation.

The superintendent indicated that:

. . . once the desegregation decision was announced, the board attempted to maintain a "neutral" policy. That is, they refused to meet with pressure groups from either race.

Among those making demands were the NAACP, which initiated and fought the entire legal battle; an unnamed organization, composed of white citizens who wanted to "educate" (white) people of Savannah to accept integration; and the White Citizens' Council. Board personnel are convinced they would not have had a successful program had they catered to any one group.

Also contributing was the cooperation of local newspaper personnel, who refrained from printing pictures or headlining articles regarding integration.

Thus, from the viewpoint of administrative personnel, their tactical moves, including the cooperation of those in control of news media, were significant in minimizing overt public reaction. It appears that tactics used by the board were effective in minimizing public demonstrations against school desegregation. And although there are a number of "hard core" segregationist elements in the community, there are also a number of individuals willing to accept and abide by the court order.

A significant number of white citizens have joined Negroes in their fight for justice and equality. Many have been outspoken at the risk of losing their social and economic security. Among the best-known agents have been the Human Relations Council and several church-related organizations. The participants include local businessmen, educators, and other professional men and women. Particularly active have been the community's Jewish, Catholic, and Protestant religious leaders.

A white minister was forced to resign from his church as a result of his liberal views on race. His congregation consisted of middle-class persons living in a sedate residential section of the city. Another young minister has been under heavy attack by his parishioners who live in a rural suburban area catering to the so-called "Georgia rednecks." Other ministers have participated with little or no resistance from their congregations. One has provided space in his church as well as tutorial assistance for integrating students.

In all due fairness to Savannahians, including those who never make headlines, one cannot overlook those who follow their convictions at the risk of being alienated and ostracized.

To What Extent Has Desegregation Occurred?

A number of parents and members of the NAACP were unhappy with the original "top downward" desegregation plan.

Mrs. Esther Garrison, a Negro parent and a member of the school board, expressed the belief that:

> It was unfair to expect students to transfer [in] their senior year . . . it was [the school board's] way of discouraging large numbers of Negroes from transferring to white schools.

These parents brought another suit, thus sending the case back to the courts. The court ordered bottom and top grades desegregated so that by 1968 all grades would be integrated. As of the 1965–1966 academic year grades one, two, nine, ten, eleven, and twelve were integrated. It should be noted that an additional provision permits pupils transferring into the Savannah public schools from other school systems—private, parochial, or outside Chatham County—to enter any school.

Starting with the nineteen Negroes entering the twelfth grade in 1963, the number increased to ninety-seven in grades one, eleven, and twelve in 1964. Unofficial figures for 1965 showed approximately four hundred Negro students in formerly white schools. There were no white students in predominantly Negro schools. In Catholic schools, which followed the decision of the board to integrate, there were about twenty-five Negro children.

At the end of 1965 there were approximately forty-two thousand students enrolled in the Savannah-Chatham County public schools; approximately eight thousand were in private and parochial schools. Of the total in the public schools, over sixteen thousand were Negro—about 39 per cent. There were only around four hundred Negroes in integrated situations: just a little over 2 per cent of the Negro school population is attending formerly all-white institutions. The superintendent commented:

> NAACP officials are disappointed because more Negroes have not tried to attend white schools. Negroes prefer their own schools because they are just as good as white schools from the viewpoint of the physical plant as well as personnel . . . there are more Negro teachers with masters' degrees than whites.

To evaluate and compare Negro and white teachers' credentials, one must inquire into the kinds of degrees and the caliber of institutions in which they were awarded.

As for the claim that "Negroes prefer their own schools," in large measure this may be true—and the argument may sound convincing until other relevant questions are raised. *Preference* presumes a choice between alternatives. To what extent does the overall situation in fact permit a realization of and an opportunity for choice on the part of students?

If the desegregation plan is closely examined, the low level of integration may be seen as linked to the successful gerrymandering of school districts. The board of education created a phenomenon called an "attendance area" that encompasses other former school districts which existed prior to desegregation. These "areas" may include both white and Negro schools that were at one time in distinctly separate districts. Students are free to attend any school within an "attendance area."

Normally students attend schools in close proximity to their homes, and this is the general rationale by which most school districts are determined. However, with the "area" plan a white student living very close to a Negro school, which would ordinarily fall within his district, is free to attend a white school within the "attendance area."

This is quite significant—when one considers that many residential sections of Savannah have been "integrated" for years. In some neighborhoods the two races have lived side by side, across the street, or in back of each other (Negroes usually living in the lanes and courts). Before desegregation, however, Negro and white youths were normatively bound to go their separate ways, regardless of residential proximity.

Today an increasing number of Negroes are moving into formerly all-white neighborhoods in the central city. In the usual pattern, the whites are making their exodus to the suburbs or other "safe" residential sectors. In large part this change-over may be attributed to the urban renewal program which has uprooted hundreds of Negro families, disrupting established Negro communities and providing no means for purposeful resettlement and re-establishment of these people and communities.

What happens to the schools in the new communities that are formed? The board acts quickly, usually at the initial stages of the transition. White personnel are moved out and Negro principals and teachers are assigned to the institution, the signal for remaining white residents to send their children to other white schools in the "attendance area."

This kind of situation has been quite noticeable in the heavily populated west-side area of the central city. Whites have moved out to make room for Negroes displaced by the urban renewal projects which have been in full-scale operation since 1959. Similar developments have taken place in public housing projects, clearly demonstrating the effects of residential segregation on public school segregation.

In other areas of the educational system no more than token integration has occurred. In 1964 two Negroes were appointed to the school board. One is a mother and part-time secretary, and the other is a local banker. Their terms expire December 31, 1970. Currently there are two Negro supervisors in the division of instruction, one elementary and the other secondary. From all indications they administer Negro schools only. Their offices, however, are in the board's downtown office—a first in Savannah.

One teacher did acknowledge that principals and curriculum division groups mix when they have general meetings, whereas traditionally they were separate—there was once a Negro group called "principals and counselors," and its white counterpart was "principals and supervisors." Currently both whites and Negroes constitute the latter—all meeting at the board. But in everyday administration and teaching, at the principal and teacher level, there is little integration.

The Web of Definitions and Consequences

Public school desegregation came to Savannah in an apparent aura of calmness. The extent to which it has actually been accepted is an empirical question. In any case, it has had a number of consequences for teachers, students, parents, and other relevant groups and individuals.

If Savannah follows the pattern of other school systems that have desegregated, a significant number of Negro teachers will lose their jobs. Events have not yet developed to the point where these teachers feel threatened, nor do they appear to be overly concerned with the direct consequences.

Several Negro teachers indicated that their organization, the Chatham County Teachers Association, is not discussing the ramifications of desegregation. A principal expressed the opinion that these concerns should be foremost in the group. He further indicated that the "leadership" had not defined this as essential, and only a powerless minority seems to be concerned.

This organization is relatively ineffective. It has not functioned as a pressure group, demanding and securing significant changes or programs for teachers. It has operated more as an outlet for general discussions of educational problems of limited import. Perhaps its limitations may be attributed to the overall position of the Negro teacher in the larger educational system. What, in fact, has been the position of the Negro teacher?

Until the early fifties teaching was the major outlet for the educated Negroes, particularly women. They occupied privileged positions in the community, and in most cases came from the homes of "old Savannahians." This was not necessarily a sign of wealth, but one of tradition and whatever prestige and influence it carried.

For those anticipating employment, two elements were important. Although not required in all cases, one should have obtained a college degree. Apparently, however, this wasn't always possible. Between 1939–1940 only 47 per cent of white teachers and 22.1 per cent of Negro teachers employed in Georgia had four years of college training.[3] Next, one had to have someone to intercede for a job. In most cases jobs were made possible through influential whites, for some of whom the parents of these teachers had worked or whom they knew through other channels.

The rate of turnover was not high and a teacher usually remained in the school where he was placed initially. Jobs were relatively secure as long as one did the necessary work and maintained the kind of complacency expected of the Negro.

During this pre-World War II era these teachers were often subject to a number of humiliating experiences. They were indeed fearful of "The Man," a term used by themselves to refer to their white superintendent or his assistant. Following the antiquated Southern custom, they were never addressed properly, even in front of their students: Never "Mrs. Forde" or "Mrs. Thomas," but "Carrie" or "Ann" or "Tom."

In the last two decades the overall makeup and character of the system have changed considerably. The entire system has been constantly expanding. There have been more than fifteen elementary schools, three junior, and two senior high schools added to the "Negro complex," which is staffed by over 566 teachers and 27 supervising and assistant principals.

At the present time principals are allowed a great deal of flexibility in the hiring of staff, a practice that has created a kind of "spoils system." The four-year college degree and teaching certificate are required, but in addition one must establish some kind of "in" with the principal, or have other influential contacts. This pattern may be linked to two main factors. First, state colleges and other Southern higher educational institutions still produce large numbers of graduates with degrees in education. Even students who major in other subject areas still take enough hours in education to qualify for teaching certificates. Second, teaching in metropolitan Savannah has been defined as desirable. As a result more individuals apply for jobs than the system can absorb.

[3] Caliver, *op. cit.*

This situation has a number of implications for the entire educational structure. Very often the most qualified individual does not get a position. Objective measures, such as a score on the state examination, are secondary to the proper contact. Many a bright student has sought employment in nearby rural counties or elsewhere. Others have turned to alternate sources of employment, permanently or until they can get in the system. Practices of this type tend to limit the range of available talent and minimize the efficiency of the general teaching staff.

This practice also creates quite a bit of friction among co-workers and makes for a widespread feeling of insecurity. The lack of objectivity in hiring also functions in the reverse context. It is not unknown for teachers to be sacked because of character slander invoked by co-workers attempting to win favoritism and further secure their own positions.

In any case, the object is to get a job and security. In the early period, when there was less mobility, teachers informally established a hierarchy of desirability. One particular school, for example, was located in an area which once catered to the more bourgeois Negro families. Those who taught there defined their status more favorably than their counterparts. The same holds for those who taught in the central city as compared to those teaching in the rural or fringe areas of Chatham County.

There are few opportunities for promotion; therefore, most teachers retain their original job status. Those who wish to make their jobs more secure usually work toward advanced degrees in the summer. As new schools open, a few jobs open up for principals, usually appointed from the regular teaching staff. Lately, supervisory and consultantships have been opening up to Negroes, whereas before they were generally occupied by whites.

The president of the Georgia Educational Association recently called upon white teachers to include Negroes in their membership. At this writing a merger has not been attempted. A spokesman for the NAACP expressed the view that Negro teachers are not likely to encourage the merger. A number of teachers are not qualified and are not interested in integration because of competition and the fear of losing their jobs. In 1964 only three Negro teachers passed the national teacher's examination.

Indeed, some Negro educators inhibit the desegregation

process: A Negro principal had been directing routine Negro student transfers to schools far from their own neighborhoods rather than to nearby white schools. Other cases involve coaches who discourage athletes from transferring to formerly white schools.

Consciously or unconsciously, these actions reflect the fear of the teacher and/or principal faced with the loss of students, and the possible loss of job security. Furthermore, this kind of behavior reflects the teacher's awareness of the situation, even though direct discussion of the situation is avoided in organized groups.

Perhaps it is unwarranted to generalize the contention that Negro teachers are not qualified. There are some excellent and well-trained Negro teachers, and there are mediocre Negro teachers just as there are incompetent white ones. Nevertheless, there is little question that a larger proportion of Negroes are inadequately prepared. They are products of the same system which they now perpetuate. Those who attend inferior schools cannot be expected to produce the maximum, nor can one expect them to be the best-prepared teachers. Furthermore, the situation is not likely to be improved when those in control condone and maintain the existing state of affairs.

It is reported that at one of the court hearings the Intervenors accused the board of discriminating against white teachers. According to their testimony whites must score five hundred or above on the state teacher's examination before they are hired. Negro teachers may be employed with a score of four hundred. If this information is accurate, it is a clear representation of the school board's traditional double standards. W. W. Law, president of the NAACP, puts it succinctly:

> The superintendent doesn't care who Negro principals hire. But when Negro teachers start teaching white children, he will care. . . .

Actually no one knows the system better than the Negro teacher. It has been a tradition in the community that they send their children to other school systems. Unofficial sources estimate that 89 per cent of Negro teachers send their children to private or parochial schools.

The Reverend L. L. Stell, acknowledged that Negro schools

have improved greatly within the past ten years, but they still trail behind white schools. Furthermore:

> If our [Negro] students are going to qualify for jobs that are opening up to them, it is essential that they get the best education, and the best happens to be "white" right now. . . .

On the other hand, the views of a white teacher, in responding to school integration, were reported in the Savannah *Morning News,* September 21, 1963:

> . . . the ability of the Negroes to keep up in [my] class indicates that they had equal opportunity at their present schools.

There is room here for gross misinterpretations of the situation. It should not be interpreted that institutions catering to Negroes are altogether below standard. It is public knowledge, however, that while Southern schools have ranked below the national average, Negro schools have ranked even lower. As late as 1959, for example, there was not a single accredited Negro high school in Savannah.

It is simple to ascribe a noninferior status to Negro schools, using as evidence the increasingly large number of students pursuing higher education. Yet a more basic factor is the extent to which Negroes can compete with whites in the various arenas of participation, particularly the job market. This is a key problem as perceived by Mr. Law:

> A number of job opportunities are opening up for Negroes that were not open to them before. Now we have department store clerks, cashiers, and other jobs available in private industry and in governmental agencies at the local and state level. The problem is to get qualified Negroes to fill the posts. Our high school and even some college graduates don't know the material. They cannot pass the [civil service] exams.

All other things equal, one cannot help but surmise that part of the blame lies in the schools. Therefore, it is necessary to examine the basic curriculum as well as the caliber and qualifications of the teaching staff. Basic course material is becoming less divergent, but there are other factors to be considered, such as the depth, intensity, and coverage of material.

A mother who has four children attending integrated schools made this observation:

In their present school they cover twice as much material as they did at their former school . . . in the same period of time. When they were attending . . . they would come home and listen to records, hardly looking at a book. Now they are doing much more reading.

A Negro male student, seventeen, presently attending Savannah High School, said:

It is quite an experience and so different from what I was accustomed to at Beach. The books are more difficult and I can't get away without studying much more than before.

There are those for whom integration has been an extremely painful experience—those representing the hard-core conservative elements. Among these are the followers and supporters of the White Citizens' Council and two other groups referred to as the Conservatives and Door-Step Savannahians. Informed sources maintain that members of these groups include some of the parents who filed a countersuit against the board of education. These are the Intervenors, who, at the end of 1965, still had their case in the courts. These whites appealed to the court order to desegregate. In the early part of 1965 they submitted a plan which would require that students be assigned to schools on the basis of qualifications and abilities. Negro parents (plaintiffs in the case) objected to this plan and attempted to obtain an order requiring the board to comply with the original decree. Finally, on September 1, 1965, the board (defendant in the case) filed a motion for a new trial and a motion to discard the scheme advanced by the Intervenors. The board had previously been content to sit and watch the two contrasting forces fight the battle, the result of which would have wide ramifications for school policies.

Another hearing was held on November 3, 1965, in the United States District Court of Appeals, presided over by the same judge who had overruled the Georgia State Supreme Court in 1963. At this time the Intervenors submitted another scheme, "Order on Desegregation Plan." The attorney for the school board accepted it, without permission of the board, and agreed to withdraw the motion for the new trial filed in September. Following this development the plaintiffs (Negro parents) requested an extension of time to study the plan, which they eventually rejected. According to E. H. Gadsden, counsel for plaintiffs:

> This arrangement would amount to a pupil assignment plan under which pupils would initially be assigned to segregated schools and/or classrooms. Pupils desiring transfers would be subjected to onerous requirements, and such transfers would be subject to so many tests and subjective standards as to permit no objective review of the basis for such assignments.

On December 29, 1965, plaintiffs, along with representatives from the U. S. Justice Department, renewed their motion for dismissal of the Intervenors' case and issued an appeal for a more encompassing desegregation plan, one in which students would have freedom-of-choice in all grades to select the nearest formerly white or formerly Negro school. The plan also requested the removal of racial restrictions in all school activities, including extracurricular activities and a specific plan for hiring and assigning teachers and all other faculty personnel on a nonracial basis. If approved, such a plan would go into effect no later than the beginning of the 1966–1967 school year.

As school integration approached the end of the third year, the court fight continued. The two forces, at opposite ends of the ideological pole, carried the banner of their respective causes. White supremacists, with the money and traditional social forces in their favor, are convinced they will win out. On the other hand, Negro parents, backed by the NAACP, have no intention of relinquishing a cause for which they have fought for more than twelve years.

A more recent controversy focused on the problem of vocational education. In May of 1965 the board of education announced the building of two new vocational schools. Both are to be constructed in the extreme northwest section of the city bordering on the suburban fringe area, one adjacent to a Negro elementary school in the newly developed Cloverdale subdivision, the other a little further west in Garden City, a predominantly white rural suburb. This is defined as an attempt to further segregate the races. One minister analyzed the situation this way:

> If [the board's] intentions are good, why not build one centrally located school which would be accessible to all residents in the general locale?

According to unofficial sources the plans call for a "minimum of duplication." One is supposed to be highly technical and the other of "lesser technical stature." The latter is designated for the Negro area. Although this information is unofficial, it is consistent with 1965 course offerings in the Savannah Vocational School (white) and the Harris Area Trade School (Negro). The former offered business education, including cashier training, bookkeeping, accounting, interior decorating, and electronics; the latter offered business education, radio repairing, shoe repairing, bricklaying, carpentry, and auto mechanics.

A young woman, around twenty, who attends Harris, offered the following information:

> I am studying business education. We do not have one desk calculator or even a mimeograph machine . . . no accounting or cashier training.

The "place" of the Negro has been defined—manual laborers, service workers, and so on. Although the needs and demands of the labor market are changing, the attempt to perpetuate "Negro jobs" and "Negro education" is a blatant reality.

The following is an excerpt from a letter written to the Georgia State Department of Education by Rev. Herbert M. Turner, a former member of the Ministerial Alliance.

> Our past experience with the "separate but equal myth" leads us to suspect that if the courses in the two schools represent a "minimum of duplication," that the superior equipment and the more advanced technical training will be found in the school located in the white community and the school with the least technical and scientific training will be found in the school in the Negro community.

According to the state superintendent of schools the situation is defined differently:

> . . . any qualified applicant who is a resident of Georgia may attend any occupational training for which he is qualified in any location, providing a similar occupational training program is not provided nearer his place of residence.
> . . . if there are courses offered in the vocational-technical school for which a Negro student is qualified to enroll, he may enroll in the course at the school that is nearer his place of residence.
> . . . the state board of education and the state department of

education do not look upon the two area vocational-technical schools in Chatham County as being segregated facilities. . . .

In referring to the subtleties which operate in the educational arena, Reverend Stell sums up the situation:

> The intention of the board appears to be an unquestionable attempt to perpetuate segregated and inferior training of Negroes. . . . We plan to boycott the school in Cloverdale even if we have to buy a bus to take potential Negro students to the Garden City School.

Traditional customs of segregation, determined elements of the status quo and forceful exponents of change, gerrymandered school districts, token integration, a web of uncertainty for students, teachers, and administrators—these and other factors have had a decisive influence upon the structure of education in Savannah, Georgia. What, then, is its future?

The Plausible Future

We have seen that the traditional power structure of the Savannah community, in which the Negro has had from very slight to no representation, has responded to the demand for integration in a piecemeal fashion. The Savannah school board most directly affected by the Supreme Court decision of 1954 did not exercise effective leadership. Instead, they sat and waited until events came to pass which rendered this immobility no longer possible. These events took the form of agitation by representatives of the Negro community, and crystallized in the form of a lawsuit brought against the Savannah school board by the NAACP.

Other events were occurring simultaneously in the community. There was the economic boycott of local white merchants who had always given their consent and assistance to those elements within the community desiring maintenance of the status quo. The more direct representatives of the traditional power structure were no less guilty of aiding and abetting this situation, *i.e.,* segregated public facilities and negligible Negro representation in positions of responsibility within city government.

Then urban renewal—in Savannah as in other major cities —proved an ideal means of uprooting and dislocating established Negro communities. Furthermore, relocation of these displaced persons was done in such a manner that the status quo regarding racial segregation was unlikely to be disturbed.

One white community leader did point out that part of the answer lies in the future leadership of the community with respect to the power structure:

> . . . proper "attitude control" has a lot to do with the success and progress of integration. Now, more so than ever, key people in Savannah's industries come from places such as Wisconsin, West Virginia, Oregon, and Minnesota. Their attitude is more liberal and their reaction to problems of integration follows a much more reasonable and workable line.

A director of the newly established Economic Opportunity Agency in Savannah suggested that their program may have some net, although minor, effect on school desegregation:

> Teachers volunteer to work under the program, part of which is contracted out to the board of education. Because it is completely integrated, the program exposes children and adults of both races to teachers of both races. More importantly, it provides the board and the community with an opportunity to see how integrated schooling can work.

Although relevant, these perspectives provide limited views of the total social setting. Savannah is a community of individuals engaged in a number of diverse activities. It is composed of individuals with various capabilities and potentialities, some of whom are Negro and some of whom are white. Unfortunately the latter fact seems to cause greater concern in Savannah than all the questions or ideals heretofore expressed.

It is quite likely that the future of Savannah with respect to "democratic ideals" will continue to develop in snail-like fashion. This means that the Negro community will have to continue responding to injustice with unequivocal demands for justice. Negro leaders, like Mr. Law, have expressed their determination to continue this struggle:

> What Negroes have achieved thus far merely penetrates the surface . . . the NAACP is the power of the Negro commu-

nity and we shall continue to fight . . . furthermore, we must continue to exercise our rights and participate fully in those areas which have already opened . . .

A Negro member of the school board, Mrs. Esther F. Garrison, said:

Being on the school board is almost like a full-time job for me, but Negroes must be represented. We must make our presence in the community realized . . . help make decisions which affect our children, our homes and our schools.

The following changes have taken place during the 1966–67 academic year in the Chatham County (Savannah) public school system.

All grades in the school system have been desegregated. Both of the area technical-vocational schools have been completed. One is operating at present; both the staff and student body are integrated. Five Negro students at Chatham Junior High and one at Groves High are honor roll students.

All predominantly Negro high schools are now members of the formerly white athletic council. This has resulted in competitive sports activities between Negro and formerly white schools. Basketball and some track meets have taken place. Football games will start during the 1968–1969 academic year; the delay is attributed to contracts or commitments made several years in advance. The Negro high school teams played in local basketball competition. The Alfred E. Beach High School basketball team (Negro) won the 1967 AAA championship for the state of Georgia, and one of their players was awarded the Most Valuable Player trophy.

Negro students enrolled in formerly all-white schools are participating in all extra-curricular activities. However, sororities and fraternities within the formerly all-white schools have been eliminated. Officials maintained that they were too much trouble and they did not approve of the hazing. On the other hand, there is some speculation that this was directly related to school integration and the anticipation of problems with these sodalities.

Three Negroes have been appointed to positions formerly held by whites: (a) Coordinator of Visiting Teachers Program, (b) Itinerant Corrective Reading Teacher, and (c) Supervisor of Librarians. They are responsible for all schools in Chatham County.

The first Negro psychometrist has been appointed to work in predominantly Negro schools. It seems that this decision was reached in view of the fact that whites holding the position were unable to work effectively with Negro children.

Two Negro counselors have been assigned to the integrated neighborhood youth corps program in the public schools.

One of the two original Negro supervisors is now administering both Negro and formerly all-white schools. The other is still working in Negro schools. There is still no integration of the general teaching personnel although it is expected to take place within a one- to two-year period. There is one Negro teacher at the integrated Richard Arnold Vocational Tech.

Both of the new vocational schools are integrated. Furthermore, night school classes for Negroes formerly conducted at the Alfred E. Beach High School have been abolished.

Groundwork is being completed for the merger of the Chatham County Teachers' Association (Negro) and the Georgia Educational Association (white). The latter has dropped its color ban. Representatives of the two organizations are meeting to iron out difficulties in anticipation of the merger which is expected to take place within the next two years. According to one informant, Negro teachers perceive the merger as desirable but are uneasy regarding the long-range consequences. They want to be "integrated but not absorbed." Moreover, they do not want to lose their autonomy. They feel that by being outnumbered by the whites they will lose some of their official positions and will have a diminishing voice in the decision-making process.

The leadership of the Negro community must continue to find means of making real for all Savannah the reality of the Negro's condition and their determination to alter it. Since this leadership must come from the same community, this brings us to the question of leadership potential. Can the same persons, particularly the youth, provide continuing leadership of the sort required?

Rather than speculate as to the possibilities, it would be better perhaps to recall what has happened in the case of the Negro across the country, namely, his active pursuit of equality of citizenship, equality of responsibility, and equality of opportunity.

Historically Negro leaders have either sought equal representation and right of participation in various institutional spheres, or they have sought to estrange and rupture already strained racial relationships. Responsible activity by the power structure in Savannah might very well favor the former type of leader. This is the prospect for the future, concerning not only education but other areas of activity potentially able to alter the traditionally segregated patterns of social life in Savannah.

IV

Integration in Newark,
Delaware: Whatever Happened
to Jim Crow?

Herbert R. Barringer

In government offices which are sensitive to the vehe-mence and passion of mass sentiment, public men have no sure tenure. They are in effect perpetual office seekers, always on trial for their political lives, always required to court their restless constituents. They are deprived of their independence. Democratic politicians rarely feel they can afford the luxury of telling the whole truth to the people. And since not telling it, though prudent, is uncomfortable, they find it much easier if they themselves do not have to hear too often too much of the sour truth. . . . They hold their of-fices for a short time, and to do this they must ma-neuver and manipulate combinations among the fac-tions and pressure groups. Their policies must be selected and shaped so as to attract and hold together these combinations. . . . (Walter Lippmann, The Public Philosophy).

Sometimes people complain about race problems here, but you should have seen this place ten or fifteen years ago. We couldn't eat anywhere on Main Street, all our children went to Negro schools, and Negro housing was pitiful. There were only thirteen toilets with plumbing in the whole Negro community. I remember one of my neighbors, an old man, who used a bucket, and threw it out his window when it was full. We may still have complaints, but we've come a long way (*Negro leader*).

We are all very proud of the way integration has been handled in Newark. Some of the other communities in this state have not been so fortunate. I think the reason for our success is that, as in other matters, we have done what we had to do in a quiet, reasonable manner. In my experience, the best way to fail on a controversial issue is to make a fuss about it. I have always found that it is best to go ahead and do something, then ask questions later. If we had made an issue of school integration here, we would still be segregated (*Former school board member*).

It was too bad that we integrated the high school first. We had about thirty Negro students the first year. None of them were up to the standards of our white students. So I asked all the teachers to adjust their standards a bit for the Negroes. Many of the teachers weren't too happy about that. They complained, but all of them seemed to go along with it. We managed to get through that first year with nothing more than a few unpleasant telephone calls from white parents. A parent threatened me at my home one Sunday, but we knew each other, so I put him down easily (*High school principal*).

Yes, we did integrate the high school first, because we had no Negro high school in town. They all went to a Negro school in Wilmington. Their parents paid a considerable fee to bus them [by regular bus—there was no school bus], so we had quite a few complaints. We decided that the situation did demand correcting, especially since the colored students had to go right by our high school on their way to Wilmington (*School superintendent*).

They tell everyone that story. The real reason they integrated the high school first was because Wilmington integrated all its schools that year, and served notice on the rest of the county that they would take no more Negroes from out of their own school district. Newark had no choice. They either had to integrate or refuse education to Negroes. Besides, another family and myself had suits before the State Courts, both concerning Newark (*Negro community leader*).

Well, you know, this state is still pretty much Southern in many ways. After the fuss about integration in some of the downstate communities, we decided to move quietly. Actually, we had already integrated our faculty facilities. In fact, the staff was completely integrated, except they taught in their respective schools. We were just waiting for the Supreme Court to reverse the state laws on segregation. The University of Delaware was behind us on this. In fact, groups at the university used our facilities for biracial meetings because they could not use university property. As a matter of fact, the university was holding us back (*School superintendent*).

Oh, we had unofficially integrated some time before the public schools. We had invited several outstanding Negroes to the campus before actual "integration." There was considerable resistance to integration in the state legislature. As you know, it was dominated by the Southern counties. Finally, the president [of the university] invited a court ruling on the university. This was immediately after the Supreme Court decision. I hope you will remember that the president comes from the Midwest himself —he has been accused of prejudice, but obviously that is not true (*University spokesman*).

They are always involving the "state legislature" to cover for the trustees. This university, as you know, is a private university with state support. The truth of the matter is that the board of trustees was afraid to buck public opinion. They weren't any more anxious to integrate than the legislature. They were simply waiting for the Supreme Court decision to give them an excuse (*Protestant minister*).

I don't think that is completely fair. After all, the university does receive about one-third of its operating funds from the state. Not only that, but the status of the university was not at all clear until 1964, almost ten years after integration. As long as I have been here, the administration *has* had to be careful about the Legislature (*University chaplain*).

We have had superb cooperation from the community on this problem. Right after we integrated the high school, someone called to inform me that Bryant Bowles [National Association for the Advancement of White People] was coming to Newark for an anti-integration rally. The superintendent and I immediately called the police, the mayor, and the university for help. The city police had every road to Newark blocked within half an hour. Bowles didn't show up, but we were ready for him (*High school principal*).

I suppose it is true that the city has kept agitators out of the picture. They've done their best to keep things quiet, but sometimes they act as if they were afraid of their own shadows. During the summer of the Philadelphia race riots, they watched us like hawks. You can bet that the NAACP and CORE would have a hard time in Newark (*Negro resident*).

Yeah, the Klan burns crosses every once in a while. The police always come to keep things quiet. It's just a big show (*White resident*).

Of course we don't like school integration, but there's not a lot we can do about that now, except to hope that people wake up to what is happening. The reason we still operate is to show these blacks that they can't have everything they want. We're quiet in Newark, but we're just waiting for race mixing. Then we'll have support enough. People around here have stood a lot, but they'll never stand for having their girls touched by niggers (*Klansman*).

We have tried to cooperate to keep race issues as quiet as possible. We feel that the less publicity we receive, the better things will go. The Klan has never been organized here. The NAACP tried to organize, but they were pushed out by their own people. The president of the local NAACP is a P.T.A. member, but the other members keep him quiet. I get a few indignant calls from parents who don't want their children sitting next to Negroes in class. We just ask the teachers to rearrange the whole class seating, and let it go at that. We try to avoid entanglement with pressure groups on either side. (*High school principal*).

If they're so damned sincere, why don't they hire more Negro teachers? They have only three or four, and they are all Uncle Toms and Aunt Jemimas—they have nothing to do with the other Negroes in town. I know for a fact that the superintendent of schools tries to keep Negro teachers out. He's not prejudiced, but he's too afraid of trouble (*Negro leader*).

Actually, we have only token integration here. The powers that be all feel that they've done their little bit, and don't want to make waves (*Civil rights leader*).

The school system has done a marvelous job. They just redistricted the school system, and without fanfare or hoopla, they gerrymandered a line through the Negro residential district to even the Negro distribution in primary schools. By the way, every school in Newark is integrated, even those in the better housing areas (*White housewife*).

I have no complaints. No one has ever given me any trouble, except for a few prejudiced kids. I'm getting a good education, and a good experience here (*Negro high school student*).

Some colored kids try to cause trouble—they ask white kids to carry their trays in the cafeteria, and then ask for a fight if they say no. Some try to date white girls, but they are just troublemakers (*Negro high school student*).

I don't think Negro kids are any worse than whites. There are some good, some bad, but we don't make any distinction. The president of our sophomore class is a Negro, and they are all active in sports (*White high school student*).

This is ironic, given the stereotype, but I do feel that sports were important for acceptance of Negro children in the schools. I know of several cases where children really made it through athletics (*Negro parent*).

One thing has been disappointing. We are now getting Negro students who have gone completely through integrated schools. It doesn't seem to make any difference—most of our Negro students are still not very good. I think it is because they receive no support in their homes (*Junior high school teacher*).

Perhaps I shouldn't say this, but after ten years of integration, I am puzzled about one thing. It seems to me that Negro children don't have the same conscience, morals, or whatever you want to call it, as we have. Some have been models, of course, but generally speaking they aren't honest (*School principal*).

One of the real problems is that our children don't really trust the whites in school. They can't tell if a white person is prejudiced or not. They hear stories from their parents at home, and carry it over to school (*Negro housewife*).

Actually, we have no real complaints about the school system. The only thing I object to is that no one will go out of his way for Negroes. You have to remember that it is quite a step for a Negro to really move into the white world, and a few helping hands would be an improvement. We don't expect preferential treatment, but our children do need special guidance. I know that the school counselors are overloaded, but our eldest son sees his counselor only once a year. He seems to be doing okay, but I can't really tell (*Negro parent*).

I make no distinction between whites and Negroes. I believe that individuals must make their own way, regardless of race (*White teacher*).

Of course we do watch Negro progress carefully—it *does* make a difference. But we're not even supposed to know how many Negroes we have in the schools. We do keep such records, of course, but the fiction is that we don't pay attention to race, either way (*Primary school principal*).

I've tried to give my Negro students the extra attention they need, but it does cause problems in the classroom. Other children seem to resent it. I agree that we must try to bring the Negro students up to our standards rather than to lower standards, but it is difficult (*White teacher*).

Most of the teachers never use the word Negro. They think in terms of social class (*White teacher*).

If you make separate standards for white and Negro students, you can expect trouble. I have talked to other teachers about this, and nearly all of them agree. Maybe the Negro students will just have to try harder (*White teacher*).

I only know of one teacher who is prejudiced. She always makes fun of Negroes in class. My sister complained about her to the principal. Anyway, she is being kicked out next year. I have never even heard a teacher use the word "Negro" (*Negro high school student*).

Most of the teachers here come from small rural towns in Pennsylvania. They don't have Southern-type prejudice, but they all believe in Horatio Alger. I suppose you would call it the "Protestant ethic." They go around pretending that race doesn't exist, at least until someone tries to talk about it reasonably. They can get away with this here, because we have so few Negroes (*White junior high school teacher*).

I have seen some figures on the relative progress of students in the different schools. If anything, I would say the schools with the most Negroes do better than those in the outlying districts (*University education professor*).

The only problem we have had with teachers on school assignments is when we start a new school outside town. They want to stay in town, for the most part. And that's where we have the greatest number of Negroes (*Superintendent of schools*).

I guess some of the schools have a better class of students than others, but all of them have *some* problem children. Some of the teachers like to get away from the areas around industrial workers, but we don't usually have much choice. For the most part, we have a pretty good bunch of kids throughout the town (*Negro teacher*).

I don't think Negro students are much of a problem. We get quite a few lower-class families in this area, and most of them are holy terrors, white or black (*White primary school teacher*).

The whole thing is simply a problem of class. Most of our Negro students are simply from poor families. They act pretty much the same as white lower-class children (*White teacher*).

I wish they would quit thinking of us as some kind of savages. Actually, many of the Negroes in Newark are not lower-class, thanks to our minimum housing laws. But most of the teachers think we are (*Negro leader*).

One thing we can be thankful for, most of the Negroes in Newark are fine, respectable people. Our schools have been steadily improving, and integration has made no difference (*White housewife*).

It seems to me that integration has just caused dissension in the community. It certainly doesn't seem to be doing any good that I can see. I don't see many Negro students improving their lot (*White housewife*).

I really would like to go to college, but I don't think I can afford to go to the University of Delaware. Its standards are too high, and my folks can't afford to send me (*Negro high school student*).

We have stated again and again that there is no reason why any student in this state who sincerely wants an education can't get one right here. We have sufficient money to support any poor student (*University spokesman*).

That's the first I've heard of it. They don't go out of their way to advertise their policies. I suppose they're not bigoted, but they could at least make an effort to reach Negro students (*Negro leader*).

Most Negroes I've talked to say the university doesn't welcome students. I get that feeling too. I plan to go to Delaware State College [a predominantly Negro school] (*Negro high school student*).

Negro high school counselors downstate discourage students who want to go to the university. Even well-meaning counselors in Wilmington try to dissuade Negroes (*Negro university student*).

We are aware that many counselors discourage Negroes from going to "tough" schools, so we have worked entirely by individual capacities. It does seem to me, though, that the university is a pretty cold place for Negroes. If I were colored, I'd think twice before going there (*School counselor*).

We know the university has a bad image among Negroes, but we do not plan to lower our standards. Anyone, white or Negro, who wishes to come here is welcome if he can meet our standards. Our position has simply been that we will make no special effort to attract Negroes (*University spokesman*).

Well, that's true in general, but actually, the university has initiated some programs to improve its image. There is a new "preschool" program, and I understand that some effort is being made to increase the Negro staff, both faculty and administration. Perhaps you know the president has attempted to gain control of the Delaware State College in order to break up its racial composition (*University faculty member*).

Aside from the university, we certainly can't complain about the quality of education here. It is good, and the schools are mostly white, so colored children are expected to meet high standards (*Negro parent*).

I think that we are on top of the integration problem here. We have met all our problems successfully and we will continue to do so as long as outside agitators keep out of our affairs (*School principal*).

We are aware that the Negro population in Newark may increase in the future. We have made no special plans to meet that eventuality, because we have a growing school system that will be able to handle it when the time comes. Frankly, I resent the interference of the government. Every time they begin a program, they establish controls. We have tried to meet all our problems quietly, with a minimum of outside interference. You know, when we first integrated, several people suggested that we form a parents' committee to handle any problems. Instead, I organized the kids in the student council. I have found that they can take care of most of their own affairs. Every time you let a bunch of nosy old women in on a problem, you can expect trouble. The same goes for other groups (*School official*).

One of the big problems in this town is that everything is done quietly. The "old guard" make quiet, private agreements, and no one knows what is going on. One of these days they're going to run into a problem they can't sweep under the rug (*Civil rights leader*).

You have to remember that this county is a shining beacon of enlightenment in a pigsty of a state. It's no wonder the school system is afraid of public activity. We have many bigots in town, and the state legislature still provides much of the money for education. I think the community and school system are right in acting quietly (*White P.T.A. member*).

Things are certainly better than they were, but I can't help feeling that the school officials and community leaders are just doing what they have to do. They never initiate anything. Underneath, this is still a stinking, rotten town (*Negro leader*).

I think this is a wonderful place to live. Can't think of a better place in this state or any other (*Negro housewife*).

The Community

The object of these comments, Newark, Delaware, is a bit of small-town Americana with severe growing pains. Located in a border state on the Atlantic seaboard, it was once a crossroads farm town, which found itself the center for the University of Delaware. For many years it remained a small university town. Then, after World War II, nearby Wilmington began the centrifugal suburban and industrial development so familiar among American cities. Suddenly Newark found itself surrounded by industries, shopping centers, and a rapidly expanding population. Simultaneously the university began expanding rapidly from within, producing a squeeze, in more than a literal sense. For a number of reasons to be discussed in more detail later, Newark responded eclectically: like Topsy, it "just growed."

The result of all this is occasionally startling. Driving the twelve miles from Wilmington to Newark, one is aware first of California-like shopping centers, complete with neon signs and modernistic façades, all surrounded with seemingly endless asphalt-paved parking lots. The Spirit of 'Seventy-six lives in laundromats, restaurants, and real estate offices decorated in variations on Independence Hall. Red brick and white steeples are juxtaposed with stainless-steel diners advertising Chesapeake Bay seafood on hamburger buns. Between, behind, and surrounded by trees and /or modern buildings can be seen stately old churchyard cemeteries, powder mills, and other artifacts of Revolutionary times. Further back one can glimpse the solid and imposing walls of mansions built by the state's duPont family, small farms, and the enormous factories and office buildings of the expanding Wilmington industrial complex.

Closer to Newark, the country almost reasserts itself, only to give way to a modern used-car lot, a railroad trestle, and the Victorian frame houses of Newark's Main Street. Frame houses gradually turn into bakeries, real estate and doctors' offices, the whole suddenly giving way to a shopping center, churches, and solid-looking red-brick commercial establishments. More independence halls jostle with trees, modernistic boxes, false-front stores reminiscent of Western movie sets, more Victorian gingerbread, and imposing blocks of stone and brick. Main Street stretches for blocks, intersected by narrow streets lined with row houses straight from the nineteenth century, giving the impression of a community spawned from the marriages of Philadelphia, Peyton Place, and Tonopah, Nevada. Suddenly one comes to the elm-lined Georgian elegance of the main campus of the University of Delaware. Exploring randomly from this point, one can find eighteenth-century brick houses, more university, modern apartment complexes, more row houses, split-level housing developments, ranch-type housing developments, Cape Cod housing developments, an automobile factory, more university, truly lovely residential areas, railroad tracks, a Southern States Co-op mill, a Negro ghetto, a Negro housing development, fraternity houses, elm trees, dogwood (in season), chemical factories, more Victorian gingerbread, supermarkets, corner grocery stores, liquor stores, modern churches, Colonial churches, elm trees, and more university.

This eclectic but nevertheless fascinating setting is inhabited by old white men on benches, five thousand college students, ten thousand public school students, eight hundred Negroes, foreign students, a few Italians, but mostly blondish Americans of comparatively old stock. One can also find Cadillacs, chrome-plated Oldsmobiles, old Fords, a goodly number of pickups driven by farmers, factory workers, college professors, businessmen, bankers, clerks, engineers (after 5 P.M.), housewives in New York fashions, housewives in pedalpushers, housewives in Montgomery Ward prints, high school teachers, and more Ph.D.'s than illiterates. At the proper time of day a goodly proportion of the town's public school students find their way to Main Street, in successive waves of Negroes and whites. Occasionally one can see Negro and white of the same sex walking together, but there is little evidence of miscegenation in Newark.

The community stops just short of provincialism at one pole, and just as short of cosmopolitanism at the other. One university faculty wife, seeking lox, called a delicatessen and was told she wanted a hardware store; but that evening she attended a concert given by the Juilliard String Quartet. If Friday night brings out overalls, Sunday night features the latest Ingmar Bergman film. On the surface, this is Newark.

The Penetration of Newark

Newark is located in the extreme northwest section of a small border state. The northernmost county of this state, containing both Newark and Wilmington, exhibits most of the characteristics of Northern industrial America. The southern counties are noted for their Southern orientation, in a very literal sense. Wilmington, with an approximate population of ninety thousand, is the seat of a large and internationally known industrial complex dominated by a single family. The considerable economic and political influence of this family has, until very recently, been confined to the northern county of the state. The southern counties, on the other hand, have been rural, agricultural, and largely isolated from the industrial empires to their north. Between them, the southern counties accounted for only 31.1 per cent of the state's population in 1960, while composing roughly two-thirds of the state's area. After 1950 the state's industries and a large Air Force base began to change the composition of one of the southern counties, but the northern county nevertheless comprises over two-thirds of the state's population, nearly all its industrial wealth, but only one-third of its area.

Politically, this situation has been disadvantageous for the northern county, with the state legislature virtually controlled by the rural, agricultural interests of the southern counties. Among other problems, Wilmington has never been able to secure state tax proceeds commensurate with its needs. Social welfare, urban renewal, and a multitude of other typically urban, industrial institutions were slow in coming to Wilmington, as compared with other Northern cities. Despite erratic (though sometimes generous) gifts from her industrial entrepreneurs, Wilmington has tended to flounder in the less pleasant by-products of industrial urbanism.

For other cities in the northern county, even less reliance could be placed upon entrepreneurial good will. Most communities were financially dependent upon the state for education, city projects, etc., over and above city property taxes (which traditionally have been low anyway). Something of this situation can be gleaned by driving through the state: barely adequate roads in the north often widen to beautiful highways at the southern county line. The result of this situation has been to produce an understandable hypersensitivity to the attitudes of southern legislators. Northern politicians and civic leaders tend to look over one shoulder to see if the state legislature is watching, and over the other at the industrial giants in their midst. Recent reapportionment of the legislature will eventually change this situation, but as one Newark official observed: "Our new legislators from Wilmington don't know their way around yet. Some of the old politicians from the south are still twisting them around their little fingers."

As suggested earlier, Wilmington's problems bear directly upon Newark. Although Wilmington's population declined by 13.2 per cent from 1950 to 1960, its periphery expanded rapidly. During the same period, its unincorporated suburbs increased in population by ninety-five per cent. This change reduced Wilmington's portion of the northern county's population from two-thirds in 1930 to approximately one-third in 1960. Although its geographical expansion has not yet quite reached Newark, shopping centers, real estate offices, suburban housing developments, and industries are all shared by Newark and Wilmington. The effect of all this has been to increase Newark's awareness and independence upon Wilmington *vis-à-vis* the southern-oriented state legislature.

The northern county itself has grown from a population of 218,879 in 1950 to 307,446 in 1960, an increase of 40.5 per cent overall. Excluding Wilmington, the population growth of the county has been approximately 95 per cent for the same period. Census areas of the county outside Wilmington show growths from 130 per cent to almost 800 per cent. Six of the seven areas of greatest growth in the county are located in the Newark region.

Newark itself expanded boundaries between 1950 and 1960, increasing the population from 6,731 in 1950 to 11,404 in 1960, a growth of 69.4 per cent. The 1950 boundary, now the center of town, increased only from 6,700 to 7,300. The present population of Newark is approximately 14,000, with at least 25,000 additional persons living within a three-mile radius. Population analysts in the state indicate that there is no reason to expect a slackening of this growth.

The largest minority group in the northern county is Negro, accounting for 26.2 per cent of Wilmington's population, but only 5.4 per cent of the balance of the county. In 1940 approximately 12 per cent of Wilmington's population was Negro. By 1960 this figure had increased to 26.2 per cent, and is still rising. The balance of the county experienced a relative loss in Negro population, from 9.1 per cent in 1940 to 5.4 per cent in 1960. Much of this change can be accounted for by the flight of whites to Wilmington's suburbs, rather than to any dramatic influx of Negroes to Wilmington. For the balance of the county, it is significant to note that while the white population increased by some 100 per cent, the Negro population declined by 3.7 per cent. Newark's Negro population, 745 in 1960, accounted for less than 7 per cent of its population. This figure is estimated at 800 for 1966, accounting for approximately 6 per cent of the total population. The Negro population of Newark, then, is small and declining in percentage of the total population. No other minority groups of social significance exist within Newark. Jews, Italians, and other ethnic categories can be found in small numbers, but they do not constitute socially defined out-groups for the city as a whole.

The relative decrease of Negroes in the northern county, exclusive of Wilmington, still allows a slight gain in absolute numbers. From 1950 to 1960 the absolute number of Negroes increased by 2,760. Of these, only 719 were in-migrants; the rest were accounted for by natural increase. During the same period Wilmington experienced an absolute gain of 7,800 Negroes, of which 3,755, or almost half, were in-migrants. These figures indicate that while Wilmington has had a substantial increase of Negro in-migrants, many of them from the South, the balance of the county has maintained a relatively stable Negro population. This is true generally of Newark: recent change has consisted mostly of out-migration, balanced by natural increase. A recent study conducted by the University of Delaware's Urban Affairs Center indicated that over 62 per cent of Negro housing in one area of Newark is occupied by lifetime residents of the state. By far the largest number of Negro in-migrants came from adjacent states, with approximately 22 per cent from Virginia. Most of these in-migrants came to Newark in the 1955–1959 period. Negro out-migrants during this period moved almost entirely to large urban centers.

The age distribution of both whites and Negroes for the northern county, excluding Wilmington, is quite young, reflecting the youthful nature of in-migrants and whites moving from Wilmington to its suburbs. In 1960 the median age for the white population was 27, compared to 39 for Wilmington. The corresponding figures for Negroes were 25.4 and 26.3, respectively. Newark itself shows a similar pattern, although its Negro population with a median age of approximately 27.5 is slightly older than the white population with a median age of approximately 24. Both Negroes and whites, however, have a large proportion of their respective populations in the 5-to-19-year-old bracket, indicating high fertility for both groups. On the basis of these figures, population analysts predict little change in the proportion of Negroes in Newark. If Negroes should join the exodus of middle-class whites from Wilmington, the picture might change, but this is not considered imminent.

Newark's population is well educated. Median school years completed is 12.4 in Newark, compared to 10 for the northern county as a whole, and 9.9 for Wilmington. Whites in the northern county, exclusive of Wilmington, are much better educated than Negroes. For whites, the median number of school years completed is 12, compared to 8.6 for Negroes. While one out of every seven whites holds a college degree, less than one out of twenty-five Negroes has completed college. Even more striking, while 54.8 per cent of whites have completed high school, only 21 per cent of Negroes have high school degrees. In 1950 the corresponding figures were 47.4 per cent for whites and 12.7 per cent for Negroes. These figures indicate that despite dramatic improvements, Negroes are still much more poorly educated than are whites.

In 1964 in a selected area of Newark containing a large proportion of Negroes, median personal annual income for Negroes was found to be $3,135, compared to $4,081 for whites. The corresponding Census figure for Newark as a whole in 1960 was $4,094. Since the area studied contains the bulk of Newark's Negroes, it is safe to assume that median personal incomes for Negroes is $1,000 less than for whites. More instructive, perhaps, are figures showing that 28.4 per cent of Negro adults in Newark earn personal incomes of less than $2,000 a year, compared to 13 per cent of whites. At the other extreme, 19.1 per cent of the area's whites earn over $6,000 annually, compared to 10.3 per cent of the Negroes. These figures were gathered in an older area of Newark, and do not reflect the wealthier residential areas of the town.

Occupation is probably the best indicator of relative status in contemporary America, and data for the northern county, exclusive of Wilmington, are instructive. In 1960, 35.8 per cent of Negroes and 7.1 per cent of whites were employed as service workers. Fifteen per cent of Negroes and 2 per cent of whites were employed as laborers. Only 5.4 per cent of Negroes, as compared to 29 per cent of whites, were professional or managerial personnel. Clerical and sales personnel accounted for 25 per cent of whites, and only 6.1 per cent of Negroes. Likewise, craftsmen and foremen comprised 18.1 per cent of whites, and 6.7 per cent of Negroes. In other words, over half of the Negro labor force were employed as laborers and service workers, while only 10 per cent of whites held such jobs. Comparable figures were not compiled for Newark itself. There are reasons, to be discussed subsequently, to suspect that the eight hundred or so Negroes in Newark represent a somewhat higher occupational level than Negroes in other parts of the county.

In the predominantly Negro area of Newark, approximately 20 per cent of a total of two hundred and ninety housing units were in poor or dilapidated condition in 1964, compared to 12.7 per cent for the town as a whole in 1960. In one area especially, sixteen out of thirty housing units were in poor condition. Of fifty-nine substandard houses in this area, fifty-four were occupied by Negroes. Only 4 per cent of the white residents lived in substandard housing, compared to approximately 33 per cent of the Negroes. One section, however, all Negro, contained twenty-two homes in good condition, three in fair condition, and none in substandard condition.

It is hoped that the reader's patience has not been unduly strained by the foregoing demographic data. They were introduced to document some observations about Newark and its social environment. To summarize, the town is caught up in a suburban growth of grand proportions. In this respect it is probably representative of many small communities throughout the United States finding themselves engulfed by the outward expansion of nearby urban centers. However, because of the nature of this growth, the racial minority of the town has *decreased* proportionately, unlike typical central cities with rapidly increasing minority categories. Nevertheless, the town is faced with a miniature "race problem," if we may use demographic materials as indicators of the "objective" consequences of discrimination: Negroes in Newark and the surrounding area clearly do not enjoy the same social-class standing as whites. At the same time, it should be noted that the relative standing of Negroes has improved in the decade from 1950–1960, particularly with respect to education. Just how much of this is due to school integration itself is not clear from the census data: we shall have more observations on that subject presently.

Politics in Newark

Newark is governed by a city council of six members, including an elected mayor and an appointed city manager. Officially politics in the town are bipartisan, but depending upon one's informants, the city council is seen as "reactionary," "too conservative," or "damned near socialist." Republicans and conservative Democrats do seem to predominate in the council, the "real" power group. The mayor's position is largely ceremonial (aside from his seat on the council), but some residents of Newark seem to think he wields a good deal of unofficial power. The city manager, ostensibly the administrator of the town, is poorly paid. As one active politician put it: "The city manager will never amount to beans until he is offered a decent salary. As it is, we get retired engineers for the job." There is a good deal of talk about the "old guard" as the invisible power wielders in Newark, particularly among Negro and liberal white informants. Informed observers agree that there is such a group, composed of landowners and local retailers, but there is little agreement as to their representation in the decisions of the city council. The "actual" power group in town is presumably a group of liberal conservatives and conservative liberals, typified by one observer as "carbon copies of Eisenhower." There is also a third group of professionals, including some University of Delaware faculty members, represented by an organization called the Newark Better Government Association. This group is, at the time of writing, ostensibly liberal Democratic in composition, and is pushing its own candidates for city councilman. Although there is considerable disagreement about the political alliances of the city council, it is likely that Gilbert and Sullivan's observation applies to Newark: they're "either a little liberal, or else a little conservative." Current election statements do indicate a split along these lines.

According to the popular view, both white and Negro, there is also a cabal ("a nest of cobras") composed of the "old guard," representatives from the duPont family, the president of the University of Delaware, the superintendent of schools, a Negro businessman (a junior member), and whoever else happens to be the target of controversy at any particular moment. "Insiders" debunk this notion but acknowledge the occasional private communications between leaders of various institutions in the town. Alliances between leaders probably actually shift according to issues. One businessman observed: "Anyone who puts the university president in the same bed with the city council ought to have his head examined."

The University of Delaware, occupying about a hundred acres of land in the center of Newark and nine hundred acres more within the city limits, does present a relevant power group to the city. It pays no property taxes and is constantly accused of "gobbling up land and taxes." The city council recently proposed a business-parking plan along its main street, which is widely expected to bring property values up. According to reports, a Wilmington trust company (controlled by the duPont family) opposed the plan. The board of trustees of the University of Delaware is widely supposed to be identical with the board of the trust company, so the story spread that the university and its president tried to kill the proposal. Whether or not the university wields such power is a moot point for present purposes, but it is widely viewed as a major component of the local power structure. This appears to be especially true among Negroes, one of whom called the university president "the mayor, city council, and city manager of Newark." The university has discouraged faculty participation in local politics, but recent criticism has apparently modified this policy. Clearly the university itself, its faculty and some five thousand regular students, do present a relevant category for power considerations in Newark.

Much of the belief in a power conspiracy in Newark stems from the very real power of the duPonts. They clearly have played a major part in the economic growth of the northern county, and reportedly control some of Newark's finance. It is not at all certain that they are as concerned with Newark's politics as is popularly supposed, but it is quite probable that Newark jumps when certain fingers snap. In any event, the industrial giant does present at least a potential audience for Newark's power structure. If for no other reason, rather generous "charities" are occasionally forthcoming to deserving parties. Some communities in surrounding areas have built fantastic public projects as a result of such grants. As we shall see, this influence has been diluted in recent years by an influx of other industries.

The state legislature, as mentioned earlier, provides another relevant out-group for Newark's power structure. The conservative nature of this body has already been discussed. Suffice it to say here that the interests of the state legislature, the university, and Wilmington's industrial giants do not always coincide. One former city councilman observed: "The politically responsible people in this town are always concerned about conflicts of interest among groups outside the community. They can't afford not to be. Our local tax rate isn't high, so we depend upon outside support for almost anything we attempt."

. . .

The voting public in Newark is extremely varied, as our description of the population might lead one to suppose. It varies from old Newark residents with a downstate orientation, to industrial engineers and to university faculty members of generally liberal predispositions. The net result of rapid industrial expansion, large in-migration, and opposing outside interests has been to penetrate the community, diffuse its boundaries, and present local power with diverse political audiences. Public reaction is predictable, and might best be expressed by residents of the community themselves:

> We try to keep conflict to a minimum. In my experience, the best way to do this is to act quietly on controversial issues, with as little public to-do as possible.

> Well, obviously they can't afford to bring the KKK and CORE in on every issue that comes up. They've problems enough as it is.

> I suppose it is difficult to handle sensitive issues in this town, but it seems to me that underhanded dealing has become a way of life here.

> They act like a bunch of scared rabbits. You'd think socialists and the John Birch Society were camped at opposite ends of town with guns loaded.

It might be expected that one of the "sensitive issues" in Newark concerns Negroes. Before 1954 there was almost complete segregation. Negroes went to Negro schools (by state law), ate in Negro restaurants, and were not permitted in movie theaters. The pattern was very much Southern, except that local politicians bought Negro votes "with booze and parties." Negroes were encouraged to vote, but of course for white candidates. The Negro vote is considered important, particularly for one council seat. Fairly recently one Negro was elected to the city council, an act interpreted by some as indicative of the liberal nature of Newark's politics. Others, particularly Negroes and liberal whites, interpreted the situation as an attempt on the part of whites to co-opt the Negro community. The Negro in question was often mentioned by white respondents as the "leader of the Negro community." However, Negroes point out that he failed to gain re-election, largely as the result of the Negro vote. The reasons for this will be clear subsequently.

With the advent of federal legislation on civil rights and "increasing Negro militancy," Newark's council established a "Bi-Racial Committee," appointed by the mayor, to act in an advisory capacity on civil rights matters. Whites see the committee as functional, in that it had recommended or supported a number of policies interpreted as favorable to Negroes. Negroes interviewed were not so enthusiastic: one called it "a bunch of fair-weather liberals." Some were more kind, but all Negroes felt that the committee had really failed to exert influence of any major consequence.

After Newark's Negro city councilman was elected, a minimum housing bill was pushed through the city council. As a result of this act, a number of homes, involving some two hundred Negroes, were demolished. The Negro councilman's firm was apparently quite active in demolition and transportation during this operation. Furthermore, he was able to use materials from this operation to build new homes on the demolition sites. He takes credit for pushing this bill through the city council, and sees the whole operation as a boon to the city in ridding it of many of its Negro slums. "I didn't make a cent on the new homes. Some people think I am a rich man, but every penny I have is tied up in loans." Whites seem split in their interpretation of the matter, but the consensus seems to be that "ridding the city of an eyesore" was more important than the side issues of Negro displacement. Negro opinion, however, is that the man in question "feathered his own nest" and "played into the hands of the old guard" by his actions. Defending himself, the former councilman points out that he has "provided Negroes with decent homes, and made at least two areas of town pay their own way in taxes." Whatever the truth of the matter, the Negro in question undoubtedly lost support as spokesman for much of the Negro community. As another Negro noted: "We believe [he] was sincere enough, but he only hurt himself and the Negro community." It is worthwhile to note that many liberal whites are aware of this situation, but most of the older community leaders interviewed still see the former councilman as unofficial spokesman for the Negro community.

The displacement of two hundred Negroes in Newark's miniature "urban renewal" apparently bothered some, for there was widespread talk and plans by the city council to build a housing project to replace persons dispossessed by the minimum housing law. The plan provided for more than enough units to replace those already destroyed, so opposition grew rapidly on the grounds that "it would attract a poor class of Negroes to Newark." A number of Negro landlords also opposed the plan, presumably because it would pave the way for further demolition of below-standard homes, most of which are in the Negro section of town. Chief white opposition to the bill was led by a city councilman whose home apparently bordered on the land chosen for the project. Considerable ruckus was raised publicly. The city council approached the FHA for funds, and were told that the project must provide units for aged, including some persons not affected by the minimum housing law. This increased the public fervor, presumably because the affected aged would be predominantly Negro. The whole project was placed before the electorate in a referendum, passed, and was approved by the FHA. Work on the project is now underway. The city council, by the way, did not want to use federal funds for the project, but could find no other sources of finance.

The minimum housing bill provides that residents of substandard houses cannot be dispossessed if their salaries are below a minimum point. The consequence of this, according to a Negro informant, is low declarations of income by the occupants of substandard housing. The same informant observed that "if people were honest about their incomes in this area, you would find their family income to be about the same as whites in the same neighborhood." One observer at the University of Delaware denies this, indicating that the informant in question, active in civil rights, is "concentrating on proving that Newark allows only middle-class Negroes to live here."

One of the interesting aspects of this problem is that Negro landlords in the area (Negroes own nearly all Negro rentals) have enough vested interest in their own properties to prevent any concerted Negro backing for city housing. In fact, the Negro informant just quoted was once president of a local chapter of the NAACP, whose advent apparently caused considerable alarm among some white civic leaders. This chapter strongly supported the city's housing bills, and was, as one white respondent commented, "chucked out of Newark before it had a chance to cause trouble." Ostensibly because of dissension within Negro ranks, the chapter is now defunct, although interestingly enough a number of white leaders still refer to its former leader as "president of the NAACP."

A plan to establish a civic swimming pool promised to provide further contention. At least one group opposed it because it did not provide guarantees for interracial swimming, and another because it did. The plan was dropped. It seems that misinformation can exist even in a small community such as Newark.

The Negro "community" in Newark has no single political structure. Negro respondents indicate that no one person is able to gain enough support to provide a Negro interest group. One leader, the former NAACP president, is apparently the most active Negro in town on civil rights matters. He belongs to the local P.T.A., and is a leader in the Newark Civic Association, a biracial group, which "attempts to keep Negroes *and* whites informed on issues concerning them." This association meets once a week, with attendance varying from twelve to more than a hundred persons, mostly Negro. Discussions at these meetings "are 99 and 99/100 per cent pure talk about education." Although some attempts have been made to broach political matters, the membership is clearly concerned with the problems of educating its youngsters.

At least one other Negro is credited with some following. Although he is not known widely throughout the community, his views are reported to be "more militant" or "more liberal" than either of the others discussed. The majority of Newark's Negroes, however, seem quite content with their present lot. As one elderly woman put it: "We remember the days when we couldn't go to decent schools, couldn't even talk pleasantly with white folks. Now why do all these Young Turks want to stir up trouble? We're doing all right. A man's a man, either good or bad, and if he wants to improve himself, he can now. We don't want no truck with these civil rights movements. They are up to no good." This may not represent all the "old guard Negroes" in Newark, but several Negro students concurred. "It's against my religion to support civil rights movements," one maintained. Another indicated that at least two Negro clergymen urged congregations to avoid involvement in political movements.

Whites with some knowledge of the inner power structure

of Newark clearly see cleavages among whites. Some also perceive cleavages among Negroes. However, the vast majority of whites interviewed perceived both the white and Negro power structures as coherent and monolithic social groups. Even the most sophisticated of whites slipped into dialogues about "the Negro interests," after discussing their cleavages. Nearly all of the older community leaders viewed the Negroes as forming at least a potential interest group. Likewise, Negroes were most apt to employ terms like the "old guard," "they," and "white power" when discussing Newark politics. Both white and Negro leaders evidenced awareness of cleavages among themselves and the respective out-group, but the fear of a possible civil rights movement or anti-civil rights movement nevertheless persists on both sides. The importance of this phenomenon in structuring school racial policies will become clear as we proceed.

It is not our purpose here to pass judgment or to evaluate the political scene in Newark. There are, as we have indicated, a number of power groups with opposing interests affecting Newark's politics. One of the national Ku Klux Klan leaders is reported to reside some ten miles from Newark, across the Maryland state line, threatening to strike at the "right moment." Very recently a University of Delaware student was identified as a Delaware Klan leader (he was arrested for carrying a concealed weapon). Members of CORE, NAACP, etc., occasionally make loud noises from another neighboring state. Local power leaders worry about the conservative state legislature, and most of all about local opinion. It is not at all clear that they have gauged the latter accurately, but as one official said: "Accuracy hasn't much to do with it. All it takes is for one Negro liberal to get up and start a fuss, and you'll have all the bigots in the surrounding countryside down our necks." He added, "I'm just as concerned about some of the white liberals. They just don't understand our problems." It is clear that much decision-making in Newark is secretive or "quiet," largely due to fears of perceived opposing external and internal interests. The fact that these interests are often perceived as more coherent than they appear to be from other perspectives ought to surprise no one: sociologists are fond of pointing to this phenomenon in terms of "out-group" perception. Nevertheless, its prevalence does not diminish its influence on Newark's racial issues.

Other Institutions and Race in Newark

Newark's economic structure has also been affected by the penetration of her boundaries. Traditionally the town possessed only those retail businesses one would expect in a small, quiet university community. Nearly all were locally owned, although Wilmington's banks and trust companies reportedly controlled "high finance," such as it was. Between 1950 and 1960, however, a large automobile plant, several chemical firms, a cosmetic factory, and numerous other industries began to spring up around the periphery of the city. This brought an influx of population augmented by Wilmington's suburban expansion, producing a building boom of housing tracts, suburban shopping centers, and other accoutrements of modern life. It also produced a class of wealthy landowners, some of whom were landholding farmers caught in the boom. It also brought chain groceries with outside ownership, and a large number of engineers and skilled laborers, producing an urban overlay on an essentially rural community.

Many local businesses responded to this change and profited, but many Newark merchants complain that much of their business has been hurt by huge shopping centers between Newark and Wilmington. In general, it is clear that Newark's retail stores retain a small-town atmosphere, while the new, modern shopping centers are all outside the town. It is probably safe to say that the boom has helped Newark's merchants, but it is certainly true that much of the town's population trades at out-of-town discount stores, chain markets, and so on.

Local merchants, for the most part, exhibit a curious ambivalence concerning integration. Very few Negro clerks are in evidence in local stores, but neither are they obvious in the giant superstores outside of town. Several merchants indicated that they did not "cater" to Negro trade for fear of losing white customers, but on the other hand, those interviewed were unanimous in their belief that "any man's dollar is a dollar, regardless of the color of his skin." A few stores hire Negroes, one rather obvious as a waitress in a soda fountain, another as a stock clerk in a retail store. One high school principal reported that a number of industries around Newark have requested qualified Negroes for "visible" white-collar positions. A counselor in the same school, however, reported that she has had difficulty in placing qualified Negroes in local businesses. She indicated that industries required "impossible" qualifications for Negroes, as compared to whites considered for the same or similar jobs.

Negroes have been refused service in a few restaurants and bars during the past few years, but recent civil rights acts have brought only "controlled hostility" on the part of some proprietors. Negroes do not feel that Newark stores go out of their way to discriminate, but neither do they feel particularly welcome in some. One merchant who invites Negro trade commented that several Negroes have expressed appreciation for his attitude, intimating that they were not comfortable in some other establishments. The small numbers of Negroes in Newark do not really present much of a problem one way or another to Newark merchants, however, so little is made of it. "Besides," as one Negro stressed, "If we're too poor to buy in Newark we can go to [a discount store in Wilmington], and if we're well enough off, we don't have any interest in the local merchandise anyway." Another Negro, commenting on a local bar known to discourage Negro trade, said, "I wouldn't be caught dead in that dive, and not many Negroes I know would, either."

The giant industries surrounding Newark brought with them considerable Negro labor. Unable to find local housing, or disinterested in residing in Newark, most of them live in Wilmington. There is some feeling that many Negroes would "invade" Newark if housing were available. The many suburban housing tracts surrounding Newark are overwhelmingly white, but middle-class Negroes (one or two families in each) have very recently moved into these areas. It is reported that one real estate agent has been quietly placing "respectable" Negroes in these developments. Wilmington's duPont family, among others, has reportedly been seeking qualified Negroes for white-collar occupations of late, so the slow movement of middle-class Negroes into the area will probably continue. Civic associations exist in most of the suburban areas around Newark. They are reported to plan a number of community projects, including projects aimed at segregation. One informant suggested that some of them exist for the sole purpose of maintaining segregation.

A large number of Negroes in Newark are employed by the University of Delaware—males as janitors, females as dormitory maids—and work side-by-side with whites; both are paid very low wages. This apparently accounts for a part of the Negro hostility toward the university. A number of Negro respondents noted that Negroes are very visible as laborers around the campus. There apparently is no discrimination employed by the university in hiring labor, so the situation simply reflects the overall social status of Negroes. A disproportionate percentage of road crews, city garbage collectors, domestics, etc., seem to be Negro, but whites in Newark seem to agree that discrimination in employment is minimal.

The city tax rate is quite low, and the presence of the university reduces tax revenues even further. One economist estimates that every new home to be built in Newark must be valued at nineteen thousand dollars or more to pay its way in city taxes. This reportedly provides some pressure to prevent low-cost housing, effectively barring most Negroes from the town.

Real estate agents in Newark react to interracial housing as they do in most parts of the country: with horror. The familiar subtle and not-so-subtle forms of discouraging Negro buyers or renters are practiced. It need not be detailed here—but it should be pointed out that very few Negroes in Newark have tested the system, and those employed as engineers in nearby industries have generally been successful in avoiding difficulty. "Incidents" have occurred in some housing tracts, but again, quiet generally prevails in Newark. In one apartment complex built partially with FHA funds, the owner was reportedly shaken upon hearing his maintenance man loudly assuring a tenant that "niggers will never move in here." The owner does not encourage Negroes either, but reportedly employs much more subtle means to prevent their entry "with the exception of a few special cases." Negroes are very much aware of the situation, but those interviewed agreed that the time was not ripe for "pushing the system too far."

In general there is little interpersonal contact between Negroes and whites in Newark. Several Negro respondents indi-

cated displeasure with this situation, but many Negroes interviewed appeared to be complacent about existent casual
contacts. One Negro husband and wife complained: "We are
never invited to white homes. If the mayor or [faculty member
of the university] want to see us, they always come here. We
feel that most Negroes would appreciate an open hand from
whites. It is awfully difficult for us to make the overtures." Another Negro old-timer chuckled: "Many of the 'old guard'
here still have their pet niggers. Once in a while I think I have
some white friends, but I guess I'm one of the pets." One receives the impression that liberals in town are puzzled by Negro
awkwardness in interpersonal relationships with whites, conservatives "are afraid of what their neighbors might think," and
reactionaries "are afraid we'll rape their daughters." Whites do
express considerable fear about intermarriage "or worse," as
one prim lady put it. This concern underlies much of the parental concern expressed about integration in the public schools and
at the university.

A paradoxical situation exists in Newark with respect to
churches. White clergy have been among the most militant anti-
segregationists in the community, and yet, as one public official
observed, "The churches have only token integration, if any at
all." He continued, "I don't approve of segregation in the
churches, but some of the ministers around here have been especially loud in their condemnation of our school policies, and the
schools are a damned sight further along than they are. I keep
coming back to the same point: The best way to handle these
affairs is to do what you have to do, quietly and without publicity."

This is not completely fair, although clergymen do acknowledge resistance on the part of many of their laymen to
integration. Most white churches have some Negro members,
but as one clergyman indicated, "It was a long, uphill fight
in our case." In at least one church an usher had been found
turning away Negroes long after the congregation had affirmed
its stand on integration. In another the minister had managed to
"trade choirs" with a Negro church, but had not yet dared to ask
Negroes to join the congregation. According to one source
"moderate Protestants led the way, followed by Catholics and
fundamentalists," in that order. Negroes acknowledge the con-

cern of clergy, but several informants indicated that whites were "obeying their consciences, but not their hearts" on the matter of church integration. Two Negro leaders also complained that while they appreciated the concern of white clergy about the integration problem, they were appalled at the "naïveté" of some of them about "power realities" in Newark. Excepted from these criticisms was the Society of Friends, for whom Negroes had only favorable comments.

School Integration in Newark: The Public Schools

We have taken a long hard look at the overall social environment of Newark before concentrating upon the school system. This is entirely deliberate: one cannot grasp the factors operating in the process of school integration without first understanding the context in which it took place. This would be true of any community of course, but it is infinitely easier to point to the interrelationships of different groups in a city the size of Newark than would be the case in, say, New York or Chicago.

It should be recalled that, prior to the 1950s, Newark was almost completely segregated in a very Southern fashion. At that time, however, the community began to feel the effects of urban expansion. New industries, complete with personnel, moved into the area. Urban, Northern-oriented people made their presence felt. At the same time the University of Delaware began a dramatic expansion. The community faced an entirely new environment, and could not have isolated itself had it wished to do so (apparently some residents were in favor of that course). Gradually old interests, particularly the state legislature and Wilmington's old entrepreneurs, lost influence relative to incoming powers. The response of the city in general was to meet these changes as they came, without, as one observer put it, "rocking the old boat." Caught up in the opposing forces about them, civic leaders made the best of what for them was generally perceived as an unfortunate, but nevertheless real, situation. Their policies were generally devoid of any perceptible long-range goals or planning, but rather seemed to be "functional" responses to environmental change. True or not, the decision-making process in this context is seen by most residents of Newark as being rather "secretive," "furtive," or "quiet," depending upon their respective points of view.

Newark is small, permitting a goodly amount of informal decision-making. Its Negro minority is also relatively small, comprising less than 7 per cent of the population. Attitudes and interest groups in and about the community present extremely varied points of view concerning racial issues. Given this general atmosphere, we might expect to find that the school system has reacted to integration in a manner similar to the polity. In fact it has, and in the eyes of Newark residents, with generally satisfactory results.

The school system in Newark reaches beyond the city's political boundaries. Education in the state traditionally has been financed and controlled by the legislature, with relatively little local financial support. An exception was Wilmington, with its extreme underrepresentation in the state polity. There the city's duPont family made possible a reasonable financial base for the schools, and incidentally provided a good deal of local autonomy in school affairs. It is not surprising, then, that Wilmington was the first community in the state to integrate its schools. Other communities viewed the expected Supreme Court decision on school integration with apprehension, particularly because of their financial dependence upon the Southern, segregation-minded state legislature. State laws forbade school integration, miscegenation, and other racial iniquities. Although Newark's leaders were aware of coming integration, their traditionally low tax base and their dependence upon the state for school financing apparently dictated caution.

The Newark Special School District is at present presided over by a locally elected school board and an appointed superintendent of schools. In view of the lack of local economic independence, it is not surprising that the local school board was, at least before 1950, relatively powerless. Prior to 1958, it was appointed by a superior court judge, and was reported to be favorably predisposed to integration during that period. According to both Negro and white informants, Newark's school board is generally enlightened on social matters, but conflicts of state and local interest appear to have diluted its power. Consequently, the superintendent of schools has emerged as a relatively powerful and autonomous figure, a situation paralleled, as we shall see, in the office of the president of the University of Delaware. Local informants attribute these powers to the personalities of the men themselves, but it should be pointed out that the social situation is at least equally responsible. In any case, integration of the Newark schools was planned and administered by the superintendent and his individual school principals, with the support of the local school board.

As was indicated in the quotations at the beginning of this chapter, there is some difference of opinion among Negroes and whites as to the exact origins of school integration in Newark. School officials maintain that integration was anticipated as early as 1945, when the present superintendent of schools came to Newark. Before integration Newark had a Negro school with Negro teachers. Negro high school students were forced to pay their own way on public buses to a Wilmington Negro high school. At the same time in Newark there were four Negro teachers in a small building serving the total Negro enrollment of somewhere between two and three hundred students. "No one even pretended Negroes were getting a decent education, and very few cared." One of the first acts of the new superintendent was to integrate his staff in teachers' meetings, etc. According to a white teacher, "A few eyebrows were raised, but most of the teachers on the staff thought it was a good idea."

Anticipating integration, two Negro families in Newark brought suits before the state supreme court, beginning in 1953. One of these suits was being heard when the U.S. Supreme Court ruling on segregation was handed down. During this period the Newark school board was planning for the eventuality of such a decision, but most Negro informants attribute the fact of integration to Wilmington's sudden decision to desegregate its schools. According to Negro sources Wilmington announced that it would take no more Negroes from outside school districts. This ostensibly forced Newark to desegregate its high school. School officials indicate that the decision to integrate the high school had been made before Wilmington's announcement. The fact that Newark's Negroes were forced to go outside town for their education was used as an excuse for the decision.

The atmosphere in the state at that time was clearly not hospitable to integration. In Milford, a nearby small town, national attention was focused upon community-wide racial demonstrations, near-riots, and almost complete disruption of the community. The Milford school board had precipitated integration in the fall of 1954, apparently failing to judge accurately the mood of its predominantly rural constituency. State and national press coverage was compounded by the arrival of the self-styled leader of the National Association for the Advancement of White People, one Bryant Bowles. Attention throughout the state was focused upon the ensuing disorder, reinforcing the fears of school officials and civic leaders in nearby communities, including Newark. Publicity was used also by downstate segregationists to demonstrate that "public opinion is not yet ready for integration."

Newark had already committed itself to the desegregation of its high school, so with considerable apprehension forty Negro students were admitted to its student body. In preparation, the student council was given several pep talks. Teachers were told that their standards might have to be lowered somewhat for Negro students with a substandard education. This apparently caused a good deal of consternation among teachers, but as the principal indicated, "they went along with it." None of the teachers appeared to be concerned with the fact of integration itself, but they too expected difficulties. Apparently to everyone's surprise, "the operation came off without a hitch." The superintendent of schools attributes this fact "to the kids themselves. They were magnificent." A number of Negroes interviewed attributed the success of this initial integration to the principal of the high school, who "handled the whole affair beautifully." According to the principal, no administrative changes were made, and "no special point was made about it. We just carried on as if nothing had happened." One informant indicated that Newark was lucky that the bigots' attention was on Milford. "If they hadn't had that to think of, they would have been in Newark."

At one point, in fact, Bryant Bowles did apparently plan to

come to Newark, but reportedly changed his mind at the last moment. During this first year of integration, the school did receive a few telephone calls from irate parents. One man removed his child from school, and another threatened the principal at his home. But no organized resistance appeared. "The community backed us all the way," recalled the principal.

Two Negro informants and several school officials noted that athletics provided many of the Negro students with a natural "in" with whites. "In fact," stated one official, "a number of alumni expressed considerable pleasure at the presence of Negroes on the football team." Despite the stereotype implications of "Negro athletes," sports did apparently provide a basis for easy interaction between white and Negro students.

The school system had shown (and still does) considerable concern over interracial dating. Immediately after integration a white girl was seen in a Negro boy's automobile. The girl was "given a good talking to," and the boy was "cautioned not to make trouble over that issue." The first interracial school dance also occasioned some concern, but the superintendent of schools asked Negro boys not to dance with white girls, to which they agreed. Since then, all dances have been "desegregated," if in a peculiar sense. One official indicated that he had no doubts that miscegenation would occur in the future, but hastily added, "we aren't ready for it around here yet." Parents have called the school to ask that teachers refrain from seating their daughters next to Negroes. In these cases school officials ask teachers to rearrange seating completely, in order to comply "without offending the Negro students." Whatever else their attitudes, at least some Newark parents do seem to be concerned about possible interracial dating.

In successive years the sixth grade, followed by the seventh and eighth grades, and finally primary schools, were integrated. In each case integration was accomplished without fanfare and without unpleasant incidents, "other than the few parents concerned over their children's association with Negroes." According to school officials the question of integration's effect on quality of education has never come up with parents or teachers. The few complaints received concerned the fact of association with Negroes.

Initially Negro primary school students were bused to two

different schools, a practice discontinued with the building of more schools. The old Negro school was closed down and is still boarded up. Of the four Negro teachers at that school, three were transferred to integrated schools and one was dropped "for sheer incompetency." "I suppose she was incompetent," complained one Negro commentator, "but you have to admit it's damned strange that issue never came up until she was considered as a teacher for whites." Two or three more Negro teachers (depending upon one's informant) have been added to the staff since 1957. The fact that so few Negro teachers have been hired serves as an irritant to Negroes, judging from the numerous comments made about it. Negroes interviewed were almost unanimous in accusing the superintendent of schools of "throwing perfectly good applications of Negro candidates into the wastebasket." One informant claimed to have a letter "proving" the superintendent's resistance to hiring Negro teachers. Another informant stated that the president of the school board had taken to reviewing all applications over the superintendent's head, in order to "keep him from excluding Negro teachers."

Whatever the truth of the matter, the superintendent is sensitive to this criticism. He argued that he had "done everything humanly possible" to recruit Negro teachers, and had in fact instructed his recruiter to seek out qualified Negroes. He indicated that he had repeatedly asked the president of Delaware State College, a predominantly Negro school, for qualified personnel, but had been told time and again that "there simply were none he would send us." I asked a number of professors of education at the University of Delaware about this, and was told that there was indeed an acute shortage of Negro teachers in the area. "Most of the Negroes in the urban centers want to stay there, and even Philadelphia and Baltimore report shortages of Negro talent." "Anyway," said one, "Negroes see this state as Southern, and avoid coming here." One of the Negro critics of the superintendent on this issue lent some support to this contention by relating that he knew of "two or three local Negroes who are teaching in cities in surrounding states." His interpretation was that "they knew they would be turned down in Newark."

The superintendent of schools, principals, and most of the teachers interviewed shared at least one trait in common: they all gave every indication of adhering to beliefs in local self-determination, individual achievement, and, in general, the "Protestant ethic." As one official observed: "We believe in tolerance, not license. We want to tolerate Negroes, but we don't want them jammed down our throats indiscriminately." Except for a few teachers, civil rights movements and anti-civil rights movements alike were castigated by those interviewed. This attitude was carried far beyond the race issue to "nosy parents" and others with public or private interests in school affairs. The superintendent of schools was quite adamant on this issue, including the federal government and the U.S. Office of Education in his criticism, "And you may quote me on this." The general impression received was that the issues of race were conceived only in terms of individual prejudice, and not in terms of social forces. For example, one principal maintained: "We hear a good deal about the plight of the Negro and what must be done about him socially. But I can show you enough examples of colored students who have done well to convince even you [a sociologist] that any Negro can make it if he just has what it takes." A more moderate view was held by the principal who initiated the first integration in Newark: "I know that Negro kids don't have the same advantages as whites, and I've repeatedly asked the staff to take this into consideration, but you can't go all the way with this. Somewhere you must evaluate the individual."

All of the school officials and most of the teachers interviewed initiated discussions by maintaining in one way or another that Negroes were given no special attention in the schools. Probing revealed that Negroes were in fact given special attention, at least when "necessary," but clearly the official position for public consumption is that race is simply not considered. Only one principal was willing to produce records showing the number of Negro students in his school, although the superintendent acknowledged that such records were kept. It is not really clear as to how much this refusal to discuss race as an issue is due to personal conviction, and how much is due to fear of public reaction. Several observers noted that most of the teaching staff and administrative officials came to Newark from rural areas of Pennsylvania, suggesting that they probably do "believe that race is not important." On the other hand, officials and teachers alike openly acknowledged that in view of the "town bigots, the less said about race, the better." Also, as one principal observed, "The NAACP and some of the liberals in this town are just waiting to jump down our throats about something." Incidentally, the lack of organization in the Negro community was not considered by any of the school officials interviewed. It is true, to be fair, that some Negroes and some white liberals appear to be very critical of the school system, but their criticisms tend not to be very specific. On the other hand, organized groups such as the Bi-Racial Committee and Newark Better Government Association are generally supportive of school policies regarding race. In general, the impression received was that the system as a whole is hypersensitive to public criticism on matters concerning integration, and it is not always very clear as to which public this sensitivity reflects.

The school system does appear to be quite autonomous in a number of other respects, so perhaps some of its resistance to pressures on racial matters is simply a reflection of a general posture of independence. A number of white and Negro parents interviewed indicated some displeasure at the "arbitrary" or even "snotty" way school officials treated parental complaints. "Nosy old women" was employed by several school officials in describing parents, giving some indication of their position. P.T.A. members had no specific complaints on this issue, and in fact acclaimed the independent stance of the superintendent. The superintendent himself indicated some pride in the fact that his administration had initiated and continuously increased local school taxes to provide, among other things, more independence from the state. School taxes in Newark, higher than city and county property taxes combined, are used for purposes over and above "basic operating expenses" provided by the state.

At present Newark's school system employs approximately 480 teachers. Over 10,500 students are served by 9 elementary schools, 3 junior high schools, and 2 senior high schools. All of the schools contain some Negro students, although the distribution of Negroes varies considerably. Exact figures are not available for this study, but numbers range from a low of two in some elementary schools to over fifty in others. One high school is known to serve 48 Negro and approximately 1,150 white students. Students are distributed strictly by residence, "with no exceptions." Several observers outside the school system indicated that a recent redistricting of school boundaries, occasioned by the building of new schools, deliberately gerrymandered the Negro residential district to provide an equitable distribution of Negroes in primary and junior high schools. This fact was not mentioned by schools officials, even after considerable peripheral questioning. The act is interpreted by outsiders as completely voluntary. Negroes and whites alike agree that "every attempt has been made to provide reasonable integration." A Negro observer commented: "Any further improvement in that situation will require a turnabout by [a real estate agent]."

Likewise, according to the superintendent, teachers are assigned to schools with the goal of distributing seniority equally. Teachers do apparently gravitate toward schools with a "better class of students," but this has not been affected by racial composition of schools. "We did have some concern about the new high school when it opened a few years ago," commented the superintendent. "But it certainly had nothing to do with race. The new school is on the outskirts of town and has very few Negro students. Contrary to what you might believe, all of our teachers and students wanted to stay at the old high school. One school board member, in fact, tried to get me to keep his daughter there. I refused, of course. We selected a good principal, divided our teachers evenly, and the whole thing went off beautifully."

Teachers interviewed did indicate that some schools were more desirable places in which to teach than others, but they unanimously agreed that this was "simply a matter of the background of the students." It should be pointed out that Newark's Negro population is concentrated near the center of town, and that many of the white industrial workers, apparently the "less desirable element," are concentrated in other areas. Consequently, there is no reason to associate school desirability with Negro concentrations, especially given the small numbers of Negroes in Newark.

A few teachers expressed desires to move to some of the private schools in and around Wilmington, including a Friends school which is integrated. One teacher who had made such a move, however, expressed a quite different view: "They're foolish to think they can escape discipline problems by moving into private schools. We get a large share of problem kids who were kicked out of public schools." The turnover rate of Newark's teachers is quite low. In twenty-one years only fifty teachers have left Newark to go to other school districts, a record which pleases the superintendent of schools. Teachers interviewed were generally favorably inclined to the system, though many were less enthusiastic about the community itself. Teachers compared facilities and salaries favorably with other nearby school districts, including those in Wilmington. They all agreed that facilities were well distributed throughout Newark's various schools. Professors from the University of Delaware's School of Education verified these observations. One commented: "Newark's system is clearly as good as any in the area. Unless a teacher wants to go into another state, she's well off here. Furthermore, teachers like the advantage of having the University of Delaware here close at hand." There is, by the way, no positive evidence of any teacher's leaving the Newark school district because of integration.

Parents of students and other residents of Newark, white and Negro alike, are generally satisfied with the quality of instruction in the public schools. Some parents send their children to particular urban centers for secondary education, but they readily admit that this is mostly a matter of "sentiment" or "origins." Evaluations of University Education staff varied from "average" to "very good." There was, as suggested previously, no evidence that integration was interpreted as related to quality of teaching. Any parental complaints about integration concerned interpersonal contacts and visible discipline problems rather than quality of education itself. White students interviewed paralleled this observation. Students exhibited varying attitudes toward Negroes, but none of these were associated with education itself.

Among teachers and administrators opinions varied considerably about the "problems" presented by Negroes. As the quotations indicate, most teachers attributed both educational and disciplinary problems to "social class" ("sociologese," to use *Time*'s term, *is* becoming known after all). This is morally toned, of course: teachers accuse parents of "not providing the background for a child to be a decent person." Most showed awareness of peer-group influences, but very few seemed aware of social forces operating independently of the student. If anything, school officials were more aware of the latter, perhaps in part because of their own position. Teachers and administrators alike demonstrated concern about discipline problems with "some," "about half," or "most" Negro students, in most cases qualifying such statements with the observation that it really is a question of social class. One high school teacher pointed out that teachers *do* discuss the "problem of Negroes" as such among themselves. One of the school administrators most cited for his liberality among Negroes expressed concern about Negro "immorality" and "lack of honesty": "I have noticed over the years that even the worst of white children have consciences, but I am really beginning to wonder about Negroes." When asked about specific cases, administrators hastened to assure me that discipline problems were evenly distributed among Negroes and whites. Whatever their personal convictions, teachers and administrators clearly attempt to avoid overt discrimination. Negro students complained about one white teacher, but otherwise maintained that Negroes were not singled out as Negroes.

Considerably more concern was expressed about the quality of Negroes as students. High school officials are puzzled that integration in lower grades has not raised the general level of Negro students. Everyone pointed to one or two exceptions among Negroes in junior or senior high schools, and again the interpretation of this problem has to do with class or parental support for education rather than with any notion of inherent racial inferiority. Teachers feel that attempts to "lower their standards" in order to give special attention to poor students, including Negroes, would lower the overall quality of education. Consequently, Negroes are faced with much the same expectation level as whites. Several teachers modified this by noting that grading might be "more liberal" with Negro students. Also, there seems to be some hesitation about failing Negro students or holding them back a year, unless the need is clearly indicated. For these reasons one teacher doubted "that Negroes are getting quite the same education as whites."

The practice of dividing students into classes by achievement level, or dividing any one class into such levels, is not universally practiced in Newark. Such decisions are made by individual school principals. Both Negroes and whites agreed that the use of such teaching methods was not common, and showed few signs of segregating white and Negro students within the schools. One elementary school teacher did comment that she has "difficulty in reaching some Negro children. They don't seem to trust me." One Negro parent also commented on this point, concluding, "We really can't blame teachers for that. It is the fault of general prejudice and mistrust."

In general, it appears that integration has been relatively smooth and problem-free in Newark's schools. Much of this can be attributed to the small numbers of Negro students, penetration of the community by urban residents, and the growing autonomy of the local school district. The policy of the school system has been to meet problems as they come, without special plans for the future. A combination of pragmatism and individualism seems to lie behind the school system's actions. It is extremely sensitive to public opinion, and tends to insulate itself against such opinion and other outside pressures. In such a small community, however, there is little chance of isolation.

———•———

Integration in Newark:
The University Case

Because there are such striking parallels in reactions to integration among Newark's polity, school district, and the University of Delaware, and because the university plays such a large part in Newark's affairs, we should briefly examine its problems with school integration.

The university, a land-grant college, possesses a unique status in some respects. It is officially defined as a private university with state support, although the state legislature is not especially happy about that designation. The state provides approximately one-third of the school's annual operating funds. Other funds derive from private donations, federal grants, etc.

By far the largest private investor in education is the Wilmington duPont family, widely supposed to "completely control the university's board of trustees."

The president of the university, like the superintendent of schools, is seen as an autonomous, powerful figure, especially because of his statewide audience. He came to the university in 1950, and is noted for his success in building the physical plant to very respectable proportions. According to many sources, including official university spokesmen, this has been accomplished "with a goodly amount of conflict with the state legislature." The president himself is known to be concerned about the rapid flow of communication around the state. He clearly sees his office as the pivot between the rural, southern interests of the state legislature, the industrial interests of Wilmington, and local interests of Newark. Like the school system, the university is sensitive to criticism, and prefers to make decisions without public fanfare. It is widely believed in Newark that state newspapers refuse to publish articles or letters critical of the university. As was indicated by quotations presented elsewhere, the president of the University of Delaware is often described as one of the "real powers" in the local as well as state polity.

The university has long been the target of both civil rights advocates and segregationists. Before 1954 a few "exceptional Negroes" apparently attended the university illegally, but the state policy was clearly to segregate Negro and white college students. In 1954, according to informants, the president invited legal action against the university, consequently opening the front doors to Negroes for the first time in 1955. The response of Negroes was and continues to be slow. Although official records are not kept, it is estimated that no more than thirty Negroes have attended the university in any one year.

Initially, out-of-state Negro graduate students were excluded, presumably because the administration feared an influx of Southern Negroes. This policy caused a good deal of public dissension, including at least one unpleasant and widely publicized confrontation of the president and a Newark civil rights leader. In 1957 admission forms were revised to exclude racial identification. Subsequently the university was attacked for segregating room accommodations. At present this is apparently not so, but one spokesman acknowledged that the university does notify parents of students who are assigned or who ask to be assigned to accommodations with Negroes. "This is due to the large numbers of students from southern counties," explained the official. "They are still quite backward about these things down there."

Clearly the university does not wish any form of publicity on matters of race, and is openly hostile to any form of civil rights activities, especially among students. This attitude extends to other forms of "civil disobedience" or "demonstrations like those in Berkeley." Officials do not appear to be overly concerned about the Negro minority in Newark, but watch potential pressure groups throughout the state with a practiced eye.

The university's official posture is: "We will make available our facilities for any qualified student, regardless of color or creed. But we do not make any special effort to attract special categories of students." It is paradoxical that at the time this statement was made, the university was, in fact, establishing a pre-college program to disseminate information about the university of underprivileged students (actually, Negroes), and it is reported that other attempts are being made to change the unfavorable image of the university among Negroes. The officials are apparently committed personally to individual equality, but seem resistant to social movements or pressures. Administration officials generally disclaim any progressive role for the university in local affairs, maintaining that it is the "obligation" of the university to "maintain the current values of the community," which, as one outside observer pointed out, "presents a question as to their perception of the current moral standards." On the other hand, they are clearly aware that faculty and students do play a leading role in social change. "Short of accusing them of stupidity, I would say that they are still afraid of the conservative elements in the state. They themselves are quite enlightened, but just don't want to make waves," observed one longtime faculty member.

The university clearly is not perceived as a congenial location for Negroes. A number of Negro college and high school students interviewed indicated that they were not "comfortable about the university." Reasons for discomfort ranged from the small number of Negroes on campus to beliefs that "some of the faculty and most of the administrators are prejudiced." High school counseling also bears upon this situation. Both Negro and white counselors throughout the state are said to discourage Negroes from attending the university, apparently because they feel that standards there are too high, or that students are not welcome there. Negro students are often encouraged to attend Negro colleges, especially Delaware State College. Newark counselors are aware of this situation and, according to Negro informants, often suggest out-of-state colleges. For this and other reasons both the president of the university and the governor of the state have urged that the Delaware State College be incorporated with the university. They apparently have been unable to convince southern legislators of the merits of this plan, however.

The University of Delaware is one of the chief targets for Negro criticism: "The university is one of the most powerful elements in this state. Why can't they take a leading hand in helping Negroes? They just don't do anything more than they have to." It is probable that the university has been influential, either directly or indirectly through its personnel, in bringing about a good deal of change in the state, but university officials are very emphatic about not courting publicity to that effect. "The problem is," one resident of Newark complained, "it's becoming a habit for them to jump at the snap of fingers in the state legislature. Why don't they bite back?" Indications are that the president does occasionally "bite back," but the university evidently considers southern elements in the state a powerful pressure group.

Summary and Conclusions

To answer the question posed in the title, Jim Crow has not disappeared from Newark, but neither does he find an official welcome there. School and public officials in the community, irrespective of their personal convictions, appear to define both friends and enemies of segregation as potential threats to the peace and stability of the community. Perhaps the best example of this attitude came about as the result of this investigation. I interviewed one Negro high school student, on his own time, who was subsequently called into his principal's office for interrogation. According to other students present at the time, "when [the student] came out of the principal's office, the vice-principal called him a 'troublemaker,' and knocked his books out of his hand." It turned out that the student in question had been overheard by a teacher telling another teacher about the interview. Questioning elicited deliberately vague answers (the student wished to protect me), so the teacher informed the principal. Apparently it took some time for school officials to connect the interview with this project. In the meantime, a good deal of consternation was expressed over the possibility of a "budding civil rights movement." It should be pointed out that the same thing might have occurred had a white student been involved, but it is obvious that the schools act rapidly to prevent possible "trouble."

Liberals at the University of Delaware and in the community in general complain about similar incidents. In the process of "mediating conflicting interests," officials appear to feel entitled to use authoritarian methods. In any event, secretiveness and authoritarianism on the part of officials are perceived by the community, particularly among Negroes. Respondents were especially critical of "arbitrary actions" on the part of university officials. Public officials meet such criticism with frankness in private, but generally decline to discuss matters of policy in public. This response appears to serve as reinforcement for public criticism. The effect is to leave many Negroes with an apparently sincere conviction that there is, in fact, "a white conspiracy" in the community. This view is shared by many white liberals, but disclaimed by whites with "inside knowledge."

On the surface at least, integration has come to Newark. Reactions vary from favor to horror, but in general the community seems to accept the fact of Negro advances with equanimity. There are still loopholes: the silent nature of the whole change and the refusal of officials to take open stands results in considerable uncertainty as to what expectations actually are. Some teachers complained that they were not certain about what they were "supposed to do about Negroes." Restaurant owners, real estate officials, etc., still find ways to discriminate. It certainly cannot be argued that equality exists in fact, but *official* barriers to Negro advancement have been removed. Only doubt and uncertainty among public officials appear to stand in the way of further progress.

Part of Newark's success with school integration is due to the small numbers of Negroes in the community. Selective economic factors have operated to reduce the Negro population, and even to produce a relatively stable and "acceptable" Negro community. Perhaps even more important, the penetration of Newark by urban economic and political interests has altered the political climate into something more amenable to change. Although there are clearly conflicting views about integration in Newark, the prevailing climate is at least favorable to personal equality and individual rights. There does not appear to be much awareness of more subtle (and powerful) social forces, or perhaps Newark feels that such issues should not be made problematic. Whatever, there is very obvious and sincere fear of civil disturbances, regardless of their sources. The NAACP is disliked as intensely as the KKK.

The future of Newark's integration looks generally favorable. As the state legislature adjusts to its recent reapportionment, and as urban in-migration continues, the anti-integration interests in town are almost certain to lose influence. There is some question as to how long it will take officials to assess these changes accurately, but no doubt they will react to evolving publics. The school board is reported to have reflected changes already, and the city council is said to be facing increasing criticism from "liberal" elements in town. The university appears to be changing its stance cautiously, as it initiates programs to attract Negro students.

The only foreseeable disruption in this evolution might be a sudden influx of Negroes to Newark. This appears unlikely, except in the event of a Negro movement from Wilmington. This would most likely occur among middle-class Negroes in any event, so presumably it would cause little disturbance. Minimum housing laws and the small size of the community will probably operate to prevent the movement of lower-class Negroes to the community. Dissension in Negro ranks makes it unlikely that Negroes themselves will initiate any sudden change.

The only real barriers to further Negro advancement appear to stem from vagaries in the democratic process itself, hence the quotation from Walter Lippmann at the beginning of this chapter. Newark's school system, its polity, and the University of Delaware all tend to react to issues they perceive to be publicly sensitive by removing the decision-making process from public view. The result of this is twofold: externally, it creates suspicion and hostility on the part of the publics involved; internally it produces an almost anomic situation, lacking in open, firm guidelines for policy on such issues as race. The organizations appear to exaggerate or distort the intensity of public opinion on matters of integration, removing themselves even further from open public debate. The "self-fulfilling prophecy" clearly operates in Newark. One might legitimately ask how any useful consensus on racial issues is achieved under the present conditions. Fortunately, the situation is mediated by the small size of the community itself, its small Negro minority, and perhaps most important of all, changing public reactions to racial integration.

There is negative reaction to integration in the community, quite strong in some quarters, but it no longer appears to reside with power. The "old guard" unquestionably is losing ground. As one university official observed: "Some of these old bigots are pretty loud, but they're dying off, thank God." Those who have not yet "died off" are still voluble, but they appear to be preoccupied with "race mixing" and similar issues not likely to be of immediate relevance. An appropriate, if grisly symbolic conclusion to all of this was provided inadvertently by a white respondent: "The old guard meets every Sunday, regular as clockwork, in a Newark funeral parlor to discuss what ought or ought not to be done about issues before the city council."

V

Segregation and Suburbia

———•———

Rosalind J. Dworkin

NEGROES HAVE NOTHING to complain about here. . . . They have the same books and teachers as the white kids (*Negro woman educator*).

Sure, people are very conscious about race here. We have our race problems like every town and city in the United States. People say, "We are all equal; Negroes have a right to have a house or set up a business—but not in my backyard." We've got to make people accept the Negro. You can pass all the laws you want, but they won't make people change how they feel and believe (*White middle-aged man*).

I'm very happy with the situation now; it is very peaceful. There is no problem as we see it today. There is a beautiful, healthy climate here (*President of the school board*).

It may sound like an unusual thing, but *de facto* segregation is worse than real segregation. Because they say one thing—that you are all equal and so forth—but they do something quite different. At least in the South, the teachers say you're inferior and they do as they believe (*Negro housewife*).

T he walls of segregation are crumbling in the South and the great Northern cities are aflame with the struggles of the Negro revolution. But in the suburban Northeast life goes on with the tranquility of the eye of a hurricane. Here the issues are vague and poorly defined. Here few parties are aligned and interest groups have fuzzy boundaries. The Northeast has just begun to awaken to the consequences of the American dilemma.

So poorly defined are the issues that the statements which began this chapter represent the divergence not within the entire Northeast, but within the Negro and white worlds of a single suburban town. This town is neither the nation's pride nor its shame. It has not initiated the extension of civil rights to its ethnic minority, but neither has it fought vigorously to retain the traditions of the past century. Rather, it has remained submissive, passively lying in the path of the storm and waiting to be caught up in its power.

A Suburban Profile

Settled by English colonists, Hempstead has experienced almost continuous population and economic growth since its founding three hundred years ago. Located on the Long Island plains less than twenty miles from Manhattan, Hempstead farmers once cultivated their land and raised their sheep and cattle. With the extension of transportation facilities in the beginning of this century, the village began to lose its agrarian personality and acquire a new one.

The level plains which once seemed suited to sheep and potatoes also proved ideal for aircraft. Just beyond the village limits, aircraft factories as well as Mitchell Air Force Base sprouted up, providing vast employment opportunities.

Today Hempstead is affectionately nicknamed "The Hub" by its residents. Because of its nearness to New York City and is central location in Nassau County, the village has become a transportation center for the area. Bus routes and railroad lines converge here from the eastern Long Island towns before fanning out again to diverse parts of New York City.

This partly accounts for Hempstead's early growth as an important commercial retail center on suburban Long Island. Contrasted with shopping areas in the wealthier communities to the north, Hempstead stores and transportation facilities attracted lower- and middle-class customers who enjoyed the convenience of inexpensive merchandise that was also easily accessible. However, with the increase of suburban shopping plazas, Hempstead is now only one of many commercial retail centers in the county.

Hempstead's "hubness" has served to attract not only retail customers, but also the suburban commuter. Formerly dubbed "the bedroom for Garden City servants," the village might now be more accurately described as a bedroom community for New York's white-collar workers. Nearly one-fourth (22.7 per cent[1]) of the employed population work outside of Nassau County, most of them driving or using public transportation to travel daily into New York City. That this is a salient reason for choosing to live in the community becomes apparent from conversations with respondents. "Hempstead is all right. It's convenient for my husband's work" and "We don't like it too much, but it's a place where you can get to where you work easy" are not unusual statements to be made by residents.

Hempstead's central geographic position has also placed it in the path of eastward migration from the center city. Beginning with the land speculations in the thirties, the community has experienced several migration waves. Three of these have been most significant: the influx of families of Polish descent, followed soon after by the urban Negro, and finally today, a heavy migration of Negroes from the South.

The Poles and some lower-class Italians settled in the center of the village. As these groups spread south, Negroes moved into the vacated areas, and finally they followed the Polish migration pattern, shifting southward into substandard housing. Another population shift resulted in some movement of Negroes to the northeastern neighborhoods of the village.

There still exists a rapid shift in population. Of the total village population in 1960, 20.3 per cent moved into their present dwelling units after 1958. This constitutes one of the highest such rates in the county. According to the Village Clerk, "A larger proportion of Negroes than whites are moving in. Some of them are from the city, and more and more are coming from the South." Another resident sees the situation this way:

> The whole town has been turned upside down. There's been a tremendous shift in population. They are even losing the professional Negro. A wave of welfare Negroes came in and the town really doesn't know what to do.

"Southern Negro," to the white residents, means any Negro who came to Hempstead from a state south of New York. Hence, migrants from Pennsylvania are classified as Southern.

Many white residents attribute the influx of new Negroes to

1 This and all subsequent statistics were calculated from the 1960 Census.

the direct work of Negroes already living in the community. For example, a prominent doctor states:

> There are so many Negroes moving in. The Negroes run ads in the papers in Jamaica, and even in the South. "Come to Hempstead," they say. "We know we have a good thing here."

Actually, I cannot attribute the present migration to deliberate Negro campaigns to entice others to the community. Some Negroes are attracted to Hempstead simply because it already has a large Negro population, and newcomers know they will be able to buy homes there. As one Negro stated:

> I like it here. The people mind their own business. . . . And I'm with my own kind. I'm with other colored people.

Formerly, Southern Negroes migrated to New York City and only after meeting with some economic success did any move eastward. Today the process is shifting from a two-step flow to a single step. The data indicate that the present Southern Negroes moving into Hempstead are attracted directly to the suburb because of kin already in the village. Typical are the following stories told by two young housewives:

> We've lived here for about three years. We lived in Pennsylvania first. When my husband got out of the army, he couldn't find any work. He got his unemployment checks for a while and then he decided to come up here because we had relations here.

and

> I came up from West Virginia over Christmas. I've been here several times before because my family is here. We decided to stay here at my mother's until we find a place of our own.

In addition to experiencing a perceived onslaught of Southern migrants, the village is experiencing the initial planning stages of urban renewal projects. It plans to redevelop a part of the central business district and some of the adjacent residential areas. The plan includes an enlargement of automobile parking facilities to accommodate shoppers and commuters, erection of new office buildings, and new retail establishments. In addition the program "will result in new, better income apartment housing, with added local population in higher income categories." [2]

[2] *To Help You Decide,* a publication of Hempstead Chamber of Commerce, p. 17.

That is, slum neighborhoods are being replaced with relatively luxurious apartments that will eventually be rented to higher-income persons than are now occupying the land.

In profile, Hempstead today is a community of nearly thirty-five thousand people. This represents a population increase of 19 per cent in the past ten years. The population density is computed as 9,362 people per square mile. Some 21.9 per cent of the population are nonwhite; virtually all of these are Negro. This constitutes the largest Negro population on Long Island and east of New York City. The Negro population inhabits the northeastern area of the village and the southern part (including the neighborhood known as The Hill Section).

The Negro population is statistically younger than the white. The median age of the white population is 36.1 and 38.5, for male and female, respectively. The median Negro ages are 25.1 and 26.6, for male and female, respectively.

The average population per household in the village is 3.24. Negro households average 4.18 persons. Not only are there more children per family, but extended familism characterizes many Negro households. For example, it is not unusual for a household to include parents and two adult children with their families.

Negro income also compares unfavorably with the income of the white population (see Table 1). The former's median in-

Table 1: Family Income*

INCOME	WHITE:	NONWHITE:	TOTAL:
	7,450	1,677	9,127
<$1,000	130	90	220
$1,000–3,999	801	375	1,176
$4,000–5,999	1,248	425	1,673
$6,000–7,999	1,660	370	2,030
$8,000–9,999	1,321	179	1,500
≥$10,000	2,560	238	2,798

* Source: 1960 Census.

come is $5,746; the white median income is nearly a full three thousand dollars a year greater—$8,567. This suggests that the income distributions of Negroes and whites are skewed in the opposite direction. Only 14.2 per cent of the Negro family incomes total $10,000 or more, while fully one-third of the white population have an income exceeding this amount. On the other hand, 27.8 per cent of the Negro families have an income of less than $4,000, compared with 12 per cent of the white population. It should be added parenthetically that nearly 12 per cent of the white population are over sixty-five years of age. To conclude that there is a causal relationship between the number of whites past the retirement age and the percentage of whites earning less than $4,000 a year would be committing the fallacy of ecological correlations. The data do not indicate that the categories represented by the two figures are the same. However, they do suggest a possible relationship that may prove tenable through further research. If this is so, then the income distributions of white and Negro working wage earners would be even more skewed away from each other.

The distribution of occupations presents a similar picture to the income distribution. The Negro unemployment rate is 7.5 per cent; the white unemployment rate is 3.3. The employed Negro is heavily overrepresented in certain occupations. Of all positions held as personal household workers (*i.e.,* servants), 80.5 per cent are held by Negroes. Similarly, 38.7 per cent of the other service workers are Negro, and 71.1 of the unskilled workers are also Negro.

Conversely, Negroes are underrepresented in the professions (7.9 per cent); managers and proprietors (3.8 per cent); clerical positions (11.4 per cent); and sales workers (4.5 per cent).

Educationally, Hempstead's traditional standards are high. The median years of complete school for the white population over twenty-five is 11.7 years of school completed. The Negro median is lower, 10.2 years. However, Negro expectations of their children's education are generally higher than the accomplishments of their own generation. Unskilled workers who themselves received only elementary school education assume their children will finish high school:

> My daughter is sixteen now and she is going to finish. We can't afford to send her to college, but she is going to graduate high school!

Correspondingly, mothers who themselves had some high school training predict that their children will not only complete high school, but may also attend college:

> She's really a bright child with books and reading. She wants to go to college and be a teacher.

> That [taking an academic curriculum] was mostly my father's doing. I don't want to go to college, but he said I might change my mind and I should be prepared.

Most of the school-age children attend publicly supported schools (Table 2). However, there are several private schools

Table 2: School Enrollment

EDUCATION	WHITE	NONWHITE	TOTAL
Total enrolled	5,788	1,742	7,530
Kindergarten	353	252	605
(public)	324	252	576
Elementary (1–8)	3,360	1,082	4,442
(public)	2,623	1,082	3,705
High School	1,574	331	1,905
(public)	1,404	303	1,707
College	501	77	578

in the area, most of them Catholic parochial schools, which absorb 16 per cent of the white elementary school-age children and 10 per cent of the white high school students. None of the Negro children attend private elementary schools.

Astride the village boundaries stands Hofstra University. Formerly a commuting liberal arts college, it is now expanding massively into a residence university. The academic establishment has not made a great impression upon the community. Hempstead is not like the stereotyped college town, whose cultural life, employment opportunities, indeed whose very existence depends upon the presence of the college. Rather, the university represents just one of the several facets of community life.

The dominant educational institution of the village is Hempstead School District #1. The boundaries of the district were established by the state legislature in 1868. Beginning with one school in the village, the district progressively grew until in addition to its high school it maintains seven elementary schools. The racial distribution within the elementary schools ranges from 90 per cent Negro in some schools to as low as 20 per cent in others. More detailed description of the school system will be given in a subsequent section.

To summarize, Hempstead's silhouette is similar to the profiles of many Northeastern suburbs. It has experienced almost continuous population growth hastened by building booms, land speculation, and successive waves of migrants from the center city. Although still tightly bound to the center city through its migration patterns and commuting population, the suburb is not totally dependent upon the city. For example, large industries relocating in or near the village provide employment opportunities outside of the city. Retail commercial centers further enhance its apparent independence from the nearby metropolis.

Concluding, the Negro residents in Hempstead, although more numerous here than in other towns in the surrounding area, are similar to Negro populations throughout the Northeast. They are a younger population with larger families, less income, less formal education, and lower-status jobs than the white majority next to whom they live.

———————•———————

Growing Discontent

The white population in Hempstead is becoming increasingly conscious of ethnic minority differences within the village. They are becoming aware of problems, which some attribute to race and attempts at community integration. This growing focus upon the racial dichotomization of Hempstead has made itself manifest among the white community in three ways.

The first manifestation of this awareness has been overt defensive action attempting to stall the influx of Negro migrants. The Hempstead Neighbors Committee, in its attempts to preserve all-white neighborhoods, "have been considerably successful in their anti-blockbusting campaign," according to some observers.

The second reaction appears to be the reverse of the first. Some white residents do not admit to the existence of any racial problems. Their denials, however, remind one of the "lady doth protest too much." It was especially apparent during interviews that race is a salient issue to these individuals when respondents initiated the subject of race without any previous reference by the interviewer. For example, a real estate agent became quite upset:

> I suppose you want to know about segregation. Well, I want you to know that if a person comes in here and is qualified to buy a house, I don't care if he is blue, black, or green, I'll show him the houses that I have.

And an employee in the village's Department of Public Information responded, when asked for census information:

> We don't keep records about Negroes and whites separately. We consider all as just residents of Hempstead.

Negroes claim that this attitude is the prevalent one among white townspeople. A Negro leader is reported to have stated:[3]

> [the village] has systematically ignored the Negro population of Hempstead and the village authorities have turned their backs on safety and health violations.

The president of the Youth Council addressed the Village Board:

> . . . either the board refuses to acknowledge that a problem exists, or the board is not concerned with eliminating discrimination and fostering race relations within the Village of Hempstead.

The third reaction of white citizens to the "racial problem" in Hempstead is the more typical reaction among the white residents. People usually agree that the village has some racial unrest. However, they add that the problem has really been solved (or is nearly solved), and that Hempstead's problem was different from and never was as serious as the problems in other

3 *The Beacon,* March 31, 1965, p. 1.

towns. A statement cited earlier is a pefect example of this kind of reaction:

> Sure, people are very conscious about race here. We have our race problems like every town and city in the United States. . . .

A variation of this, admitting to a problem but attempting to minimize it, is:

> A lot of towns around here, like Malverne and Baldwin, have de jure segregation. They set up the school districts politically; they gerrymandered around so that they have segregated schools. Hempstead is different from the other towns. They don't do that here. In Hempstead we may have de facto segregation, but there was never any de jure segregation here.

The official governmental reaction to minority problems in the village has been of this last type. In January 1964 the village formed a Human Relations Commission to deal with racial tensions. This constituted an unmistakable recognition of situations in the community that are potential strains. The reaction, however, follows the pattern just outlined. Recognition is given with a concomitant minimization of the stresses which produced the reaction. The annual budget allotted to the commission is minimal. For the most part participation on the commission is voluntary and services unpaid. Almost two thousand dollars is allocated for the salary of the executive secretary. The village is having some difficulty gathering applicants with satisfactory qualifications for managing the organization. The present secretary volunteered to hold the position temporarily on a part-time basis. Yes, Hempstead has a race problem, but evidently only of half-day intensity.

Thus, the reaction to Hempstead's "problem" has been varied but patterned.This growing race-consciousness has been almost literally pushed upon the white community by various civil rights organizations in the village. The two most active have been the NAACP, including a subsidiary, the Youth Council; and the Long Island chapter of CORE. Other small local groups have formed to face particular issues, for example: the Citizens Committee on Hempstead Schools; People for Educational Planning Committee; and the Hempstead Citizens Committee for Education. However, NAACP and CORE have been the continuous voice of the Negro community.

Beginning most notably in 1962, these groups have vocalized complaints and waged campaigns against the incidences of injustice and discrimination they perceived occurring in the lives of Hempstead Negroes. Many of the issues raised, although idiosyncratic problems with details peculiar to local conditions, have a form common to many civil rights issues. These included attempts to invite more Negroes into the fire department and police force, and to institute rent controls. These complaints, voiced before the Village Board and punctuated with marches and small demonstrations, received little more publicity than a phrase in a news article in the local paper, *The Beacon*. Nevertheless they represent battles; some won, some lost.

In the past four years three issues have been sources of irritation and tension around which much of the organizational action has been focused: rezoning, urban renewal, and education. The main concern in this paper is the question of discrimination in the schools. However, to understand the Negroes' attempts at desegregation, it is necessary to outline action occurring around the two other loci.

The conflict over rezoning was waged by the Negro organizations in a more overt, aggressive way than the conflicts over urban renewal and education. Furthermore, Negroes were more successful in this fight than in the other two.

Located south of the village center in the middle of one of the Negro neighborhoods was a virtually empty ten acres of land owned by one of the older white families. In 1963 application was made to the Village Board to rezone the land from residential to light industrial. In June of that year the board passed such a resolution. The trustees on the Village Board agreed with the owners that such a change would increase the tax base of the community and provide more employment opportunities.

Upon the passing of the resolution, the Negro residents of the surrounding area raised various objections. Such a change, they maintained, would cause immeasurable harm to the entire neighborhood. Property values, already low, would fall sharply on the low- and middle-class homes; a factory atmosphere would pervade the area; automobile and truck traffic would increase on the roads, presenting a danger to the children; and crime rates would probably increase. Furthermore, they objected, the rezoning would reduce the area available for Negroes to live.

The board declined to reverse its decision. Finally the Negro leaders threatened and ultimately carried out a week-long boycott of Hempstead retail stores. The intended purpose was to put enough pressure on the board via the merchants so that the land would be re-rezoned to its original residential classification.

The tactic of concerted, overt group action was a success. In early August 1963 the land was returned to its original status. As an official explanation, the mayor stated that the board's decision was not influenced by the ethnic composition of the neighborhood involved. He charged that:

> . . . threats were made to destroy Hempstead by those who seek to make a race issue out of an action by the board that in no stretch of imagination could be construed as a race problem.[4]

Furthermore the mayor insisted that the board would not recognize the race issue because this would encourage demonstrations and riots. "We have read too much about this in other communities," [5] the mayor pointed out.

Here again we see the tendency to compare Hempstead with other towns to the former's benefit. Note also in the mayor's speech the attempt to minimize, if not deny completely, the racial aspects of the problems. It matters little in this case whether the objective facts actually support the minority leaders' hypothesis of deliberate attempts to devaluate the Negroes' land to benefit the white community. What is salient here is that the behavior of the board was perceived and interpreted as an action of deliberate racial discrimination. This definition of the situation necessitated an approach to the conflict that included recognition of racial interests.

The second source of conflict has been the proposals for urban renewal projects, of which some mention has already been made. The central irritant is the allocation of much of the land for middle- and upper-income apartments. In other words, lower-

4 From a speech reprinted in *The Beacon*, August 7, 1963.
5 *Ibid.*

class homes in slum condition are being demolished and replaced by apartments which the displaced families could not
afford to rent. Charging that the intent to build only high-rent
apartments discriminated against the lower-class Negro who
now resides in that area, Long Island CORE coordinated a protest march through the center of the village to the Village Hall,
where the Village Board was meeting, to lodge a complaint.
The march involved approximately three hundred individuals,
but did not appear to make an impression upon the mayor or the
village trustees. Up to the present time, the issue is still unsettled.

The third major source of racial conflict is the one that is
most intense, involves more people, and has been fought longer
than the other two previously mentioned. This is the campaign
waged against the local school board using the battle cry of *de
facto* segregation. This is the war in which the first battle
erupted as a lawsuit against the school board, permissive transfer was instituted as an uneasy truce, and the final solution has
not yet been discovered.

The charges of *de facto* segregation and the problem of the
validity of these charges can only be understood through a
knowledge of the history of the town and the development of the
school district. When Hempstead was founded in 1643, it was
virtually alone in the wilderness of what is now Nassau County.
Since there were no towns nearby to confine its growth, the village was able to spread itself out as the increase in population
demanded.

In 1868, the state legislature established Hempstead School
District #1 to educate the children of the village. The district
boundaries were set at that time, and only an act of the legislature can modify or rearrange them. To this legislative act
establishing district boundaries is attributed many of the present problems in the racial imbalance in the Hempstead schools.
After the establishment of the first district the county became
more dense with other small communities, so additional districts
were formed to serve families in areas adjacent to Hempstead.

The first school to be built in the Hempstead system was
Prospect School, located in the center of the district. As the
school-age population increased, more schools were added to
accommodate them. These elementary schools were built in patterned locations. With Prospect in the center, the additional

schools were located in a circle nearer the outer limits of the village. Some of the schools were only two or three blocks away from the district border. The school planners constructed the schools in this patterned way to provide "neighborhood schools," and to eliminate the need for bus transportation for the children. In 1949 the state education department issued statements which further encouraged this procedure. The high school was built in the center of the district near Prospect School, making it easily accessible for its students. Thus the pattern of school locations today resembles a large wheel, with Prospect and the high school forming the hub. An older resident of the community recalls:

> When I came here before the First World War, there were only two schools—Prospect, in the center of town, and Washington. I went to Prospect. As the town grew, they built more schools and added on to others. Now the high school is just about in the middle of town and the other schools around it. So no one is more than two miles from the high school; anyone can walk that. And all the children would go to the school right near them. It's less dangerous that way—they don't have to cross crowded streets and it's quicker and easier for the kids.

As the housing patterns shifted, the ethnic characteristics of the individual school enrollments shifted accordingly. Prospect School was one of the first to change. Located in the center of town, Prospect became the neighborhood school for first the Polish population, and then the nonwhite population as Negroes began to settle there. When the Negro residential area spread southward and then northeastward, other schools experienced a change in ethnic distribution. The previous respondent continued to reminisce:

> The Poles and some poor Italians moved in, followed by Negroes. And they all settled right around Prospect School, and that's where they went to school. Then they started to move south and then up north. Soon some of the schools were 90 per cent black.

The principal of Franklin School recalls:

> About thirty years ago there were twenty-five Negroes in this school. Now it is predominantly Negro. There are less than forty whites here now.

In addition to Franklin School in the south and Prospect in the center, most of the other elementary schools in the district also experienced shifts in pupil composition. Jackson Street School in the northeast corner of the district was affected in about the same way as Franklin. On the other hand, Fulton Street School to the west experienced a shift in the other direction. Located in what was once a predominantly Negro neighborhood, the school serves mainly white students today because of these population shifts. Washington Street School in the north was affected in much the same way as Fulton. Ludlum School at the far eastern end of the district remained nearly the same.

Hempstead schools are organized on an eight-four system, that is, the elementary schools contain kindergarten and grades one through eight; grades nine through twelve are completed in high school. Hence there are no junior high schools as would be the case if Hempstead had a six-three-three system.

There is only one public high school in the district. Traditionally, all high school students have attended this school with the exception of some who are enrolled in private schools, about 10 per cent of the high school population. Thus, Hempstead High School has always served both white and nonwhite pupils. The only change that has occurred is in the ratio of nonwhite to white, which has been getting progressively higher.

Excluding the high school for the present time, in 1960 there were three schools that were nearly all white: Fulton, Ludlum, and Washington. The other schools were nearly all (95 to 99 per cent) Negro: Prospect, Jackson, and Franklin-Marshall. Of the latter, Jackson and Franklin-Marshall were overcrowded, while Ludlum and Fulton were underpopulated. This imbalance in both racial composition and in space available became the leading issues behind events which erupted in 1962.

Hempstead employs over three hundred teachers. The personnel turnover in the district is minimal; no more than an estimated 10 per cent of the teachers leave the system. The superintendent of schools describes the employment practices:

> We recruit from all over the country—even California. I guess we get more of our teachers from New York State and the state universities. We have a good reputation. The publications

—*NEA Journal*—rank us high. We give a good salary and good working conditions. We even get street applications— people who walk in and apply for a job. We usually have about thirty openings a year. . . . We have three hundred twenty-five teachers all together. But Hempstead is a growing district. We never have the same amount of teachers. Those thirty positions are partly to replace teachers who left, and partly to fill new positions.

We lose about 5 per cent, or maybe from 5 to 10 per cent every year. That's a very low rate. These are teachers who actually leave—usually because they are getting married or their husbands move, or pregnancy or retirement.

A former teacher in the district concurs:

Hempstead keeps their teachers until they either retire or drop dead. They have some women there who have taught in the same school for twenty or thirty years. I only left because we bought a house in Suffolk [County] and the hour traveling time was too much every morning.

The school administration is proud of the schools. In the past few years several articles have been published in professional journals about the school system. These articles, primarily in *New York State Education, School Executive,* and *Music Educator's Journal,* describe various programs in Hempstead schools that have been successful. For example, their elementary school library program has been depicted in detail (*School Executive,* Vol. 78, February 1959) with recommendations for other districts to follow.

Their pride stems from other sources, too. In addition to their success in professional journal publications, the district has become known in the state through its experimental programs. For example, the high school sponsors a work-study curriculum in which the student obtains part-time employment related to his school curriculum and his future aspirations. At first this enabled students in merchandising to participate. In 1963 the program was enlarged, permitting some pupils in other fields, *e.g.,* industrial arts, to obtain part-time employment to extend the education they were acquiring in the classroom. The program, even at the time of its enlargement, was an innovation in Long Island schools.

More recently the district has begun a pre-kindergarten program that is highly respected by the parents:

I'm sending my boy to pre-kindergarten. He's such a hand-ful. I have a friend who is sending her child there, too. It's real good. He'll go so that when he gets to first grade, he'll learn a lot.

The program is still quite new. Hence, it is difficult to assess its accomplishments so far.

The district has also begun a third experimental program. With the influx of Southern Negroes, the administration decided that these children needed special training. About two years ago the district started an "interim program" for "especially cultur-ally deprived children." A principal of one school conducting such a program reports:

> We have a large student turnover here. Many Southern Negroes are moving into the neighborhood. We have had to set up an interim program for these children. We put them into a spe-cial class to help them catch up with the rest of the children. Their backgrounds are so bad that they couldn't get on in a regular classroom. Some come in here twelve years old and they have trouble writing their names. They are physically old enough for school, but not emotionally mature. We have to do something for these kiddies.

As a result of this curriculum the school system was cited in September 1965 by James Allen, New York State Commis-sioner of Education, for its concern for and aid to the disadvan-taged migrant. Unfortunately, this plan is also too young for its success to be assessed. It is still too soon to evaluate student progress in these classes. It will be especially salient to ascertain if these children ever do catch up, and if they ever are placed in regular classrooms. Programs like this one can result in the complete separation of these children from the others in the school rather than in increased integration into the school com-munity.

Programs like the three just described are subsidized by state aid and federal support. In addition to the normal state aid based upon average daily attendance, the district receives funds for the special projects. One doubts if the system wishes to lose this additional aid for any reason.

The school administration and the school board claim that they want to maintain a standard of education which they perceive to be very high already. They say they want "the best" for the children—the best of facilities, the best of teachers. The superintendent of schools tells of the search for good teachers:

> We just look for the best qualified [teachers]. We want the best. We want well-educated, experienced people. If we get them straight from college, we look at their academic record, their student-teaching records, and how they participated in college affairs. That gives a good indication of how they will teach.

The president of the school board describes the proposed new high school:

> This building will have everything the very best—the best lab equipment, the best facilities. The present high school will be a "middle school." The building was originally built in 1920, and it is somewhat outmoded for a high school. It's okay for a middle school, because younger children don't use all that equipment. But we need a new high school, and it is going to have everything the very best.

The principal of Franklin School brags:

> Of course, you know that Hempstead is one of the ten best schools in the country!

The local newspaper also reflects this general pride in the schools' accomplishments and standards. Nearly one-quarter of every issue has to do with school news and announcements. It is not unusual to find the school board proceedings reported upon, and the school athletic page in addition to items about activities of specific schools and/or classes all in one issue. Furthermore, announcements are continually made of college acceptance, scholarship awards, and other honors bestowed upon the high school seniors. This kind of reporting is common in small communities, where the school plays a central role in social life. However, one cannot avoid noting that these rather standard news stories are reported with an obvious air of pride and enthusiasm.

This satisfied attitude in the work they are doing that is held by the board members and the administration may be an explanation for their subsequent attitudes toward the problems which arose challenging their judgments and intentions.

---•---

Action . . . and Reaction

In 1962 the school board was indeed challenged. Their judgment and their intentions were indeed questioned. They were told, in essence, that they had no reason to be proud of their district. In 1962 a lawsuit was filed charging discrimination and *de facto* segregation in the public schools.

In March of 1962 the school board had scheduled the voting on a referendum concerning a bond issue of $1,385,000 for the construction of additional classroom facilities. Two of the district elementary schools, Jackson and Marshall Schools, had become extremely overcrowded: conditions were serious enough for the board to have considered placing the first and second grades in these schools on double session. (In this kind of arrangement a child attends school for only half the school day, either in the morning or the afternoon. In this way two shifts of students, one in the morning and one in the afternoon, can be accommodated each day.) To avoid the necessity of this action, the board proposed a plan to build temporary additions onto each of the crowded schools. Jackson School was to have four more classrooms and Marshall School was to have thirteen more.

In protest the NAACP filed an application to the State Commissioner of Education, James E. Allen, Jr., requesting the postponement of the referendum vote. Simultaneously, Dr. John Branche, under the auspices of the NAACP, filed suit against the school board charging the district with permitting discrimination and *de facto* segregation. It should be noted that during 1962 and 1963 in some sixty-nine communities—many of them large cities, and others smaller towns and villages—the NAACP filed suits charging school boards with either actively fostering segregation in the schools by gerrymandering intradistrict lines, or by passively permitting *de facto* segregation. Hempstead was one of six communities on Long Island to be so charged. Of these six districts, Hempstead had the largest enrollment of non-white students.

The Negro leaders in Hempstead objected to the proposed classrooms and maintained that additions to already crowded Negro schools would only increase the fact of segregation in the system. They suggested adding the temporary facilities onto other schools, thereby providing more space in these white schools to permit Negro children to attend.

In the face of this apparent hostility toward the board's plan—hostility that was manifested in not only the lawsuit and the appeal to the commissioner of education, but also in parent demonstrations—the referendum vote was canceled.

Consequently, Ewald Nyquist, Acting Commissioner of Education, dismissed the appeal made to his office, because the board had yielded and canceled the bond issue vote. The board, in the meantime, requested that the federal court dismiss the lawsuit filed by Branche. The request was denied and the court action remained pending for the next three years until the suit was dropped in 1965 with the stipulation that it could be reinstated in the future.

In addition to the cancellation of the referendum vote, the school district's budget was twice rejected by the voting population that year.

The president of the school board relates his impressions of the events:

In 1962 a lawsuit was filed by the NAACP charging segregation and things. I don't know what happened to the suit. In July 1963 Commissioner James Allen sent a letter to all the school boards, asking [them] to inform him about what we intended to do about desegregation. Many people misconstrued this letter. It was not an order to desegregate. He just wanted to know if we were thinking about it. We proposed a plan. . . . We were going to add on to three schools.

By 1970 we will have no seats for the children. Kindergarten and first grade are jumping from three or four in a school to seven. So we've added seventeen or eighteen temporary classrooms. They put quite a strain on the budget—$5,000 a year goes into them. It puts extra strains on the heating and maintenance. We try to save the taxpayers' money, so we had our own men—the custodians—build the classrooms. That can get us in trouble with the union.

During this time Commissioner Allen directed that a study be made of the intradistrict boundaries. After examining the results, Allen was fairly satisfied with the manner in which the children were distributed to the various schools. Only one districting policy was found unsatisfactory. The investigating committee decided that one small strip of residential property, districted as belonging to the Ludlum School, would be more appropriately served by the Prospect School. The school board complied. Otherwise, the committee concluded, the district lines had not been manipulated to produce the existing racial imbalance.

If political gerrymandering did not cause the racial imbalance in the schools, what, then, can account for it? Both Negro and white leaders agree that the problem lies in the housing patterns. A former president of the school board explains:

> It's a case of congregation, not segregation!

The present president of the board adds:

> *De facto* segregation develops naturally. It's not that things are done politically. It just grew naturally as people moved.

A village official comments:

> It just happens that way. People move around and it just happens that the Negroes all live together.

The Negro advisor to the Youth Council sums up:

> *De facto* segregation certainly does exist. The problem is that old bugaboo—housing patterns!

Although no official information is available on the overall ratio of white to Negro children enrolled in the district, estimates made in 1963 suggest that the total enrollment in the elementary schools at that time were 61 per cent Negro and 39 per cent white. Estimates made by community leaders today indicate an increase in the imbalance. A former member of the board estimates:

> Now all the schools have at least 20 per cent Negro, but three have 90 per cent. The way things are, it's 70–30.

A Negro leader offered a more conservative estimate:

> We have a ratio of about 65–35, and getting worse all the time.

The administration declined to offer their estimate.

With such an ethnic ratio, it is obviously impossible to distribute the children so that all schools have an equal number of whites and nonwhites. This unfortunate fact is recognized by both parties in the disagreement. The former board president continued:

. . . The way things are it's 70–30. Not even Einstein can spread the whites around so each school has 50–50.

And the Negro leader previously quoted agreed:

We have a ratio of 65–35. . . . Now how are you going to even that up in the schools? It just can't be done.

The ecological basis for the racial imbalance in the school enrollment in Hempstead is complicated by some rather peculiar circumstances. It was mentioned previously that Negroes make up some 22 per cent of the total village population. Using the more conservative estimate, however, we have seen that 65 per cent of the school children are Negro. We might expect a Negro school enrollment to be over 22 per cent because census data indicate that the Negro population is somewhat younger than the white and have slightly larger families. Nevertheless, the large discrepancy in the two figures could not be explained by this one factor.

It was also noted that some 16 per cent of the white school population attend private school. This phenomenon would raise the proportion of Negroes in public schools somewhat. However, in itself this factor could not account for the discrepancy either.

Consulting the village census data (refer to Table 2), we find a more startling fact. In grades kindergarten through eight there are 5,047 village children enrolled in public schools, of whom 1,334 are Negro. Calculated into percentages, only 31 per cent of the elementary children in Hempstead are Negro. Thus the village census presents a picture the exact opposite of the estimates made by knowledgeable individuals. The explanation for this incredible difference lies again in the history of the school district.

In the previous section I stated that the district boundaries were set by the state legislature in 1868. This was more than half a century before the tremendous spurt of growth experienced just after the Depression. As the village population grew, the demand for more village lands increased. Hempstead was able to expand its political boundaries outward, and particularly to the east. Although the village was able to push back the established political lines, the school district could not do likewise.

As a result, a glance at a street map of the village reveals that the district and the village boundaries are not identical. Rather, there are areas of land which are not included in one, but are included in the other. In particular, the entire eastern end of the village—a strip about a half mile wide and nearly two miles long—does not belong to Hempstead School District. Instead, the children living in that area are served by schools in other districts. The neighborhoods in this strip are almost completely white. Herein lies the explanation of why there is a majority of Negro students in the Hempstead schools: a large number of village children attend public schools outside the Hempstead district.

The community recognizes this factor as a major one contributing to racial imbalance in the schools. One of the plans proposed to compensate for this problem suggested merely extending the boundaries of the district to coincide with the village boundary. An alternate suggestion was that all the districts in the area unify into one. In this way, it was felt, some kind of racial balance in that part of the township could be achieved.

Unfortunately, both of these plans are considered impossible to activate. The past president of the board explains why:

> The district is fixed by the legislature, but the village kept growing. So now the district boundary is not coterminous with the village. So someone just over the district line can't go to the closest school because it's not in his district.
>
> What should be done is to extend the district boundaries to the village boundaries. That way more whites will be included and some kind of even population can be gotten.
>
> These people in Garden City or Rockville Center or Uniondale district don't want to send their kids to Negro Hempstead schools. Only the legislature can change the districts, and those towns have a lot of powerful members in the legislature. They won't let the districts be changed. [Why not?] When someone sees a school that is half black, he thinks it's all black and he doesn't want to send his children there.

A prominent Negro agrees:

> They had a plan to unify with other towns, where we would go to Garden City Schools. Now you don't think Garden City will like that, do you? They're rich white, and they will fight any change as hard as they can.

Finally, the president of a school board in an adjacent district said publicly:

> I doubt that the State Education Department would seriously consider merging Hempstead District with Hempstead Village to relieve racial imbalance. It would be political suicide for legislators to support a bill that would be needed to put such a plan into effect.

This solution to the problem, which is felt by the villagers to be the ideal answer, nevertheless is discarded by them as unattainable.

With meetings and proposals being rapidly generated, the school board in 1962 and 1963 was still under a great deal of pressure from the NAACP to improve the racial imbalance. The board decided not to redistrict completely within the system by dividing up the white population into equal proportions for each school. Explained one high-ranking school official:

> If we were to spread the white around, there would be so few in each school it would defeat the purpose of desegregation.

This respondent seemed to imply that the purpose of desegregation is to produce schools with a more perfect racial balance: fifty-fifty if not a "balance" in favor of the white enrollment.

Instead of effecting an even distribution of whites in the various schools, the board decided upon a plan they call "permissive transfer." An elementary school principal describes the plan:

> We started this permissive transfer to meet the demands of the Civil Rights Movement. . . . This way, if there is an empty seat in another school, a parent can apply to have her child sent there. We have thirty children, some of them white, on the waiting list. When there is a seat available, the name is picked from a hat, almost literally. They are drawn by lot. No one has ever complained about how the children are picked. . . . No, I don't know how many whites are on the list . . . a small proportion.

Additional probing could not disclose exactly how many of the thirty children on the waiting list of this school were white. The respondent did say that fewer than half on the list were white. In this school, where there are only forty white children to begin with, having even three or four on the waiting list would be a high percentage of the white enrollment. Having these three or four actually move would result in permissive transfer producing more racial imbalance rather than less!

The district superintendent of schools describes some of the results that he has noted of the transfer plan:

> All the schools now have at least 20 per cent Negro. Some have more. . . . Well, the proportion goes from 20 per cent to 90 per cent. That's the range. . . . Three years ago we started this permissive transfer. Students are allowed to go to a different school if they want. Some parents want the transfer because they say they want to take advantage of different ethnic situations—some whose children weren't doing well in one school wanted to see if they could do better in another school. But that's silly. All the schools are the same here.
>
> Anyway, both white and Negro students transfer. But they have to pay for their own transportation. We don't discriminate.

A Negro leader describes some of the other results omitted by the superintendent:

> They say, "You want him to go there, you get him there." I'm middle-class black. If I want, I can afford to send my kid to another school; I can drive him or call a taxi. But my neighbor next door, for example, is black-middle-class black. He can't afford to spend his money on foolish things. So what you get is permissive transfer causing more segregation. Only now it's segregation of the classes. The middle class can all transfer to one school.

The following summarizes another result the Negro leadership perceives:

> It's taking the leadership away. If I transfer my child away from his school, I'm not going to be nit-picking or raising hell in that school. I'll just pay attention to his new school which will be better than the old. Otherwise I wouldn't have bothered to transfer him.

Hence, while the school system officials appear to be content with the transfer arrangement—

> We have this housing that seems to be solving the problem.

—the Negro leaders are viewing the situation cynically:

Permissive transfer is doing more harm than good.

The residents of the village—those who are not actively involved in the NAACP-school board disagreement—have diverse feelings about the transfer plan. A village trustee is enthusiastic about the decision:

We are whole-heartedly in favor of the board's plan.

A private citizen expressed his opinion:

We have this transfer that seems okay.

Conversely, another white resident is less convinced:

The board decided on the permissive transfer. But that isn't going to solve anything.

Still another argues:

This busing—I'm against it. It's not right for a child to be sent to a school three miles away when there's one on the next street. And then another child is bused in to occupy that empty seat.

Another white parent states:

When I moved here and picked out a place to live, I looked at the school very carefully. I checked their rating and talked with the teachers. Then I checked about the library, theaters, and stores after I was satisfied with the school. I moved here for a purpose. I don't want my child to be sent to another school miles away.

A middle-class white man summarizes the reasons of many of the subjects, both white and Negro, for not transferring his child:

A child doesn't just work in school; he plays, too. That's how he gets to know a lot of different people. You can become very close to some of these friends. If your child goes to school two miles away, he has a group of friends there. But he doesn't stay at school all day until six o'clock at night. Who can he play with when he comes home? There's no one. So he'll have two circles of friends: one here and one there. That's not good for him.

The Negro community is also divided in their reactions to the possibility of transfer. Many say they would not transfer their child. Some say they have. But most state their motives, for whichever course of action they decided upon, not in terms of the racial balance, or in terms of the ethnic characteristics of the schools, but in terms of uniquely child-centered reasons—the play group. A lower-middle-class housewife expresses it this way:

> They send a note home every year when school is over. But I'd never send my girl to another school. All her friends go to her school. If I send her somewhere else, she wouldn't know anyone there. I like this school fine.

An upper-lower-class mother comments:

> I did think about [transferring] once. My boy knows so many of the kids in his school. All he wants to do is play. I was afraid he wouldn't learn. So I thought about transferring him to another school. My husband said to wait. So I did, and I haven't thought about it since then.

The implication from these two comments, and others like them, is that the children, when transferred to another school, may be unable to make new friends. This was viewed as a bad and good thing by the first and second mothers, respectively. The reason for this concern could not be uncovered in the interviews. That may be an artifact of my race—white; it was noticed during the interviews that with the exception of the community leaders, Negro respondents were polite but reluctant to discuss racial issues even when I directly suggested them. Therefore, one possible interpretation of the foregoing remarks is that some Negro parents do not wish to send their children to white schools because they fear the child will not be accepted there; but to admit this to a white interviewer would be a breach of good manners. This hypothesis to explain the low transfer-request rates is an interesting contrast to the explanation offered by a principal:

> Our waiting list is short because the children here have a pride in their school and in their community. They don't want to go to another school for that reason.

There was one case which deviated from the pattern by, first, not being reluctant to transfer her child, and second, doing so for purposes other than immediately child-oriented reasons. Her motive was more concerned with the future significance of the act. The subject, an upper-middle-class Negro woman living near the Marshall School insisted her son would never go to the local school:

> He's going to Ludlum, not Marshall. I don't want my boy to have the stigma of going to a Negro school. Everyone thinks Negro schools are inferior. If my son has that on his record, it will make it difficult for him.

Permissive transfer has done little to reduce the racial imbalance in the system. The proportion of Negroes has risen to 20 per cent in formerly all-white schools. However, the proportions have remained the same in the predominantly Negro schools. For this to occur, white children would have to transfer into these schools. I know of no instance where this has happened.

Some members of the school board claim that the reason for the relative ineffectiveness of the transfer policy is that not many children can transfer because of a shortage of classroom space into which they could move. Actually, children may apply for transfer only if they are in a classroom of over twenty-five children and they may be transferred only to classes having fewer than twenty-seven students. Fewer than three hundred students can be transferred. It is therefore perfectly conceivable that a child in a small class may never transfer out, even if his parents are willing and even if there are empty seats in another school.

The board does expect that there will be an increase of available seats in the elementary school by converting the district to a five-three-four system after the construction of a new high school for which the bond issue will be up for approval some time this year. The president of the board explained the proposal:

> The board has been working on another plan. There are thirty-eight acres on Peninsula Boulevard near the parkway. It's watershed property owned by New York City. Try talking to New York about something to do with water now! If we can, we want to buy this land. Nassau County gave us the okay. We're negotiating with New York, but we haven't gotten anywhere yet.
> We want to build a new high school there. That would be the ninth, tenth, eleventh, and twelfth grades. Then the present grade schools will be cut down to grade five. They'll just be kindergarten through fifth. The present high school will be

a "middle school." This middle school will take the pressure off the grammar schools.

Some townspeople are quite optimistic about the proposal. A village trustee states his approval:

> This high school will enable us to also have a middle school— sixth, seventh, and eighth grades. This will give us more class-room space in the elementary schools. We'll have more room to juggle kids around and get this segregation thing settled.

Others are not so enthusiastic. A white mother with a child in high school complained:

> The whole bond issue could be rejected because of the loca-tion [of the high school]. Well, it's as far away as possible. Some of the kids have to walk home in the dark. A lot of parents would feel better if the school were in the center of town. There's a lot of bars and things along Peninsula Boule-vard. Let's be frank . . . it's a colored slum. It's broken down and in terrible condition. Parents don't want their chil-dren walking there at night. I'm not speaking just for myself. Some of the colored who live near me have the same com-plaint.

Just as the board refused to take the responsibility for bus-ing students who transferred, they also are not willing to trans-port high school students. The president of the board feels that busing would be unnecessary:

> There would be no busing because everybody lives within the required two and a half miles. That's the two and a half miles to ten miles required by law.

It should be understood, however, that not all school dis-tricts on Long Island require students to walk two and one half miles to school. Several districts provide bus service for students who live half that distance away from school.

This proposal is similar to the plans offered by Dr. Branche in 1962 which advised the construction of either a junior high school (giving the district a six-three-three system) or the plac-ing of all the primary grades (*i.e.,* kindergarten through third) into separate schools. The suggestions were dismissed at that time because it was felt that land for a junior high school was not available in the center of the district; building elsewhere would necessitate bus transportation, as would separate build-ings for the primary grades. It seems that three years later, the board has reversed its decision: now it is decreed all right for children to walk two miles along a busy highway to get to school.

It appears that this proposed bond issue is going to be a source of future strain in the community. The referendum will bring to the forefront many of the issues which have lain silent for the past year: permissive transfer, busing, location of future schools, and the intentions of the school board.

Today, Negro leaders accuse the school system of providing an inferior education for Negroes, not just through *de facto* segregation but also through differential treatment of students and the differential placement of personnel.

In 1962, at the time of the announcement of the lawsuit filed against the school board, the Negro leadership also protested that the schools did not employ enough Negro teachers. At that time less than 10 per cent of the faculty were nonwhite.

Although there appears to have been some increase in the number of Negro teachers hired, minority leaders are still unsatisfied:

> In 1962 they certainly did not have enough Negro teachers. Since then they have hired more. With a ratio like we have, we wouldn't get the right proportion of Negro teachers. But we should have 30 or 40 per cent. It's nowhere near that now.

The superintendent of schools defends the hiring practices:

> We have some Negro teachers. I don't know how many. We don't discriminate. We just look for the best-qualified. This is nothing new or recent. It's been a matter of policy to hire some Negroes.

On the other hand, the president of the school board, who has been a member of that board for three years, in response to a question about the practice of hiring Negroes answered with surprise:

> We have no policy—this is the first I've heard about it. There are plenty of Negro teachers. There is no discrimination in that area. Never gave it a thought.

It appears from the above statements that there is a minor breakdown of communication between the board and the administration.

Not only has the initial hiring practices of teachers come

under attack, but also the quality and placement of these teachers in the schools. Regarding placement, there is little evidence of mobility from school to school within the district, according to one teacher:

> Years ago teachers could request a transfer to a school they thought was nicer. But they put a stop to that. When they place you in a school, that's where you stay unless they tell you to transfer.

A former teacher agrees:

> You get the same teachers teaching in the same schools for years. You don't get much movement around. Even the principals usually don't change schools. When they assign you to a school, it's because they want you there.

The superintendent presents the following reason why there is little interschool mobility:

> There is very little movement from school to school. There's no point to anyone moving. All the schools are the same— same facilities, same curriculum—so there's no advantage to it.

There is some disagreement among my respondents over this latter point. Many people, both Negro and white, have indicated that the schools are not identical and that there are very real differences between the schools. A former board president says:

> Prospect and the other schools are all alike. But Prospect does get the best teachers, has the most audio-visual equipment, but has the same text books as all the others. The best teachers are needed there. Let's face it; the school has to make up for the poor families these kids come from.

A teacher agrees:

> Prospect has some of the best teachers.

A substitute teacher explained her preferences:

> I usually taught in Franklin because that's where my kids went to school. I also did some teaching in Jackson and Prospect. Prospect has more trouble getting substitutes than the other schools. Well, it's almost 99 per cent colored and they have these special classes. The classes used to be based only on intelligence scores, but that's going out of fashion now. . . .

222 · Rosalind J. Dworkin

They have four of them. But it's the best school to work in. The classes are smaller, so it's nicer.

From this we may conclude that teachers also perceive the differences in the schools. Also, teacher preferences for particular schools are not exclusively based on the school's ethnic characteristics. Much of the judgment is based upon such educationally relevant factors as classroom size. A Negro leader continues the debate:

There is one school in the district that is maybe 95 per cent black that I wouldn't mind sending my kids to. That's Prospect School. It has good teachers, good facilities. . . .

He compares the other schools with Prospect:

[In Prospect] the teachers really seem to care. They want to do a good job. In the other schools they don't give enough attention to the children. I'm talking about the man at the top—the principal—he just doesn't care.

His solution?

We need teachers who care. I'm not just talking about this brotherly love jazz either. But teachers who want to do a professional job well.

Negro critics also find differences in the physical plant of the district schools.

I don't keep a lawn, but a school should have a nice lawn. Have you seen the front of Franklin School? There's papers all over the yard. They should keep the place at least looking neat. They have some broken windows there too. Jackson School needs repainting, or maybe they just keep painting it that dingy color from year to year. I don't see why kids should have to sit in gray rooms. They need janitors who have pride in their work, who want to get that floor polished like a mirror. In Prospect they do a pretty good job, but in the other schools, it's a mess.

It is well accepted in Hempstead that there is differential treatment of students. However, the interpretation of what "differential treatment" entails varies widely according to the position of the person with whom one speaks. Asked about differential treatment of children, an elementary school principal outlines the interim training program for recent Southern migrants. A high school administrator will talk about the vocational training curricula and the work-study programs, both receiving state and federal support.

Teachers view differential treatment in another way. Rather than expounding upon systematic programs instituted by the administration, a teacher will speak about her experiences in the classroom:

> You have to treat these kids differently, especially the ones from the South. They are tough! I suppose they were shipped around in the Southern schools, but they come up here acting really tough, saying, "You can't hit me" and "You can't do that to me." They say that because they know we can't.

and

> You have to treat them differently because of the homes they come from—those deprived backgrounds. Some of them come into first grade without understanding a full sentence or being able to speak one. The teachers can't change the family. The children are with their families most of the time. How can the school change them? We can try to help, but that's all.

The Negro community interprets the meaning of differential treatment in still another way. When talking about differences in the treatment of whites and nonwhites, Negroes speak of such phenomena as these:

> It's demoralizing to be in a learning situation where everyone thinks you're an oddball. Where even you think you're an oddball; some kind of freak!
>
> And the teachers . . . they're prejudiced too. In the beginning of the year, they point at you and say, "I don't like you," and then you're in for trouble for the rest of the year.
>
> At the high school they have really archaic counseling. They have directed really bright kids into nonsensical shop courses. They think Negro kids can just be cooks and waiters, so they put them into shop.
>
> All the white kids know about the Regents examination. But some of our kids never heard of the Regents. And you can't get into college in this state without taking the Regents.

Conversely, many Negroes do not criticize the counseling system. These people are not only satisfied, but they suggest that parents have the opportunity to be vocal about their wishes when a child's high school curriculum is being planned:

> We can't afford to send her to college, so I thought a business course would be best. Yes, I spoke with the guidance counselor.

I told her what I thought was best, and we decided she should be in a business course.

and

I'm taking history, English, geometry, Spanish, and driver's ed. [How come it's an academic course?] That was mostly my father's doing. . . .

The last four comments highlight one of the aspects of the Negro community in Hempstead: the first two voice extreme dissatisfaction with one aspect of the school system; the third conveys a contentment that critics disapprove of; the fourth presents a situation that critics would approve of. The critics were middle-class respondents who had received some college education and who had lived in the North for most of their lives. The fourth statement was made by the son of a lower-middle-class family whose father had finished high school. The third was taken from a conversation with a lower-class woman with an elementary school education who migrated from West Virginia five years ago. Her ambitions for her daughter are high ones compared with her own achievements; she anticipates her child's becoming a white-collar worker, although she, the mother, is working on an assembly line.

The arguments of the Negro leaders suggest that they have higher ambitions, not only for their own children, but for the children of these lower-class families. That is, where lower-class parents are contented and actually proud that their children are taking some kind of vocational training and finishing high school, the Negro leaders, all of whom are middle-class, interpret vocational training as "nonsensical" and degrading. While some parents are pleased that their children will become secretaries and mechanics, others want these identical students to begin professional careers.

This particular disagreement over appropriate definitions of the situation is only one of many that divides the Negro community into those who are hostile critics and those who are either mildly or strongly in favor of the schools. The following is another example of such disagreement. (The following data analysis is not presented as a proof of a hypothesis. Rather, its function is to generate hypotheses that may prove tenable after using large samples and more thorough questionnaires.)

The boy's room is odorous (*Middle-class man*).

No, they keep the building very well. It's not like where I worked at the Euclid School for nine years. There the kids used to write all over the walls and we would spend hours washing it off. But the principal here don't let no one write on the walls or do anything like that (*Lower-middle-class woman*).

The school seems a lot different than where I went to school. We didn't learn nothing. But my son is learning arithmetic, how to add, and how to read (*Upper-lower-class woman*).

My little girl is learning a lot this year. She's really a bright child with books and reading. She gets better and better each year (*Lower-middle-class woman*).

The teacher is very nice and so is the principal. Well the teacher really wants to teach the children a lot (*Lower-middle-class woman*).

But the other schools don't give enough attention. I'm talking about the man at the top—the principal—he just doesn't care (*Middle-class man*).

The principal, I only met him once at a meeting. I like him. He's an ordinary kind of fellow—like one of us (*Lower-lower-class woman*).

The teachers are okay, I guess (*Lower-middle-class man*).

I don't know too much about the schools. I work so I don't go to the P.T.A. meetings. But I like the teacher, and the principal is nice (*Lower-lower-class woman*).

They have some teachers who are really incompetent that they should get rid of. They really have some duds (*Middle-class man*).

Negroes have nothing to complain about here. . . . They have the same books and teachers as the white kids (*Middle-class woman*).

The previous statements were all made by Negroes. They were all referring to the same school. Three of the statements are overtly hostile toward the school and toward the personnel. The others range from pleasantly neutral to a criticism of the critics. What can account for such a wide variation in the perceptions of the same situations?

A possible factor that could account for the variations in perception is the length of time in the community. It could be argued that the longer one lived in the district, the greater opportunity he had to become familiar with the district schools; hence the more time he would have to become acquainted with the faults of the system. This, however, does not appear to be tenable. Admittedly all the critics are older residents. Each has lived in the village for over seven years. The remainder, however, are not all newcomers. The range of length of residence is from two to twenty-one years. It appears, therefore, that the critics of the system tend to have lived in the district for some years. The converse is not true: long residence does not necessarily produce discontent.

Using socioeconomic status as an explanatory variable, we find that we can account for more of the discrepancy. All of the critics are middle-class Negroes. Only one other, the critic's critic, is middle-class. The others are all either lower-class or (using the terminology of one subject) black-middle-class-black, a term that implies two parallel stratification systems: Negro and white. Black-middle-class-black refers to the individual who is middle-class in the Negro stratification system; translated to the parallel white system, the individual would be ranked lower-middle-class. Hence, with the exception of one deviant case, all satisfied customers are lower- and lower-middle-class persons, and all critics are middle-class.

Closely correlated with economic status is another variable that may provide the link between class and attitudes toward the school: the amount of education. All the critics were above the median on the educational variable. That is, all had completed high school and two had some integrated college and university education. The critic's critic is again a deviant case; she is a Negro educator who has had education beyond the master's degree. All the other cases were below the educational median.

Dismissing the deviant case for the moment, we have a clear dichotomy of individuals who are middle-class, well-educated critics, and persons who are lower- (and lower-middle) class and poorly educated. What, then, is the connection? Studying the complete interviews of these persons, one emergent pattern is the use of comparisons with other schools as a basis of evaluation. Comparisons are made between the schools presently attended by their children and the schools that the parents once went to or that the parents had once worked for.

This suggests that comparison with a relevant group is the intervening variable between socioeconomic status and dissatisfaction with school policies and personnel. I would hypothesize that the relationship is thus: Negroes of high socioeconomic status can afford to attend college more frequently than those of lower-status backgrounds. While in college, they become familiar with the white culture and especially the white educational system. In this way they come to expect much of the schools and measure their present situation against this newly acquired standard.

The lower-class Negroes who did not complete their education have as a relevant comparison those schools with which they are familiar through actual attendance at one time: many were old New York City schools; many were segregated Southern schools. Whichever the case is for a particular individual, Hempstead schools look a good deal better than what they were accustomed to. In other words, those satisfied persons look at what once was; the critics look at what could be.

The use of these comparison groups as the intervening variable can also explain the deviant case. A person of high education and socioeconomic status, this woman is an educator who has worked for white administrators and with white teachers. It is most likely that she has identified with these groups and has accepted their value system and "party line" that the schools are better than others. She thus is comparing the district with what is occurring in other areas of mixed population and finds that indeed Hempstead "Negroes have nothing to complain about here."

Using the variable of comparative relevant groups, one can explain the diverse evaluations of a situation by understanding the way in which these evaluations are being made: that is, through comparison with other groups or situations perceived as relevant. This concept is similar to the concept of reference groups.[6] The essential difference between the two is that the subject at the time of his comparison is not a member of the relevant group, but nevertheless uses it as a standard for evaluating his present situation.

It has been shown that the Negro critics of the school system are a vocal and action-oriented group. Their attendance at board meetings to debate issues and their threats to block the

[6] For example, see Robert K. Merton, *Social Theory and Social Structure* (New York: The Free Press of Glencoe, 1957), chapters IX and X.

acceptance of budgets and school bond issues, not to mention the lawsuit filed in 1962, all represent pressures placed upon the school board and administration. As in other school districts, Hempstead is subject to pressures from local groups which do not always have racial segregation as their focus. Rather, political groups, private citizens with special goals (*e.g.*, the reduction of taxes), and parents with specific complaints about their children's education all attempt to exert enough pressure upon the school board so that their demands will be met.

These problems that plague the school system are compounded by the fact that people define the schools as "public property" and wave the banner of "local control." Thus, these groups view their desire to pressure school boards as a legitimate right of "any interested and concerned citizen." Hence, the school system is deemed open to scrutiny by parents, newspapers, civil rights workers, federal and state governments, and social scientists.

A complex organization cannot function effectively while under the constant surveillance of many interest groups, nor can any complex organization, including a school board, yield to all demands, many of which conflict with each other. To attempt to do so would be organizational suicide. Rather, an organization must develop certain defense mechanisms whereby it can function in a semi-hostile environment. The kinds of defenses open to an organization depend, of course, upon the characteristics of the particular structure. Two mechanisms that could be used in an organization are secrecy and the surrender of token concessions. In a public institution secrecy is especially difficult to maintain because of the assumption that what is supported by public funds is legitimately open to public scrutiny and control. Professionalism can be viewed as an attempt to take an organization, such as the schools, out of the public domain. By claiming that only professional specialists are equipped to operate the organization, some of the legitimacy of public control is removed.

The Hempstead school board and administration have attempted with some success to employ these two protective techniques—token concessions and secrecy—in their effort to "cool the mark out." Erving Goffman first borrowed this phrase from the vocabulary of professional confidence men and employed it to describe a phenomenon in the everyday world.[7] "Cooling the mark out" refers to the process by which a victim (the mark) is convinced by others that his fate is not as bad as it had originally seemed to be. The method of cooling out might be stalling, offering of a different status, or a kind of bribery in which the victim is given a token prize in return for withdrawing his complaint.

Using this concept metaphorically, one could depict the Negro in Hempstead as a "mark" and the board and high administration as attempting to "cool him out." Pushing the metaphor a little further, one could describe the use of permissive transfer as a bribe—a token concession designed to offer a reward reciprocated by a decrease of Negro pressure on the board. Indeed, busing has been viewed in just this way. The school board president stated:

> We proposed a plan that everyone—or at least the people who were concerned with it—were satisfied.

A Negro leader's view of this is:

> Permissive transfer is doing just what the school board wants. It's taking the pressure off. It's satisfying the people who complained. But what about the others?

The school system has also attempted to protect itself by a modified use of secrecy to suppress publication of any information that my be interpreted as school mismanagement. The administration claims not to keep records of any kind that would indicate that Hempstead is a biracial district. Thus, members of the administration refused to supply the following information:

> How many Negro teachers are employed?
> There are plenty of Negro teachers.
> What proportion of transfer applications are made by white parents?
> I don't know. (Half?) No, less than that. (One-fourth?) No, it seems less than that, but I can't be sure. We don't keep track of that kind of information. We don't discriminate.

Not only is access to records denied, but access to the physical building is also closely guarded. There are planned "open houses," when parents may visit during the day. At other times, parents may confer with teachers by appointment. All other out-

[7] Erving Goffman, "On Cooling the Mark Out," *Psychiatry,* Vol. 15, No. 4, November 1952.

siders are not permitted to tour the schools or speak with teachers unless permission is first granted by the principal. Such permission does not seem to be usually granted. A former teacher
in the system observed:

> They think they have this integration thing settled now. They
> don't want anybody making any disturbances. You won't get in
> to see any of the teachers. They want to keep everything quiet.
> The teachers are scared out of their wits to talk frankly to any-
> one.

Secrecy is also fostered by telling half-truths or by feigning
ignorance. However, as in many bureaucracies there is often a
breakdown in communication between the various levels of the
hierarchy. The result of this is that occasionally stories don't
quite agree. Consider the following two responses explaining the
reason why permissive transfer was begun in 1962. Says the superintendent:

> We had some schools that were very populated—Franklin and
> Jackson; and some were underpopulated—Fulton, Ludlum, and
> Prospect. Just sheer population growth, that's all.

and the principal of Franklin School:

> We started this permissive transfer to meet the demands of the
> civil rights movement.

Other communication breakdowns have previously been
described: comparability of faculties across schools, and the existence of policies involving the hiring of Negro teachers.

Thus has the system adopted mechanisms to "cool out" the
opposition and keep the surface of organizational life apparently
smooth and trouble-free. However, this peace can only be temporary. When the Negro community is no longer satisfied with
the token concession of permissive transfer and when new issues
arise that cannot be remedied through this technique, the still-
ness of the surface will be broken. The organization will be im-
periled until a new adaptation can be generated. In the meantime, the present protective mechanisms are inhibiting communication between the school administration and the Negro
community, thereby making a new crisis imminent.

Conclusion

The administration and the board of education have consistently claimed that they do not discriminate. They do not control the proportion of white and nonwhite pupils applying for transfer. They have no policy of hiring a quota of nonwhite teachers. No policy equals non-discrimination.

The system is clearly working under a very narrow definition of what constitutes discrimination. It is true that the district has not actively initiated practices with the intent of subordinating one group for the benefit of the other. However, there is more than one way to discriminate: by remaining passive, by allowing "chance" and undue opportunity to operate, or by evaluating only the manifest intention of a policy without regard for the latent functions of the same policy, as much discrimination and segregation can occur as if the village relocated all Negroes into one ghetto.

Therefore, the school system cannot legitimately claim that they do not discriminate because they do not actively sanction such policies. In order for the school board to be able to justify their claims, they must take an active role in fostering equality of educational opportunities. This can be done in several ways.

First, because the classroom teacher is the key individual in the process of formal education, special attention must be given to hiring and placement practices. The district needs a specified policy to guide the hiring of new employees. Part of this policy must be an active campaign to recruit more Negro teachers. It is understood that there is a shortage of well-educated certified Negro teachers in New York State. The labor market most probably cannot supply a ratio of white to nonwhite teachers that would match the ethnic ratio of the students. However, interracial understanding must be fostered through interaction between the members of the ethnic groups. This cannot be accomplished when interaction occurs exclusively between a white superior and a Negro subordinate. Nor can a Negro child be supplied with adequate role models when the only Negro adults in a school are the janitors. Therefore, it is necessary for the social education of all children of the district that they be supplied with opportunities for interaction with minority members who are in high-status jobs as well as those in low-status positions. Therefore, it is advisable that enough Negro teachers and/or administrators be employed so that all students are taught by at least one Negro teacher at some time during their formal education.

Second, the low interschool mobility rates, already established, should be further encouraged. Moreover, there should be no systematic stocking of one school with "the best teachers." Transferring a teacher who has been unusually successful teaching a particular kind of student to a school where her job would be working with children with different problems would be self-defeating. Superior teachers should be retained in those situations where they have been successful in order to predict with more certainty their future success.

Third, the school system must begin a program of equalization of facilities. Providing the same text books in all schools is not sufficient. Each school must be provided with proportionally equal facilities. Although different emphasis may be placed upon such materials due to individual school personnel, the distribution of such durable items as audio-visual equipment must be appropriate to the characteristics of the particular classroom situations. Hence, the children in the interim program or the educable retarded children would have different facilities available for their education. It must be remembered that under some circumstances, the same education is not equal education.

Fourth, a clear and conscious effort must be made to keep the interim program functioning as an *interim* program. That is, the grouping must be flexible enough to enable a child to progress from the special class to a normal class as soon as he has acquired the minimum skills necessary to allow him to participate. This might be done even if it entails placing a ten-year-old child into a fourth-grade class with children a year younger than he. The interim program must be designed to encourage this mobility rather than deter it. Otherwise, a child would be condemned to remedial classes for the duration of his school career as a result of a circulative and cumulative causation pattern.

Fifth, capable high school students should be encouraged by the guidance counselors to enter college preparatory courses without consideration to the child's socioeconomic status. It is the guidance counselor's professional duties to make known to and to assist the capable child in obtaining financial aid to complete his schooling if his family is unable to assume the burden.

Although improving the quality of education, these measures obviously would not improve the racial balance in the district. A merger of school districts mentioned previously would provide a better racial balance, not only for Hempstead but also for the other participating communities. This cannot be done in the immediate future because well-formed political interest groups oppose the change. However, the school district can maintain pressure on the legislature both directly and indirectly through the state's department of education.

Sixth, as the district stands today, much can be done to improve the situation. The district cannot have fully integrated schools unless it assumes the responsibility of transporting students. This would no doubt mean an increase in school taxes, but quality education never was cheaply bought.

The district cannot rely upon integration through the individual efforts of isolated families. That is, in order for the transfer system to work, it cannot be permissive. Since Negroes do not transfer because they fear non-acceptance in another school, and whites infrequently transfer to Negro schools which are overcrowded, a compulsory integration program is necessary. The most efficient way to accomplish this would be to build the proposed high school and provide bus transportation for the students. The present high school would then be used as a middle school, and the elementary schools would then be paired. Two schools, such as Prospect and Ludlum, which are relatively near each other, would be joined together; combined, they would have a ratio representative of the total school enrollment. These paired schools would share the responsibility of educating the children within their combined territory. The children would be distributed to the schools on the basis not of residence but by grade. The primary grades would be taught in one building and the intermediate grades in another. Thus, *de facto* segregation caused by housing patterns could be overcome.

I do not believe the school board will independently initiate any progressive, action-oriented policies. Past performances suggest that the board yields only when it appears necessary for the passage of budgets and bond issues.

As Negro expectations continue to rise, issues become clearly defined, and interested parties become aligned, social action will become more continuous and more effective. Through the joint emergence of economic sanction and awareness of its role in the larger civil rights movement, the Negroes of the Northeast can effectively challenge the legitimacy of segregation in suburbia.

VI

Desegregation in the Midwest: The Case of Kalamazoo

John Pease

It may very well be that the race issue cannot be solved apart from solutions to other problems: urban renewal and housing, and poverty and technological unemployment, for example. An ideology of integration, then, may need to be an intellectual assessment that starts with the fact that the vast majority of Negroes suffer from class position as well as racial status (James B. McKee, "The Ideology of Moderation: Some Assumptions about Conflict in American Society"—an address delivered in the Provost's Lecture Series, Michigan State University, February 1964).

The first thing you should know is that I'm not a Negro. I know that you can see for yourself, but I want you to write it down in your notes before I say anything else.

You know, I think that most white people often forget how much difference that makes. I mean that you always wonder how much madder you'd get, and then there's all those little occurrences that never happen to you and that you never see just because you're not a Negro. I really think it makes a difference. (*White male, about forty-five*).

Negroes won't tell you how they feel. They've learned to tell the white man what he wants to hear. I think Baldwin's right; the Negro knows the white man better than he knows himself. . . .

The white plantation owner used to tell his Negro slave how much he liked him, and then he would promise the slave that he would be buried in the family gravesite. The Negro would smile and the white man would recall to himself how really happy that Negro slave was. What that white man didn't know is that that same Negro slave was out in the kitchen, spitting in the soup (*Negro male, about forty*).

It sure is great to be in this bastion of freedom, this great melting pot of the world that tells you that your son can't push a broom, can't be nothing. . . . They say we're "good boys," but I'm tired of being good boys (*Negro male, about thirty-five*).

Life is good in Kalamazoo (*Kalamazoo Chamber of Commerce.*)

This town is so steeped in paternalism that it isn't funny (*Negro male, about forty*).

Oh, I think the Negroes' contention that this town is paternalistic is a natural viewpoint in this community. The Negro population is only about 7 per cent and it's easy for the Negro middle class to get detached from the Negro community. Negroes in the community haven't much power, and there isn't much definite that they can focus complaints about (*White male, about fifty*).

I know they don't trust me but I don't care about that. I'm interested in results. They can call it paternalism. I don't care. If they've got a solution I'd like to hear it. Where are they? (*White male, about forty-five*).

They don't understand that you do with and not for. They always call us up, very politely, and inform us what they are going to do for us. There's never any discussion. Sure, they always have some Negroes on the committees, but they always pick those who won't rock the boat (*Negro male, about forty*).

One of the problems in this community is with the Negroes themselves. They can't get themselves mobilized. Before, we knew who the bastards were. However, now that more and more people in the white community are trying to help, the Negroes don't really know what they want to have done and they can't get themselves mobilized (*Negro male, about fifty*).

I think that if a Negro has the money, he can live anywhere in the city that he wants to. It may not be as easy as it is for you and me, but he can do it. Even though the Negro population is still concentrated in one area, there is no census tract that doesn't have at least one Negro family (*White male, about fifty*).

Today in Kalamazoo we are experiencing a rapid growth of the Negro population. That is, people are coming in from the South with a number of limitations—they are primarily unskilled, have little education, and little in economic resources. Consequently, they are only able to get jobs on the bottom of the ladder. Therefore, these people from Southern rural backgrounds, who have it so much better than they had it before, are apathetic and, because of their backgrounds, don't motivate their kids to do well in school. It's all part of a vicious circle (*Negro male, about fifty*).

Life is supposed to be good here, but at present the good is just in some places and not all over the city. I think I should enjoy some of the good in Kalamazoo, too. I'm sure you must know the housing conditions that are so terrible in such a large part of the north side. When visitors come to Kalamazoo they don't see this part though. They see all those places that can be admired, yet seldom see the place that's most talked about, written about, but not done about (*Negro female, about forty*).

I wouldn't give five cents for him. . . . I've got no use for black professionals who don't help (*Negro male, about thirty-five*).

No, as a matter of fact, one of the problems is that the Negroes' most able and articulate people won't help (*White male, about forty*).

The NAACP here is primarily a middle-class club (*White male, about fifty*).

Well, right now the Human Relations Council isn't doing much. As a matter of fact, we're looking for a project. I think it's going to be housing (*White female, about thirty-five*).

Listen, the Community Relations Board isn't doing a damned thing and it can't. The director's got his hands tied. He works for the city government and you know that they're not going to let him do anything (*Negro male, about thirty-five*).

We've got *de facto* segregation at Lincoln school and there's no sense in pretending we don't (*White male, about forty-five*).

I maintain that anytime you've got segregation, you've got inferior education (*Negro male, about forty*).

If you can end *de facto* segregation and improve the quality of education, then I'm all for it. If, on the other hand, you end *de facto* segregation and the quality of education isn't improved, then I lose my enthusiasm (*White male, about fifty*).

It's not the school board's job to do everything—they didn't create the ghetto-like condition. They can only go so far and then it's out of their hands (*White male, about thirty-five*).

I honestly think that every effort has been made to bring the best possible education to Lincoln school (*White female, about thirty-five*).

There's a good deal of community pride in Lincoln school and the board of education has worked hard to make it good (*White male, about fifty*).

I was the first volunteer teacher at Lincoln school (*White male, about forty*).

I think that being a Negro gives you a break in the public schools since then you are defined as part of a problem. For instance, when NASA sent in a team to explain the space program to public school students, the administration, quite expectedly, selected the "nice" elementary schools of the middle- and upper-class areas. Then they needed to select one school on the other side of town, and they picked Lincoln school. Actually, it's the high-status schools and Lincoln which get the preferential treatment. What I'm concerned about are those schools in between, the ones which aren't defined as "problems" (*White female, about thirty*).

The school administration has made a real effort in the past few years to hire Negro teachers. This is not tokenism and the teachers are not concentrated in one school. They are spread throughout the school system. Kalamazoo is a very good community. There are a lot of people here who are very concerned. There have been a lot of research studies regarding the Negro situation, and I think the town is very receptive to change (*Negro male, about forty*).

This is a fairly conscientious community (*White male, about fifty-five*).

The tragic thing about this town is that despite a better attitude about race relations, the community is becoming more segregated (*White male, about sixty*).

I am convinced that most Negroes suffer from class position as much, if not more, than they suffer from race position. In fact, if you're middle-class or upper-class, it doesn't make a hell of a lot of difference what race you are (*White male, about thirty*).

If you're poor you're a nigger, but if you're rich you're only a Negro (*Negro male, about thirty*).

Kalamazoo

According to a local historical marker, Kalamazoo was built on what once was a reserve of the Pottawatomi Indians. The Indians, as every schoolboy knows, were squeezed out of the area, "removed" to land west of the Mississippi which was known at that time as the "Great American Desert."

Kalamazoo's first permanent white settlers were Yankees, and at the time of their arrival (about 1830), the area was simply a small fur-trading post in the wilderness. In large measure it was the favorable location that attracted these pioneers to Kalamazoo, for here was the center of a rich agricultural area with black prairie soil in every direction, and here the river was conveniently forded and relatively easy to bridge.

The community's early economic growth was similar to that of other Midwestern communities; similar to the extent that Kalamazoo's early economy was dependent upon agriculture for its main income, followed by the development of a diversified industrial complex. By 1870 the community income was balanced between agriculture, commerce, and industry.

During the latter half of the nineteenth century the population increased substantially, from twenty-five hundred in 1850 to nearly twenty-five thousand in 1900. Much of this increase was due to the influx of foreign-born whites. In 1890 approximately 17 per cent of the city's population were foreign-born, but the relative size of this group has decreased steadily from that time; at present less than 6 per cent of the population are foreign-born. Approximately 75 per cent of these foreign-born residents are from Northeastern Europe and Canada. About one-third of all foreign-born are Dutch.

The city population increased rapidly during the early 1900s. By 1911, when President Taft laid the cornerstone of the local Y.M.C.A. building, the population was slightly more than forty thousand. Only during the decade of the 1930s was there a decrease in the city's population, a loss of 1.5 per cent. During the period from 1940 to 1950 the population increased nearly 7 per cent, and from 1950 to 1960 the increase was 43 per cent, mainly as a result of annexation of suburban areas. The population of Kalamazoo in 1960 was slightly more than eighty thousand.

Presently, Kalamazoo has a relatively diversified economy. There are over three hundred manufacturing and processing firms in the area and as recently as 1959 no one firm employed more than 6 per cent of the labor force. The paper and paper products industry is the most prominent in the area. The second largest industry is the chemical, mainly pharmaceuticals and petroleum. Other industries of substantial size include transportation equipment, construction, electrical machinery and equipment, and fabricated metal products.

Many of these plants, subsidiaries of national firms, were located in Kalamazoo because of the city's proximity to Chicago and Detroit markets, adequate labor supply, and the community wage scale. Some industries, such as chemicals, engravings, paraffin, and printing ink, moved to Kalamazoo to be near the paper mills. Retail, wholesale, construction, and service industries have grown along with the manufacturing industries.

According to 1960 census data, approximately 40 per cent of the city's civilian labor force were employed by industry, 18 per cent were employed in retail and wholesale concerns, 8 per cent in educational services, and 8 per cent in other professional services. Approximately 9 per cent of the labor force were self-employed, and about 12 per cent were government employees. The paper, retail, service, and chemical industries employ about 55 per cent of the labor force. According to a study completed in 1957, there were approximately twenty-seven hundred employers in the community, although only four hundred of these employed more than eight persons.

Relative to other Michigan cities of comparable size, Kalamazoo has usually had a low rate of unemployment, and many authorities believe that this is attributable to its diversified economy and the fact that its major products are finished products which are not seasonal and which find worldwide markets. One large chemical firm, for example, "has not had a 'lay off' in this century."

Kalamazoo residents are proud of their community. They point with pride to the fact that in the mid-1950s the city was presented with awards for being "one of the twenty most desirable residential cities" in the country. Twice in the late 1950s Kalamazoo was selected by the United States Information Agency as "The Typical American City" for its overseas exhibits. Just recently the National Municipal League designated Kalamazoo as an "All American City." Residents of Kalamazoo are also proud of the fact that the community was one of the first in the United States to rebuild the heart of the downtown section. According to one longtime community businessman:

> . . . this typifies the progressiveness of Kalamazoo. The community slogan, "Life is good in Kalamazoo," is not just a Chamber of Commerce phrase. It's really a good description of this town. Just ask anybody.

Negroes in Kalamazoo

When the Indians were being "removed" to their new home in the "Great American Desert," the first permanent Negro residents arrived in Kalamazoo at the invitation of a town official who maintained an underground railway station for runaway slaves. Some twenty years later Abraham Lincoln arrived in the city to speak of the troubles over slavery in Kansas. At this time, Negroes constituted approximately 4 per cent of the city's 5,000 residents. By the end of the Civil War the Negro population was about 350, approximately 6 per cent of the population. They included stonemasons, farmers, cooks, cabinetmakers, barbers, laborers, blacksmiths, shoemakers, and housewives.

At the turn of the century Negroes were only 2 per cent of the population, for although the number of Negroes had increased by one-third since the end of the Civil War, the non-

Negro population had increased four times over. During the first ten years of the twentieth century the Negro population in Kalamazoo increased 45 per cent, and it seems that this sharp increase was primarily due to the cityward migration of Negroes from surrounding communities plus some natural increase, rather than to the influx of Southern migrants. The Negro population in the city increased only 9 per cent between 1910 and 1920, which was, of course, the period of the great northward migration of Southern Negroes. The Negro population in Kalamazoo increased 30 per cent in the 1920s and 16 per cent during the 1930s.

Kalamazoo did not experience a significant Southern Negro migration until World War II. In 1940 Negroes comprised only 2 per cent of the total population. During the next ten years the Negro population increased 121 per cent, an influx that continued during the 1950s, when the Negro population increased 114 per cent. In 1960 Negroes were 6.4 per cent of the city population. If this wartime rate of migration and increase in the Negro population has continued through the 1960s, and we have no reason to believe it has not, then the Negro population of Kalamazoo is probably about seventy-five hundred at the present time, and will more than likely number between eleven and twelve thousand by 1970.

This postwar increase in the Negro population is crucial to understanding the "situation" in Kalamazoo. Many, if not most, of the residents define the general problem in terms of the rapid increment of a large and unsophisticated population, crippled by a rural, Southern existence, and therefore unable to participate in the larger community. According to this definition, the "problem" is based upon the inadequacies of individual members of this migrant population. One of the Negro leaders, a longtime community resident, expressed it this way:

> Today in Kalamazoo we are experiencing a rapid growth of the Negro population. That is, people are coming in from the South with a number of limitations—they are primarily unskilled, have little education, and little in economic resources. Consequently, they are only able to get jobs at the bottom of the ladder. Therefore, these people from Southern rural backgrounds, who have it so much better than they had it before, are apathetic and, because of their backgrounds, don't motivate their kids to do well in school. It's all part of a vicious circle.

These residents point out, for example, that the city did not have a predominantly Negro school until the 1950s, and that there were few or no exclusively Negro residential blocks until early in the 1950s, which is to say that the city had no "Negro problem" when it had no Negroes. It is significant that many of Kalamazoo's residents, sympathetically concerned with the difficulties Negroes experience, discuss the ways in which the Negroes' Southern history contributes to these difficulties and fail to mention the inequities of the community social structure.

According to the 1960 Census 3.4 per cent of the population of Kalamazoo County were Negro. However, 92 per cent of these fifty-eight hundred Negroes lived in Kalamazoo, and 43 per cent of all city Negroes lived in a single census tract; 86 per cent lived in just four tracts. As of 1960, Negroes lived in each of the city's eighteen census tracts, but in six of these they numbered less than a baker's dozen.

In 1945 the Social Action Committee of the Kalamazoo County Council of Churches and the Kalamazoo Council of Social Agencies, in cooperation with the Race Relations Department of the American Missionary Association and the Social Science Institute of Fisk University, conducted a comprehensive survey of Negroes in Kalamazoo. According to the report of that survey, Negro families lived in nearly every major section of Kalamazoo, and there were few, if any, exclusively Negro residential blocks. Nonetheless, there was "strong evidence of a trend toward residential segregation." Negroes were not evenly distributed throughout the city; indeed, the largest concentration of Negroes at that time lived in a "congested area wedged between the New York Central and Pennsylvania railroad tracks."

The 1945 report also identified the major factors responsible for a trend toward residential segregation. These factors included racially restrictive covenants, real estate agreements, and the policies of private loan companies and federal loan insurance agencies. According to the report:

> In recent years, there has been evidence of a growing policy toward residential segregation of Negroes. Such a policy was almost nonexistent in former years, a fact well substantiated by the presence of many scattered Negro homes outside of predominantly Negro areas. As recently as 1940 there was no exclusively Negro block in the city, according to a local social worker.

Two Kalamazoo attorneys who are engaged largely in real estate transactions estimated that between 85 and 95 per cent of the residential plots in the city are covered by racially restrictive covenants. This would appear to leave from 5 to 15 per cent of the residential plots to 2 per cent of the population. But there are other limiting factors: to begin with, covenants constitute merely one method, albeit the chief method, used to exclude Negroes from desirable areas. To this must be added the "gentleman's agreement" by which real estate men pledge to rent or sell to Negroes only that property designated as "colored." Under this arrangement many uncovenanted houses, which Negro families could afford to buy or lease, and which are listed for sale or rent, are unavailable. Furthermore, racially restrictive covenants are used only by those owners who feel that Negroes are likely to move into their neighborhoods. It is not usual for such restrictions to be found on property where the price or rental precludes occupancy by any but the most affluent Negroes.

In addition to restrictive covenants and informal real estate agreements, there has been support for a segregation policy from the Federal Housing Administration which refuses to insure loans for Negroes in predominantly "white neighborhoods" or for whites in predominantly "Negro neighborhoods."

These data regarding the trend toward residential segregation and the factors which were encouraging it are twenty years old. They were collected and publicized under the sponsorship of some of Kalamazoo's leading citizens because, says the report, these responsible residents of Kalamazoo were mindful of stresses in intergroup relations that needed solution. "Prior to World War II," the report continues, "relations between the two groups were relatively amicable; there was little evidence of overt friction and civic leaders could say that in Kalamazoo race relations were stable."

Nonetheless, the increased residential segregation of the Negro population which the 1945 study foresaw has obtained in fact. The area which in 1945 had the largest concentration of Negroes is today more than 58 per cent Negro. Moreover, the census tract on its western border is 21 per cent Negro; the tract on its eastern border is 20 per cent Negro; and the tract on its southern border is 12 per cent Negro. These four tracts account for 86 per cent of the Negro population of the city. Equally significant is the fact that these areas experienced a sizable out-migration of whites during the 1950s. For example, tract two was 77 per cent white in 1950. During the ten-year period from 1950 to 1960 the white population decreased by 57 per cent, while the Negro population increased 100 per cent. In 1960 this tract was 58 per cent Negro.

Most Negroes in Kalamazoo are limited not only in place of residence but also in quality of residence. For example, the area which was 58 per cent Negro contained only 6 per cent of all housing in the city, and yet it included one-half of all dilapidated units and 13 per cent of all deteriorating units. Within this tract two-fifths of all housing units were defined as unsafe, and two-thirds were either dilapidated or deteriorating. Whereas 15 per cent of all whites lived in deteriorating or dilapidated housing, 50 per cent of all nonwhites did. Twenty-one per cent of the nonwhites lived in crowded housing compared to only six per cent of the white population.

Comparison of White and Nonwhite Population with Respect to Housing

COLOR	CROWDED (PER CENT)	DETERIORATING (PER CENT)	DILAPIDATED (PER CENT)
White	6	12	3
Nonwhite	21	29	21

The situation regarding the quality of housing for Negroes has changed very little in the past twenty years. "In 1940, more than half of the dwelling units occupied by nonwhites were in such poor state of repair they constituted a menace to the structures and to the health of their inhabitants." The source of the housing problem for Kalamazoo's low-income Negroes has not changed much in the past twenty years either. In 1945 a citizens' committee reported that:

. . . local leaders interested in the housing problem claim that public housing has been opposed consistently and successfully by persons who have a genuine suspicion of government sponsored housing, or are protecting short run and often selfish interests in speculative and exploitative real estate ventures. Most of the families in low-income brackets live in jerry-built hand-me-down houses—structures constructed to turn a quick and substantial profit either by rental or sale. The comfort and health of occupants are secondary considerations. The hand-me-down houses were built for persons with adequate means

who later moved and are still moving to "better" sections of
the city or suburbs. These buildings, while often quite adequate for the original owners, are usually unfit to live in by the
time new tenants are ready to move in. Despite the deteriora-
tion, these houses demand more rent than single low-income
families can pay or, if purchased, cost more to maintain than
the new owners can afford.

In 1964 the local League of Women Voters reported that:

> Tabulation of assessed valuations in tract two showed evidence
> that there are people in Kalamazoo who own large amounts of
> property in rapidly deteriorating areas. Two men in particular
> each own at least twenty structures. They may own more than
> this, but this many have been identified. Other individuals own
> smaller numbers than this. One of these buildings has been
> divided into eight apartments; it brings the owner a gross rent
> of over $700 a month. In this house, one four-room apartment
> is rented by a woman with nine children, at $22 per week. Not
> all of these properties have been divided into this many apart-
> ments. However, even a conservative guess at total annual
> income from this source is staggering. As the assessed valua-
> tion on these properties goes down, the net income increases.
> These landlords, then, are profiting from the loss to the city,
> and the other taxpayers in other areas of the city are actually
> contributing to their profits.

In 1960 about one-half of the segregated Negro families
were paying rents equal to those in nearly every part of the city.
In the most residentially segregated tract the median gross rent
per month for all units was $62, but for nonwhite units only the
figure was $77 per month. The median gross monthly rent of all
renters in Kalamazoo was only $74.

From all indications the housing situation for Negroes, particularly those with limited economic resources, shows little
chance of improving. According to the League of Women Voters survey, "Negroes in Kalamazoo have a housing problem
which, while aggravated by the economic factor, is fundamen-
tally based on segregation."

In an effort to obtain detailed information regarding
discrimination in rental housing, the League's research staff tele-
phoned a number of owners who had advertised housing for
rent. In answer to the question, "Would you rent to Negroes?"
most of the owners were indefinite. In a sampling of twenty-two

completed calls, four said "yes," four "no," and fourteen were indefinite. Here are some sample replies:

YES:
I don't see why not.
It makes no difference to me.
NO:
I never have. I'm afraid you wouldn't be happy. A Negro asked about it a while back. He didn't want it as there were no other Negroes around. I think it is regrettable things are hard for you. I knew a clean Negro family. . . .
We wouldn't because the people downstairs are white. I don't know whether it would be congenial or not. You would have to use the same entrance. I don't know. We have another couple who looked at the apartment this morning. The other tenants have a little girl who doesn't know about Negroes. . . .
INDEFINITE:
Well, if I liked you. I guess so. I never rented to colored. I'm not against it, but we have no colored in the building. I don't know about the other tenants. I would show it to you. Your money is as good as theirs.
We have a family who is interested. But I see no reason not to. I'm checking the references of this other family. You could come and look at it. You could call back.
Well, this presents a problem. I myself have no objections but my neighbors . . . I believe that there is good and bad in everyone. I sell real estate, so I'm not prejudiced.
I don't think I should rent it to you but maybe I should take a look at you first. I'll check with my neighbors. . . . You have a big problem. . . .

These data notwithstanding, most residents define the housing problem primarily in class terms, although acknowledging that the situation is manifestly worse for low-income people who are Negro. Indeed, one Negro merchant thinks that the large proportion of indefinite responses which the League of Women Voters received is clear evidence that people in Kalamazoo do not discriminate on the basis of color, but on the basis of income:

If those people were going to discriminate, they wouldn't beat around the bush, they would have told them "no" flat-out. But they didn't. They want to know if you're a "nice" Negro, and what they mean is that they want to know if you're middle-class.

Other residents, both white and Negro, essentially share the same view. As a Negro housewife put it:

> They don't care what color you are, they just care about the color of your money. Anyone will rent to you if you have the money.

The new Michigan state constitution (1963) has a civil rights clause which forbids discrimination to even one tenant. A year ago a Negro schoolteacher filed a complaint with the Civil Rights Commission. The resultant publicity and attempts at settlement led to meetings with realtors and apartment owners who were made aware of the law and the penalties. Most large apartment managers now rent to Negroes because of this, but some set aside one building in the complex for Negro tenants and will rent one or two apartments to them. Moreover, there is some evidence that the ease with which middle- and upper-class Negroes are able to buy and rent homes outside of the Negro ghetto has changed in the past few years. According to one Negro upper-middle-class resident, there has been a substantial change regarding housing for Negroes:

> When we bought this place, we had all kinds of trouble. But just last month I was asked by a person, a Negro, who is going to be living in Kalamazoo to find an apartment for her and her son. I called and visited a number of places, and never did I get the impression that race was a factor. I was really happy to see how much this town has changed in just a few years. I don't mean that there aren't a few people who would refuse to sell or rent to Negroes, but I asked about fifteen different apartments and didn't have any difficulty.

Various members of organizations concerned with community relations are also in agreement regarding the increasing ease with which Negroes are able to purchase homes in Kalamazoo. As one of the community relations workers put it:

> There is no census tract area which does not have at least one Negro family. Realtors respond to the pressure of the green. In the last couple of years about thirty-five Negro families have moved into predominantly non-Negro areas. Well, at about $1,000 commission, that means about $35,000 for someone. . . . I think that if the Negroes have the money, they can live anywhere in the city they choose.

As a matter of fact, when Negro professionals arrive in Kalamazoo, they are usually specifically told that it is an integrated community and they are free to live anywhere in the city they choose. They are usually encouraged to live outside the Negro ghetto, thereby providing at least some token integration for the community. According to one of the community leaders:

> . . . the purchase and rental of housing for middle- and upper-income Negroes is generally unrestricted. The big problem ahead of us now to provide adequate housing for low-income families, and especially for low-income Negro families.

The general economic situation of Negroes in Kalamazoo is markedly worse than it is for whites. In 1959, for example, the median annual income of Negro families was about $2,000 less than it was for white families. Forty-six per cent of Kalamazoo's Negro families in that year earned less than $4,000 compared to 17 per cent for white families. The differential was greatest however in the $10,000-plus range. While nearly one out of five white families earned this amount or more, only one out of every twenty-six Negro families did. At the lower end of the income continuum one white family in fifty earned less than $1,000 compared to five in fifty among Negro families.

Whereas the unemployment rate for whites in 1960 was about 5 per cent, it was about 10 per cent for Negroes. In addition Negroes are most overrepresented in the low-income occupations: private household worker, service worker, and laborer. They are most underrepresented among sales workers. Similarly, Negroes are considerably overrepresented in occupations such as personal services, entertainment, recreation, and construction. According to a local resident:

> Factory employment did not open up to Negroes until rather recently. World War II had very little effect on changing long-time patterns of discrimination against Negroes.

This situation was frequently expressed by Kalamazoo's working-class Negroes. "We've got jobs," one man reported, "but we're all concentrated in the bottom and we're not moving up." Another semiskilled worker reported that "the requirements aren't the same across the board" when it comes to employment and promotion.

However, several people, particularly middle-class Negroes and whites engaged in social service and education, reported that employment opportunities for Negroes have improved noticeably in the past three or four years. Three years ago the NAACP picketed a white drug store in a Negro neighborhood that had never hired Negroes. This shocked the community into the realization that *nowhere* were Negroes visible as employees in any stores, offices, and only in very few factories. Employers suddenly became fearful of the NAACP and picket lines, and made a concerted effort to hire Negroes. Negroes responded by bringing their trade to these places. According to a local social worker, employers advertising for personnel now frequently identify themselves as "equal opportunity employers. They've found that it's smart to do it—it's good business, and more and more employers are doing it." Another person working in the social services pointed to the fact that one of the area's largest employers had only one Negro employee ten years ago, and not more than a dozen Negro employees as recently as five years ago; it now has

. . . agreed to take a select number of Negroes in at the bottom [*i.e.*, as janitors, etc.] and train them. Then, as they see people who are motivated, they will move them into better-paying jobs.

A number of people pointed out that the city police department is trying to hire Negro officers but without success. The city has only one or two Negro policemen at the present time. In fact, several whites in government and business referred to the difficulty in getting Negroes to apply as police officers as strong evidence of the fact that the community employment for Negroes is available on a nondiscriminatory basis. Moreover, they argue, this also illustrates the fact that the employment problems of Negroes in Kalamazoo are primarily

. . . the fault of the Negroes themselves. I think that the fact that you can't get them to apply means that they are either not qualified or not motivated. I don't know which. But I do know that it's not because of discrimination on the part of the city.

Other community leaders reported that they had personal knowledge that various members of the city government had honestly tried to get Negro applicants. According to one respondent:

> Not only were the positions advertised in the usual source, but several of us called Negro acquaintances and asked them if they knew of people we could contact. Nothing. We still haven't got anyone.

One Negro leader, commenting on Negro-white relations in general, and the attempt to solicit Negro applicants for the police department in particular, remarked:

> They think that every time a job comes along, the Negro is going to jump at the chance. They always act as if they're doing you some special kind of favor. No Negro is going to be a cop, not now anyway. . . . Every day he hears of police brutality somewhere, and if he takes the job, he knows that he's selling out his people.

One local businessman, active in organizations concerned with bettering the life of Kalamazoo's Negroes, reported that he recently had a job opening and attempted to hire a Negro for the position, but with no success.

> It wasn't the world's best job, but it was steady and paid about forty bucks a week. If a guy wasn't married it wouldn't have been such a bad job. The only qualifications were that he would have to be a high school graduate and couldn't have a police record. I thought that if I could get some young guy, he could work around here for a year or two and get some experience at holding a job, and then I would help him try and get on the police force. Well, I called a number of Negroes and asked them to get me someone. After about a week, I called them back and they told me that they didn't know of anyone with the qualifications who was not employed.

—————•—————

Education in Kalamazoo

By and large, the people of Kalamazoo are quite proud of their public schools. They describe the school administration as progressive and competent, the members of the school board as dedicated, and the professional quality of the instructional staff as very high. Kalamazoo, for example, was the first district in the state to provide a public school for trainable mentally retarded children. In recent years the public school system has won national recognition. It was selected by the National Joint Council on Economic Education as one of the ten pilot systems for the development of economic education, and the *Woman's Home Companion* cited Kalamazoo as one of the "Top Nine Cities" in the nation doing the most to house its schoolchildren properly.

The first public school in Kalamazoo was opened in 1833, and the first school building which provided both primary and secondary education was opened before the Civil War. At the turn of the century there were nine public schools in Kalamazoo, with a combined enrollment of more than three thousand students. By 1903 a full music program was offered without special fees; kindergarten, manual training, and home economics were a permanent part of the curriculum; in-service classes for teachers, special education classes for the deaf, and night-school for adults were a regular part of the public school program.

The increase in population and a series of annexations in the 1950s greatly spurred building expansion following the Second World War, and from 1950 to 1960 the school district enrollment doubled. In 1945 there were only twelve school buildings in the system; today there are thirty-nine. Currently the school district population is approximately a hundred thousand and there are between eighteen thousand and nineteen thousand students enrolled in the Kalamazoo Public School System, in twenty-nine elementary, five junior high, two senior high, and three special education schools.

Kalamazoo is also the home for three institutions of higher learning: a small liberal arts college with a national reputation, a Roman Catholic girls' college, and a large state university, which offers bachelor's, master's, and doctoral degree programs. There are also three parochial school systems in Kalamazoo, two operated by Protestant denominations and another operated by the Roman Catholic Church.

All of Kalamazoo's public school teachers are required to hold a four- or five-year degree from an accredited college or university and a state teacher's certificate. Moreover, 44 per cent have master's degrees. Teachers are recruited almost entirely from states in the Midwest. According to a source close to the superintendent of the system, Kalamazoo has about a hundred positions for the coming year, and about fourteen hundred preliminary applications for these positions.

Most residents of Kalamazoo are convinced that the public school system is fully committed to equal education for all. Members of the school administration point out, for example, that the Kalamazoo school system won national recognition for its public pronouncement on equal educational opportunities "before the civil rights movement was fashionable." In 1947 the board of education pledged its "educational resources to the imperative of building a peaceful world by teaching and practicing democratic human relations in the schools." To this end, the board affirmed the following general policies:

(1) The promotion of unity and understanding among all peoples of all kinds, so that they may live and work together harmoniously.

(2) The development of awareness of the interdependence of all peoples of the earth, and the instilling in mankind of the urgency and responsibility for working for a decent life for all.

(3) The encouragement of educational practices designed to eliminate evils and contradictions in our social, economic, and cultural life.

(4) The provision of opportunity for all to participate in the democratic process, so that man's opportunity shall be based solely upon his character, competence, and training.

Specifically, the statement continued, the board of education shall attempt to carry out these aims:

(1) by continuing its policy of choosing all personnel on the basis of character, competence, and training, without regard to color, creed, or national origin;

(2) by continuing its policy of having each child attend the school provided for in the district in which he lives;

(3) by encouraging the establishment of a program of in-service training of teachers, directed, in part, toward the assimilation and implementation of these aims;

(4) by providing increased opportunities for adult education in each school neighborhood;

(5) by assuring that all activities and facilities shall continue to be open to all children.

Children in all grades shall be given the opportunity to develop an understanding and respect for democratic ideals by practicing in day-to-day living principles of cooperation, fair play, acceptance of personal and social responsibilities, and respect for the rights and properties of others.

Teachers (meaning all employees—principals, supervisors, and teachers—who have concern for the instructional program in the Kalamazoo public schools) in all grades shall be concerned with the maximum development of all children:

(1) by encouraging equal opportunities for participation in school activities;

(2) by seeking to understand the causes of emotional disturbances;

(3) by helping children to develop a wholesome respect for self;

(4) by helping boys and girls to distinguish between fact and propaganda, between truths and half-truths, particularly in the field of human relations, and to use these new findings to bind our peoples more closely together in mutual understanding, appreciation, and opportunity;

(5) by building, in the classroom, attitudes of respect, good will, and concern for the welfare of all;

(6) by giving consideration in the classroom to the problems, rights, and responsibilities of all people in the school, community, and world;

(7) by participating in community groups which are actively engaged in promoting better understanding among people, and in the consideration of solution of social and economic problems;

(8) by acquiring a richer background in anthropology, sociology, and social psychology;

(9) by critically re-examining their own practices in the light of tested principles of human relations.

Nevertheless, Negro youth experience some difficulties in attempting to obtain a full and complete education. Most community residents, school officials, and teachers are quick to point out that the problems which besiege the low-income Negro are more familiar to the low-income white than they are to the middle- or upper-income Negro. Most residents, teachers, parents, community leaders, and school officials believe that the difficulties of some Negro students in acquiring an education is due primarily to the inadequacies of the Negro population, or more correctly, to the inadequacies of low-income people who are also Negro, because, as one man put it, "if you're poor you're a nigger, but if you're rich you're only a Negro." According to one teacher:

> There are three main kinds of kids that we get. There is the middle-class student, the poor whites, and the poor Negro. Whichever group the person falls in makes a difference, I think, on how the teacher treats him.

It is significant that this teacher perceives awareness of race differences among the lower class, but not among the middle class. Nonetheless, most of the teachers believe that there are only two main types of students, those who are poor and those who are not. The story of the "vicious circle" of troubles which plague the lower-class child is legend, its followers legion among the instructional staff of the Kalamazoo public school system.

In addition to the "lack of motivation," "home problems," and other such reasons which account for a differential educational experience in the public school system, community residents also discuss the impact of the pattern of residential segregation (again a manifest difference depending on one's economic-class position) and economic discrimination. Last of all, and to a very minor degree, the prejudice of teachers and the official policy of the board and administration of the public school system are mentioned as reasons for differential treatment. Although most of the teachers and school officials agree that the system harbors, albeit involuntarily, some teachers who are prejudiced against Negroes, many are of the opinion that the school administration has transferred staff members from one school to another to ensure that Negro students would not have teachers who might discriminate against them. One local leader alleges to have personal information that the school administration has in fact quietly removed teachers from the system who were prejudiced and/or discriminated against Negroes.

Although several teachers reported encountering a colleague who was prejudiced or knowing of an incident of racial discrimination, many regard this state of affairs as inevitable and often naïvely unintentioned. According to one Negro teacher:

> Many of the teachers who fail to teach the Negro student fail for the most unintentional reasons and they're surprised to find out that they've been doing something wrong. For instance, a lot of the Negro students are way behind in abstract perception,

and if you point it out to teachers they usually try and do something about it, but most of them have never even thought about it.

On the other hand a large number of teachers in the system, particularly the younger teachers, are unequivocally fair in their treatment of students, and many parents, teachers, and school officials are aware of this.

The consequence of residential segregation for the racial composition in the public schools in quite clear since school attendance in Kalamazoo is based on residence. In 1945, for example, Negro children were enrolled in all the public schools in Kalamazoo, although the number ranged from one each at two suburban schools, to 175 at Lincoln Elementary and Junior High School, where the concentration of Negroes was the greatest (17 per cent). In the fall of 1947 two of the twenty public schools had no Negro students. Ten years later there were twenty-six schools in the system of which eight were all-white. In the spring of 1959 nearly one-half (43 per cent) of the thirty-five public schools did not have a single Negro student enrolled. In point of fact, 94 per cent of all Negro elementary and junior high school students in 1959 attended just six schools.

Although a deliberate effort was made to obtain accurate and detailed information regarding the racial composition of Kalamazoo public schools from 1940 to present, the effort was only partially successful. According to two high-ranking school officials, the school administration does not have and has never had information regarding the proportion in any year of Negro students in any of the public schools. One of the officials has been an employee of the Kalamazoo public school system for more than twenty years, and he contended that he had never seen any data regarding the racial composition of schools. However, previous reports (1945 and 1957) about the education and employment of Negroes in Kalamazoo included a count of Negroes in each of the schools. Through the cooperation of one of the community leaders a copy of a table entitled "Number of Negro Children Enrolled in Kalamazoo Schools by School Communities for the Years 1945, 1947, 1951, 1957, and 1959" was made available for discussion in this report. The table, prepared by a former director of the Department of Research and Pupil

Personnel of the Kalamazoo Public School System, shows how the racial composition of the public schools had changed over time.

Lincoln Elementary and Junior High School, which was 17 per cent Negro in 1945 and 21 per cent Negro as recently as 1951, was 55 per cent Negro in 1957 and approximately 68 per cent Negro in 1959. According to the estimates of teachers, social workers, school officials, local town officials, and other community residents, Lincoln Elementary School is now approximately 85 to 95 per cent Negro. As a white community leader acknowledged, "We've got *de facto* segregation at Lincoln School and there's no sense in pretending we don't."

Although Lincoln Elementary School did not become predominantly Negro until the last ten years, it should be pointed out that it has always been "the Negro school." That is, according to available information, Lincoln educated between 54 and 61 per cent of the Negro elementary and junior high school students, at least from 1945 to 1959.

Since 1959 four elementary schools, two primary schools, one senior high school, and one school for the mentally handicapped have been added to the public school system. Also during this period two elementary schools were subducted as well as junior high programs at two other schools. These changes reflect primarily annexation and the changing population composition. As one would expect, all of the additional schools are in the suburban and outlying areas, while the subductions were in areas nearer the center of the city with relatively declining populations.

The most significant of these changes was the elimination of the junior high program at Lincoln School, since the student body was predominantly Negro and since most of the community residents interpret this change as a deliberate attempt by the school administration to desegregate. In the spring of 1963 the Kalamazoo board of education appointed a citizens committee to study the educational housing needs of the Kalamazoo public school system. Following their investigation, this committee recommended, among other things, that the junior high school program at Lincoln be discontinued and that students be transferred to adjacent junior high schools where space was available. The

committee reported that there were various "unfavorable conditions regarding the junior high situation at Lincoln" which necessitated its recommendation:

> In the first place, Lincoln has by far the smallest enrollment.
> Last year [1962–1963] only 314 students were enrolled. It can-
> not accommodate any more students because the elementary
> school is also housed in the same building. This restricts the de-
> velopment of both the elementary and junior high programs,
> and frequently results in competition for space. The housing
> of elementary and junior high students in the same building is
> not educationally desirable. It has, in fact, been discontinued
> at all other junior high schools except Hillside, where the hous-
> ing of a primary unit is a temporary expedient.
>
> Because of the limited enrollment, the educational program
> is restricted and below the standards which exist at all other
> junior high schools. Library facilities are limited and are shared
> with the elementary school. There is no foreign-language pro-
> gram. Offerings in mathematics are extremely limited. Ninth-
> grade algebra is not available every year. The number of elec-
> tive subjects is also limited. There is only one counselor for the
> entire student population. This should not be so in an area
> where counseling is greatly needed. A counselor who is unsuc-
> cessful in helping certain individual students cannot refer them
> to another with whom they may be more compatible. In this
> age of technological and scientific development, the Citizens
> Committee believes very strongly that no student in the district
> should be prevented from obtaining a balanced education by
> being deprived of the opportunity to elect courses in any area
> including those of mathematics, science and languages.
>
> Lincoln is the only junior high school without cafeteria
> facilities—an area where perhaps they are needed the most.
> The playground is too small and is shared with the elementary
> school, creating an undesirable situation.
>
> The Citizens Committee is, therefore, convinced that the
> students attending Lincoln Junior High School, do not and
> cannot under existing conditions receive an adequate junior
> high school education.

The committee therefore recommended that the junior high
school program at Lincoln be discontinued and that the board of
education "consider the use of the present junior high facilities
for such purposes as special education, nursery school, adult education, and the Community School Program." The committee's
recommendations were accepted.

Although it is not mentioned in the official documents regarding the discontinuance of the junior high program at Lin-

coln, the racial composition of the school played a large part in the decision. As a leading member of the study committee acknowledged privately:

> The fact that Lincoln was a segregated school was in the minds of all of us. We saw here an opportunity to provide a more efficient school program and at the same time to "nip segregation in the bud."

Other residents, teachers, parents, school board members, and officials of the school administration also indicated that while race was not mentioned in the official report, it was an important deciding factor. Many Negroes are of the opinion that race was not mentioned in the official report because the community did not want to acknowledge the fact that it had a segregated school. On the other hand, most white community leaders believe that the reasoning was more practical than that. It was thought that since the change could be legitimized on the basis of money and the quality of education, there was little reason to mention the race factor and thereby take a chance of eliciting a reaction from whites who might contend that the system was "favoring" Negroes. All these reasons were probably involved in the decision and the white community leaders and school administration were and still are quite careful in their handling of the race issue in fear of polarizing community opinion. While this is sound conservative politics, it seems unnecessarily timid for a community like Kalamazoo and is viewed as hypocrisy among many Negroes.

The decision to end the junior high program at Lincoln school did not meet with universal approval. As one school official reported:

> The closing of the program at Lincoln was not a happy day for us. We had to work hard to convince several people that it was the best thing.

Other residents confirmed the fact that there was some disagreement about the decision. Initially some teachers and some social service workers in the area, most of them Negroes, were opposed to the plan. To some extent it seems that their lack of support was an indication of their displeasure over what they term the "paternalism of the power structure." According to one Negro leader:

They don't understand that you do with, not for. They always call us up, very politely, and inform us what they are going to do for us. There's never any discussion. Sure, they always have some Negroes on their committees, but they always pick those who won't rock the boat.

For the most part, however, the initial lack of support by some Negroes was because of their concern for the possible consequences that the change would have for the Negro students and their families. Although a few Negro families would prefer "the old way," most of the community leaders, both white and Negro, are convinced that in the long-run view, the phasing-out of Lincoln was the only thing the school board could do.

Nevertheless, the change has imposed a number of hardships upon some of the Negro students and their families. According to one of the social workers in the Negro ghetto, "many parents were opposed to the desegregation of Lincoln." First of all, since cafeteria facilities were not provided at Lincoln, it meant that the children usually went home for lunch. Now that they would be attending a junior high school outside of the neighborhood, it meant that distance would require them to take lunch at the school. At just thirty cents a day, this would mean $1.50 per week per child.

Many parents also foresaw problems regarding transportation: "Most of the students were going to be transferred to junior high schools, which would mean a forty-minute walk or they have to get motor transportation." Although school administrators made arrangements with the local bus service to provide transportation from the Lincoln School area to new junior high schools, this solution has been less than satisfactory. For one thing, local bus service costs fifteen cents for a one-way ride, which means thirty cents per day per child, or $1.50 per week. Thus, the change means approximately $3 per week per child, and many families have to provide for more than one child. Moreover, these are the families who have the lowest average annual income of all city residents. Although the school administration has some money for "hardship cases," and most of that money is used by these families, the amount and coverage are woefully inadequate and do little to offset the additional burden for most families.

A social worker who spends a good deal of time with the Negro junior high students from low-income families believes that another consequence has been an increase of absenteeism because of the transportation problems:

> A lot of the kids from this area have to walk and many of them don't have boots. Because of the distance, they sometimes get to school a few minutes late, and many of the kids have told me that they would rather not go to school at all if they have to go in late. It's always embarrassing, of course, if you come in late, and most of these kids don't have clothes which are as nice as some of the other kids' and it makes them feel all the more self-conscious. At Lincoln there wasn't much of a difference between what you and the other guy wore because his folks were poor too.
>
> If they do walk and get to school late, and they don't have an excuse, they have to go back home and get one, so most of the kids, if they think that they're going to be late, just don't go.

Some of the Lincoln Elementary area residents thought that the school system should have provided free transportation for students, but the Kalamazoo system is not a busing system, and according to a school official, if they provide transportation for some of the students, they have to provide transportation for all students, and present operating funds aren't adequate. One school official also pointed out that many other students travel even greater distances to school, and no special transportation arrangements are made for them. For the most part these other students are from middle-class homes where sufficient money is available to provide public transportation for the schoolchildren without hindering the family budget, and where private transportation is more readily available. Although the school system provides special arrangements for students who are physically handicapped, it does not provide special arrangements for those who are socially and economically handicapped. "People," Michael Harrington once wrote, "who are much too sensitive to demand of cripples that they run races ask of the poor that they get up and act just like everyone else in the society. The poor are not just like everyone else."

Some people think that the difficulties regarding the need for extra money and transportation were the proper responsibility of the Negro parents themselves, and that had they wanted to, they could have solved the problem. The Negro president of one of the local organizations concerned with equal rights for all people of Kalamazoo argues:

> One of the problems that parents in the area had when they phased out Lincoln Junior High was transportation for the kids; but they didn't band together and put on cookie sales or anything to raise money. They left it for someone else to do.

A number of people indicated that "some of the parents didn't want their kids to compete with whites." Another, more prevalent concern was that although the formal educational opportunities would be improved by transferring the students, the net result might be a less meaningful educational experience because of a change in the opportunity to participate in the non-academic social activities. Teachers vary in their evaluation of the extent to which Negro students formerly of Lincoln participate in extracurricular activities, but by and large Negro and white teachers who have taught or are teaching in schools which are more than 5 per cent Negro, report that the junior high school change has meant that Negro students do in fact participate less in non-academic events, with the possible exception of the participation of boys in sports events. They also indicated that

> A few students whose parents have cars participate more in activities like the science club, but for the most part, they have less chance than they did at Lincoln to be in the social affairs at their school.

Since many of the social activities, club meetings, etc., are held "after school," students who live outside the area and whose parents do not own cars are seriously disadvantaged. Whereas the public bus is available to provide transportation immediately after school, it is not available when other school events end at a later hour. Social activities held at night and on weekends present similar difficulties for Negro students who live in the ghetto.

Size is another factor which contributes to the more limited social participation of Negro students in the "new" junior high schools. Lincoln Junior High had an enrollment of approximately three hundred students, whereas the school which most of the students from Lincoln now attend has an enrollment of approximately a thousand students. Although there are more activities with slightly larger memberships available, most social organizations have a limit on membership—a football team still has eleven members—consequently fewer Negro students now participate in extracurricular activities than was the case at Lincoln.

Another reason that some parents and teachers were dismayed about the discontinuance of the junior high school program at Lincoln was that, according to one observer, "there was a good deal of community pride in the school and most people thought that the school board had worked hard to make it good." For example, one parent thought that "Lincoln was the top school athletically and academically." Several people pointed out that Lincoln consistently won athletic championships in the city. Many people also stated a preference for the neighborhood school. One parent who was against the move noted that the main basis of his objection was the change in the teaching staff:

> At Lincoln many parents knew several of the teachers on a personal basis and the teachers would go out of their way to let you know how Johnny was doing. If your kid wasn't doing his work, the teacher would stop around the house and let you know.

Although most of the teaching staff of Lincoln Junior High "transferred" to the same schools as the students, most of the staff at the three schools where students from Lincoln Elementary attend junior high school were new not only to the students but also to the parents. Moreover, the parents viewed the teaching faculty at these "new" schools as predominantly white, middle-class, and insensitive to the problems of their children, if not outright prejudiced. Another parent remarked:

> The teachers at Lincoln knew the parents and spent time outside of school hours visiting families and trying to encourage the kids. The parents knew the teachers and felt easy dealing with them. Negro teachers do more than just teach.

However, with the exception of some parents—especially those with low incomes—most of the community residents now view the termination of the junior high program at Lincoln School as a "positive step in the right direction." The upper and middle classes see it as a conscious attempt to end *de facto* segregation. Several people emphasize the positive effect the change has had on the elementary program at Lincoln in terms of increased space, lack of competition for the playground area, etc. Others refer to the fact that these students from low-income families are being exposed to the larger community for the first time. One teacher reported to me that he still keeps in touch with some of his former students and that "all of the kids that I knew at Lincoln that moved to South are doing fairly well. At least they seem to have more self-confidence." Similarly, the change has also exposed some teachers to the larger community. One Negro teacher commented that when the school administration first announced that the Lincoln students would attend other junior high schools, there was much anxiety and discussion among the teaching staff at one of the junior high schools where the teachers had not had very much experience with Negroes as students:

> There was real panic out there. So they had a few of us go out and give a short talk under the guise of talking about the students, although it turned out to be a discussion of the teacher's attitudes and feeling—which is what it should have been in the first place. Anytime a middle-class-oriented person teaches a lower-class student, there is a real need for an orientation program.

Most white community leaders and some of the Negro leaders point to the discontinuance of the junior high program at Lincoln as another indication of the school system's commitment to provide an equal education for all students. This move toward desegregation was not, they emphasize, requested by the parents, the teachers, or any civil rights organization, but was voluntarily initiated by the school administration.

At the present time there are five high schools in Kalamazoo. Two of these are parochial schools, two are part of the public school system, and the fifth is a state-supported campus school attached to the university. The parochial schools do not have and never have had a significant number of Negro students. From all reports this is entirely a function of the religious composition of the community.

Similarly University High, the campus school, has had only a very few Negro pupils. University High, which is now being

phased out of existence, has primarily been a private preparatory school for the children of the upper-class. According to at
least one resident, the major reason that University High is
being eliminated is that the board of trustees regard it as more of
a private prep school than a training facility for the university's
College of Education. The school's almost exclusively upper-
class clientele is a function of a number of factors. First, the
school used to take faculty children tuition-free, which meant
that a sizable portion of the student body were children of university professors. Secondly, there has been a widespread belief
that the instruction at the school was better than average, which
encouraged parents of professional families to send their children there. Third, University High has a nominal tuition fee,
which although not large, has prohibited a number of children,
particularly lower-class children, from attending. In addition,
the school has given priority to applicants whose relatives have
attended the school. These policies have tended to produce
graduates from middle- and upper-income families. Therefore, although the school has never had a formal policy of discriminating on the basis of race, discrimination on the basis of class, as
most students of American race relations know, is frequently just
as consequential as discrimination on the basis of race. It is
sufficient to note, perhaps, that a handful of Negroes have attended University High, and that almost without exception they
have been children of the "better" Negro families.

Consequently, all but a small handful of Negro students
have been dependent on the public school system for their high
school education. Moreover, one of the two public high schools
is only five years old and is situated at the southern edge of the
city in a predominantly, indeed exclusively, white middle- and
upper-class area. Although there are five high schools in the
community, there is only one high school for approximately 95
per cent of the Negro youth.

There was considerable community discussion regarding
the site for the new high school. Some members of the Negro
community thought that the site was selected deliberately to exclude Negro students. Other residents pointed out that the site of
the new school was in a relatively undeveloped area and, in fact,
excluded everyone. It seems that the school system wanted to
build a campus-type school and owned property which, in-

cidentally, was outside both the city limit and the school district. The campus-type school requires considerable space, and since this land was available and since much of the community's growth had been to the south, the present site was selected. At the present time there is a citizens' committee to investigate the need and possible site for a third high school. It was the consensus of the community leaders that the site for the next high school will more than likely be in the western part of the city, which means that if the present pattern of residential segregation is maintained, the new high school will be a facility for only white students.

Many members of the Negro community are just as concerned about the racial composition of the instructional staff as they are about the racial composition of the student body. It is noteworthy that the first Negro teacher in the Kalamazoo school system was not hired until 1945. At the time when the board pledged itself to "continue its policy of choosing all personnel on the basis of character, competence, and training, without regard to color," there were only two Negro teachers in the system. In 1957 there were eight Negro teachers in the public schools; today there are approximately twenty to twenty-five Negroes employed as teachers, counselors, specialists, and administrative personnel (about 2 per cent of all employees in these classifications). Almost all of the Negro community leaders believe that the school administration has made substantial improvement in employment practices in the past few years, and all believe that the school administration should continue and speed up this process in the coming years.

Several Negro leaders contend that the school administration is even more discriminatory in regard to employment of Negroes in such non-academic positions as secretaries, boilermen, etc. Many Negro parents and teachers are also disgruntled about the lack of Negroes in administrative positions and the lack of Negro counselors. Part of this is a result of the mobility patterns of the system. Among most teachers in the system, the "better jobs" are the non-teaching jobs, such as assistant principal, principal, counselor, and various special auxiliary positions. The present superintendent is a former assistant superintendent, former principal, former department head, and former classroom teacher. Virtually all of the school principals and assistant principals are former teachers, as are many of the counselors. At the present time there are two Negro counselors and two Negroes in administration, and they are all former classroom teachers in the Kalamazoo public school system.

Benign Paternalism

At the present time the school administration seems to be working deliberately to obtain a more equitable distribution of education for Kalamazoo's youth. "The school administration," one man testified, "is particularly sensitive to the needs of Lincoln School and has worked hard to get good instruction there." According to a social worker:

> Most of the parents think their kids are getting a good education at Lincoln. They have a pretty good special education department and they are trying to lower the student-teacher ratio, which is already lower than it is for most schools.

Moreover, most of the teachers at Lincoln are "volunteer teachers," that is, teachers who asked specifically to be assigned to Lincoln, and consequently, "the morale of teachers at Lincoln School is very high and the administration is continually trying to provide the best for the special needs of students there." As one longtime teacher remarked, "every effort has been made to bring the best possible education to Lincoln School."

Yet according to parents, teachers, and high-ranking officials in the school administration, the student body at Lincoln is at least 85 percent Negro, and one or two other elementary schools in the area are also reputed to be 50 percent Negro or more.

Most of Kalamazoo's residents, both white and Negro, are not especially concerned about the segregation at Lincoln Elementary School. One white community leader who has long been active in the fight against discrimination expressed the position of many when he said:

If you can end *de facto* segregation and improve the quality of education, then I'm all for it. If, on the other hand, you end *de facto* segregation and the quality of education isn't improved, then I lose my enthusiasm.

He and many of his neighbors are of the opinion that the former is not very likely. They are quick to point out, for example, that the school administration has successfully lowered the student-teacher ratio at the school and that they are continually spending time, money, and energy to maintain high standards there. At the present time the school system is in the process of using some three to four hundred thousand dollars of federal funds, and most of this money is being used to improve the quality of education at schools with high proportions of the student body from low-income families, and in Kalamazoo that means schools with high Negro enrollments. According to one high-ranking school official, "It costs more to educate a pupil at Lincoln School than it does at any other elementary school." Still other community leaders argue that:

It's not the school board's job to do everything—they didn't create the ghetto-like condition. They can only go so far and then it's out of their hands.

The question which continues to face Kalamazoo is, How much more is the community willing to spend to maintain a segregated school? "I maintain," said one Negro teacher, "that anytime you've got segregation, you've got inferior education."

The future of Kalamazoo will bring continued attempts by perennial community organizations—like the League of Women Voters, the Board of Community Relations, the National Association for the Advancement of Colored People, the Human Relations Council, the Big Brothers, the Jaycees, the Labor Council, the Human Relations Committee of the Regional Association of Social Workers, the American Association of University Women, the Council for Civic Responsibility, the Social Services Council, the Neighborhood Improvement Association, the Area Council on Civic Affairs, the Council of Churches, the Human Rights Committees of the Democratic and Republican parties, the City Education Association, the Interfaith Council and on and on and on and on and on—to end discrimination in all phases of community life.

Yet these organizations have worked hard in the past to eliminate discrimination. Even if they are necessary for the elimination of discrimination, they are clearly not sufficient. In fact, for the most part, these organizations tend to be token affairs at best. Rather than changing the community patterns of segregation, they tend to solidify the status quo by acting as escape routes for the "white man's guilt and the black man's shame." They tend to discourage support for spontaneous grass-roots attempts to address the problems effectively because their very existence suggests that "something is already being done." These organizations serve as means for the community leaders to control the situation since they acknowledge the legitimacy of conventional middle-class processes of social change. And they are all incapable of making any consequential alteration in the situation because, if nothing else, they lack the intellectual radicalism to see the problem as a complex, many-sided one. They all persistently view the problem in the narrow paternalistic perspective which defines the problem as "The Negro Problem."

The changes which have occurred in employment patterns and in housing have come about as the result of overt acts (picketing and filing of complaints) by members of Kalamazoo's Negro community. Until these pressures were brought, the whites had gone on for years believing that "our" Negroes were well treated and had no major complaints. The uproar arising from Negro demands illustrates how complacent the white community has been.

Gradual change is taking place in Kalamazoo race relations —too much change to suit a few, too little change and too slowly to satisfy others. Change will undoubtedly continue to occur, and its rate will be heightened by the increasing activity and more efficient organization of the Negro community.

VII

Chicago Voices:
Tales Told Out of School

———•———

Charles and Bonnie Remsberg

The young teacher pushed open the door of his elementary school building north of Chicago's Loop and stood for a moment surveying the setting as big flakes of snow melted into his blond hair. There probably never was much formal education accomplished in this neighborhood, he speculated.

Back in the dry and lawless years when Prohibition gang wars put Chicago on the map, this was the alcohol cooking belt. The intersection where now his school stands then was called Death Corner. Forty-two lives were rubbed out here by the Sicilian Black Hand in one eighteen-month bloodbath. The assassins thoughtfully posted the names of their intended victims on an old elm tree so the prospective widows could plan ahead.

All are gone now—the nickname, the tree, the immigrants' boozy shacks, the immigrants themselves. Even one of the street names has been changed, as if to erase its tarnished past forever. Around the school now rise huge public housing skyscrapers, crowded with Negroes and a few Puerto Ricans.

But in the teacher's mind, death still frequents the old intersection—in another form. With a gesture to the stark projects, he said, "Education is life to many of these children. Without it their lives are just as dead as if you cut them down with machine guns or put them to death in a gas chamber. Already we are putting to death thousands of children. There are people here climbing to the tops of their professional careers over the dead educations of children."

This sentiment, phrased in dozens of different ways, became a familiar refrain to us as we moved across the Windy City with a tape recorder, listening to teachers talk about their schools, their problems and their expectations.

It is, perhaps, not surprising to hear it said of the Negro ghetto. As education writer Bernard Asbell has pointed out:

Schools in the central sections of our major cities [including Chicago] are factories of failure . . . The slum child is a child of another world. Our laws do not bind him, our standard middle-class ambitions do not inspire him, our IQ tests do not measure him, and most of all, his teacher is not reaching him. Rules she learned in teachers college clearly don't work in the slum school, but she clings to them, for no one has taught her different rules. Teachers in first to third grades feel the child slipping away. By the fourth grade he has fallen behind. By the eighth grade he may be as many as three years back, his mind closed, his behavior rebellious. By high school age, he is more than likely a dropout, headed for chronic failure.

But in Chicago we heard the despairing quote echoed about "good" schools on the white fringe of the city, as well as schools in the black inner city. Even a member of the city's board of education in submitting his resignation last March [1966] referred to the "tragic consequences for *all* our children" in the way Chicago runs its schools.

In short, the Chicago school system—some 570,000 students and 22,000 teachers in about 600 schools—presents a striking case study of the chain reaction of urban decay and neglect. It demonstrates that the deficiencies that germinate in the ghetto, often fertilized there by segregation and prejudice, spread in time like a strangling vine through the rest of the city; a system that permits some children to be written off finds eventually that it cannot control this negligence. Thus, teachers told us about a Negro school where a white principal refused to permit a white teacher to conduct a special tutoring program, with the observation: "Remember, these children are Negroes first and students second"; a white school where teachers turn up the heat so students will go to sleep in their seats and thus not present a discipline problem; a Negro school where students were arbitrarily put into classes for the mentally retarded—without testing—including one child with a 131 IQ; a white school where severely emotionally disturbed children were allowed to remain in regular classes, making teaching impossible; a Negro school where children are forced to watch TV all day while their teacher stands at the back of the classroom with a ruler to enforce discipline; a white school where an elementary-grade class had eight different teachers within a single term.

This is not to say, of course, that all Chicago schools share equal quality, or lack of it. For reasons explored in detail in the interviews which comprise the bulk of this report, the 42 per cent of students in Chicago schools who are white, generally, at this point in time, still experience better education than Negroes generally, although isolated Negro schools are considered superior to many white schools and there are important gradations within each group. But to a growing number of observers, *all* local schools, white and colored, are inferior to what should be expected in the city that is second in size and importance in the world's richest nation. As one college professor puts it, "I have taught hundreds of white graduates of Chicago high schools, and my conclusion is that the whites receive a second-rate education while the Negroes receive a third-rate one."

In this context, then, integration as a means of raising Negro education to the present level of the whites' is no longer the ultimate goal of many advocates of change. They are interested uppermost in improving quality, and integration is seen as but one step in lifting the education of all Chicago children higher than its present level and in preventing the education of any from dropping lower.

In Chicago, where the schools are among the most segregated in the nation, successful integration of classrooms would require more than a declaration by the board of education that it be done. The present pattern of segregation in the schools, like the matter of quality, is shaped by a multiplicity of influences. These too are probed in our interviews. As a prelude, however, let us look briefly at some of the basics about the city and its school system which pertain to the problems at hand.

Chicago, an industrial giant of 3.5 million people, sprawling for twenty-eight miles along the Lake Michigan shore midway between the coal beds of the East and the ore veins of the West, on the edge of the nation's rich agricultural belt, has long suffered a certain defensive embarrassment about being the nation's second city. New York flaunts its size, its culture, its sophistication, its international savoir-faire; Chicago has often been regarded as a gangster-ridden, corruption-riddled, shirtsleeves-and-undershirt hick town. However, in four respects all germane to its school problems, as we shall see, Chicago has no equals:

1. It headquarters the nation's most populous Roman Catholic archdiocese and boasts a majority Catholic population consisting mostly of Polish, German and Irish descent;

2. It has the world's largest public-housing project, a monument of sorts to its 700,000 citizens who have been termed "poor" by representatives of the federal anti-poverty program;

3. On its South Side is the densest concentration of Negroes on earth, a ghetto that is slowly expanding while the city's white population is dwindling annually;

4. Its schools were first in the nation to be boycotted by civil rights groups protesting segregation and discrimination in the North.

Negroes have been a part of Chicago's history almost from the beginning. In the 1790s after French explorers opened up the swampy, garlic-dotted Indian shoreland, a Santo Domingo Negro, Jean Baptiste Pointe DuSable, built a trading post where the city later rose. Before the Civil War, Chicago was a terminal point for the underground railroad. And as the nation hurtled toward World War I, city fathers literally begged Negroes to move in. The high wartime demand and the sudden end of European immigration left Chicago's industries hungry for labor. Recruiters zig-zagged through the rural South, promising cotton choppers and river rats finer living conditions and better jobs if they came North. Negroes responded by the thousands. By 1920, Chicago's Negro population had leaped 150 per cent—to nearly 110,000, or four out of every 100 residents.

Before this great influx, Negroes had been scattered over the city in a number of small settlements. More than half lived outside the South Side's then small black ghetto, and as a whole they were less segregated than some of the clannish Eastern European ethnic groups. But the transplants from the South, insecure in an urban environment and filled with Southern-bred apprehensions about whites, flocked largely to the ghetto, and white pressure groups moved quickly to see that they and all future arrivals remained there.

In 1917, a committee of the Chicago Real Estate Board laid down a basic policy on segregated housing: "The old [Negro] districts are overflowing and new territory must be furnished . . . In the interests of all, each block shall be filled solidly and further expansion shall be confined to contiguous blocks . . . The present method of [Negroes] obtaining a single building in scattered blocks [shall] be discontinued. Promiscuous sales and leases here and there mean an unwarranted and unjustifiable destruction of values." This pattern persists today.

From July 1, 1917, to March 1, 1921, according to the Chicago Urban League, "Chicago enforced racial segregation in housing by systematically bombing an average of one home every twenty days. Some of these bombed homes belonged to Negroes outside the ghetto, others belonged to whites who had sold to Negroes, or said they would, or helped Negroes buy a home." Also in this period, the city found time for its worst race riot—twenty-two Negroes and sixteen whites were slain. Arrests were made in breaking up the melee, but only one arrest—and no conviction—was made in the bombings, although Negroes were warned in advance where the explosions would occur and police were stationed at some sites.

In the 1920s, bombs gave way to brains; violence was supplanted by racial restrictive covenants, by which white property owners agreed not to lease or sell property to Negroes in otherwise white areas of the city. This move too was supported and praised by the Real Estate Board. By the 1940s, an estimated 80 per cent of all-white residential property in Chicago and suburbs was off-limits to Negroes, thanks to covenants.

Thus, the second great wave of Negro immigration, corresponding to the industrial production needs of World War II, splashed almost entirely into the already crowded black ghetto. Between 1940 and 1950, the city's Negro citizenry increased from 278,000 (8 per cent of the total) to 492,000 (14 per cent), yet this population explosion was contained almost exclusively in the same amount of space that was available to Negroes when the war broke out.

Since the war, Negro immigration has increased steadily. Negroes pour off the trains and buses that run up from Mississippi, Louisiana, Alabama, Arkansas and the Carolinas, hoping in Chicago to escape the Four Horsemen of Southern oppression: terrorism, poverty, immobility and inferior education.

Today, Negroes constitute nearly one-third of the city's total population, and newcomers as well as long-time residents —regardless of income, occupation or social status—are still concentrated in the ghetto, which has expanded to the West and near North Sides. Some 76 per cent of all Negroes in Illinois and 96 per cent of all in Cook County, of which Chicago is the seat, live there. For Chicago's pattern of housing segregation, permitting the ghetto to expand like slowly falling dominoes, block by contiguous block only, has continued largely un-abated, despite passage of a local open occupancy ordinance and a Supreme Court ban on restrictive covenants. Says the Urban League:

> The real estate industry still stands out as the major institu-tional bulwark of residential segregation . . . [It] continues to subsidize local groups that oppose housing integration and itself opposes fair housing legislation. Overwhelmingly real es-tate brokers refuse to show Negroes properties outside the ghetto and lending institutions refuse to grant mortgages to them for properties outside the walls of the ghetto . . . Since the [first] great [Negro] migration, people who violated the policy of racial segregation [have] suffered repeated and severe economic reprisals—no financing, no insurance protection, no tenants, no income. Brokers, managers, owners and inspectors have worked persistently to preserve racial segregation.

As for life in the ghetto, statistics speak for themselves. A University of Chicago study shows that eight out of ten Chicago Negroes want to live some place other than their present resi-dence. In 1960, two out of five—41 per cent—of all Negro-occupied units were classified as dilapidated, deteriorating, or lacking plumbing facilities, compared to one out of five—18 per cent—occupied by whites. The same year, one out of every four —27.4 per cent—non-white families lived in households with more than one person per room, compared to one out of every twelve—7.8 per cent—white families. Moreover, according to the findings of one survey, Negroes pay roughly $10 a month more in rent and an average of $1,500 more in purchase price than whites for comparable housing, in addition to generally higher interest rates on mortgages and/or contract purchases. Yet Negro families in 1960 earned one-third less than did white families, who are not burdened with any such "color tax."

Many observers, as we shall see, believe the Chicago school system has abetted the city's housing segregation in a number of subtle and blatant ways. No one denies that the schools mirror it. Indeed, school segregation in Chicago is intensifying. During the 1963–64 school term, the percentage of Negro pupils attend-ing predominantly or all-Negro schools under Chicago's "neighborhood school" policy was 87.8 per cent for elementary schools and 63.8 per cent for high schools. During 1964–65, the figures rose to 89.2 per cent for elementary schools and 68 per cent for high schools.

Of the city's 508 elementary schools and branches, fewer than 10 per cent—48—are integrated in the sense that they have more than 10 per cent of both Negro and white students. This is a decrease from 51 such schools in 1966. There are 156 elementary schools and branches that are 100 per cent white and 156 with more than 99 per cent Negro enrollment. *The National Observer* pointed out recently that in order to have completely integrated neighborhood schools in Chicago, "you would have to move 92 out of every 100 families."

The Negroes' isolation is demonstrated by the experience of a white teacher who took his small son with him one day to his class in a ghetto elementary school. One of the Negro students asked if he could take the visitor home for lunch, explaining, "I want to show him to Mama." He had never seen a white child before.

Similarly, the majority of white public-school children are attending predominantly or all-white schools in white neighborhoods. Some of the statistics related to this confinement, like those concerning the ghetto, are illuminating. In Chicago, 140,-000 high school students are crowded into space intended for 100,000. The five most crowded high schools, operating at 150 per cent or more of capacity, are 90.8 to 99.9 per cent Negro. For the ten most crowded high schools, construction of an addition was planned for only one in a typical, recent year—the one with the least (5 per cent) colored population, the one less overcrowded than any other.

Among the city's elementary schools, there were in 1966 an estimated 453 vacant classrooms, mostly in white schools, and a need for 564 classrooms in other areas, mostly Negro. No interschool transfers were planned to effect a balance.

In sampling Negro, white and integrated elementary schools, one survey team found that Negro schools, especially in the ghetto, have more noncertified teachers and fewer teachers with at least five years' experience and master's degrees than do white schools, with integrated schools "falling . . . between . . . in quality of staff."

Every day in Chicago an estimated 300 to 700 classrooms have no teachers whatsoever because of absences that are not covered by substitutes. In a week's sampling by the Chicago Teachers' Union, it was discovered that of the ten school districts with the greatest percentage of unfilled teaching positions, nine were in predominantly Negro schools. In one of these districts embracing seventeen schools 83 per cent of the teacher absences were not covered.

One statistic affecting all the city's schools is worth noting —the expenditure per pupil. In 1964 Chicago spent $448 for each student in elementary school, $565 for each in high school, and $726 for each in vocational schools. The corresponding figures for New York were $713, $857, and $1,270. Chicago received roughly twice as much money from the federal government as New York, but less than half as much from the state. Indeed, Illinois, ranking fourth among the states in per capita wealth, was supporting only 22 per cent of the expenses of the public schools in 1967, compared to a national average of about 40 per cent. This placed it 42nd among the states. That same year Illinois dropped from 47th to 49th in the nation in the percentage of income spent on elementary and secondary education.

What money is allocated by the state is not distributed on the basis of need but in relation to the amount of industrial property and high-value real estate located in each school district. When large corporations settle in suburban areas with relatively few students—and this trend is very noticeable in the Chicago area—the corporations profit by having to pay lower local taxes and the residents benefit by getting more state money for their district's schools because the tax base is enriched. Consultants to the Chicago Board of Education asked recently, "Who can blame the successful young parents who decide to leave for the suburbs where their children will receive an education worth maybe twice the dollars and with a tax burden often considerably below Chicago's? The departure of such families from the city drives another nail into the coffin being fashioned for the integrated society." Yet the chance of the state legislature changing the method of school funds distribution seems slim for, the consultants noted, "the present system discriminates in favor of the most powerful interests in the society . . . [and] the people of all districts above the state average in wealth would find it to their disadvantage to equalize the system.

In the history of Chicago's schools, probably no person has been more controversial or blamed for more of the system's ills than Benjamin C. Willis, who resigned in 1966 after nearly thirteen years as general superintendent of schools. At $48,500 a year, Willis was the nation's third-highest-paid public official, and his years in office undoubtedly were stormier than those of any other school superintendent in the country. Civil rights groups sometimes oversimplified Chicago's school problems by implying that with Willis removed, all would be well. But to understand many aspects of local education the impact of his personality and policies certainly must be taken into account. The atmosphere of his reign was summarized in *Renewal,* a magazine of urban problems published by the Chicago City Missionary Society:

"They say the man himself—his personality and his methods of administration—stands in the way of obtaining and maintaining quality education for every child in the city schools. . . .

"[After Willis first arrived here] he embarked on a multi-million-dollar school-building program, which in 1963 resulted in the end of the double-shift for many school children.

"The low, sleek, yellow brick buildings which replaced [some of] the more traditional red-brick fortresses throughout the city's school districts are a dual symbol of Willis' capacity as an administrator.

"His supporters note proudly that Willis wrung the financial sponge dry to get the most out of the school-building dollar. His opponents say the new schools, while physically adequate, were placed in such a way as to perpetuate segregation and contain Negroes within an ever-enlarging ghetto. . . .

"It was prodding by dissatisfied citizens groups . . . that led to the initiation of what was to become [known as] the Havighurst Survey of Chicago Public Schools (a critique of local school problems by University of Chicago Professor Robert J. Havighurst).

"Willis did all he could to delay the report. When the board finally after an eighteen-month delay approved the initiation of the report in May 1963, Willis insisted he be made part of the survey committee. The board acquiesced, and what was supposed to have been an independent survey now included the . . . head of the system to be surveyed.

"Then the real trouble began. The low rumble of newly formed civil rights groups grew to a roar of protest against *de facto* segregation in the city's schools in the summer of 1963.

"Scores of persons were arrested during turbulent scenes at . . . the [South Side] site of proposed installation of mobile classrooms: air-conditioned, modern trailers, that civil rights militants dubbed derogatorily Willis Wagons. Their gripe was that the trailer classrooms were being installed unnecessarily, because just a few blocks away in primarily white schools there were empty classrooms that could accommodate Negro students. . . .

"Willis . . . prefers to maintain the school as an island of education, separated from the turbulent problems of the community in which it is located.

"However, Havighurst, in his report, has recommended the abandonment of this 'four-walls school' concept for a 'community school' concept, in which school administrators open up channels of communication between themselves and others in the community—parents, civic groups, and the like—to provide a solid basis for solving neighborhood problems.

"Chicago is 'sick and getting sicker,' warns Havighurst. Only a new approach to running the schools can help save the city from economic and social disaster, he says. . . .'"

Since that article appeared in March 1965, neither Willis' educational policies nor his approach to public relations has changed. Consider these random illustrations from the Chicago newspapers:

Late in 1965, for the first time in the city's history, residents of an all-white Chicago neighborhood asked for Negro teachers in its public schools. Explained a spokesman for the group, "It is our feeling that like every other white community in Chicago, we are going to have some [Negro] move-ins. We think we can help prepare the community and help the residents get over their stereotypes if they have some contact with educated Negroes." But, the spokesman told reporters, a meeting with

Willis proved "fruitless" because the general superintendent said that neither he nor the school board could do anything to notify Negro teachers that they were wanted there.

Last March 1966 the outgoing president of the Chicago P.T.A. announced that in her two years in office, she had never been able to get an appointment with Willis to discuss school problems, nor had he ever appeared before the P.T.A.'s delegate assembly. "We have asked," she said, "but Dr. Willis has not found time for us."

That same month a white member of the board of education said in a letter to Mayor Richard J. Daley that certain of Willis' persistent "traits" had made working on the board "impossible" and had placed in educational jeopardy all Chicago students, white and Negro. He itemized such traits as Willis' "contempt for the judgment of any board member who has the temerity to disagree with him"; his "habit of effecting a pocket veto of board . . . policies and orders with which he happens to disagree"; his "refusal to give the board timely, complete and reliable information"; his "rejection of the traditional concept of citizen control of the public schools as embodied in the statutes of Illinois"; his "overriding anxiety to defend everything the Chicago public schools have done since he took office . . . instead of using his energy to identify and meet today's problems as effectively as possible"; his "stifling of creativity in teaching"; his discouragement "of simple communication from principals and teachers concerning their current problems and needs"; his "refusal to accept the official board policy [of integration] adopted over two years ago"; and "his lack of . . . any real respect or understanding of today's concern on the part of Chicago's parents, both white and Negro, who want the best possible education for their children."

Willis' lack of cooperation has extended to the federal government. In 1965 he flatly refused to allow any Chicago schoolchildren to be given achievement tests and background information quizzes in connection with a nationwide survey by the U.S. Office of Education, required by the Civil Rights Act. In February 1966, he ordered Chicago principals not to answer civil rights questionnaires received from Washington as part of the same survey. Meanwhile, in January, the board adopted "guidelines" stating that "All contacts from Chicago public-school system to staff representatives of the Department of Health, Education and Welfare and/or the U.S. Office of Education shall emanate from the general superintendent of schools."

In the wake of these moves, the Chicago system was characterized by some observers as "the system that won't let itself be tested." Indeed, it was difficult even for local authorities to determine how Chicago children ranked in comparison with others across the nation, for Willis changed the method of recording students' achievement test scores. The existing system of grade-level scores with *national* norms was replaced by a nine-point "stanine" scale with *citywide* norms. In other words, teachers, school officials and parents now can tell only how their youngsters are doing in comparison with youngsters in other Chicago schools.

With this kind of insulation, Chicagoans are sometimes startled by face-to-face performance between their children and those from other systems. In a letter to the Chicago *Daily News* last November, a white mother wrote:

"At [a predominantly white] high school [on Chicago's South Side] an honors chemistry class didn't open a text book the first ten weeks of school. An art major teaches physics, and an advanced math class is taught by a shop teacher. Students with IQs in the highest percentile sent to a regional workshop in Latin didn't even score. With third- and fourth-year Latin students sharing room space and teacher with second-year students it would be hard to expect any real enthusiasm to ensue. One wonders what the same students would have scored had they attended the suburban schools of their competitors . . .

"Ask any parent of a college-oriented child what the attitude of college admissions personnel is when they hear a child is from a Chicago public high school. Even the best becomes average in the sight of the colleges, with this background . . . It is interesting to note that the mayor and most members of the board of education do not and have not sent their children to Chicago public high schools. . . ."

The question "How did Willis get away with it?" has been asked frequently. The answer is fairly simple: Among all the individuals and organizations he fought, there was one significant exception—he did not fight City Hall, and vice versa.

As we explained recently in an article for the *Saturday Review:*

> Because of an old scandal in which the school system was exposed as a'haven for patronage hacks, the running of Chicago schools, in theory, is buffered from politics. Yet like everything else in the city that hosts the last great political machine, the schools are, in the final analysis, politically influenced. . . .

> Chicago has always been first and foremost a businessman's town, and no machine mahatma has taken shrewder advantage of this fact than Democratic Mayor Daley. . . . Daley, one City Council member explains, "is essentially a broker," catering to the needs and desires of big business and finance, in trade for their political support. . . .

> The schools superintendent, like other potential movers-and-shakers in the city's superstructure, must be compatible with both the Daley machine and its business angels, and the mechanics to see that he is [or is made] compatible have been provided. Members of the Board of Education, which hires the superintendent and is supposed to set policy, are appointed by Daley. The fact that he draws exclusively from a list of nominees drafted by a twenty-member commission "representing civic and professional organizations and educational institutions" allegedly inoculates against "politics." But the commission [is] itself appointed by Daley . . . and remains in existence only at [his] discretion.

> Not surprisingly, the school board in composition is almost a Lilliputian reproduction of the Daley-controlled City Council. Token representation is given to minority groups. . . . Frequently, Negro appointees have been compliant. . . . Another role characteristically provided for on the Board is that of vocal liberal dissenter. The majority of the Board . . . remain, in [one member's] words, "votes the Daley administration can control."

> Thus, even though Willis dictatorially usurped the Board's powers—effecting pocket vetoes, indulging in acid petulance, resigning briefly at one point to get his way—his four-year contract was three times renewed and then extended until his retirement. The reason . . . was simply that Willis served the city's power structure. . . . Largely because he made himself a symbol of racial segregation, he also was lionized by whites in the city's blue-collar population. This group has traditionally attached the least importance to quality education, and it is perhaps the most valuable grassroots buttress to the Daley ma-

chine, particularly in light of the usually lethargic Negro vote. Finally, and perhaps most important, [Willis] convinced the business community that Chicago could get quality education at bargain-counter rates.

Critics argue that the business interests have never demanded much from Chicago schools. Ringed by some of the best suburban school systems in the nation, home of a dozen major colleges and universities, still a magnet for the talented young of the Midwest and the Great Plains, Chicago has not been threatened by any letup in the steady stream of professionals and aspirants to the executive suite feeding in from the outside. With their own children by and large attending parochial, private or suburban schools, "the principal concern of the influential business leaders for Chicago schools," contends Alderman Leon Despres, a liberal lawyer elected to the City Council from the University of Chicago area of Hyde Park, "has been keeping costs—and taxes—down." In the context of the system's size Willis's budgets were always relatively appealing. . . .

Daley claims that once appointments are made he keeps hands off board matters. But the hard nose of power politics has been stuck from time to time into school matters.

When unhappy parents announced that a student boycott was planned at a Negro elementary school to protest conditions there, Democratic precinct workers are reported to have gone from door to door in the public-housing projects that feed the school, advising mothers that their welfare checks would be cut off if they participated in the protest.

A well-publicized incident occurred in the fall of 1965 when the Department of Health, Education and Welfare withheld some $30,000,000 in federal aid from Chicago schools under a provision of the Civil Rights Act until charges of deliberate segregation in the system could be thoroughly investigated. Before the would-be investigators even reached the scene, Daley, considered by experts the most influential Democratic politician in the U.S. aside from the President, was reported to have telephoned the White House. The order was rescinded.

In the fall of 1966, the vacancy left by Willis's resignation was filled by Dr. James Redmond, former schools superintendent for Syosset, New York. In contrast to Willis's Pollyanna pronouncements, Redmond soon acknowledged in his public speeches that the system he had inherited was fraught with major problems. Before he finished his first year in office, startling substantiating evidence was being made public.

For instance Redmond presented the Board with a district-by-district report on pupil reading skills which the Chicago *Daily News* said "proclaims an emergency." In one Negro district, for example, the report shows that only 8 per cent of the sixth grade pupils can read at the accepted norm for their grade level; 92 per cent are retarded readers. Only two districts, both at the north (white) edge of the city, had fewer than one-third of their sixth graders in the retarded reader category. Only three others could boast that more than half the sixth graders were up to average in reading ability. In short, in twenty-two of Chicago's twenty-seven districts from 51 to 92 per cent of all sixth graders are below par in reading—"the skill basic," the *News* observed, "to acquiring almost every other skill in the years to come."

Tests at other grade levels have proved no more encouraging. On third grade achievement tests, Chicago youngsters fell below the national median in reading, word knowledge, spelling, word discrimination, language and arithmetic computation and problems. The average eighth grader was below national norms in reading, language, arithmetic computation and problem solving, science and social studies information and study skills. Compared to the national average, high school freshmen and juniors did better than elementary school pupils, but were still below normal. Redmond reported that freshman scores are getting worse instead of better.

"Time has run out for the Chicago public school system," he said. "The neglect is decades old and has reached a point where it cannot be denied."

One thing is obvious, he added: the need for more counselors. At present, Chicago schools harbor 40,000 children who need but are not getting psychological help.

Also made public after Redmond's arrival were some disquieting facts about Chicago's teachers. Six thousand of the city's 22,000 teachers, it was disclosed, have never passed the written and oral exams necessary for teacher certification. (All Illinois cities except Chicago rely on state requirements and personal interviews in certifying teachers. Chicago operates under a 1916 law designed to "take politics out of education" in an era when ward heelers peddled teaching certificates. A semi-autonomous Board of Examiners conducts six-hour written tests, and five-member oral exam panels then question certification applicants. A high percentage of those who fail the oral exam, and therefore must repeat the written on their next certification attempt, are Negro. The reasons for failure are never explaind to the appli-cant.) Of Negro teachers (who comprise one-third of the total teaching force), one out of three is not certified, compared to less than 10 per cent of the white teaching complement. About 30 per cent of all teachers are full-time substitutes, and three-quarters of these, Redmond announced, have never even *tried* to be certi-fied. In one entire district on the predominantly Negro West Side, fewer than 46 percent of the teaching positions are filled by certi-fied teachers.

Certification after three years brings tenure. And statistics pertaining to tenured teachers suggested possible cause for con-cern, too. In 1967, for instance, only two tenured teachers in the entire system were fired, causing some observers to charge that Chicago is "blanketing in" incompetents.

Meanwhile, a study by outside experts funded by the U.S. Office of Education charged that Chicago's schools have grown "dangerously inflexible, with little interest in the innovation and experimentation required to meet the city's changing needs and population." Of six big-city school systems explored in depth by the research team, Chicago (along with St. Louis) was adjudged poorest in innovative accomplishment.

Redmond explained that his administrative staff lacks "the time and energy to give serious thought to planning education programs to prepare students for a changing social and economic era. Our staff meetings should be concerned with ideas. [But] as of now [we are so] busy reacting to the day-to-day problems that I wonder at times when and how we will be able to get to the demanding educational tasks."

In another report, the Office of Education announced evi-dence of Civil Rights Act violations in Chicago schools, charging that "current school policies result in unequal treatment for mi-nority group students." Action was necessary, the O. E. said, to change the patterns of teacher assignment (more than 95 per cent of Chicago's Negro teachers—a higher percentage than in any ma-jor city outside the South—are assigned to predominantly Negro schools, as are a high proportion of the least qualified teachers); school boundaries, which have produced "extreme separation of children by race"; enrollment in vocational and trade schools, which often is of only one race; and the admission practices for apprenticeship programs run jointly by the Board of Education and labor unions (twenty times as many whites as Negroes are allowed to participate in such programs).

For months it seemed that Redmond was making no effort to meet the problems, despite his avowals. Then as the first anniversary of his appointment approached, he offered a revolutionary blueprint for change. His one hundred forty-four-page report, promptly adopted "in principle" by the Board, proposed to promote integration and quality education through: the creation over a number of years of educational parks serving a full grade range of up to twenty thousand pupils apiece, ultimately supplanting the city's traditional neighborhood school system and providing what Redmond calls "the ideal milieu for cultural and racial integration"; the development of "magnet schools," whose staff and student bodies will be racially mixed and whose specialized academic offerings will draw students from all sections of the city and will be so exemplary that white families will move back to the city from the suburbs so that their children may attend; the busing of students to maintain strict racial quotas in "fringe area schools around Negro ghettos in the hope that a stable racial ratio in those schools will keep whites from fleeing the neighborhoods; the establishment of exchange programs between Chicago schools and white suburbs; a change in personnel transfer policies which will compel teachers to remain in "difficult" schools and distribute certified teachers evenly within the system; the integration of all school staffs (there are now only twenty-four Negro principals in the system) and, among other things, the introduction of special classes for slow learners and students who present disciplinary problems in ordinary classrooms.

As a starter Redmond proposed and the Board ordered that the city be carved into three giant school jurisdictions with nearly autonomous administrative powers, to "bring the responsibility for decision-making closer to the local schools" and to help decentralize the monolithic bureaucracy that mushroomed under Willis. For the first time, lay personnel were hired at some schools to relieve teachers of record-keeping and other burdensome, non-educational chores. Other changes, the superintendent promised, would be effected as soon as possible.

With his first effort early in 1968 to implement any of his integration proposals, however, Redmond went down to swift defeat, and one reporter was prompted to note that "public education in Chicago is still spelled t-u-r-m-o-i-l."

What Redmond proposed was a modest plan whereby about one thousand students, mostly Negroes, would be bused out of their overcrowded schools into 17 white schools on the Northwest and Southeast Sides. Reaction to the proposal was instant and overwhelming. Twenty Republican state legislators threatened to stall school money bills if the busing were approved. Mayor Daley said extensive public hearings should be held on the proposal and that no action should be taken without majority approval of the city's residents. A faithful Daley minion, U. S. Representative Roman Pucinski, came to town to lead opposition to busing. At subsequent public hearings, proponents of the plan were loudly booed and fights between pickets and counter-pickets erupted frequently. A civic association on the Northwest Side hired a lawyer and threatened to have him draw up secession papers for that section of the city if the plan went through.

When the matter finally came to a vote before the Board, busing for the Northwest Side was rejected and the other plan was referred back to Redmond for "revision." Board member Warren Bacon, a liberal Negro who backed both plans, told reporters bitterly, "The Board did not have faith in its commitment, so piously made, to adopt any reasonable plan (to aid integration). All the pious utterings do not hide the fact that this Board does not have the will, the resolve, the commitment to make the necessary changes."

Added Edwin Berry, director of the Chicago Urban League, "To turn down such a small plan makes Negroes lose hope that anything will be done about Chicago's education problems."

After some speculation in the local press that the Office of Education might again have cause for withholding funds, the Board reconsidered and decided to implement one of the busing plans on a greatly modified scale. Public opposition remained high, however. As a new strategy, some whites threatened to persuade hundreds of their neighbors to take their children out of parochial schools and enroll them in public schools to fill up the empty seats that otherwise would be occupied by bused Negroes. On the first day the plan went into effect, a fire bomb was thrown into one of the schools involved, but no one was injured. All in all, school officials said the busing got underway "peaceably," but at this writing (early March 1968) the situation still appears volatile.

Redmond says he has not given up hope for his master plan. But most of its ingredients for integrated, quality education seem a long way indeed from materializing. Under the most favorable circumstances, some elements are not expected to be realized even under Redmond's own time-table for thirty years or more. Those with short-range target dates face formidable obstacles. Some civil rights groups have threatened renewed pupil boycotts because the plans, for all their integration-consciousness, offer no relief from segregated schools in the foreseeable future for the vast majority of black youngsters in the heart of the ghetto. Angry white homeowners have urged political pressure to get the superintendent ousted; some realtors are lending their support to protests about his "dictatorship." Redmond has conceded that he and his consultants did not consider the legality of various proposals when they drafted the blueprint, so drawn-out court battles seem a certainty. Union leaders have expressed opposition to the intended changes in teacher placement. Many of the administrative staffers whose responsibility would be to put the plans into operation are the very administrators who fiercely buttressed Willis and so avidly embraced his philosophies.

And overwhelmingly there is the basic question of money. Even if the current school budget of some $462,000,000 a year were doubled, it would not be sufficient to meet the minimum needs. Redmond says more than $1.2 billion will be needed for new and remodeled buildings in the next decade. For the 1968–69 school year, he says the system's educational fund is falling $24,000,000 short of minimum requirements and that about seven times that amount should be added to the budget to achieve an "adequate" education program. "We are almost overcome," he says, "by the magnitude of the needs and the complete absence of resources to meet them." But so far, neither local business interests, individual taxpayers nor state legislators have been persuaded of the desperate need for escalated spending—despite the fact that the annual expenditure per pupil could be tripled and still not equal the cost of maintaining a person in state prison or a family on relief.

Finally, there is the question of whether the plans, if put into effect, will actually heighten integration and improve quality. Variations have been tried in other cities with few spectacular results. Anyway, integration may be a moot goal long before Redmond's plans fully blossom. The city's Negro population is swallowing up new territory at the rate of nearly three blocks a week, and demographers can see an all-black Chicago on the not-so-far horizon. Already if the racial ratio in the public school system as a whole were reflected in each school, 54 per cent of the children in every classroom would be Negro.

Deficiencies in the school system are helping to flush out from the city important economic and social leadership and leave behind fewer citizens who can or will protest. Many middle and upper-middle class whites who suspect the system have moved or are planning to move to the suburbs, or are sending their children to private schools. Nearly half the white children in Chicago attend parochial schools. Many white parents left in the system have convinced themselves that so long as their schools are kept white, everything is fine.

Negroes, for whom the option of moving away is more complex, have developed alternative courses. Some, as indicated in this report, are converting to Catholicism for the sake of their school-age children; more than ten per cent of the parochial system's 225,000 students now are Negro. Others have organized private schools to escape the public system. In one of these, more than one-third of the parents are public-school teachers. Even in this era of militancy, the concept of protest is far from the ken of many lower-class Negro parents to whom the school still represents "Whitey" or the power structure. Numerous teachers report that many Negro mothers' sole concern with their children's school performance is based on deportment. "You whip him if he don't behave," they tell the teacher, echoing centuries of Negro-white relations. The seeds for this were sown in the segregated South, but the harvest is being reaped in Chicago today.

Our idea of letting teachers tell the Chicago story was inspired by Dr. Willis. Shortly before leaving office, he publicly rebuked a Pulitzer Prize-winning newspaperwoman for her published observations in a Negro ghetto school. He chided her for quoting teachers and announced, "We wouldn't go to a hospital and interview interns. We would certainly go to the administration of the hospital and then we would write a story in that vein." People at the top, in Dr. Willis' eyes, were the important ones in the educational process. When the school board once cut pay raises for top administrative personnel, Willis argued, "You're talking about the heartthrob of the school system."

But common sense says that it is the "interns," present in the parts of the "hospital" where the action is, who are aware of things an administrator may never hear—or tell—about. They know the institution's pulse beat, weak or strong. For instance, "official" figures place average class size at thirty-three students per teacher. But a teacher told us that at her school, the principal splits up classrooms of teacherless children among other rooms, then "forces" those teachers to fill in attendance books for empty rooms so she can keep her head-count looking low downtown.

Although our interviews were conducted shortly before Willis left as superintendent, an overwhelming proportion of the problems discussed remain. What these teachers have to say demonstrates at once the pressing need for the kinds of changes Redmond has suggested and the tremendous forces within the system working for the defeat of any effort for reform. The unpleasant truths revealed here apply not only to the Second City, but in varying degree to an increasing number of school systems across the land, threatening us with what one observer calls "a generation of untaught children."

The "interns" quoted here are male, female, Negro, white, substitute, assigned, kindergarten through high school teachers. They were contacted privately and interviewed in their own homes, on their own time, their comments recorded verbatim. They were guaranteed anonymity and they were given no reward for participating. Some pleaded that their names not be disclosed; others were willing, even anxious to be identified publicly with their views. In all cases, we believe they were frank.

First is a young blonde, thirty maybe, thin and willowy. Every school day for five years now she has left her apartment in an old converted mansion on the North Side and has pointed her Volkswagen toward a Negro ghetto school on the fringe of Chicago's artists' colony. In a first-grade classroom shadowed by rat-run tenements and stark public-housing high rises, she brings "Dick and Jane" to the masses. Every afternoon driving home along the lake she says she thinks about the Chicago school system, its cause and cure:

"This is a system based on fear. It has become sicker and sicker and sicker and is at death's point now, both at white and Negro schools. It has become so sick that God help [Redmond]. I don't know what his chances are.

"Teachers are really afraid. Principals are really, really afraid, and district superintendents are really, really, really afraid. The fault lies, I feel, with [Willis]. He is a man of dictatorial personality who has made it quite clear that he does not want this school system thought of as having any problems. Ironically, this attitude ultimately *generates* problems.

"Consider the matter of passing children. Nowhere in the rule book does it say that you have to pass children if you do not believe they accomplished what they should. Yet the unwritten rule here is that you may flunk only 3 per cent in any school. One year our principal told us, 'You can't fail more than one person in your class, and preferably none. Especially in the sixth grade. We don't want any of them coming back.' The vast majority of teachers are too frightened to stand up against this.

"You've got to keep the kids going, you see, otherwise Willis' image is destroyed. His image is that he has maintained a certain class load; the children are moving along; more children are getting high school diplomas so you have children at [a nearby high school] doing third- and fourth-grade arithmetic in physics class. They call it physics and pass them on—some with high grades. When these children are unleashed on society and try to get jobs they suddenly realize they are not qualified and that all their grades didn't mean a thing. The teachers have deceived them. The system has deceived them.

"A breed of principals has arisen who use fear as a weapon. They live in fear themselves and are constantly worried about what 'downtown' is going to think. They've become administration-oriented instead of education-oriented, and it has bombed the system.

"Teachers too are terrorized. And once you live in fear you can no longer teach, because you'll sacrifice every good program if you're asked to. And you'll be asked to, because good programs sometimes have their rocky moments and often go a little bit outside the rule book. You sell out. You begin to blame the children and their parents instead of asking what is there in the system that makes us unable to teach these children.

"Another significant element of Willis' program is the deliberate effort to break down the P.T.A. If the P.T.A. is weak, then the chances are greater that parents never will know what is going on in the school.

"At the same time he has rigged up certain decoys to distract from the real problems. For instance, our school has in-circuit TV which supposedly features educational programs. The teachers have lied about it for years, filling out phony reports for the higher-ups about how great it is. In reality, they never turn on the programs because they are so inferior. Yet Willis can bring in influential suburban people, the white power structure, and they say, 'Oh, look, you have something that even our white schools don't have. You have in-circuit TV.'

"The good teachers are not fooled. The number of assigned teachers in Chicago has increased something like only 70 per cent since 1953, while the number of substitutes has shot up more than 500 per cent. We are literally bankrupt of teachers. The good, creative, dedicated teachers are fleeing this system for the suburbs, and the suburban women in turn are coming into our schools as substitutes. Our teachers go to the suburbs because they want to teach. The suburbanites come here because they want extra money without having to expend any real effort.

"Underneath all the statistics, our white schools are in bad shape, as well as the Negro schools. What is happening in the inner-city schools is spreading like a cancer throughout the entire city and eventually will reach the suburbs. You already have —— High on the North Side where the principal locks herself in her office all day and watches television. This school is in a very excellent area, but it's a perfect example of a badly run school where children are not being properly educated.

"While the average white child in the Chicago system is not nearly as well off as he should be, he is, of course, much better off than the average Negro child. There is discrimination and segregation here, despite official pronouncements to the contrary. Some is subtle, some not so subtle.

"This neighborhood-schools business is not always an honest system. I've studied the school district maps very carefully, and the human eye picks up the gerrymandering. Some districts are real long and narrow. —— Elementary School is an outstanding example of gerrymandering. The children from [a large white upper-income housing complex] go there, although it is a good mile from them. Their nearest neighborhood school, two blocks away, is —— School, which is Negro. This district is gerrymandered deliberately to accommodate those kids. Everyone knows about it; nobody does anything about it.

"To really change things in Chicago, in my opinion, you have to start by changing the top. Right now we have a Catholic mayor. The Catholic Church essentially controls him, and through him, the city. Teachers have talked about this for years, even the Catholic teachers. Now when you talk to Irish or Italian or Polish Catholics, their hatred for the Negro is generally evident. The more educated ones cloak it in code words like, 'The Negro parents should discipline their child,' or, 'Negro parents don't motivate their child,' instead of saying, 'When a parent does not fulfill these functions, the school must then be the dynamic force in doing so.' I come from a long line of WASPs, and I know these ways of saying, 'We hate niggers.' This sentiment, I think, flows from the people through the Church to Daley, to the school hierarchy, and ultimately into school policies, spoken or unspoken.

"Right now Daley also controls a powerful, powerful machine. The Negro vote is important to him and he controls the Negro aldermen. But this may not last forever. Rising up within the Negro population is disenchantment with the Daley machine. We've got a young group of Negro activists now rising up on the West Side who are willing to literally die to change what is happening here to the Negro.

"Assuming an eventual change at the top, then certain specific changes will be needed in school policy. First, I think we should milk out of our ghetto schools those children who can compete on middle-class ground. We have many who could hold their own in North Side white schools and who would be better off there educationally. Out of the 2,000 kids at our school, maybe we have 200 like this at the moment. Get them out of there so they can contribute something back to society. You don't even have to bus them; their parents will pay their transportation.

"Then for the discipline problems, the mentally retarded, the severely disturbed, the slow learners who are left, take government money that is available and cut down the class load to something like 15 students to one teacher. Bring your best teachers—teachers who say they really want to teach and are dedicated—into the ghetto areas. Gradually we can work these children into society, too.

"Efforts also should be made, however, to integrate Negro teachers into white schools. The Negro teachers now in Negro schools despise their own low-income people. They themselves have arrived; they are middle-class now. They don't want to be reminded of where they came from. They tear hell out of the Negro kids. They rule by the whip—slapping, hitting, making children stand with books on their arms.

"Also they have the terrible fear that they will be the first to go in any teacher cutback, and I think it's a legitimate fear. Most of them are not certified. Their own backgrounds go against them. A lot are from Southern schools, and they have difficulty passing the certification exam. They may pass the written but they can't pass the oral because their speech is too bad.

"But we could help them. Put white teachers down in the Negro schools and put some of the Negro teachers up in the white schools so they can mature themselves intellectually. Most of them are very sharp. They're natively bright or they wouldn't be teachers to begin with. But they need to be out of their own environment.

"Somehow we need to recruit a better grade of teacher generally. Now we have a vast group who are supporting their husbands through various endeavors—law school, med school, and so forth. They only intend to teach two or three years. They don't really take anything home to work on after school. They don't grade papers. They don't care. They sit and read the newspaper in class, and the class runs wild. Also you get the older woman who comes back to teaching after many years and confronts a whole new breed of children. When you say sit down, quietly, they just don't sit down. You must use other methods, yet there is no effort to retrain these people.

"It's time we faced up to our problems. It's hard work to plan a program to alleviate the sickness that is in our schools, the inner-city schools especially. It takes every creative thought you have. It's hard to recruit psychologists, train people to handle discipline problems, find ways to help disturbed children, find ways to motivate children to learn, and improve reading methods. It's easy to put in in-circuit television and never have it turned on."

The path of least resistance is familiar terrain to another teacher, too. A short man, balding, he teaches civics in a Negro high school planted on the West Side among a forest of tenement hutches, welfare stations, chitterling groceries and taverns that tout Bullfrog beer. A newspaperman once nicknamed his school "Slum High." As many as 75 per cent of its students, he speculates wearily, will drop out shy of their diplomas. And after four years in the Chicago system, he thinks he has clues to the riddle why:

"You take a Peace Corps job and you go where the challenge is greatest. I haven't met many teachers at my school like that. Generally teachers in Chicago want to go to schools on the fringes of the city, where you have students from a higher income bracket, from homes where they have more encouragement and come to school eager to learn. When they give you several schools to choose from, usually the ones you choose last are inner-city schools like mine. Students there are more difficult to handle and your teacher turnover is much greater. Teachers get the message right away that they [the administration] don't think of these schools in the inner-city as educational institutions. They're custodial institutions. The whole attitude is that the kids aren't going to learn; we are just keeping them off the streets. Nobody comes around to see if you are doing a competent job or to help with the problems you face when thrown into a situation like this. After a while you start to feel that if nobody cares how you teach, why should you care.

"Nobody appreciates if I do anything special. For instance, I saw that my kids were not responding to the freshman civics class, which is set up to give them something practical since so many won't finish school. Everybody has to teach at least one course with these low readers, and in this civics class you cover things like home management, teenage problems, and how to get along in the world. Even this is hard to present in a way that will hold the kids' interest. There isn't much material available at the level where they can read, so you use talks and movies. Then I had the notion that if you want to teach the kids about civics, get them interested and involved in something in the community. Give them an idea of what it means to be civic-minded. So I made some contacts in the neighborhood and lined up some work projects for the kids. It worked out very well, and the people from the Chicago Housing Authority and the Boys Clubs were very enthusiastic. I also took the kids out on bike trips and other outings in recognition of their doing this. The beneficial results were immediately apparent.

"I thought we should make this a regular sponsored school activity and get the wholehearted cooperation of the school and recruit more kids and maybe get permission to spend some of my school time on this work. I met with completely negative response. I was told I was exposing the board of education unduly to risks in which the school would be legally liable. Therefore the risks did not equal the value to the kids. The neighborhood agency people had experienced this negative attitude from the school people before. It was nothing new to them.

"It's not just color, either. Our new principal, who is colored, has the same attitude toward the kids as previous white principals. It all reflects the attitude of downtown central administration. They lack the imagination and creativity to deal with the problems that confront them, so they try to pretend that they don't exist. This attitude relates to the poor white kids, the Puerto Ricans, Mexican and Indian kids on the North Side as much as it does to our lower-income Negro kids on the South and West Sides.

"I don't think it's so much a race problem as a poverty problem. You find that many middle-class teachers have the same attitude of dislike and animosity towards white poor as they do to Negro kids from the same background.

"The behavior of these kids in inner-city schools, which the school people base their attitudes on, is not due so much to race but to their upbringing at a low income level. This is a slum way of life. These kids are brought up in crowded houses where they have to shout to be heard or have to learn how to close their minds to all stimuli in order to survive the noise they are exposed to continually, or who never sit down to eat with their parents at any regular meal, or who have no privacy to study or a room to themselves.

"In school one of our biggest problems is lack of space. In many cases classes have to be canceled because there aren't enough rooms. There are kids in my division [homeroom] who were cut out of art or music classes because of this. They have to hold classes in the auditorium, and you can't conduct classes in there.

"Even then our school isn't as bad in some cases as —— [a "good" white school], where none of the departments have offices, where the nurses and speech therapists don't have private conference places, where the halls are so narrow they have to have one-way traffic. Libraries have to be used as study halls in some schools. Kids wait in line so long for lunch they never get a chance to eat. The outer schools and inner-city schools are both crowded, but the Negro often worse than the white.

"I think there has been gerrymandering to keep Negroes out of white school districts. The school board has to reflect the sentiments of the public, and they haven't convinced the public that it's desirable to racially integrate the schools. I think it is their responsibility to do so if they consider themselves top-flight professional educators. One of the basic ingredients in quality education is providing the kids with the environment that is as much like the world in which they are going to live as they can, and we don't live in a lily-white world.

"Also, I think in these inner-city schools you have to recruit teachers who are as interested in social work as they are in teaching—teacher-social workers who are willing to visit homes, to get involved in recreation projects and show responsible leadership to the kids in a non-classroom situation. If there were more emphasis on working with kids in the whole setting, after as well as during school, I think they could do a lot more toward getting these kids to want to learn and in overcoming this mental image that all of them seem to have that school is a jail and teachers are wardens.

"You need a general superintendent whose attitude is not that of running the school system as a big business enterprise with monetary values, but who comes to a big city like this with a background of social work and then in terms of educational administration puts the emphasis on curriculum and subject matter rather than physical plant and the business aspects.

"Principals are not selected for the way in which they have displayed leadership qualities in working with other teachers. There is no in-service training program for giving teachers opportunities to work with other teachers in the system, so they take a written test comprised mainly of multiple-choice questions which parrot back a lot of routine answers to routine questions. This method seems to select the least imaginative, mediocre, time-serving type of people to become principals instead of people with some imagination, creativity and sensitivity to human values.

"Principals need a social-worker approach, too. They need to be out in the community, getting to know the people and seeking help with some of the problems we have. But nowadays, being a principal is just like being in business. You have a nine-to-five job and then you're through. Or else you go into another job, moonlighting. Our principal has a job four nights a week at a vocational high school. He has no time for the community. Having P.T.A. meetings at night would be an intrusion on him. So there is no P.T.A. to speak of—maybe 15 or 20 parents out of an enrollment of 3,500—because most of the parents work in the daytime and can't get to afternoon meetings. That's just one of the instances of lack of sincerity to get the parents really interested.

"Some principals couple their indifference with a reign of fear and intimidation, directed at both students and teachers. At [a white high school] they had a principal who used tactics more appropriate to a warden of a penitentiary than the principal of a high school. He opened teachers' personal mail. He pulled teachers away from tutoring students to stand corridor duty. He said, 'You have to devote your full time to being a policeman here.' He said teachers could not meet with clubs after school, so a lot of clubs had to be dropped. He also locked the doors of the building to keep the students out until about five minutes before their first classes. He locked the teachers out, too. On rainy days they stood in the rain.

"These people know they are not educators. Yet they remain untouched in the Chicago system. Once people with any intelligence or creativity get into the system they find out what they are up against and get out as quick as they can. They find that the quality of education is way below what it is in any of your best suburban systems, either for those kids at the bottom of the economic ladder or those at the top. At the white schools on the fringes of the city and in upper-income neighborhoods, the level is vastly better than in our inner-city schools, primarily because of the caliber of students, because your most experienced teachers are there and because the parents are concerned and keep an eye on what is going on. But if you compare what's going on in these 'good' white schools to what is going on at Evanston or New Trier or Niles [suburban high schools], there's as much difference between them and Chicago's 'good' schools as between these good schools and the inner-city schools. The methods in Chicago schools are the ones the suburban high schools used twenty-five years ago and which are so outdated that it's really pathetic. The kids in Chicago's white schools are being short-changed just as much as our kids in the center of the city, because they are really going to run up against a rough time when they try to get into college. You don't find any of this variety of activities that go on in the suburban high schools in Chicago, except in the athletic field. And here in Chicago in the athletic field they don't schedule the games on Saturdays and nights because they can't pay the coaches for staying after school or on weekends for this kind of work. So they take the kids *out of class* to be spectators at football and basketball games regularly, throughout the schools in the city. How much are they really concerned therefore with academic achievement?"

He is not alone. Elsewhere on the West Side, at a once-white girl's vocational school where nine out of ten faces now are Negro, a baby-faced history teacher estimates that his colleagues will "turn over" 30 per cent or more this year. Half the faculty already is substitute and he knows "very few" who are planning to stay longer than three years. He has been there two; he knows how they feel:

"It is not the kind of place you would make a career of teaching at. A large percentage of the teachers become discouraged after a relatively short time. They feel they're not accomplishing much and adopt the attitude that they're going to present the material and if the kids don't take it, that's too bad. Nine-tenths of the kids won't take it. Some of the better kids I've talked to realize it's a vicious circle. They seem to know that in that kind of neighborhood, with their breeding and the attitude of the teachers, they're going to end up as bad as their parents.

"At first, teachers may make an attempt to adjust their presentation to the receptive capacity of these kids. It's called simulation—educational games, really, trying to get them interested without it seeming to be an educational situation. But most teachers feel it's probably not worth the five or six times as much effort it takes to work out something creative. It's considerably easier to keep the kids busy with assignment reading, plodding through miserable busywork. Easier on yourself, and in many ways on the kid, probably. If you can keep them occupied that way, they're not bothering each other.

"Because a lot of teachers do this, students become used to having some kind of routine work sheet for every class. It seems to me it would be awfully boring to have six class periods a day occupied with filling in the blanks, although it appears that in the majority of cases boredom is the ultimate response no matter what approach you use.

"It's very difficult to place the blame. These kids spend considerably more time on the streets than they spend in school, and it colors everything about them. Then there's their previous schooling. The largest problem I have teaching history is that a large number of kids can't read or write beyond a fourth-grade level. Then there are the high school teachers. Many regard teaching as just an extra income and hold other jobs after school which are their main occupation. In the fall and spring, one man in our business department takes off for three or four weeks to tend to his farm. In class he's always talking with a certain group of the girls, usually about sex. The rest of his class is running rampant—crawling on their hands and knees out the door and then getting out in the halls and running around.

"Some teachers are movie kings and queens. They show as many as five movies a week. It doesn't matter what subject they teach or what the movie is about.

"One of my colleagues taught summer school at [a predominantly Jewish high school] this summer and says he wouldn't like to teach there full time because it was much more demanding; you had to work harder to keep one jump ahead of the kids all the time. This certainly says something about his ability. No matter how bright a student you have, no high school student should be intellectual competition for a teacher. Of course, here you can get away with almost no content level. Just bluff your way through. The kids won't call you on anything, or the parents either. (

"The Negro teachers aren't any more dedicated than the white teachers. In some ways they're probably more middle-class-value oriented than some of the white teachers. Most of them are leaving. Some want to get into a college or university. Some just want to transfer to a better school, preferably on the North Side, where there's a reputation for academic excellence. They may have trouble getting in there. I know Negro kids have a great deal of trouble. There's one extremely bright sophomore who's in my class this year. When she graduated from the upper grades, she was given the choice of going to [two Negro high schools or the girl's vocational school]. She said she didn't want to go to any of them, that she wanted to take advantage of a voluntary transfer plan then in effect and go somewhere else in the city. Her mother—a college graduate, very educated woman —has been downtown several times over a two-year period trying to get her daughter transferred—unsuccessfully. Just a big run-around. She's still trying and everyone she sees sends her to someone else. So here's this really very bright girl in a vocational school, academically the best of her three alternatives.

"Whether this girl's experience is the result of race or a reflection of the fact that no one in this system seems to know what's going on, who can say? Everything happens like this. Take the way the after-school reading program was set up. I have one of these classes. They started on a Monday, and it was the Friday before that they asked me if I'd do it. Materials are starting to come in now—after eight weeks. Up to now it's just been pretty much trying to use as many gimmicks as you can to keep the kids interested. The assistant principal's main objective was to keep class attendance up because, you see, they're rating the various schools on pupil attendance, not on quality.

"The counseling system is another area of chaos. We have four counselors for two thousand students, and two of them actually are part-time office clerks because they are taken off their counseling duties and given odd jobs almost continually. So you send a behavior card down and you'll be lucky if the counselor sees the kid in two weeks. By that time any punishment or attempt to reason with the kid doesn't mean much because almost everybody has forgotten about the incident.

"Racial prejudice definitely plays a part in the counseling program. All the counselors are white, and when they get information about scholarships or honors or awards—things of that nature—only on rare occasions are Negro girls ever called in. The majority of times they call in a group of white girls to tell them how to apply for whatever it is they've heard about. Often Negro girls who do go to college have to learn about opportunities through their churches. The school is of no help.

"Even all the student aides in the office are white, with a school population that is more than 90 per cent Negro. In some classes no Negro girl will ever get higher than a "C" because the teachers are so very prejudiced. In other words, the bright Negro student who has a potential for more than a life in the slums is fighting an uphill fight."

> Academic wanderlust does not nag another man, a Polish Catholic who teaches science at an upper-grade center, the local euphemism for junior high school. He matriculated at parochial schools, but his professional loyalty lies with Chicago's public system, and his Holy Grail is a niche in administration. In his limited pyramid-climbing—four years in the system—he has encountered faults with the schools, he says, the greatest being the students. The memory of the months he spent at a Negro elementary school comes back to him like a living page from *The Blackboard Jungle:*

"It was my first assignment. There wasn't much being offered, mostly schools in Negro neighborhoods. I figured you have to put in a certain number of years in a rugged school before you get to better schools anyhow. And I had a lot of friends on the faculty there. I didn't mind putting up with some abuse, the old humane, I-will-be-a-martyr bit. So I chose this West Side school.

"I hate to say it, but the fault for the problems I found on the West Side lies mainly with the child—the way he is brought up, his attitude, his indifference. The vast majority of these kids are bad, just bad. They won't do school work or conform to rules. There is hostility toward any white teacher, any authority symbol. It is manifested by defiance, insults, the usual four-letter words mumbled and shouted at you in and out of classrooms, people throwing things at you just for kicks. There are always two or three kids who are sleeping in class, either because they have a job or they've been out on the streets all night. A large percentage are totally indifferent to school and don't want to be educated. You have some students who make an effort, but then the problem is self-control. There are too many things to distract them. They are more interested in what is going to happen at the next game, or in some fight, or in what happened to little Mary. This you find in any school. But it was different there because little Mary was probably getting pregnant.

"We could have used ten full-time psychologists for all the psychological problems. I had one kid, fourteen, so mentally retarded he couldn't even tie his own shoelaces. I spent one entire day trying to teach him to work a combination lock. I said to the assistant principal, 'Couldn't we send him some place?' He said, 'Mr. ——, there are no EMH [educable mentally handicapped] facilities in District ——— for boys.' So there he was in my classroom. I had another kid in my class with a 65 IQ. They told me nothing could be done. We graduated a number, incidentally, who could barely read and write. Our principal used to be a psychologist. He felt it did no good to flunk a kid, so you just passed the kid on, regardless. These kids grow up tough. Their own solution is to fight, and they do. The race line didn't enter into it. If a Negro teacher expects them to study, learn and do work, the hostility builds up against him, too. We had one Negro teacher struggle with a girl who had a fork wrapped around her hand with the prongs sticking out so she could carve up his face.

"The funny thing you find in these schools is that the *Negro* teachers come storming into the teachers' john every so often and say, 'Those damn savages!' echoing your sentiments exactly. The Negro teachers for the most part were dedicated teachers. We got many from Southern universities, however, and some of these could barely read and write. From Mississippi they could barely talk. But it really didn't matter much. Teaching was almost a secondary thing.

"The primary concern in such a school is to keep order. This is hard. I found out one thing after another that you could not do in terms of discipline. You couldn't stand a kid in the corner because it disrupted your class too much. You couldn't have him stand in the hall because he'd run around. You could not keep him late for his lunch hour because the principal frowned on the kid not eating, though I managed to sneak around that some. You weren't supposed to keep kids after school because they shouldn't cross the streets without crossing guards. You could give them punishment assignments, but they might not do them and they didn't care if they flunked. You could always threaten to send them to the office and have their mothers come in, but in many cases the parents were indifferent or afraid of incurring the child's wrath. Or they'd drag out the old cliché, prejudice: 'Yo' prej'dic'd 'ginst my chile. That's why yo' pickin' on him.' These parents aren't even interested enough to bother with P.T.A. We sent letters home with the kids about an open house in the afternoon to inaugurate P.T.A. and only about six parents came, out of an enrollment of eight hundred. Anyway, taking the kid to the office was practically impossible. One of the first weeks I was there I took a girl downstairs, and while I was gone somebody threw a chair through my book-cabinet window. The principal said I must never leave my class unsupervised, which I've never done again.

"I finally transferred out voluntarily after I got hit on the head by a kid with a big stick while about three hundred kids stood in the hall screaming for him to kill me. The police were never called, but it wouldn't have helped much.

"On the West Side, it's a status symbol to have a prison record or a probation officer. I was told by a counselor that of the 2,000 students at [another Negro high school] over four hundred are on probation now. With four hundred young, practically hardened criminals, how can you get much done? My solution for the whole problem would be to just take these kids away from their parents when they're born. Isolate them from that social environment. By the time they reach school now they are well down the road to hopelessness.

"I recall one kid who was bright and good and worth saving. His father was a drunk and his mother hated him. He ran away from home and she had him arrested for being incorrigible. He was working as a busboy and living on skid row when they picked him up. He could have been a college graduate easily, but he flunked out in the eighth grade—when he was reading everything he could get his hands on at the level of college fresh-man. The confusion in his life just overwhelmed the potential he had.

"Anyway, I asked for a transfer and moved to the —— Upper Grade Center. It's about 60 per cent white, 25 per cent Puerto Rican, 10 per cent Negro and the rest Indians, Filipinos, you-name-it-we-have-it. Most are from low-income families.

"I consider the move I made a move up. Not a hell of a long way up. If I had any sense I'd have my name on a transfer list right now, but I have my own project—the federal after-school reading program, which I supervise. It'll look great on my record if I ever take the principal's exam. Since this came along I decided to stay. If it hadn't, I would have gotten out, into a better school. This is a much better school than the other, but it's still no picnic. You still find a large percentage who won't work. Where on the West Side you could teach maybe 50 per cent of what you could in a good school, here you can teach 60 per cent.

"We don't have supply problems here, though. On the West Side, we got an awful lot of old, out-dated books. They'd ship new books to a white school and keep them five to eight years and then send them to us. The kids just destroyed them anyway. Here we get mostly new texts.

"If I had my choice I'd probably teach in one of those far North Side or Northwest Side schools, where the biggest prob-lem is the kid who chews gum everyday. These are the only places in Chicago where a kid can get a really good education. There the school is congenial to good teaching. You have inter-ested parents. By the time teachers get there, they are experi-enced. And those schools have stable faculties; the person who has been there for ten years is referred to as the 'new girl.' You can walk down the hall and hear a clock tick or the kindergart-ners singing. On the West Side, you hear screams and shouts and yells in the halls. Look into the kindergarten and there is Jeffrey throwing erasers at another child.

"Since we don't live far north, we'll probably send our kids to the local Catholic school. The people upstairs aren't even Catholic but they send their little girl to Catholic school. If we weren't Catholic, I'd probably move. There aren't Negroes in this district, but there are hillbillies, and I don't want my children coming home muttering four-letter words or to hear the realities of life at age six, seven or eight. Those colored kids and hillbillies know what it's all about in second and third grade. By the fifth grade, they're trying it.

"I think if school officials ever adopted a busing system or another system to really mix up the school system racially, you would not have to worry about integration any more—because you wouldn't have any white population left in the city. . . . I think the vast majority of white people would pack up and leave for Evanston or Highland Park. And the reaction would be a lot quicker than some people imagine.

"Someday I'd like to become an assistant principal or a principal. My ultimate goal is administration. If I were in a position where I could, I would build a social adjustment school in every rough district on the South, West and Near North Sides. These would have ten to fifteen children per classroom, and they would be strictly supervised, with policemen on duty. This would take out many of the problems that you have to contend with day in and day out. Then I'd cut the class size of West Side schools in half. I'd have twice as many schools with twice as many rooms. This would make for much better teaching situations. I would give the teachers more weapons to use in forcing good conduct, such as staying till 4:30. I'd force poor readers to stay in after-school reading programs without parents' consent. In many cases the kids go home now to babysit so mama can go drinking. We need more counselors in the schools. I'd also increase the number of psychiatrists. I'd constantly try to carry on a cultural enrichment sort of thing. We just had our first bus (field) trip with the after-school reading program, and it was three months in coming. This stuff should be carried on constantly in culturally deprived neighborhoods. Take them to the Chicago Symphony, to quality movies. Expose them to the rest of the world. Give them ideals. Have a doctor come in and cut up a cow and make them wonder how he learns all this. I don't think you get anywhere having them march around school singing freedom songs. Better to march them down to a library.

"Actually, this is the first time I really thought of what I would do to improve things. Schools are going to continue to go downhill. Violence will increase and people will be wringing their hands. But what can the schools do?"

An echo comes from a tall, graying, white woman, four years from retirement from the Chicago system. The near-Loop school where she teaches third grade was once a bridge on which the offspring of Italian and German immigrants crossed into American society. Now the neighborhood is almost wholly black. In rag-curtained rooms above sagging store-front churches, some families burn old auto batteries to keep warm in winter. The teacher walks past these places every day to reach the school, and she feels they stand like a wall between herself and the children in her charge:

"I don't think communication in these homes is what it should be; for one thing, even the parents speak only in short words and sentences. And I just wonder if they ever sit around and really carry on a conversation about world affairs.

"I don't imagine there's a great deal of reading, either. I have not been in the homes and really don't know, but this is my assumption. If you ask for magazines or newspapers, right away they [the children] say, 'We don't have any.' So I'm sure that this is due to the fact that they just don't buy them.

"They have TVs, I think. For years *we* didn't have one; in fact, everyone in the class had a TV but the teacher. However, I dare say not very many of them would turn on Channel 11 to listen to some good educational programs. And that makes it difficult for the rest of us who would like to have more good programs on TV because they go by the ratings, and so there you are.

"Another thing: you give a child a book and at the end of a term it isn't fit to pass on to another child. It will come back with tears, colored crayon marks, pages cut out. They're just not taught to take care of things. Many times I have seen a child come in with a brand-new pencil and leave at the end of the day with a stub—from sharpening it all day long.

"Yesterday about a dozen children lost their pencils. Three left their books at home, and one left a workbook at home. I said, 'All right, we will put our work away and we will sit with folded hands because it's evident to me that you are not interested in learning.'

"The most discouraging thing is the apathy of these parents. It disheartens me at times that the parents keep these children out of school to babysit with the others while they go out to shop or whatever they do. And they don't feed the children balanced meals. I brought a beet top in to grow in class, and the children didn't know what it was. They had never eaten beets.

"If the parents were interested in giving their children as good an education as teachers are, they could at least furnish them a few of the tools. But try to get the parents to supply pencils or crayons or materials like that. The children come to school loaded with candy every day. They drink soda pop instead of milk at home. If these children can be furnished those things, a pencil and a box of crayons is not too much to ask. After all, we furnish the paper and their textbooks.

"I think they're going to have to learn that you have to work for things. Everybody should realize that we get out of life what we put into it. And if they're not going to put forth an effort to give their children an education, then you can't expect the schools to do it all. The more you make a person depend on you or on the aid they get, the less that person is going to put forth an effort to work out his own problems. Each time I give a child a pencil, am I not taking the responsibility away from his parents? These simple things multiply, and the more responsibility you take away from them the more they're going to be irresponsible.

"I grant you that for many years Negroes were held down. Their responsibilities were taken away from them. They needed a doctor, and the doctor was provided; they needed clothing, clothing was provided. But now we've got to teach them to take back that responsibility. What part can the schools play in this process? Well, I don't know. That's something I'd just have to kind of think about."

A lively young brunette has done some thinking. A few months ago she came from a Midwest tank town to a Chicago neighborhood where "you can buy dope practically anyplace" to teach while her husband finishes his professional schooling. Her inner-city upper-grade center is roughly 10 per cent Puerto Rican, 40 per cent Negro, 50 per cent white—and 100 per cent poor. Many of her students would not know their fathers if they walked into the classrooms. Many list their mother's occupation as "ADC." Her experiences as a new teacher have convinced her that her classes have to fight not only their environment but the school to get an education—and that they are overmatched:

"I wanted to teach in the city because I feel strongly that something has to be done about the city schools. Of course, being naïve, I thought I could do something. I've since learned that there's not much that can be done.

"They are supposedly hiring elementary-trained teachers (for upper grade centers), but there aren't enough, so they [the administration] take high-school trained, which is what I am. The first day we were there they went around to all the new teachers and asked what they wanted to teach. They didn't look at records. I got English, for which I'm trained. Another teacher got the library, for which she isn't trained.

"All of us in our departmental are new to the Chicago system. Two of us are new to teaching. But there was *no* orientation. The excuse is that there are no funds. But, when you have fifteen new teachers coming into a school, you orient them, somehow. You at least show them where the washroom is. Whatever you learn you pick up in conversations with other teachers. In our departmental, nobody was put in charge. We decided ourselves when we would pass classes. There were no schedules. Nothing. We could have done anything.

"Surprises kept cropping up. A week before the first report period went out—this was nine weeks after school started—I found out that I was to grade art and music. Up till that time I had never been told that I was to teach these subjects. I had to grade music and I had no piano. So I graded music and I graded art without them ever having it. To arrive at grades I gave them all G in music, and in art I gave them one crayon thing. Unless they refused to do it, I gave them S [average].*

"The grading is very mixed up. I taught spelling to all four of my departmental classes. Then at the end of the first report period, they said homeroom teachers were to grade spelling. I had taught it. The homeroom teachers hadn't, but they had to grade it.

"The physical setup is just as unbelievable. The upper-grade center is in the same building as ——— Vocational High

---

* In Chicago's grading system, students are marked E for excellent, G for good, S for satisfactory and U for unsatisfactory.

School. They are set up to be two separate schools, although one principal is over both. You have to work in the building to really see the significance of two schools in one building.

"I teach in the basement, which has high school shops—printing, automobile shop, all of these—and eight to ten seventh grades. Many of my frustrations have been just because of these physical arrangements, because the attitude of the vocational high school is radically different. For instance, it has the students who haven't been able to go to an academic high school. They are in an atmosphere of nonlearning. They are allowed to cut classes and nothing is done about them. You have a tremendous rate of illegitimate children being born to unwed mothers. Smoking in the school is a problem; so is setting off fire alarms. There are big fights. They pass classes in the vocational school when we're trying to hold class. They get out for lunch a half hour before the upper-grade center, so right across the hall from us are all these people milling around. We have dropouts wandering through the basement constantly, throwing bottles, drinking, anything to harass. One girl was walking around the building drunk. There's an alley outside my window and boys from the vocational school stand out there to smoke. Every now and then they start throwing bottles in the windows. One day this was going on and during the same period I opened the door and somebody threw French fries at me. One day somebody threw a big rock at me in the basement. They especially like to harass new teachers. I don't beat the children, but there are rumors going around—they go around for all the white teachers—that 'You have disciplined my little brother too much,' or 'There's going to be a big kid get you,' or 'I'm going to bomb your house or your car.' I feel physical fear. These are very emotional people. They throw chairs or anything. This affects these seventh- and eighth-graders who see what's going on, and you see them changing.

"There are so many things. We are using classrooms that shouldn't be used, they're so old. We are overcrowded. The rooms are so small and poorly designed you can't even get a whole class in. We have a *man* gym teacher with the seventh- and eighth-grade *girls*. There is no art or music teacher. The science teacher next to me has no science lab, no Bunsen burner, no books. He teaches off the top of his head. There's no playground. There's a library where they go once a week. In the whole departmental there are enough crayons for one class, so we take turns.

"In the seventh and eighth grades, we have everybody from the EMH—educable, mentally handicapped—clear on up to college preparatory ability, all lumped together. There are two special EMH classes of fifteen each, but neither of the teachers is really trained for EMH. They could only have two classes, so they took the very worst thirty and the rest had to go into regular classes, which are supposed to be at grade level. I have readers in the seventh grade who read from third-grade to seventh-grade level. The average is about 5.5. I have students who could go on to college, but I don't think they're going to get there. They're not learning anything. I have one set of English books for one hundred-forty students. They stay with the desks. They do not leave the room. I can take literature books out of the counselor's office to use in class, but they usually don't go all the way around. There are no plays in the whole building, no basic readers. These kids are in an atmosphere of nonlearning, control only, and it's terrible.

"I don't think the Negro teachers have as much trouble, certainly not with discipline. Most of them have been there six to eight years and are very dedicated, intelligent, well-groomed men—the perfect example that you put up to children who have no fathers. Nothing goes wrong in their classrooms.

"Of course, you've got to understand the difference between the new and old teachers. An old teacher knows the way Chicago runs, knows Chicago slum children. Most people [teachers] go to a school like mine despising every minute of it because they are somewhere they don't want to be, or so full of ideals for the civil rights movement that they're on the other extreme. Neither does very well. In fact, the one without ideals may do better because they are harder. I was much too easy, too understanding. I was trying to teach in a school like I attended until I found out that these children don't expect to be anything but sweared at. You don't say, 'Sit down, please.' You say, *'Sit down, buddy!'* At the beginning of the year, [men teachers] were throwing kids up against the wall.

"Control—the magic word. This whole year I'm learning it. I am teaching nothing, as far as I'm concerned. Nor is the teacher next to me who teaches science, nor the one on the other side who teaches social studies. Maybe the math teacher who has taught in Chicago one year before is. The rest of us have fought for control, for some sort of respect so that oral discussion can take place.

"The principal walks through the halls and sees what's going on, but he doesn't bring any pressure to bear. He's interested in all the small things—clean halls, no bottles around. He wants what looks like a well-run organization. We've had only three teachers' meetings this year. No one checks on what's going on in the classroom. I don't even make out my lessons-plan book.

"There's no way you can change [the school] until you get a new principal. Our assistant principal does what he can, but he can only go so far. The first year he was there he flunked about 18 per cent of our children because they were all reading so far below seventh grade that it's better for them to flunk. Officials downtown were furious. He had to come downtown and account for every child he flunked. Every one. Since then he's flunked only the bare minimum, 3 per cent.

"There are children here who have ability. We have some who could easily go on to business school or college. And you see them trying. You wonder how, sometimes, how their enthusiasm stays.

"In many ways, I feel it is too late for these children. Their parent—singular—is busy working or raising eight other children. The children in school are not interested. They can't read. You see, all of their school literature is for the white child only, either a fairy tale or too hard for them; there's nobody writing for the Negro in this type situation. You can't laugh with these children because they go out of control. If one child is allowed to get out of his seat without permission, then all day long they're sharpening pencils, shooting rubber bands, shooting spitballs, anything. It's terrible to say, but you can't give any freedom. And how can people grow up without freedom? These children have to be told everything. And if they have to be told everything, they'll never get out in society. They'll be ADC mothers, men without jobs.

Out west near the city's skid row frontier, where neon signs for fireproof rooms and 80-proof booze give way to ads for hair processors and skin lighteners, a young former social worker experiences many of the same frustrations. She teaches kindergarten in a school where half the children live in high-rise housing projects—"the colored Stonehenge," a colleague calls them. In her first year there, she feels she has witnessed as much contrast between what she wanted in teaching and what she has gotten as between her own white skin and the dark skin of her pupils:

"When I first applied for a school, I said I wanted a North Side school because people think they are the best schools. They [school personnel officials] said, 'Ha, ha.' They told me at the board that my chances of a North Side school were nil. I ended up on the West Side. I got the assignment over the phone at 10 A.M. I went in that afternoon at 12:30, waited for the principal till 12:55. She came and took me to my room, and the kids came in at 1:00. So much for orientation.

"I get most of my help from the other kindergarten teachers. One is Negro, the other white. The white one is more helpful. The Negro is trained for high school English, and isn't equipped in any way for this level.

"The principal has come to my room twice since that first day—once to ask if I could use more play equipment, and once to reserve one boy's painting because she needed some examples of creative work for a display. I feel unsupervised.

"The parents often aren't very concerned. I've had maybe half a dozen parents introduce themselves to me. They want to know how the children are doing and say if they misbehave I should spank them. They don't ask questions about the education. I don't think parents are aware of whether their kids are getting a good education. They trust the school system. They don't know enough to criticize.

"I must admit I yearn now and then for a classroom such as my friends in the suburbs describe. A school like ours needs a teacher who is a pro. I'm willing to do my best, but I'm not the best one for the job and neither are many others there. You need to be trained for this. Other teachers say what these kids need is a man. They seem to live too much in a matriarchal society.

"When I came I thought you said 'please' and 'thank you.' I found something very different when I got here. I found out why it was quiet in other rooms. They hold the rod and use it. Some of these teachers couldn't teach without a ruler. A quiet class-room is considered a good one. No one asks if you are teaching.

One teacher told me that that was all you could do—hurt them, use a ruler.

"I thought in the beginning that being white would hinder my relating with parents and children. I still wonder. Yesterday I saw two boys start fighting. I took the culprit by the arms and pulled him away. One girl said, 'You white people are always hitting us Negroes.' This hurt me. A friend of mine says this is just a defense mechanism they throw up. But the feeling still must be there.

"There are good and bad schools in Chicago. I don't know if I would consider the white schools necessarily good ones. I do know I wouldn't send my kids to the Negro school I'm in. I might take them to an integrated school where the atmosphere is not threatening, but calm, yet with good discipline. If I lived in the inner city I think I would send my children to a private school. To do otherwise would be sacrificing your children to your crusade. I talk about this to the Negro kindergarten teacher. She says the thought of her child going to this school frightens her."

Another young teacher, slender, with long raven hair, knows about despair too. She criss-crosses the city as a substitute now, but for a year she taught at a Negro elementary school in the West Side jungle "because I wanted to work with deprived children." Their deprivation, she discovered, extends to their school; in many cases to their teachers as well. She remembers kindergarten in the ghetto:

"When I arrived at the school the first day I found that the other two kindergarten teachers were Negroes. Neither was certified. In fact, there was only one certified teacher in a school of twelve hundred pupils. One of the kindergarten teachers was in her early forties, a divorcee from the South with a very, very poor education and very self-conscious about it. She had been teaching kindergarten as a full-time-basis substitute since the school opened three years before. The other was a very young thing, pleasant and easy-going, with no kindergarten training, who had grown up and gone to school in the South. She had been at this school the year before. She was working on her bulletin boards that first day. Bulletin boards are of primary importance to this school's principal because of the impression they make on outsiders. You can be a terrible teacher, but as long as your bulletin boards are shipshape the impression is that you are a good teacher. Neither girl had any lesson plans. They didn't seem to realize that the next day the children would be there and that first impressions are important.

"Well, the children came. The kindergarten rooms were designed for about thirty, but in the first two or three weeks the enrollment inched up to about thirty-five. Many people registered late, and the enrollment continued to go up. Soon we had in the high forties in each class. There were only two rooms, so I switched back and forth, helping each of the other teachers for half a day. In no time at all I was teaching two hundred kindergarten children a day. Both of the other teachers turned over their classes to me completely when I was there and either worked on records or just sat. The concept of working with me so that the children could have more individual attention was alien to them. The children did need attention, and of course having two hundred a day I didn't begin to know one from the other. The other teachers couldn't have cared less. The older one said she never got to know her children by name and didn't expect to. These children deserved the most conscientious, hard-working teachers, the cream of the crop, because they came from nothing in most cases. The importance of kindergarten can't be overstressed where there is such limited background. Everything depended upon their having something at school. Yet these teachers sloughed off.

"Neither played the piano. I do, so I taught the children songs and rhythms. These teachers had never had rhythms with their children before.

"At no time, though, did I have more than forty-two chairs in the room. What chairs there were had to be packed around the tables so that a table for six was seating ten. This meant they had no elbow room, and before the year was out these long-suffering children began to realize that chairs were at a premium. They began to snatch them from one another and grab them out from under children who were already sitting on them with not a backward glance to see what happened. These were not vicious children; they just got fed up with not having a place to sit. Actually, there wasn't even floor space for fifty-seven children.

"So all the things I had—supplementary games and all the other things for individual tables of four—I couldn't use. And I want you to know—I want to say this real loud on the tape—I had so many bright children whose greatest joy was to learn it just put me in a delirium of gladness. They were just like sponges. They would soak up everything. It was not some stultified semimorons that I had fifty-seven of. I had at least twelve that I could have had reading well before the year was out, if they hadn't been in this impossible situation.

"I suspect they have continued to be bandied about from pillar to post since leaving kindergarten. A kindergarten or first-grade child doesn't know what's coming off. But a third- or fourth-grader—they know. They not only suffer, but perceive. By sixth grade they are withdrawn, sullen, hostile, discouraged.

"Many of the Negro teachers seemed concerned about conditions in the school. But none would have ever gone to the principal to correct things. I went to the principal after I had been there two weeks and explained that we needed some crayons. We had paper and some black crayons and a few brown ones that were left over from the year before. That was all. I had already pled with both kindergarten teachers about this and they'd said, 'There's no way to get any more.' The principal couldn't believe we didn't have supplies. She said, 'Why, the storerooms are gorged. Why haven't you gotten them?' She personally brought supplies to the room—cases and packs and boxes—and these two kindergarten teachers were so grateful that I'd gone to bat for them. They hadn't tried and been rejected. They just wouldn't stick their necks out.

"I began to form some generalizations about Negro schoolteachers. They seem to have no academic background, no conception of professionalism or any abstractions that would apply to children. When I talked with most Negro teachers, there was nothing. I was talking to a void. Most of them are from the South and have all kinds of problems, but this always harks back to segregation, which has been their heritage for generations. They are each caught in one way or another.

"For instance, this older kindergarten teacher told me that her only alternative to this job was to go back home to Louisiana and work as a domestic at $25 a week to support her three children. She was so meticulous about getting no ink spots on her attendance book that she made almost a religious fetish about keeping it neat. The principal saw this book, and its appearance figured in the teacher's rating. But the principal never came to the classroom, and when it came to teaching the children this teacher didn't have anything to offer. At the end of the day her room looked like a nightmare. You'd find bits of crayons scribbled on the blackboard, all over new tables and chairs, ground under foot. There were wads of paper around the room as though it were a garbage dump. By her own admission she was a very poor speller. She sent incorrectly spelled, wrongly punctuated notes home to parents. The children copied these words for exercises. Even her alphabets were incorrectly lettered. Her main concern was just keeping the children quiet.

"I felt that faculty morale was extremely low at our school and one reason was constant classroom reorganization. The teachers just make out their record books and start to do some serious work with their children only to have classes shuffled and new children brought in. This happened several times in the first few months. Teachers who had one grade had half of it taken away and half of a different grade put in. So they had what is called a split division—a second grade and low third grade, for example. It means you're doing a juggling act all the time.

"The principal wanted no kind of parents' organization connected with the school. She was desperately afraid that people had been planted in the community to make trouble. Perhaps civil rights people, perhaps Communists. So there was no P.T.A. in the school and there had never been an open house.

"Inadvertently I mentioned to the principal one time that I had invited mothers to stay for class when they brought milk money. She seemed just terrified. 'Parents in your room!' she said. 'There shouldn't be any parents in your room! They have no business in your room!' Also, I mentioned that I had said something to a parent about there being fifty-seven children in the classroom, and she said, 'It's none of their business that there are fifty-seven children in the room. Don't tell them that or you'll have the whole neighborhood making trouble for the school.'

"I really don't think her fear is justified in that regard, and again this goes back to race. These people by and large are so distraught with their human problems, like what are they going to eat tonight and when is the Man going to turn on the heat, and where can we get money for shoes so our child can go to school—I did have children absent for a month because they didn't have shoes—they are so concerned with all this that they wouldn't begin to know what to do about overcrowded classes or begin to have the emotional energy to do anything about it. They are completely ground down as human beings.

"In subbing, I've skated around quite a bit. I've seen several Negro schools that are a botch administratively and others in just as deprived areas where the children are achieving, where they have an enthusiasm to learn. Everything in these schools is excellently ordered and supervised. I think the principal must be the deciding factor.

"On the whole, though, the minute I walk into the average inner-city school, I feel a kind of subtle tenseness. The faculty may give the impression of being very flighty and very casual. You see them going by in the halls and there are just gales of laughter, like sixteen-year-olds. They're letting off pressure, I think, trying not to think about or take seriously this serious situation that they are in. Whereas you walk into a North Side white school and the contrast is marked. There is a freedom there. You can draw a breath without being afraid that you won't get the next one, whether you are a teacher or an administrator or a child.

"I believe that if all the financial and intellectual resources we have were focused on the problems of educating Chicago's children, we would have plenty to keep us busy for years. I keep dreaming of what these children need to get out of this [slum] hellhole, and I see one of their first and only breaks in life being the public school. Then I see the Chicago public school system not giving it to them, and it makes me hate the system."

For a pale, stooped man who commutes each day to the sooty heart of Chicago's South Side, the slums have become a career. Professionally he has never left the ghetto. After thirteen years in the system he is principal of "a very normal Negro elementary school," flanked by towering, gray, public-housing skyscrapers. From this vantage point he feels he has come to know the children who enter Chicago classrooms, the adults they meet there, and the problems both weave into the educational tapestry:

"There is a vast difference in the quality of education available from school to school in Chicago. Kids do not get equal education. For one thing, you've got the family background. If the kid isn't ready when he goes into first and second grade, there's nothing you can do with him, really. Compared with the kids who've got the background and the home, he's lost. Here in the ghetto we find an anomic situation—a state of normlessness in which there is complete emotional chaos within the individual. With the Negro family, this is it, all the way through. This describes so many things in a slum school. You see a kid walking along with a baseball bat banging out windows. Why? Just because he's completely shot and has to do something. When you come to school with that kind of background, everything else is secondary.

"In a city like Chicago, race helps determine the home background, of course. Too many people damn the schools when they should damn the city. The city throws up a bunch of high-rise housing projects along State Street which are vertical ghetto slums, and destroys these people by confining them there. The kids come to school with no hope, and the schools are blamed for not producing. It's not quite fair.

"Then there is the teaching situation. In education as it is now set up, we are all trying to conform to a norm which is the white standard. Negro kids are going to have to produce to this standard to be accepted by the white society. And there they are completely left out, because they have no background in this norm in the ghetto. They see no white students, and they see very few white teachers. In short, they can't see the white norm. Therefore, they can't get the same education that a white student can.

"One of the great disadvantages to the Negro community is that the kids do not come into contact with white teachers, generally. Probably 95 per cent of teachers in Negro schools are Negro. When Negroes start moving into a school, white teachers transfer out as fast as they can. Now there's nothing wrong with a Negro teacher, but he is carrying along the Negro mannerisms that the whites deprecate. If a Negro teacher talks in dialect to a class, the class is going to continue talking dialect.

"The other thing is that Negro teachers do not necessarily come from top universities. Many come in from the South or fringe schools in the Chicago area. They go into teaching because they find status there. There is a great demand in industry for very bright, articulate Negroes, so they will not go into teaching. So often you are left with Negro teachers who have come out of the same kind of background as the students.

"However, a very important factor is that the Negroes who teach are entering the Negro middle class. I know very few Negro teachers whose wives or husbands don't also teach. This means an income of from $10,000 to $20,000 a year for this family. Even by 'white' terms they are affluent. They don't have a tendency to look down on their students—this is a fallacy being bandied around—but they are very unhappy if the Negro students do not excel. They try to adhere to standards they would normally expect in a white school. They'll take a seventh- or eighth-grader who is reading at the fifth-grade level and say that he should not graduate because he is not reading at the eighth-grade level. Then the principal has to say, 'You can't fail this kid because he's been failed twice, and next year he'll be a sixteen-year-old in the grammar school. He'll drop out immediately.' I'm sure if a Negro ran into the same problem in a white school, he'd be much more sympathetic.

"Among white and Negro teachers both, there's great transiency in the ghetto schools. This has its influence, too. In a stable school where teachers stay on to retirement, that teacher becomes better as time goes on. She builds a reputation in the community among the kids. She's got her control established before they walk in the room. In a ghetto school, your faculty is so highly transient the kids and the teachers start fresh every year. This is a major factor in quality.

"Another major matter of concern is that we don't get any substitutes, day-to-day substitutes, for when a teacher's absent. The white schools don't get all they want, of course, but we don't get *any;* well, maybe ten in a year's time. The reason is that the white subs are housewives working only one or two days a week, and of course they live on the North Side or in the suburbs. So you have a transportation factor. The sooner the sub gets to a school, the faster you have someone in the room with the children, so they generally are assigned near where they live. There aren't qualified subs living near Negro areas. Negroes who qualify are teaching full-time. So if one teacher is absent, I send in the gym teacher. If two are absent, I put in the librarian, and so on. Sometimes in the ghetto schools the librarian is subbing the entire week, which means, of course, that the kids can't use the library.

"And the counseling system—it's the rule that they are almost ineffective. Each counselor has four hundred to five hundred kids. This can't work. There's no time. Counselors are so busy doing other things—like tabulating truants—that they have almost no time for kids.

"Then there are physical factors. There's a lot of flurry in the papers occasionally that the Negro schools are denied funds that the white schools have. This is hogwash. They get more, but they have a higher loss rate through vandalism and theft. If someone breaks into your school and swipes all the projectors, it may take you five to seven months to get new ones from the board. How can a school do without a movie projector for this long? But it happens every day. Textbooks—we have kids who have gone to fifteen different schools because of the transiency rate in Negro schools; they leave one school and take their textbooks with them, and you can't get the books back. So despite the fact that we get more money we still have fewer books and supplies.

"I think there should be Negro kids in every school in the city, but it's not a function of the schools to bring about integration. Kids shouldn't be bused to racially mix a school. Instead, Negroes should be allowed to live anywhere they want so they can go to any school they want. The schools by and large are segregated racially because neighborhoods are segregated, and we have a neighborhood school system. On the other hand, schools in some cases could have been integrated by the board of education, yet the boundary lines were changed to keep them all-white or all-Negro until the immediate area around the school changed. [A formerly all-white school] is a classic case in point. As the Negroes moved west, the boundary line kept changing west. More and more kids were fed into [an all-Negro school], and fewer were fed into —— until Negroes leaped across —— Park and moved into the —— area. At that point, the high school was given up to Negroes. Give it five years and it will be a Negro school. [Another high school] is exactly the same way. It's changing so fast I would give it only one or two years before it's all Negro. There were boundary changes all the way until finally the [housing] turnover became so rapid that they [school officials] just gave up.

"In both these cases the whites in the area are not necessarily the type who would stay, so that if they held the boundary rigid and the Negroes moved into the adjoining block, the place would go like wildfire. So maybe the board had a certain point in holding the line.

"There was one school on the West Side in an old established, white, working-class area. It was once two buildings, a fairly new one and a very old one, and while they were double-shifting the Negro schools just a few blocks away, this school had empty rooms. There was a big hue and cry about this, and the board finally turned part of this school into a multidistrict physical education school for crippled kids, Negro and white. Well, the white pressure groups in the area got so active that they [school officials] tore the school down. They actually leveled it. ——— School on the West Side is another case. Heart of Chicago, a segregationist group, got in there and kept it white, kindergarten through eighth grade, while all the other schools in the area feed their seventh- and eighth-graders into a Negro upper-grade center. The upper-grade center is within a mile of this school. But this school is all white and the kids don't go to the upper-grade center. Another West Side school had a third floor which was completely empty while Negro kids were on double shift four or five blocks away. This is deliberate segregation on the part of the powers-that-be.

"There's no solution for it, either, because pressure groups are so strong. The board did build ——— High School, which was going to have a 60–40 racial ratio. There were a lot of Negroes moving out there, and the whites howled like mad. They didn't want to go to this school, but the board insisted and would not change the boundary line. So ——— became 97 per cent Negro within one year because of whites moving out.

"I feel that integration is absolutely necessary for the survival of the school system. I see no other answer. Some Negro schools are quite famous for work that's being done in them. They have special programs and field trips going day and night, dances, concerts, kids putting on plays, reading groups within reading groups within reading groups, teachers coming at 7:30 A.M. illegally to tutor, university tutors coming in in the evening.

I know principals at Negro schools who work every Saturday and Sunday for their schools. They come out in the evening and are active in all the community groups. They go around begging businessmen for clothes and money for kids. And yet, at the end of eight years, their kids aren't much higher than those in other Negro schools on an educational reading level. They learn absolutely nothing. They observe a lot culturally, yes, but what good is the cultural aspect if you can't read? The reason for this is the home, and because the kids are confined to a segregated society.

"For the really gifted child in the ghetto, there's still a very good chance. It works in lots of ways. You get so hungry for a bright kid that when you get one he gets everything he asks for. When the chips are down and the scholarships are available, the bright kid in the Negro school can automatically get one. The universities are after them. And the university may make it easier in many cases for a good Negro student to get in than a good white student. The University of Illinois, for instance, will only take students from the top 25 per cent of the graduating class because of the population pressure. The top 25 per cent at [a Negro high school] could be the bottom 25 per cent at [a white high school], so a bright kid at [the white high school] who might be in the middle of his graduating class can't go to the U. of I., while a poorer student at [the Negro school] can. In white schools you often don't spot a gifted kid till he's in his third or fourth year of high school because they often slough off and slip by unnoticed. By then you've lost them, and this is why 10 per cent of the dropouts in white schools are gifted children. In a Negro school you spot them by the fourth grade, and that kid is structured all the way through.

"One definite improvement that could be made here is to adopt the New York system of open enrollment in the high schools. In New York any student can go to any high school except for your top schools, which are screened as to IQ. Chicago has limited open enrollment at two technical high schools, one north and one south. But there is a boundary line so that Negro kids by and large cannot go to the North school.

"Also, we have to attract competent teachers into the system. I'm talking about suburban housewives, young gals who get married and are going to teach for three or four years before they have a family and then they have the kid and come back three or four years later and teach for the rest of their lives. Good stable people with a good education.

"Another thing is getting stability in the system for both the teachers and the principals. Now they are helter-skelter, transferring like mad. They are liable to become anomic themselves. Also they need special training in the specific techniques of teaching disadvantaged youth.

"I am not interested in getting into the suburbs. If they sent me somewhere else I'd go, although I prefer to stay in a ghetto situation. There's so much going on here. It's so fascinating watching all the things which you don't get in the white schools. I've often thought I could imagine nothing worse than teaching in normal schools, normal kids. It would drive me bats.

"As many problems as there are, I like it here. I'll stay and just keep hoping for a new day dawning."

The hope for better days is not peculiar to Negro schools. An immigrant's son, a swarthy young white man with flashing eyes and staccato speech, says he has taught in all types of Chicago schools, "high-level gentile, Jewish, Negro and all-around American." And from the Borscht Belt to Brownsville, he has encountered weaknesses in the system. They began, he recalls, even before he reached a classroom:

"Most people still say when they hear I taught at [a Jewish school], 'Why would you ever leave there? Jewish kids are so good, and they want to learn.' However prejudiced these teachers may be against Jews, they still view that type of school as the ideal. Even if they are lazy and may never want to go there themselves.

"Actually, I found some kids at [the Negro high school] who were as highly motivated as those at [the Jewish school]. In both, the general level of motivation was higher than where I am now, where the kids are second- and third-generation Poles and Germans mostly. Prejudice had its effect in both those places. Those kids know that education is the key, but the kids where I am now feel, 'What do I need with it?' One summer that I taught U. S. history at [the Negro school] I had those kids for one and a half hours straight, and I offered them a five-minute break because it was really hot. Often they'd stay in there and work. We used to have debates on the Revolutionary War, drawing parallels with the civil rights movement, stuff like that. But I think the general feeling among teachers there is that Negroes can't learn. There is a large number of teachers who don't really want to teach. This attitude is not unique to culturally deprived schools. At the [white] school I'm in now, the first thing I heard from the older teachers was, 'The parents won't bother you, the principal won't come in the room, nobody bothers you here. It's really nice. Just don't try to push things because that's when you'll run into trouble.' By 'push things' they mean don't demand a lot from the kids because they're pretty lazy, and don't demand a lot of discipline because the office doesn't want to be put into an uncomfortable position.

"The heart of the school system is 'Don't antagonize anyone in the system because you won't get a promotion.' That, and ' Stay out of the papers.'

"They don't want you to fail anybody, either. I'll pass kids this year in what is considered a good white school who cannot read for comprehension or significance, who can't even construct a sentence or a simple argumentative essay. There are no standards. If a kid tries, you pass him. If your failure rate is high, they tell you you are a bad teacher. And it looks bad for the principal because the district superintendent jumps on him. So in effect you end up buying promotions at the expense of the kids.

"I've been in all types of schools in the city. There isn't any question about it. It's much nicer in the white upper-middle-class schools if you're interested in teaching. At [the Negro high school], the kids and I had good rapport, but it was torture to get them to work. And the insults you had to face! I can remember I made a stray mark on a test once. To the kids this meant racial prejudice. One stray mark on a piece of paper and three hundred years of discrimination comes up in your face. You'll break your neck for those kids, but they'll never really trust you. No matter what you do, to them you are still white. Sometimes you just can't stand that undercurrent. You wonder, 'Why shouldn't I be with white kids who aren't going to be attacking every human error as deliberate discrimination?' You think, 'I give them my life down here and what do I get in return?'

"I probably had the least trouble of any teacher there. The kids were crazy about me, just to show you the trouble even I had. One kid—he was a criminal on parole, really bad news and overage—was making passes at this girl right in the classroom. When I said, 'This is ridiculous, you don't belong here,' he said, 'If you throw me out of this school your troubles are just beginning.' I didn't even say anything about it. I failed another kid and he comes into school drunk to argue about his grade. There's a class going on at this time and I'm trying to preserve my rapport and keep this kid from hitting me at the same time.

"You learn to live with things like that. You just have to judge them on a different standard of values. I don't mean that Negroes are inferior, but what's the old saying? 'Morals are a luxury only the rich can afford.'

"Once this kid brought me a beautiful magazine, a pictorial thing on the civil rights movement, after we'd done a unit on civil rights in the senior problems class. It was on my desk and I turned my back for one minute and somebody stole it. Another time a girl had to pay me thirty-five cents for some school thing and she said real loud, 'How do I know you're not going to keep that thirty-five cents?' I think emotionally is where you get hurt the most in those schools. Some days I was ready to be part of the white backlash. I didn't care how they got that way; something had made them different from me.

"The Negro teachers undermine you, too. They tell the Negro kids not to trust white teachers. If you seem to be gaining some rapport with the kids, the Negro teachers seem to resent it.

"Of course some of the white teachers do terrible things to the kids. Insults and all. The kids told me once, 'There are two kinds of teachers here: the ones who want to pretend we're not Negroes and the ones who look at us like we're freaks.' One teacher told his class, 'Before you monkeys moved into this neighborhood it was real nice. Now we have to change our tires all the time.' He'd run over some broken glass in the parking lot and that's what started it. Another time I saw a kid come running down the steps and practically knock over a teacher. The teacher looked at him and said, 'You black ape.' They really do talk to the kids that way, like Southern sheriffs. One white English teacher there told her classes at the beginning of the semester, "I know Negroes can't learn English so we don't need to do English. We'll do whatever we want.'

"It was very hard for me to believe this at the time. But now that I've taught I know there are teachers who do literally nothing. I mean *nothing*. They just sit there and read and the kids do what they want. This is true everywhere, not just in culturally deprived schools.

"In our [white] school, one man's class finished its study unit six days before Christmas vacation. He said it was silly to start anything until after Christmas. For six days they just sat there.

"One woman teacher said to me yesterday that she never takes any work home. I don't know what the hell she's doing. She teaches math. There *must* be papers to mark every night.

"But any kind of teacher—good or bad—is hard to find in Chicago, and when you're in a place where you don't even have enough teachers to physically stand in the classroom with the kids you can't start choosing and looking for quality.

"Sometimes people who *do* try to really teach there—to correct the effects of past incompetence—run into trouble. I know a college professor's daughter who taught sixth grade for a while in a really bad school in [a hard-core Negro slum area]. Her kids were supposed to be doing some refinement with fractions, but she found out they couldn't even do simple addition. She dropped the fractions and started them adding on the blackboard. The principal came in and saw this. He said, 'What are you doing? They're supposed to be working in fractions.' She said, 'But they can't add.' And he said, 'What would happen if some visitor came walking in here? Don't you dare put anything on the board like that again. You teach them fractions!' She quit right then.

"Of course, in our school the principal would never see this sort of thing because he's never in the classroom. So far as I have been able to determine, he has visited only one class in the five years that he's been in that school.

"The same laxity is shown toward the counseling system. The counselors at [the Negro high school] felt the kids had awfully inflated opinions of themselves and would guide them away from college. But this is true to some extent in all Chicago schools. The counselors generally set low goals. They haven't gone to good schools themselves, and the kind of person who went to Chicago Teachers College because he couldn't make it at a prestige school isn't going to direct kids to a prestige school. They advise the kids to go to places like Wright Junior College. At [his present white school] we had a girl in the 99 percentile. The counselors were advising her to go to the University of Illinois. At [a North Side 'Jewish' high school] a counselor was horrified because one of the girls wanted to go to Northwestern.

"Bad facilities aren't limited to Negro schools, either. My friend teaches at a Negro school and averages about sixteen students in a class, with his biggest under thirty. I have up to forty-six. We have five counselors for 2,300 kids; the kids can't even get in to see them. As far as physical plant, [a 'good' Jewish school on the North Side] is far more of a dump that [the Negro high school discussed earlier]. As for supplies, I got more supplies [the Negro high school] than I do now. If anything, the Negro schools get more. I've been in white schools where English teachers have to divide up the books. They can't even integrate grammar and literature because there just aren't enough books to go around. I've even collected money from kids in my classes —six dollars apiece—to get books we need. I have a friend who teaches at a branch of ——. It is poverty-stricken, but it is white and they don't get anything. About two years ago there was a school of deprived kids, mainly Spanish-Americans. The health department said that school was a disgrace. The toilets were about thirty years old; the lighting was damaging the kids' eyes. The board of education had actually approved funds to revamp this school. Then about that time the first real [civil rights] explosion came. The money was taken back and given to ——, which is almost completely Negro. Do you want to know why? Because Puerto Ricans aren't vocal. And poor white people aren't vocal. Through civil rights groups, Negroes are becoming both vocal and organized.

"Good teachers face all these things we've been talking about, and pretty soon they stop fighting the things they don't like. Many of those who are disillusioned leave for the suburbs or other jobs. We had a history teacher last year. He loved history and loved to teach, but he couldn't take it any more. Now he's working for a stock brokerage."

On the Southwest Side, in "a working-class neighborhood that looks prosperous but has people who are not primarily interested in education," stands a white school that is beginning to experience the same teacher emigration that characterizes many Negro institutions. A former math teacher, a heavyset woman with tired eyes and nervous hands, recalls why she left there after thirty-nine years:

"In the last ten years, there has been a terrible disintegration in the quality of education at that school, and race has nothing to do with it. The school has traditionally been all white. There are many little problems. The counselors don't understand the people they're counseling. They get into that work to get out of teaching because they think it's easier; the school is crowded, so study halls are held in the auditorium, as is the case in many Chicago schools. Also in this system, principals play musical chairs. With a principal in a school only a year or two, he can't develop much. But the biggest problem is that discipline at that school has gotten out of hand. The kids lack respect for authority. They're defiant.

"In my class they'd yell, 'Kiss her,' 'Spit in her face,' 'Pull her nose,' 'Pull her glasses off,' 'Kill her.' They organized a gang. Two notes were delivered to me containing bomb threats. These were 100 per cent white kids, so there was no racial aspect to it.

"I asked for help, but the principal wouldn't do anything to help me with these kids. He said I'd have to handle things myself. I wouldn't have asked for help if I hadn't really needed it. I sent down to his office names of thirteen troublemakers and got back a note saying the counselors couldn't function if I put such a great burden on them. If they had cleaned out sixty kids, they would have cleaned out the school of all the bad eggs. Instead the principal did nothing. He was aiming for a promotion, so it was easier for him to just go along rather than try to help solve my problems. Principals feel if they don't see and don't hear, it doesn't happen. Their own report is likely to be better if they ignore their problems rather than bring them out in the open and try to solve them.

"I appealed to the personnel office, but they insisted that I stay in that same school. They discouraged a transfer because of my age, unless my principal gave me an unsatisfactory rating. I was a good teacher, so he couldn't do that. I decided I wouldn't go back there for anything. I'd had it.

"I was sixty when I resigned. I had intended to teach another five years, and I think I still had something to offer. But I'm retired now and reconciled to the fact that I'm no longer a teacher. At least I'll live longer."

When a freckle-faced redhead recently quit a monotonous cafeteria job and turned to teaching, all her teacher friends "were just plain green with envy," she remembers. Fate led her to a white elementary school on the North Side to teach home economics, while her young friends remained locked in the inner city. In a "good, old-time neighborhood" of first- and second-generation Europeans, they declared, she'd find girls eager to learn and parents ready to back her in any disciplinary actions. They told the truth, she concedes, but not the whole truth:

"There was no room for my class at the beginning. I had twenty-eight students in the teachers' lounge from September through the last of October, and then we moved to the adjustment room which we shared with the assistant principal. There was a bookcase-and-blackboard divider. Gradually my class leveled off at fifteen. Then the principal decided to eliminate it by having the other teachers absorb it, so they now have thirty-nine students per room. Now I'm doing some third-grade tutoring. We have third-graders who scored zero on reading tests. Some of them have been moved ahead previous years because there was no room.

"The principal doesn't pay much attention to any teacher's teaching. My situation is unusual since the assistant principal is in the same room. She is paying a great deal of attention to what I'm doing. She'll sometimes tell a child he isn't reading loud enough or something. The other teachers all feel they are in it alone.

"We have an all-white faculty. We have a P.T.A. that meets during the day once a month, but the teachers aren't involved and it doesn't do much. The parents are interested in the school, though. Out of my twenty-three children, twenty-two had parents represented at an open house.

"In some ways I feel the wool is being pulled over people's eyes. We have windows broken in our school for weeks and weeks, and they get the money from the children who break them to pay the glaziers. But the glaziers have still not come. They are always on the South Side [in Negro schools].

"Also, the system is so large. I feel they just shove the kids around like puppets to fit the pattern—so many children to each school, so many to each teacher, and so on. There seems to be no concern for the individual. And very little administrative control. The district superintendents are afraid to discipline principals for fear someone above them will think they're having trouble, so the principals are almighty gods in their schools. They can ruin a school with no one stepping in.

"I think there are people in power who want to segregate the schools here because of power pressure on them. I think boundaries are moved to foster segregation. For instance, they [school officials] are willingly shoving mobile units into South Side [Negro] schools. We begged for them at our school to get more room and rather than do that they changed the district around. When our district lines changed, the racial composition stayed about the same. Similar changes on the South Side could have put Negroes into white schools. Basically, though, I think the schools are all Negro or all white because of housing."

Elsewhere up north, in a high school with a Negro population of one, a sandy-haired, pipe-smoking math teacher finds fault too. His classroom, his professional nest for six years, lies in an old German neighborhood where the floors of some stores still are set with tile swastikas, a legacy of the Bund. In recent months, he notes, the heavy fragrance of the area's old-world cooking has become laced with the smells of olive oil and hominy grits. Puerto Ricans and Southern Mountain migrants are moving in:

"There's no significant difference in basic intelligence between these various ethnic groups. The home background makes the difference. The German kids are very ambitious, achievement-oriented. Many have hopes of becoming doctors and lawyers. Lately many of the Puerto Ricans—especially those who came to this country when they were maybe two or three years old and whose parents have made some progress by now—are also achievement-oriented. It's the Appalachian whites that are the most lethargic and depressed. They have no ambition higher than, oh, maybe truck driver is the very ultimate. They're quite content with jobs like selling hot dogs at Wrigley Field. They look on that as a career.

"The bulk of the German kids got their elementary education in Chicago. Generally they are better prepared than the hillbilly kids who have come up from Kentucky or Tennessee perhaps only within the last couple of years. I've seen cases where it's no wonder those kids can't read or add or anything else. We get the school records from down there, and I remember a report written on a child by his third-grade teacher, containing atrocious grammar and misspellings. It looked as if that teacher hadn't even had an eighth-grade education herself. I'm sure there are some people like that teaching in Chicago, too.

"In Chicago schools, social promotions are prevalent. Many Chicago kids actually drop out when they are in the second grade—and just sit in the classes from then on, being pushed ahead every year. If such a child manages to stay in school long enough to graduate from high school, his diploma can't really be interpreted as much more than a certificate of attendance. It doesn't mean he's learned anything. We graduate people who are actually functional illiterates. They couldn't mix up a bowl of Jell-O following the directions on the package.

"That's one reason you can't get a class discussion going in some Chicago schools. The words the teacher is accustomed to using in just normal conversation are beyond the kids. You have to stop with about every third word, write it on the board, and define it to half the class.

"In my math classes, most of the kids understand the mathematical concepts; they know how to add and subtract. But there are many who get to high school without knowing their multiplication tables, or without even knowing the basic addition combinations. They have to add on their fingers. They can't associate these fundamental operations with the problems at all. They can't look at a simple problem like: 'A refrigerator cost $259. So-and-so has saved $150. How much more does he need to buy the refrigerator?' I find lots of them say, 'If there are two numbers in the problem you probably have to subtract. If there are three or more, you probably have to add.'

"The average class size in Chicago is supposed to be 32 point something—which is just a statistical gimmick. That actually means the teacher has between thirty-five and forty children in her class. She doesn't have time to give all of them the individual attention they need. So she just aims for the middle. The others start falling farther and farther behind.

"In some cases, home environment helps compensate for

what they don't get at the school. But in some homes, like these hillbilly homes, kids have just never seen things like blocks and papers and pencils and magazines and watching mother and father write and then trying to imitate by scribbling across the page. They come to school with quite a different orientation than what we might consider the average child.

"Of course, this becomes frustrating for a kid, especially as he develops a reading deficiency. Because of this deficiency, they're convinced they're stupid, even though they may have average intelligence basically, and they just give up. They won't try, and it's very difficult to do anything with them. Maybe if there were more time you could get somewhere with these kids. But just let me give you an idea of what my day is like.

"School starts at 8:30 A.M. I usually arrive at 8:00. Now I have the additional duty of detentions. That's a punishment system we have whereby for minor infractions students are detained after school for fifteen minutes. I don't have to sit with them—there's another teacher who has that duty—but I handle the records and track down the kids who don't show up. At 8:05 I go to my mailbox and there are all sorts of slips from other teachers: 'So-and-so gets three detentions because he failed to do an assignment,' or 'Tardy to class, two detentions.' I have to sort all these—a clerical job, really—and record them on the detention sheets. This generally takes twenty minutes or so, then school starts and I have a class. Second period is supposed to be my open period, the time when I can phone parents, check a child's record in the office, see what his reading score and IQ assessment is—the kind of thing you have to do to know how to cope with a child in your class. Normally by this time of year [February] I would have gone through each child's record and know pretty much what to expect from them, what their problems are, and how to deal with them. This year, however, my open period is taken up with more detention work, because that's the time I go around to classes and call out the kids who cut detention, lecture them, contact their parents, this sort of thing. So I often do not have time to consult even one child's personal record in the office. Then I have three classes in a row, plus study hall and lunch. I generally have to take ten or fifteen minutes off my lunch period to take care of absences from my division. Then I have more classes, and that's the end of the school day. The sheer demand on my time makes me a less efficient teacher than I could be.

"There are other problems, too. I don't think we have adequate books or other supplies—ditto paper, masters for running off tests, study sheets. I have to collect a dime from every kid in my classes and buy supplies myself. I keep a ditto machine in my apartment so I can do that stuff at home. Just a week before Christmas our high school got a movie projector for the first time. This is supposed to be standard equipment.

"This year we just went over to the new math in teaching algebra. The whole city was supposed to go over to it last year, but we were short of textbooks—couldn't buy the new math textbooks. I tried to teach it on my own, but since I was still using a traditional text, it was madness.

"This year they instituted an essential algebra class for kids who are interested in algebra but don't quite have the mathematical ability. There's no textbook of any kind available on new math for this level. I would be happy with just some decent copies of the old traditional text. Now we have twenty-eight, one for me and one each for the kids. They were purchased three years ago, and they're all falling apart. The kids are already complaining that pages are missing. I'm afraid that next year I'll have to teach the class without any kind of text, since there are no new math materials available for this level and we can't order any more traditional texts because they've been removed from the approved list.

"Incompetent teachers are in almost every school in the city. I find fellow teachers whose attitude is almost shocking. 'These kids can't learn anything'; you often hear teachers saying that. There's an older woman who teaches English at my school. She says things to her class like, 'Look at that one over there. He only comes to school because his parents collect ADC and they'd cut off the check if he's not in school.' She told a student teacher, 'Don't waste your time teaching any more. You've already taught ten minutes today. That's quite enough. They can only absorb so much. They're all going to grow up to be grill workers anyway.'

"I've come across too many teachers like this. Some just sit in class and read newspapers. Over the years they've developed the skill of making the class keep quiet, but they do not teach a single thing. Some actually go into their rooms and turn up the heat as high as possible, so the kids go to sleep. I have seen this done. There are a lot of teachers who grade on the quietness of the student. If you are the most quiet student in class, you'll receive a good grade, regardless of your ability or what you do.

"It's almost impossible to get rid of a teacher after he's assigned. Once you've been assigned three years you're on tenure, and a teacher cannot be gotten rid of then except through a civil service drop. It's a large umbrella under which many incompetents find shelter.

"In most cases, the administration has no idea what is going on in the classroom. I've been at —— six years now, and the principal, I'm sure, has no idea what kind of teacher I am. He has never visited my room. The only way he can judge me is to figure, Well, he doesn't have too many discipline problems, not a lot of kids coming from his room to the office, so he must be doing a good job.

"Every semester, twice a year, he has to rate me and tell how good a teacher he thinks I am. He rates me excellent all the time. Nearly everybody in the school is rated excellent. That's why the premium is on keeping your classes quiet. Turning up the heat gets you a good rating.

"Often trying something creative gets you nothing but trouble. A young woman friend of mine, a very intelligent, dedicated person, teaches English at [a predominantly white high school]. This year she was given a basic English class, freshmen and sophomores whose reading level is fifth grade or below. Basic English teachers have always complained that there is absolutely nothing on the market at that reading level of interest to a fourteen- to fifteen-year-old. Well, this teacher wanted to get across some basic ideas of simple narrative—character and plot and setting. She had a TV in the room, and she discovered that one day of the week a cowboy series was on TV at the very time when her class met. So she thought that for three weeks she would watch the cowboy show with the kids on TV and then they could begin to grasp a little of what you mean when you talk about character, plot, setting and so on.

"One day the assistant principal happened to check on her. She told him frankly what she was doing. The administration wouldn't even listen to any kind of justification at all. She was having her class watch cowboy shows and that was not permitted—final. Instead of being pleased to see some initiative on the part of a teacher, her rating was lowered from excellent to satisfactory. The principal's main goal, you see, is to avoid stirring up anything. Better play it safe. The few principals who are active, who really try to do something, are the ones who never get promotions. Of course, because they're trying to do something there is trouble at their schools; everything doesn't run smoothly; there is resistance from the teachers, from the parents, and so on. That sort of person gets a reputation downtown for causing trouble, so he doesn't move ahead.

"There are other serious problems. For instance, there are so many kids that we're forced to deal with who really do not belong in a normal school with normal kids. We have kids here whose records are stamped in red ink: RETARDED. One boy is sixteen, but he looks twelve and acts six. There's nothing we can teach him. His reaction to any situation is the reaction of a six-year-old kid. If he's restless he squirms around or gets out of his seat and bothers other kids, grabs their pencils, that sort of thing. If you raise your voice to him he'll begin to cry. He's extremely disruptive. Then there are kids who are mentally disturbed, actually insane. A girl in one of my classes runs around the room, dances and talks to pictures on the wall during class. She has a great acquaintance with this one Leif Ericson picture. It took sixteen weeks before we could get her transferred out to the social readjustment center for girls.

"Some schools have ungraded classrooms and teachers who are trained to deal with retarded children. But they can only take so many, and we're forced to keep the rest in regular classes until they're sixteen.

"There are other system flaws. Voluntary transfer plans, for one. Last year they had such a plan in answer to the criticism that the schools in the inner city, mostly Negro, were overcrowded while there were vacant classrooms in places like [a white, North Side high school]. This year there's no such plan. Yet if you walk through the halls of [the North Side high school], which I've done on a couple of occasions, you'll see that many classrooms there are still not being used, whereas in other schools classes have to be held in the auditorium and in the lunchrooms.

"In my opinion, the voluntary transfer plan was set up to fail deliberately. A list of schools where there were vacancies was made up, and anyone in an overcrowded school could transfer to these, provided they did not present truancy or tardy problems and could pass all their subjects. But you couldn't transfer until the first of November. Well, two months of the school year were already over. By then most kids are pretty much entrenched in the school they're in. They don't want to transfer. The superintendent could wave the figures at his press conferences and say that throughout the whole city only twenty-three people or whatever applied for transfer, so obviously people in inner-city schools don't want to go anywhere else.

"Another program that seems headed for failure is the government-financed after-school reading program. I was on a teachers union committee which heard complaints from teachers who were participating in this program, and the mass inefficiency under which it is organized is incredible. For example, every single teacher told us about being notified that they would be participating perhaps a day before the program started. We checked back and found that the president of the board of education announced last May that money was coming from the government for this, and that before December 31 they had to have something going. Yet they waited until the last minute to recruit teachers.

"Again, we find initiative being stifled. One teacher wanted to try a reading system which he and his wife, also an elementary school teacher, had been working on for several years. Since there were no specifics to the contrary laid down, they requested an opportunity to experiment with this. They were flatly told no. On the other hand, they weren't told what they could do. In fact, many teachers have complained of getting no guidance along these lines. So, many of them are just killing time."

A social studies instructor says he has no trouble teaching. At times his high school has gone for a month or more without a principal—and without a hitch—"because everybody here knows his job and does it." After fifteen years in the system, on the coveted North Side, among quiet tree-flanked streets and modest homes, he sees some differences between his "white" school and its inner-city cousins, but he begins with something they have in common—"the average Chicago principal":

"He is what we call the 'suitcase principal.' He's looking to advance himself, to move on and up to a bigger school as quickly as possible. To do this, he doesn't want to rock the boat. Anything dirty should be covered up in some way. You smile nicely; emphasize the positive, especially in your reports, and tell the next man up what he wants to hear. You definitely *don't* burden anyone with problems.

"Our school is considered a good teaching assignment, like most of the North Side schools. We have special classes for children who don't speak English, so they aren't mixed into regular classes as they are at some South Side [Negro and Puerto Rican] schools. We have speech classes for problem children. We have five categories of classes in all: average, honors, advanced placement, basic, and some even lower than that. Some inner-city schools don't have this range.

"We have an all-white faculty. Occasionally we get a sub teacher who isn't white.

"The school is very cooperative with parents and community groups. Our district superintendent seems to be out in the community and attending meetings all the time. He's very sensitive to what people want and are trying to do. He seems to be soliciting their help on school problems."

A plump, dark-haired woman on the Near North Side sees no evidence of marriage between town and gown—or even serious flirtation. She is a mother, not a teacher. She has watched her son gradually become a member of a minority group after six years at an elementary school. Today he and one white girl comprise that school's "integration.' And in the vortex of the neighborhood's swift racial change, the mother feels the school has been more than a neutral force:

"When I moved here, this [apartment] building was all white. More than half of my son's class was white. Then slowly but surely these [white] people have moved out. Often they've moved after arguments with this man [principal of the neighborhood's elementary school] in which he told them that if they didn't like the way he ran the school they could move. He'd say, 'It's better if you do because this is a terrible school. Just get your kids out of here.' Many whites left, not because they didn't like Negroes, but because they couldn't stand the school the way he runs it. Even the better-class Negroes get this treatment. One lovely Negro family—the father is a doctor—took their child over to the school and [the principal] said, 'You don't want him to go to this school.' His attitude seems to be: Let's get the higher-class Negroes and the white people out of here so we can treat all these crumbs like crumbs.

"As a matter of fact, it's not a terrible school—yet. It's got pretty good teachers and as inner-city schools go I think has the potential of being a darned good school. The quality of education is adequate. But I'm worried about my boy's physical safety in school and on the school grounds.

"The principal lets all grades out of there together the minute the bell rings, and he won't let them in until the bell rings in the morning. They're forced to stand around outside and take whatever comes by. There are no provisions made for children in cold weather either.

"My boy was beaten up badly and he's constantly shaken down for money. The children are constantly beating each other up. I mean really getting into gang fights. There are attempted rapes and sexual incidents. There's no supervision on the playground either at recess or after school or before school. One Puerto Rican mother is keeping her children out of school illegally, they've been beaten up so often. She's afraid they'll be killed. Another woman said her daughter was held by two boys while another hit her with a stick. She's six. Lots of dropouts from other schools hang around there, starting fights at basketball games, trying to beat up as many as they can.

"The principal doesn't call the police when bad things break out, apparently because he wants to avoid giving his school or himself any reputation for having trouble. He doesn't even report the sex crimes. He himself has been attacked and hasn't called help.

"When my son reached eight years of age he told me that he was no longer allowed to go to the washroom at school. He didn't know why. He wet his pants on the way home, so I went to see the principal. He told me that they had all kinds of problems—fighting, homosexual incidents—in the washroom, so he wouldn't allow the older children—this is eight years old—to go there. 'If he can't hold it,' he told me, 'you'll just have to bring a note from his doctor that he is to be excused to go to the washroom, that he has poor bladder control.'

"Several of us mothers asked the principal if he could do anything to protect the children. He just said, 'Protection is not a major problem.' We believe that if teachers are to teach, discipline must be maintained by the principal. Yet he establishes no authority to control the behavior of the children, does nothing to assert the powerful emotional impact of his office. The children in an inner-city school are marked by a lack of self-control. It requires a very firm approach. Not a rigid approach, but a firm approach of meeting the children eye to eye. This principal is far too permissive for this kind of school. He takes the position that the school reflects the problems of the community, and he sees the problems of the community as being a lot of irresponsible ADC parents who don't care about their children, parents who are uneducated and who only come to the school to make problems. He feels things can't be changed because this is the way of the community, and that the community will never improve.

"We've tried to strengthen the P.T.A. in hopes of bringing pressure to change things in the school. If we ever really unify he might have to pay attention. But it's hard to really work together. It takes a lot of time for us to trust each other, and it's a transient kind of group so you have to keep starting all over again building trust. The principal makes every effort to keep us apart. He talks about parents to each other behind their backs, and at one point because of this we all thought that each other were the kind of people who were not interested.

"According to the P.T.A. bylaws, a member of the faculty has to be the second vice-president. The principal has taken this to mean him, making him a member of the P.T.A. board. But since he refuses to come to any evening meetings and most parents on the board work and can't go to any afternoon meetings, the board can't get together to meet. The bylaws can be amended by a two-thirds vote of the membership, but we can't get two-thirds of the membership together in the afternoon because most of the mothers work. So we're at an impasse, virtually inoperative.

"The principal simply doesn't want a whole string of parents tampering with his precious school. Without parents in the school, nobody would know there weren't any assembly programs, nobody would know that there are these incidents in the halls or washrooms, nobody would know a lot of things that go on there that he just doesn't want to be known. P.T.A. members who are on A.D.C. say he has threatened them with getting their checks taken away if they cause trouble.

"The business of having no assemblies is an interesting sidelight, incidentally. When we asked why there isn't a regular assembly every week like in other public schools, we were told our kids can't do anything and wouldn't know how to behave in assembly. Last year they had one assembly, and one of the Negro mothers ran over to the principal to say, 'Isn't this great,' because her kid wanted to wear a white shirt and tie for it. Later we discovered why it was held. They had some practice teachers learning in the school, and they wanted to show them how to put on an assembly. Now we don't have any assemblies. No awards programs. No athletic teams.

"There are little things that dehumanize too. For instance, the principal's habit of referring to everyone as 'Mother.' That's the main complaint of a Negro friend of mine. She said to him once, 'At least you could learn our names. You call our children "you kids" and us "Mother." Why don't you just treat us like human beings?' He doesn't call me 'Mother.' I'm white.

"I don't perceive that anything will be done at this school in time to help my boy. I've stuck this out six years. My lease is up in June and I'll move because we have not moved this character [principal] one iota. Not even to get him to admit that there's a problem.

"The [other white family] are going to move, probably. They have a girl, and if I had a girl I would never have stayed this long.

"I'd like to say that I stayed because I'm terribly idealistic and I want to see the school integrated, but it was just financially inopportune for me to move the time my lease was up last time and the time before. This time, God willing, I will be financially able and of course I'll take off. That's the only thing to do in this situation."

Talk of "taking off" slithers through another community, a strange island in the city on the far South Side. It is Little Suburbia in many ways, almost a replica of what many city whites are fleeing to in the face of Negro encroachment— winding streets, treeless lawns, styleless houses in three models, backyard barbecue pits. But some of the hands that flip the

steaks here on summer nights are black. The continuing struggle to keep the area racially mixed, explains a slim, blond man
whose sons attend its integrated elementary school, is as much a
struggle against the school system as against the blind urge to
run:

"Our community is dedicated to maintaining integrated
housing. We have managed to achieve a relatively stable real-
estate market. We have developed a wholehearted spirit in the
area. And we always make a deliberate attempt to face racial
questions, not to avoid them.

"The school system is our biggest enemy. It is fighting us.
We are on the edge of a Negro ghetto that has been moving
inexorably, block by block. When Negroes first moved into our
community in 1962, the real crisis was not the first Negro families but a school boundary change that was suddenly announced
by the board of education. It brought a large number of Negro
children from the west into the school, at the same time taking
away a large white area to the east. So the big crisis was not
'What are we going to do about Negroes living next door?' but
'What are we going to do about the school?' Many whites moved
out.

"Since then we have worked hard to stabilize the white exodus. Then last year another boundary change was unexpectedly
announced. The school principal didn't even know about it. No
community people had been consulted, and this is a very active
community about schools. The effect of the change was to take
three blocks out of our integrated community and put them
into [an all-Negro school]. We felt that those few blocks would
certainly not remain white if their school was all Negro. Anyway, it made no sense to take three blocks out of the middle of a
community. There was great opposition and for once we won.

Right now the grade school for our area is a good one. It is
about 80 per cent Negro and 20 per cent white. It is one of the
few schools in Chicago where the teachers are all regularly assigned—no substitutes—and there is no classroom without a
teacher. We have a teacher who does nothing but handle reading
problems, and we received a $5,000 grant for a new gifted-stu-
dent program for accelerated learning. We have home mechanics, a special-assigned gym teacher, a full librarian, many things
that some all-white schools lack.

"There has been no exodus of teachers as Negroes moved in. This is because of the principal. She has a great talent for dealing with both teachers and parents. She's an extremely dynamic, exuberant, enthusiastic person, fully committed to running a good school and offering good education regardless of race. She even has substitutes coming in from the suburbs, which is unusual for the South Side. Also, she has encouraged a very active P.T.A. It is constantly buying supplementary equipment, raising money for ditto materials, movie screens and other things to help teachers. The principal always attends the P.T.A. meetings and so do some of the teachers.

"The big problem for our area is the high school. People think it's an inferior school. In any case, it is fantastically overcrowded and the racial ratio is badly unbalanced. Right now there are less than a dozen white kids in the whole school. I think this is really the big objection. Even if you were to boost the quality of [that school] and guarantee parents that it would be absolutely as good as [a South Side white high school], they still wouldn't want it because it's all Negro. If you were to have the identical program in a 90 per cent white school, my guess is they would stop seeing so many weaknesses in the academic program.

"There have been proposals for getting around this stumbling block. A cluster plan was proposed whereby parents in this area could send their kids to any one of four high schools, all of which have a white majority. If this were a sure thing, people would have no qualms about continuing to live here as their kids get older. But we're kept in constant doubt about whether a cluster plan will be in effect from year to year. You don't know what's going to happen until shortly before school starts, if then. So the only thing to do is register your kids at the all-Negro high school and hope that something will come along so they won't have to go there. This is very scary to some people, even to some of the gung-ho integrationists. Rather than live in suspense, white families start planning to move out about the time their children reach seventh grade. Under these circumstances, it gets harder and harder to find new white families to move in.

"Most people feel the success or failure of our area as an interracial community rests with the schools. Let's not kid ourselves; we still have a big problem with real estate. But the predominant problem in real estate is attracting people and the thing that attracts many people is schools. We had many people who were really determined to stay or buy, but who felt they had to go elsewhere to get into a better high school situation."

Elsewhere in Chicago, says a South Side teacher of the mentally handicapped, Negro infiltration has transformed neighborhoods with almost predictable certainty. A Catholic, with grandmotherly warmth and soft features, she teaches now in a largely Negro pocket of brick bungalows, tidy lawns and old elm trees that shade new cars. She has spent more than a dozen years in Chicago public schools—white, black, and mixed. And in more than one she has watched the classroom population become 50 per cent Negro within a year of the first colored child's arrival, and twelve months later entirely Negro. As predictable as this swift metamorphosis, she feels, are problems that ride the Negroes' shirttails:

"I have found all my schools very satisfying, but I will honestly have to say that in the Negro schools the teaching isn't as easy. The children are not as ready for learning. Many have come from the South where they've never been in schools before. I had a great big sixteen-year-old girl who was almost seven feet tall, who had a recorded IQ of 48—which is below the level we should take them; 50 is our mental level in EMH—and she had never been to school before. When she was asked to get a saucer, she didn't know what a saucer was. And this was not because she was mongoloid. I think her IQ was much higher than that, but she had never had any schooling.

"Also so few people come out for parents' night in the Negro schools, even in a middle-class school like the one where I'm teaching now. Out of a whole class, one Negro parent might turn up. Also, the school boycotts have made it hard for white teachers with Negro children. These youngsters came back with an entirely different attitude toward me. I think the rapport before was excellent and that after the boycott they really thought, 'Oh, we got the better of you white people that time.' It was harder to work with them.

"Discipline problems definitely increase as the number of Negroes in school increases. No teacher in our school would deny that. Of course, we have some terribly prejudiced teachers who are horrid to the children. One excellent teacher is always harping on the Negro children. I think she just loathes having to stay in this school, but she's nearing retirement age and is going to have to stay here to continue teaching. She had a Negro parent in and she was very flip. The mother said she really didn't know what she could do about her child's problems, and this teacher says, 'Well, lady, you hatched him, I didn't.'

"On the other hand, she had a white child who all through school has had a horrible time. He never did a lick-spit of work. But she got this child and she really helped him. She got work out of him for the first time in his life. She's dedicated to him. I'm afraid it's the color of skin that makes the difference.

"Often the administration makes all the difference in the world in a school. Before I came to [her present school] I taught in a school that I actually saw come up by its bootstraps. It was probably one of the highest-rated schools in the city before it became a Negro school. It's in a lovely neighborhood, single-family dwellings for the most part. Then as Negroes moved in, of course, it gradually went down and quite far down by the time it got to be 99 per cent Negro. When I got there it was really a struggle. The children were unruly; they came in with very low grades, and so on. Many of the white teachers had transferred out.

"Then an assistant principal who was the gym teacher was taken out of the gym and given a little tiny office, and he was the disciplinarian. He did nothing but discipline all day long. By that I mean work all the time with the kids referred to him from the classrooms because they were causing trouble. He'd call the parents and either have them come over immediately or deal with them over the phone. He'd often tell us to send bad kids home for a day or two. They hated that. It sounds a little militaristic, but really, children respond better, they mind better, the whole atmosphere is better when they're disciplined.

"Our principal there was not too intellectual a man, but he certainly understood human values. No problem you ever had was too little for him to consider. A teacher appreciates that.

"Anyway, bit by bit that school improved. We got a marvelous bunch of teachers there. Some came in from the suburbs. Some had lived in the area and had moved out. Some were the last [white] ones who had moved out. They were dedicated teachers who went beyond the call of duty in every way—in teaching, in doing remedial work with the children, in bringing them up to the standard where they should be, in taking their outside duties seriously. Today, I think the school ranks about third or so in Chicago.

"It's not true, you know, that white teachers are always going to do less for Negro children than Negro teachers will. I think of one Negro EMH teacher in another Negro school who used to sit with his feet up on the desk, reading comic books. He had the teenage girls writing *I will learn how to be a lady* time after time; *I will learn how to be a lady,* for at least a year. And the clerks in the principal's office used to say, 'Oh, he's the best.' Because whenever he handed in a book order, it was done in the neatest fashion that you can imagine. It was so easy for them to copy. They used to think he was one grand teacher.

"So much depends on the principal. The best one I ever had really kept us hopping. She expected a lot of you, and you really accomplished something, and the children learned. She gave a spelling test every semester to every child, even the EMH. She called them into her office to talk to them. If your lesson plans said you were teaching the sound *k* and she walked in and you weren't, you heard about it. She kept close watch on you. We had one assembly every month on a certain topic, such as world musicians or American poets or action songs. You just did your utmost under her. You were forever paging through something, trying to find something new. It was fun, like college days. But she was definitely the exception.

"As a school starts to integrate more, it usually grows more, becomes more overcrowded and they need more space. A school with EMH students draws them from several districts, so if they close the EMH rooms, which they have done in a number of schools, these children go back into the regular grades in whichever district they happen to come from. This is a pitiful thing, really. Whenever you have a child with an IQ of 50 sitting in a regular classroom, he just sits there. These children really prevent the other children from learning.

"I knew a fifth-grade girl in an all-white school where there wasn't room for EMH who took a spelling test every week and just wrote down a jumble of any letters that occurred to her. She had been doing this in her regular classes for years, but she wasn't a troublemaker, so nothing was done about it. After she was finally put into an EMH room she said to me, 'Oh, Mrs.——, I always hated school. Now I just love it.' The poor little thing was learning for the first time in her life. There are many kids who reach the fifth grade in the Chicago system before they're found to be retarded.

"EMH kids go to high school when they can pass fourth-grade tests or are fifteen years old. If there are special rooms, they go into them. Otherwise they go into basic courses. If there are no basic classes, they just mark time in regular classes until they're sixteen, then go to continuation school until seventeen, then drop out.

"As for integration, I don't think we have *school* segregation in Chicago at all. I think segregation grows out of the neighborhood. It's not a school situation.

"Right now I live and teach in an integrated neighborhood. But I wonder how long it will stay integrated. Many white parents have sent their high school children to [a private] school. Some find this almost prohibitive in cost, and they are pulling out.

"Many of the teachers at our school feel that the die-hard whites who stay are going to sacrifice their children. We know these children are brilliant, that they could go farther than what they're doing right now in our school under better conditions.

"For all the problems, I think a good teacher can cross the color line and reach these kids. I have to tell you this little incident. My son came over to school one day to get my car, and I said, 'Come in here for a minute. I'd like you to shake hands with some of these nice students of mine,' and one boy walked up to my son and said, 'Hey, he's white!' When they're learning and interested, they don't remember about color. It doesn't mean a thing to them!

"So when any of my co-workers complains terribly about the situation being so bad, I say 'Cheer up. This is your Peace Corps. You don't have to go to Africa or South America or the Southern United States or any place. We have problems to work with right here.' "

Twice a week on the days her maid comes, a young blond housewife with lilting voice and frail figure leaves her new split-level home in a North Shore suburb for the city. She considers herself typical of a legion of women, part-time substitutes, who daily fan through the Chicago system, working schools from the city's dark core to its white fringe and rarely lighting in the same classroom twice. Her mobility has offered a panoramic glimpse of school problems, one of which, to the thinking of some regular teachers, is the attraction that draws her and so many others to the substitute horde:

"My main motivation in teaching is getting out of the house two days a week, seeing adults, talking to the other teachers. I don't mind teaching in the inner-city schools, but I don't like getting home late. So my main consideration—the only thing that makes me happy—is being close to home.

"Before I had my own children, I was regularly assigned to a school near skid row—a very old building, about seventy-five to eighty years old—where the children are very difficult to handle because they have limited background and a very low IQ and there are very large classes. So many teachers would leave because you felt that if you were in a school where the children were well cared for, you could do a teaching job rather than a disciplinary job. But you know how some people are: once they become accustomed to a place they won't leave unless the building burns down. There were some teachers there who started when the area was a very fine neighborhood; women who were in their sixties, and they probably had been there thirty-five or forty years. They never left. They hated the school, they hated the change, they hated everything. But they felt they had a few more years before their pensions and they'd just hang on. I don't think it's possible not to convey this feeling to the children when you're there five hours a day, five days a week.

"I know they gripe to the other teachers. Not just there, everywhere in the inner city. Sometimes if you sit in a teacher's lunchroom, it's revolting because everyone is griping. I was subbing in an inner-city school, and it was a very old building. I walked into the washroom and it looked like something out of a nightmare. The walls were actually falling apart; the ceiling was coming down, and it was dirty and smelly. There was a little table, and a teacher was sitting eating her lunch in the bathroom. I said to her, 'This is such a bleak room to be eating your lunch in.' And she said, 'This is how my whole life is—bleak.' She was very bitter about her life, yet this is a woman who's teaching our children. You find a lot of this, and it's unfair.

"Nothing happens to somebody like that in the Chicago system. There's no increase in salary for being an excellent teacher. It's simply a matter of putting in your time for automatic pay increases. And if you can last for about two years, you have tenure. If you're sent into an inner-city school, the principals are so happy just to have a permanent person in the school to simply discipline the classroom and keep the children from killing each other or running into the hallway, they don't bother you.

"I consider it bad teaching when there is much rote. But in many inner-city schools this is generally what you have to resort to. If you are in a school where the children listen, where they have materials at home, where they can do something on their own, you can do more meaningful teaching. If you are in a school where the children have no reference material, where they aren't even impressed about going to a library, then everything more or less has to be by rote because this is the only way that you can maintain discipline. Copying their tables five times, copying words ten times. Everything is simply by the book. Everything is meaningless. Maybe you find five or six kids in every classroom who are interested in doing their work and could do something more creative. These are the children who are being cheated. In [a North Side lower-class white] school where I was, one family had sent seven children into the school, and not one of them came to kindergarten able to talk, because no one at home ever spoke to them. Kids like those come to school and see a book that shows a whole family sitting around a nice little table eating a nice dinner, and it's a completely different world. When these children aren't exposed to any materials—no scissors, they don't know what crayons are—you can't expect them to be able to come into kindergarten. I had a first grade at [a white southern-migrant school] and the children didn't know their colors. These were six- and seven- and I think eight-year-old children, and not one of them knew the date of his birthday.

"Your heart actually breaks. I went there on a very cold day, and I saw so many children without boots or coats. Last year I had a third-grade room there, and one little white girl, probably around eight years old, was so undernourished and so dirty. She kept looking at the clock, and I asked her if she was hungry. She said no, she was worried about her brother and sister at home. Her mother was an alcoholic and they had a new baby at home, about two months old, and her mother was incapable of taking care of it. And this eight-year-old child was worried about getting home to take care of the baby. These children actually lack a childhood.

"I find these children very easy to handle. In the Negro schools, for the most part, I think the children resent me. Still, I cannot really say that you find more teachers who have a rapport with the white poor children than with the Negro poor children. It depends on the classroom. If you have a group of poor children who really cooperate with you, you feel sorry for them because they're poor, and do your best. If you have a group of children who are very obnoxious—discipline problems and truants and always causing problems—you feel as though it's their own fault. Where the kids are just plain obnoxious and I feel they're stupid, it's their own fault because they're not doing anything to help themselves.

"So often what really makes a difference in a school is the principal. I knew a very good principal in a very low-middle-class white area with some Mexicans and Puerto Ricans. She tests in all areas. She practically knew every child in the school. She had meetings scheduled, different committees going, no discipline problems, marvelous hallway order. Another school—all white, upper-middle-class on the Far Northwest Side—had the most fantastic teaching job going on I've ever seen. Seventh- and eighth-graders were actually doing high-school and college-level work. I visited a biology class and the teacher was dissecting the heart of a calf and telling all about it. This was mostly in a Jewish area—very bright children whose parents were interested in their education—but also this principal was marvelous. Now there's one beautiful school in a very nice neighborhood, and the school is staffed mostly by substitutes because the principal is so difficult to work for. Parents in the area are very upset with him and have been trying to do something, but there isn't much progress being made.

"I'll probably always stay in the Chicago school system even when I'm able to go back full time. In the suburbs you spend a good deal more time working in the building. It's required. For me, getting in and out is important."

Another suburban mother, a petite white woman, has substituted "between kids" for some eight years. Like most seasoned subs, she has seen a cross section of Chicago schools, and with enough experience to take "a realistic view," she explains what lures her to the system two days a week and what she hopes to find when she gets there:

"I substitute just to keep active, to keep abreast of things that are going on. I find it very interesting to go from school to school to see how the various schools are run, and I think it's very interesting going from kindergarten all the way up through eighth grade, seeing what different class levels are doing. The money helps, too. I'd rate that right after being active.

"I go to all kinds of schools. They can send you pretty far west, but any North Side substitute they can't send farther than 2200 south. This has been a long-standing rule, to make it more convenient for you.

"When I go to a new school, I hope to find a class not larger than thirty-three, nice lessons plans for the day, and a well-behaved, well-run classroom. Adequate supplies, too, of course. And a principal who is a good administrator and has a nice personality.

"When I think of a bad school, I think most of bad discipline—when the principal does not have control over his teachers or his classrooms. At one lower-middle-class school where the kids are 100 per cent Negro, in the kindergarten, first and second grades, the discipline is fine. Then you get them in the fourth grade and up, and complete chaos. I feel it's from things that go on at home that you don't know about. The change comes when they are older and realize the situation. They know more fully what they are living with. The lower-grade teachers are very happy there and they wouldn't want to leave.

"I don't know why this happens, but if you have the lower grades at a Negro school you have a nice day, and if you have the upper grades you don't. You may get control for a few minutes, periodically throughout the day, but not enough to have a complete lesson. I think maybe a Negro person would have an easier time. Negro men especially can handle their classrooms well.

"For the most part, the teachers I've met are very interested in their children and trying to teach them as much as they possibly can. About 20 per cent of the time, though, I find absolutely no planning of what to do with these children during the day—no program, no plan. Also, I find that some schools just don't have the basic supplies. For what reason I'm not sure. There doesn't seem to be any economic or color pattern to it.

"One pattern I have noticed, though, is Negro teachers largely in Negro schools. You may find a Negro school with 50 per cent white faculty, but I never found a white school with 50 per cent Negro faculty. Most of the Negro teachers I've met are very competent people, very dedicated. They enjoy their work, and they seem to have a positive attitude toward the school system.

"I feel that something has to be done because you do eventually want more integrated schools. However, it has to come from your neighborhoods, through more integrated housing. Now there is definitely the predominantly Negro and the predominantly white school, and this is caused by predominantly white or Negro neighborhoods. I don't feel all Negro children are getting an inferior education now, but probably a lot of them are."

A pretty, dark-haired young white woman who has taught fifth grade in a West Side Negro ghetto for a year now also questions whether being white necessarily guarantees a Chicago child an educational break. Before settling in a school whose students "qualify for every type of poverty program there is," she taught in a suburb, then subbed throughout the city. To her, the quality of local education is not by definition a study in black and white:

"I don't think that Negro schools per se are superior or inferior in any way. So often the difference lies in the principal. And there are principals in both colored schools and white schools who simply don't care.

"As a substitute I had one small second grade in a Negro school that had had teacher after teacher after teacher through the year, no stability at all. I knew I was going to have problems, and I had everything planned. I held them for about five minutes. I tried to take it, but I couldn't keep hold of the class after that. They were throwing things, *coats,* all over the room, chasing each other, and I had absolutely no control. None! The principal's attitude was, 'I don't want any discipline problems in my

358 · *Charles and Bonnie Remsberg*

office; they cause *me* problems.' So you couldn't send anyone to him. I went out of that place in tears.

"At the school I'm in now, the children are used to being beaten at home. They're easier to handle. They love to help the teacher. They'll wash anything, put anything away—they'll all jump to do it, which you don't find very often in a suburban school, for example. It does make life easier.

"However, our principal runs a rather lax ship. It was announced at the beginning of the year that our school would be on the ungraded class system in which the kids move at their own rate. We are still not on it. Or take the new math. The principal knows she is eventually going to have the teachers come around to it, but she doesn't really want to be bothered with it. In other schools they have teachers' meetings to learn the new math either before or after school. We had a reading readiness committee set up in the fall, and we haven't met yet [February]. So long as the committee exists on paper, that satisfies downtown [the central administration].

"A lot of inner-city schools have less than 50 per cent certified teachers, while the white schools have something like 96 per cent. The principal can do a lot to influence whether certified teachers want to be in his school. Still I think we do have very good teachers here, generally, with years of experience. One sixth-grade teacher is especially good. He can handle his kids well. They like him and can laugh with him. He experiments constantly, trying new things with them all the time in every area—art, math—really very interested in what he's doing. On the other hand, a fourth-grade teacher who came this year has his own TV set and has his kids watch it all day long. I asked him, 'How do you get them to pay attention?' He said, 'It's easy. All I do is stand in the back of the room with a yardstick in my hand and they'll listen.'

"I'm not sure the principal is aware of this. She never gets around to the classrooms. Last year I saw her twice—once in the hall.

"We have physical disadvantages here. I have a small class now simply because we meet in the lunchroom. It's not a perfect situation at all. I cannot set up something for the day. But if I got into one of the regular rooms I'd have thirty-six students, which is too many. The other teachers are doing that now and before February last year they had forty-five to fifty. I prefer my twenty-seven even though this room is no good for anything.

"The big thing the kids lack here is motivation. Negro kids from this type environment have parents that have been beaten down so much that they don't really care what happens. So you have to deal with the kids differently, dangle things in front of them, give them goals. Somebody right now is experimenting giving candy if they get the answer right. You can't have a long-range goal. It's got to be day to day, question to question.

"The Negro teachers as a group don't seem to have any more success with the kids than the white teachers. It depends on whether or not they can empathize and most Negro teachers are no better at this than white. They don't rise from the slums; they rise from middle class.

"Now the white school where I taught kindergarten before coming here was one of the 'elite' districts, but we had many problems there too. The goal of the principal, a former high school teacher, was always discipline. She merely demanded respect without understanding why the children might be misbehaving. She believed that a classroom should be quiet at all times, even a kindergarten.

"I had forty-two to forty-four kids there all the time. You can't teach forty-two kids. You can't give them individual help. Of course, the school officials say there's an average of something like thirty-two in a class, but they divide the visual-aids teacher, the master teacher, the assistant principal, all into the number of kids to get such low figures.

"Whatever went on in class there didn't matter as long as the classroom was kept in order. There are teachers there who just mark report cards without grading papers. One fifth-grade teacher gave a certain kid an S [average] in arithmetic shortly before I took over the class. The kid was a lousy reader, but in arithmetic he was great. He was persistent and he did well day after day. Yet he'd been graded S because the teacher hadn't graded papers. The teacher used to say to me, 'You don't need to grade papers. You can see what they're doing.' Obviously you can't always.

"The big contrast between here and suburbia is that here you're anonymous. In many ways this is a desirable trait because you don't have a community down your neck, watching your every move like you do in the suburban schools. Parents don't come in constantly and give you little hints about things that you could do, putting pressure on you to teach their children to read or something. Where I am now I have never experienced pressure, and that's a plus for me.

"Anonymity is not good, however, if you're having problems. Suppose you don't get paid for a day you worked. You just don't go to your principal or superintendent as you would in a small system and say, 'Look, there's a discrepancy here,' and he'd fix it up right away. You have to write letters, make telephone calls and wait, and if you don't get it you go through the same process again. Last year I was teaching without certificate through some renewal mixup. Nobody knew it until March. Then when I went downtown to straighten things out, I was treated like an ant. They stepped on me and smashed me to pieces. They just tore me apart. There are teachers who work two or three years without getting their raises. You can't overcome it. There are so many people working down there, and you mean nothing to them.

"In Chicago there are definite strata of schools in the minds of many teachers. A promotion usually means going to an all-white school on the Northwest Side. A demotion is going from there to where I'm teaching. Race is definitely a factor to some. However, there's another factor coming into the picture now. That is the mountain people from the South coming up to Chicago. Anybody I've talked to wants to avoid teaching them. They'd rather be in an inner-city Negro school."

The hill people, latest ethnic group to touch Chicago and its education network, have squeezed into a dark "hollow" of ancient apartment buildings and rooming houses that lies on the mid-North Side, between the gloomy girders of the El and the lakefront's glossy wall of luxury high rises. The sagging Fords and Chevrolets that hauled the migrants from Kentucky, West Virginia, and Tennessee sit abandoned in glass-strewn alleys and grassless backyards, rusting in the gray Chicago rain. In the area's cramped taverns, truck drivers and short-order cooks somberly feed quarters into gaudy jukes to hear the lonesome Nashville sound. When the quarters are gone, the old cars head south again for a change of troubles. Schools in this section often have more than 150 per cent student turnover within a single term. Teachers come and go fast, too. A dark-eyed white woman who taught first grade in a "hillbilly" school remembers what it was like when she came—and why she left:

"When I came there that spring, seven other teachers already had had the class just that year. No one wanted to stay. There was a very strong administrator, and she was willing to back the teacher no matter what, but it was just emotionally too much for me.

"The Appalachian children are horribly neglected. I had a six-year-old who was abandoned with an infant when she was very sick with measles. Around 2:00 in the morning she realized it. She and the baby were hungry. She went out in the middle of —— Avenue until a policeman found her. The policeman took both children to County Hospital and finally found the mother. When the child came back from what I would consider a traumatic experience, she was thrilled. She had been to County Hospital and she was telling me how the sheets were so clean and the food so good and what a wonderful experience it was.

"There was another child who had poured hot coffee all over her leg. The blisters had turned green and were festering, and she had come to school this way. I felt we had to do something because she was a human being. I finally insisted that we send a nurse to the home, which was against the principal's wishes. She claimed we had no right to intrude on the sanctity of the family. The nurse was turned away by the family.

"These were the kinds of things that tore me up completely. When you like children and you see these things yet can do so little, the frustration becomes unbearable. These people are existing at an animal level. Even lower. At least animals take care of their young.

"There was a psychologist who came to the school every week, but there was never enough time to go into all the problems. Problem children went unattended for months or years. I recall one third grader with a rather thick file of troublesome incidents. He was emotionally disturbed, clearly in need of psychiatric care. Yet, nothing had been done about him. One day he jumped on another child and started to strangle him. I interfered and this boy was so violent that I was black and blue for weeks afterward. I told the principal that this child did not belong in a regular class and that he was dangerous. She did not want to make out a report on the case, and I finally had to appeal to the teachers' union to get an official report made. The principal didn't want to call attention to her school in any unfavorable light because she was interested in a promotion.

"I now teach in a middle-income school on the North Side in an old community with a high German population. In some recent study we ended up with a half of one per cent of our enrollment being other than white. This is mostly Oriental. We have one or two Negro children in the multidistrict social adjustment program.

"Last year a Negro substitute came to fill a sick leave, and we wondered how this would work out. Some of us were spoken to by the principal to prepare us for her coming. Nothing was said to the children, and there was no comment except from some of the older ones. But no other Negro teachers have come in.

"Our community seems very sensitive to Negroes. Once we went on a field trip. The parents there are too busy washing windows and cleaning house to take their children out. Because there are five classes with something like two hundred children we had a number of buses. At that time the newspapers were carrying on about busing Negro kids into these communities to bring about school integration. Well, some of the people read the headlines and then saw all our buses coming back from the field trip. The mothers lined up in front of the school, quite sure that children were being bused in from a Negro community. To their surprise, it was their neighbors' children who came off the buses.

"I like my present teaching assignment. I would not consider teaching in an inner-city school. What would be the point of having the inevitable frustrations and not achieving what I would like to achieve? The parents do not cooperate with the teacher in educating their child. The children come to school either ill-fed or ill-clothed or from a badly disciplined home where they are just existing. Upper-grade children come to school with weapons. You are not teaching there, you are being a social worker.

"Likewise, I would rather not go into some of the so-called better areas of the city. They have their problems too. You are working in very close relationship with the community there, and some of the parents' groups are most critical of everything.

You spend a lot of your time, I understand, on public relations.

"Of course, my school is not perfect. We need more social-adjustment rooms. We have three now with eight to ten boys in each. We have only three EMH rooms, and whenever there's a vacancy it is filled immediately. Meanwhile, EMH-eligible children are in the classroom. We have no classes for brain-damaged, perceptually handicapped children. And we have only one full-time counselor-adjustment teacher for 730 students.

"Teachers feel the top echelon is out of touch with their problems. The head of one department was trying to see the superintendent about funds for a specific program, and he had to send him a telegram. Now if the director of a department has to do that to get an ear about something he feels is very important, how can you expect the teachers to speak to the top brass? What contact do the top officials have?

"Apparently the top echelon is responding to pressure from somebody, though. Last year as part of the city's experiment in music, our district was asked to put on a program at the —— Hotel for the National Association of School Superintendents. Suddenly, when it came time for the group rehearsal, here came a Negro group which they [school officials] brought up from the South Side. These were not just plain Negro children. These were black, black, black Negro children. They had them do a dance.

"I was hot and bothered about this. I said if this is a music program recognizing the work of one outstanding district, then let's leave it a music program. Not every program has to have a Negro angle. But if it's a program in brotherhood, then let's call it that. Let's be honest with ourselves. It seemed that the administration was concerned because of Negro pressure at that time and fearful of how it would look if he brought a group of all-Nordic children to the meeting.

"There's another point to this, though. I understand that the Negro teacher who brought her Negro group felt they were being used. If I were a Negro I would have resented it. So then why did they let themselves be used?"

Often, says one Negro language instructor, a Negro teacher's actions spring from a reluctant weighing of alternatives. Two years ago she came to Chicago with her husband after studying at the Sorbonne and teaching for a decade in two out-of-state school systems. She wanted a "good" assignment, and the "evasive attitude" of Chicago placement officials convinced her that openings were available in some white schools. She says the only vacancy she was told about, however, was at a West Side ghetto high school, with some five thousand Negro student and a reputation for trouble. "It was take that or nothing," she recalls. She took it:

"Before I ever set foot in the door, I was prejudiced by what people said. 'Oh, you're going to ——. That's a bad school.' But when I got there I felt that on the whole the kids were not really bad or rude kids. They're warm and sociable, but you just feel frustrated academic-wise.

"The majority of the students are 'essential' or 'basic.' Basic students have very low reading scores (like third to fifth grade). Essential students are better, but they still are below what you would expect for high school. They should be reading at least eighth grade at national norm, but these students are far below that. They are there because of their age. They have to move them out of elementary school to have room for the other students.

"On the whole, the motivation is very low. I taught in Negro schools for all of my ten years, and this is the worst experience that I've had. I don't know whether they feel trapped; they just don't seem to try their best. They have difficulty getting the homework in. It's really hard to get a neat assignment, for example, or an assignment that has been thought out. You can see that it's been done hurriedly. I feel too many of my students are excused for a lack of achievement just because they are deprived. Some teachers may fear to exercise authority for fear it will cause the students to think they are prejudiced.

"Some teachers have discipline problems, and the attendance is poor. Some students refuse to come five days; they only make it three days or every other day, even the better ones. I've been used to having students cut only if they were very sick.

"I like to think I know something about the sociology that's involved in an area like this, but sometimes I have to keep reminding myself of it so that I don't fall into the pitfall of saying, Why can't they just adjust themselves and apply themselves? I imagine if they could, they would. I'm sure it must be miserable and frustrating to them to always remain underachievers.

"Because the school is overcrowded, it is on shifts. Some students start early, at 7:15, and some don't come in till 10:22. Some leave as late as 4:30. It's possible for some to leave some days at noon. So there are kids who are out of school for the entire afternoon. Many just hang around the halls, no place to go. I met some teachers from Maryland who were complaining because things had gotten so bad in their school that they had to have a policeman on duty at a fair. I was laughing because we have a policeman on duty in the halls all the time—security guards, too—and I'm glad.

"We don't have many faculty meetings. There never seems to be time for the teachers to make suggestions or even discuss their gripes. The principal is permissive. For example, when reports are due I never get the impression any time limit is set. Midterms aren't given at uniform times, so the school never has an atmosphere of testing for the kids to be aware of. I feel that professionally I'm slipping because everything seems so permissive. Nobody keeps me on my toes or tells me how high to jump.

"We have a racially mixed faculty, probably more white than colored. We have one main principal and four assistants, all white. I don't know how that affects the kids. It affects me. If they want the kids to try hard—perhaps think of going into education as a career or feel that they'd like to be a principal themselves some day—it seems they certainly should make a special effort to groom some Negroes for at least assistant principal. At least in admittedly segregated systems the students are able to identify with Negro heads and authorities. I think that's one of the problems of Negroes anyway, that idea of constant white authority. On the other hand, in white schools you don't really have interracial faculties. This could be done just simply by doing it. All the teachers couldn't flee to the suburbs; some of them have to work in the city.

"It's hard work to get a good education at our school. For example, we don't have a language lab, a room with a lot of electronics where you can listen and repeat and listen to students individually. Some students it would help. Some students would get a better education if they were in an integrated setup. Our [the Negroes'] salvation is in trying to get to the power structure, which means actually going to school with white people to learn what they think and to feel comfortable with them. You

366 · *Charles and Bonnie Remsberg*

never know whether whites are more intelligent than you are until you're in a class with them.

"Yet, it is very painful to break into an integrated situation. I asked students why they didn't go to [a white high school], one of the schools that you could go to under a special transfer plan provided you had good attendance. The answer was that it would be too much competition. Some who were pretty good students would rather be here and be top.

"Incidentally, most of the white students who were still here when I came transferred out when this plan went into effect. I look at those few who stayed and I wonder why.

"Of course, there are factors other than lack of self-confidence that keeps Negroes from taking full advantage of plans like that. I remember one senior student went to [the white school] and returned because she said they told her she wasn't going to get full credit for her French there if she transferred. Both schools are in the same system; the credits should be interchangeable. But they used this to keep down the number of Negro kids coming to the white school.

"Once in a while in our school you hear a kid accuse a teacher of being prejudiced. Possibly the teacher isn't, but the Negro student has been conditioned that if something goes wrong or if somebody says certain things, that person is prejudiced. Very often it's just lack of experience in being around whites. Some of the kids have recently come up from the South, and they are just now free—though one isn't really free in Chicago, but they feel that they are free now—and some of them really are ridiculous. They may keep their hats on or insist on going out an exit which isn't open at that particular time just to flaunt authority. I told a boy he couldn't go out a certain door recently, and he said. 'If you wasn't a Negro teacher I'd go right by you.' And he would have.

"Some don't care what the white teachers think. Others act excessively subservient because they've been taught that's the way to survive around white people. We need a happy medium. They've got to have some kind of image of themselves to act the way they should. Counselors might help. When I first went there, there were two Negro counselors for five thousand kids. There are a few more now, but they aren't able to counsel. They're concerned mostly with truants or disciplinary problems, with the testing that's required of freshmen or juniors. They're so loaded that they aren't able to just talk or even see all the students that they have.

"I have only one white student. I find her aggressive, which is the difference between white and colored, if you want to say there is a difference. Personally, I'm sorry that Negro students in that class aren't more aggressive, and it probably has something to do with this one white girl. That's one of the results of segregation.

"For the first time in two years in this system, I feel I want to do something else besides teach, and I always loved to teach before. Now I'm tired of it. But I'll probably go back to teaching. I don't know anything else to do. I don't like to stay home too much.

"I don't know if I'd be happy in a different kind of school. Anyway, I think I am limited geographically. There may be some Negro teachers in white schools, but I think that they are generally kept on the West or South Sides. So I'll probably stay where I am. The most rewarding thing about teaching where I am? The lunch hour."

Another Negro teacher, a woman with warm eyes and an infectious smile, has found her rewards increase with each transfer she has made in the Chicago system. Like many white teachers, she lives in a middle-class area of split-level homes and wall-to-wall children, but she began teaching ten years ago in the slums. In three moves, she has advanced to a chemistry class at one of the city's two technical schools. She recalls her first assignment and the schools, students and frustrations she has encountered since:

"First was an adjustment school for elementary-level children. Many of the girls were pregnant, many already had children and many had been convicted of crimes. It was all babysitting, except when the state visitors came. We were notified, and everybody began to teach for that day. When they left, we went back to babysitting. At the end of the semester I called the [placement] center and told them, 'Please send me somewhere else.'

"I was assigned to —— High that fall, a real Negro ghetto school. There were very, very few whites, and those were Appalachian whites. There was one Chinese. Oh yes, and Puerto Ricans, right off the plane. I taught general science for a year, then was assigned as a regular teacher. The students didn't change. They were very, very slow. Even the honors classes were quite mediocre. They would be regular classes anywhere else. Nothing would motivate them. The board of education says we're to 'teach them where you find them.' We had students reading at third- and fourth-grade level. How do you teach a third-grade student chemistry out of a textbook designed for high school students?

"Some kids there expected me to give them a grade just for attending class. They catch on to the system very quickly, too. The administration does not like failures. We had to turn in names of student we intended to fail. One year the principal had never been in the room to visit, yet she told me who I could fail and who I couldn't. She said I intended to fail too many, and if I submitted a long list again, she would give me an unsuccessful rating. The next year I was planning to fail twenty per cent of the bunch. They hadn't done anything other than keep the seats warm. But I wanted a transfer and I needed a good rating to get it. So I failed only two students who had been absent over twenty-five days. A kid who gets pushed through and out has a diploma of equal value to valedictorian. That seems wrong to me. But I had reached a point where I didn't give a darn, so I cut my failures back.

"You have so many discipline problems in the ghetto schools, too—actual violence. One year they rehabilitated the lunch room, made it one of the most modern in the city. The dirty plates were to go on a conveyor belt to be washed. Instead, the kids dumped them in the trash baskets. The principal was almost at his wits' end over this sort of thing. One afternoon he collapsed.

"A devout missionary might stay, but usually the better teachers leave. At one of the West Side schools where the neighborhood changed, they had at one time 85 per cent assigned teachers. Within a period of two years it just was in reverse. This means then that you get a school full of substitutes who stay a fairly short time. A student might see four different teachers in four different months. It's getting to the point where it will be solidly Negro teachers in the ghetto schools. And so many of our Negro teachers are from Southern colleges. They aren't really teachers. They don't know the subject matter, can't follow directions.

"Of course, some of the whites nearing retirement stay. And those who don't want to work hard. One of the kids often does the work for these teachers—puts stuff on the board, grades the papers. I've seen teachers just show movies all day. They feel these kids are not going any place, so they don't try. Sometimes the kid goes to school just because it's warmer than the home. Nobody cares, so long as he doesn't become too bad a behavior problem. The attitude is, Why bother? This was actually said to some of the students by counselors at [the Negro high school]. 'You won't make it into college anyway, so why take the entrance exam?' They were probably right, but some of the students were crushed.

"At [the technical high school] where I am now, the situation is quite different. It draws pupils from roughly half the city. Anyone passing the entrance exam is accepted, and they must enter with ninth-grade reading and arithmetic level, and take three years of science and math each. Now we have something to work with. Most of them are middle-class. There are many Chinese; many, many Polish; some Italian; a few Jewish; very, very few Puerto Ricans and about 19 per cent Negro. Very few are on relief, while at [the Negro high school] almost everyone was on relief. Here in almost every case both parents are in the home and in many cases both parents are working and the fathers hold good jobs. We get results.

"There are very few Negro teachers here. Out of 150 teachers, six assigned Negroes. Up to September I had not had any Negro students in my homeroom at all. In September I got three.

"Actually, I don't tolerate some of the Negro students as well as the whites, because I know that the Negro student still has to push just a little harder, be a little closer to perfection for the average job. I'm rougher on them. I hate to have them come in class and sit and expect me to do all the work, to pour it into them. How are we going to overcome slums and poverty if they are not prepared to do something? There is really no excuse for them not doing the right thing there. The school is cheerful, the teachers are young and friendly and for the most part not prejudiced.

"Of course, quality-wise we have some teacher flops. We have a teacher about three years from retirement who shows movies day in and out—movies that don't always have any bearing on the course. There's another fellow, a substitute, who raises pigs. He talks about them all the time. We wonder why the principal invites him back every year. But these are rare exceptions at this school. They would be just about average at many other schools.

"I got a refresher course in the difference between this place and a ghetto high school last summer when I taught for eight weeks at [a South Side Negro high school]. At [her regular school] we get thousands of dollars worth of books for each department each year from the board of education funds. We threw out 1959 chemistry editions last year and bought 1964 editions, along with room sets for reference books. But where I taught summer school we didn't even find the books until the fourth week. Everybody said they were locked up. When we did find them I had thirty books for sixty students and they couldn't even take them home. Every student had a different book. They were in awful condition, just rags.

"The kids there are demoralized. Of course, many Negro teachers have low morale too, because they feel they're limited to certain schools. It wouldn't make sense to put your name on a transfer list to the good white schools on the North Side if you are a Negro. I doubt that even the day-to-day Negro substitutes are ever sent there.

"Negro parents are demoralized, too, because they see evidence of gerrymandered districts. A teacher on the Near North Side told me the boundary line of her school was about one block east of the school and just east of that was a Negro housing project. The children there had to go five blocks from their homes, across a busy intersection, to another school. Yet there were empty rooms in the closer school. This teacher said when the North Central [accrediting] Association visited the school, the administration set up the empty classrooms just as though they were occupied, even put writing on the board to give the impression they were so crowded they couldn't take anyone else.

"I've heard many Negro teachers say that they would never put their own children in Chicago public schools. One Negro friend became Catholic so her kids could be sure of attending

Catholic schools, most of which are integrated. This is why there are so many Catholic converts among Negroes in Chicago. They want their kids to have something better than the public school education, and this is just the easiest way."

For another Negro, a single transfer carried her to the end of the line in teaching. For five years this young mother, a tall, angular, nervous woman, had taught physical education at an integrated elementary school on the South Side. About 25 per cent of its students were Negro; all were solidly middle-class. She was not certified, however, so when a certified teacher came along, she was "bumped" out of her job. She transferred to an upper-grade center, 90 per cent Negro, in the heart of "a public-housing concentration camp." Three weeks later, she quit teaching:

"Within that time I really felt the basic difference between the two schools. When I first went there, the upper-grade center had just recently been added to the high school. A principal was in charge of both buildings, but I never met him. Only his assistant.

"For the first week, even though I was sent there for physical education, I was going to classrooms to fill the places of teachers who were absent, because they had no substitutes available. All the teachers were Negro and maybe 80 per cent were substitutes and in passing from room to room I found that most didn't have any lesson plans. A lot of them seemed uninterested. I'll admit there didn't seem to be much to work with; in some classes, the IQs ranged from 70 to 78. The absentee rate was very high among the students, but nobody was very strict about it. There was little watch kept on the teachers.

"School had only seven weeks to go before summer, but they still had no organized program. For the previous semester, there had been no phys-ed teacher. The P.E. department had almost no facilities. There were none of the materials used for a normal phys-ed class—balls, bats, anything for games. We borrowed everything on a day-to-day basis from an elementary school or from the high school department. Even then we were basically limited to softballs and jump ropes.

"The gym was not in use at all. We had no dressing rooms whatsoever. The students did not have proper gym clothing. In each class I had from thirty-five to forty students. I usually brought them into a classroom that was vacant because a teacher had gone to lunch. We usually played seat games, word games, nothing physical; it was much too crowded and too dangerous to move around. I was just occupying their time.

"I did try to teach a little health education. Most of the students were anxious to learn. A number came to me afterwards and asked if I could in any way get them deodorant and soap. They didn't have it at home.

"I left after three weeks, which was not the end of the school term. I was not happy there at all. It was such a drastic change from the other school where I had been working. I just couldn't make the adjustment.

"That [other] school was overcrowded too. About thirty-five students per classroom, in some cases forty. But where the classes were too large, they had an assistant. It was all very well organized. And they had most of the facilities to work with. Putting the same student in both schools, certainly the [predominantly white] school was superior.

"I was the only Negro teacher there. At the main branch, that is. The school had two other branches, and there were several Negroes at the branches. I understand there was a higher percentage of Negro students at the branch, too.

"In this school all the teachers worked, really worked, and were very much interested in the students. They enjoyed their work. They didn't have the high dropout rate in that kind of neighborhood. I think about 80 per cent of the students who graduated went to college. It makes a big difference when you're trying to teach. The students were easier to work with and the parents more interested. They all wanted everything to go just right. The students tried to make the highest grades possible. And everything was so *organized*. At [the upper-grade center], you found just a handful of students who were quite interested in trying to better themselves. That's really about all. I thought even the food in the cafeteria was better at [the predominantly white school].

"Right now I have no long-range plans. I'd go back to the Chicago system if I could get an assignment I think I'd be happy with. I would like very good conditions: namely, a neighborhood where the children are in middle- and upper-class families. Ideally, it would be integrated.

"I think integration is deliberately discouraged now. The

boundary lines are very well chosen to keep the Negroes in certain districts. I really believe that this is the reason why a lot of the upper-grade centers are established—to keep them out of white schools. Parents think once Negroes start coming into a school the quality decreases, like they think Negroes moving into an all-white neighborhood lowers property values. But I think if a number of Southern schools can make integration work, certainly a city in the North, such as Chicago, should be able to do this as well."

In white schools and black, especially in the slums, there runs through many classrooms a moat of misunderstanding that separates teacher and children, and in turn blocks the children from education. Such is the view of an attractive widow, a soft-spoken white woman, who for fifteen years has worked Chicago's South Side as a truant officer. Her job is to "investigate absences, help alleviate home problems, refer appropriate cases to social agencies or the courts and work with families to create new values." She tries also to help teachers grasp what their students' lives are like outside of school in hopes of strengthening the chances of rapport. But often, she finds, teachers not only are naïve but are dedicated to their ignorance:

"The cases that come to me are not the well-adjusted children. They're the children who are deprived in one way or another. And, of course, when you go into the homes you can spot immediately why. I've never run across a case yet where you couldn't walk in and put your finger on something in the home.

"I came from a home today, for example, of a Puerto Rican family. The father died about three years ago, and the widow's left with six children from fifteen years down. Their sole income is Social Security. This afternoon it was about seven degrees above zero. There was no heat in this house. Water was dripping through the ceiling where the plaster was out. Some community agency was there taking pictures for the Board of Health. The child I had come to visit was in bed. There were no bed linens; these are unheard of. He was covered with a mass of rags. He had a very high temperature. He's been sick for about two weeks, maybe pneumonia. I asked about a doctor. The mother said she's taken him to a private doctor, but couldn't afford to return. I called the county physician and asked the association house to refer her to ADC for supplemental assistance. But now here's where I feel the teacher fails. She didn't have anybody going to the home to report directly to her. The teacher's attitude is, 'This kid's in and out all the time. It's negligence.' The attitude is immediately and automatically, They're a Puerto Rican family so they keep the kid at home at the slightest excuse. If the teachers knew about some of the home conditions that affect a child's attendance and classroom behavior they just might have a little more sympathy for the children. They might be more successful in establishing rapport.

"As it is, I don't recall ever getting into a conversation with any of them where there's any sympathy at all with the need. There is terrible prejudice from the teachers and the principals against these impoverished families, especially the ones in ADC. The minute they hear ADC they don't even want to know details. Immediately there's a stigma on this family. I don't think I ever ran across anybody [in the school system] who defended the program—ever. You hear the argument that the ADC mothers have illegitimate children in order to get more on their checks. This, of course, doesn't even work out arithmetically, having a child just to get \$20 more a month on a budget. Always comments about chiselers, about Negro children being the ones always asking for something. Teachers don't leave their prejudices at home when they come to school. In fact, about the first or second week I was in this work I got into a discussion with a principal about the ADC program. I made a defense of a kind for these people. And the next thing I knew I was called downtown to the personnel office. I was told that somebody had reported that I was critical of the school system and wanted to change things.

"Among principals and teachers, I find a very conservative or reactionary viewpoint on the whole. Sometimes you will find some milk of human kindness in some of them. They may even have a prejudice toward a certain child because he's a behavior problem, but if I come back to them and try to explain the deprived situation at home, sometimes you'll see a turnabout. Generally though, they will say, Oh, but they have a television! And I say, I'm so happy they have a television because they have nothing else. Absolutely no touch would be had with the outer world at all except through this medium. It gives them a sense of living, of some joy.

"What amazes me is that the young teachers just coming

out of college seem less tolerant than some of the older ones. I notice the yelling and the screaming at kindergarten children, at first graders. You can hear those shrill teacher voices going through the halls. So many times I can hear the same screaming before I get to the door of the child's home—the mother going at it, or maybe the father and mother at each other. When these kids come from that to the same thing at school, you wonder how their nerves aren't completely shattered. I think most of them have more skin than we give them credit for.

"I came out of school in the Depression when you couldn't help but be aware that something was wrong and you felt you had to do something about things. Most of us developed a social conscientiousness. Today these teachers coming out seem tremendously immature. You get the feeling the only reason they've gone into this [teaching] is because they're just married, it is a good career to go into for supplemental income and for something to fall back on after you rear your children. They don't go into it with any kind of a crusading effort, the way I went into social work. I mean I felt, God, we have to do something. It's not there now, with most of them.

"Most of these people come from teachers' college, and they certainly haven't been stimulated socially. I sat in the lunchroom the other day aghast. There were eight of these young gals there, in their twenties. One of them, all through the lunch hour, was making up cosmetically. And I wish you had seen what she was going through—with the white shadow and then a darker one over it and then the pencil, you know, and the undercoat—well, I was fascinated! This was somebody who after lunch was going to teach little first graders. And there was no talk at all about anything of worldly interest. Everything was immediate: when I do my washing, and how much ironing I've got to do, and how I do it. And I was just flabbergasted. The rest of them were playing cards. I think nobody's ever really given them anything to think about.

"Among principals, I would say a very small percentage think of themselves as liberal. Probably the majority consider themselves just neutral. They don't want any trouble.

"I find that many of the Negro teachers who have come from the South are not too literate—horrible spelling, horrible grammar. It's understandable; they were deprived too. But this is what they're passing on. And they are the ones who will accept the minority neighborhoods that some of the better-educated white teachers will not take. The Negroes may be better teachers, though, as far as what they have to offer the child personally. I have seen many mothers who morally are not considered good mothers and yet they have an awful lot to offer their children in the way of love and kindness and warmth.

"The majority of the teachers I've seen are white, from middle-class backgrounds. Their [job] choices would be either teaching, or social work or office work. They have no *particular* talent to make any wider choice than that. So this is a fine profession for them, with prestige and future stability. Some may find themselves good teachers after they're in, like some of the presidents we've had who go in politicians and come out statesmen. But the majority don't go in because of any great fervor for teaching. They want to go to the good neighborhoods, where there aren't as many social problems, where the children are clean and refined—and, of course, white.

"The fact that we have so many dropouts shows that somewhere along the line somebody did a lousy job. And we get some very bright children dropping out. We get them from technical high schools where it's hard to get in and from other schools where standards are very high.

"One problem, of course, is the counselors. The majority of them are not trained counselors. They drop these children left and right without too much attempt to work with them. There's often a complete lack of interest. And this is not just a racial thing, because a great many dropouts are from predominantly white schools, and many hate their former counselors.

"A large number of these kids are salvageable. I'm so busy I don't have time to do much with them. I have a backlog of five hundred cases. A kid can drop out of school illegally and be past the age limit before I get to him. Those I do reach, there's no time to follow up after just one visit. Sometimes the success story in our field means if you can get a kid to just open his mouth and talk to you without antagonism or just get a kid to smile who never seems to smile. It's a step forward."

To a psychologist, the culture gap between many students and teachers is obvious in both white and Negro schools. An attractive woman with salt-and-pepper hair and vivacious personality, she is troubled after five years in the Chicago system by what she terms "an attitude of expendability" toward students by some school officials. Often this trait is grounded in a lack of understanding, she says, but it can be related to the chess game of career advancement. She begins by telling a little about her work:

"I have all types of problems from pregnancy to homosexuality to cases where parents have cruelly abused children. At present I have a backlog of approximately two years. In fact, I have children who were referred to me much longer than two years ago. There are so many blue slips from teachers describing the child's problem, and so little service I can offer that whoever misbehaves the most is the one I get to.

"Many of the problems in the schools where I work are related to race. For one thing, many white teachers have a hidden fear of doing something that will cause hostility or acting-out aggression by the Negro child. It's not always a foolish fear. I have one boy who is the most aggressive, hostile Negro child I have ever seen. He walks around with not one but two chips on his shoulder, and if you say one thing to him he pulls up his sleeve and puts his hand next to you and says, 'That's because I'm black and you're white!' He's a typical example of a boy faced with the unrest and agitation of our times who cannot accept his role as a Negro, who is looking for a means of retaliation because he was born a Negro.

"We also have a serious problem with the Puerto Rican children. They have difficulty identifying because they feel they are not accepted by the Caucasians and they don't want to be Negroes.

"Often the problems are aggravated by school officials because of their lack of understanding about children from lower-class backgrounds, whether white or colored. They [school officials] are so forced by their own thinking to engage in [social] conformity that they can't see anything other than accepted conformity as possible for the children they handle.

"I had one white high school boy with one of the highest IQs I ever saw, but he was wearing his hair Beatle-fashion. He was a nonconformist with a very unhappy home life. The assistant principal demanded that he cut his hair. Instead of taking this boy and telling him that a certain amount of nonconformity is like salt in one's food and then ignoring the hair and developing his potential, all they did was keep him in the office and told him to cut his hair or be thrown out. Now he's more belligerent and no longer has any desire to achieve. What will happen to him? A school dropout with this potential?

"I had another white child who was so extremely withdrawn that she wore her hair in front of her face. She parted it like a curtain on a stage to look at me. Her teacher couldn't understand it and was very harsh with her. I found out that this girl slept in a room with a huge butcher knife stuck in the door to fend off attempts by her father to have sexual relations with her. Once her father had tried to choke her.

"I told the school administration that under no circumstances was this child to be sent to [the girl's social adjustment school], where you send girls who are truant and misbehaving. They have a very large Negro population there and some pretty tough kids. I wrote several reports stating how important it was not to send this girl there, this shy, neat, withdrawn, retiring little girl behind the curtain of hair who had to have a façade even to dare to talk to anybody. I arranged for her to get some psychological help if she stayed in her regular school. The child was sent to [the adjustment school] against my wishes because the regular school didn't want anyone who might bring them problems. She'll be confronted there with a tough group of girls she can't handle and a tremendous amount of sexual promiscuity. She'll get no psychological treatment. She'll have every reason to withdraw even more.

"The schools are unwilling, basically, to follow through with problem children—especially in the inner-city—partly because they are overwhelmed, there are so many, and because in this system the fewer problems you bring to the fore the better.

"In many cases the only way a problem child gets special help in an inner-city school is by becoming a discipline problem. I found an eighteen-year-old child this week with an IQ of 55 sitting in a regular classroom. This child doesn't have a high enough IQ even to be in a secondary EMH. If her IQ was six points lower, she'd be eligible for the state school. Her teacher said, 'She's working beautifully. Her work is excellent,' because she was quiet and didn't bother anyone. This child can't even read, yet she has been passed along every year because she doesn't cause trouble. She'll probably end up with a diploma.

"Out of the inner-city, the children are well nourished. They have regular physical exams, beautiful clothes, after-school activities. Papa and mama are busy with them and with their activities. This is the kind of child most teachers under-stand—and care about.

"Inner-city children, troubled or untroubled, are consid-ered expendable. Let me give you one example involving EMH rooms. First, you realize that not every school has EMH rooms. They're something of a status symbol, and also you get addi-tional money for each EMH child in the classroom. Now I know of one principal, Miss ——, who placed elementary-school Negro children in EMH rooms *without* exams to determine whether they really belonged there. She just arbitrarily decided. In some cases she just picked kids who were discipline problems with no indication that they were mentally retarded. I discovered this last May when I came around to test the EMH children at her school. I discovered one child with an IQ of 131 in an EMH class. She even asked me to help her out by giving inade-quate tests in hopes of keeping the number of EMH children high. She was expecting the state visitors shortly and she wanted them to see what a fine job she was doing with retarded children.

"The superintendent of the EMH rooms, a Negro, knew what she was doing, too. He and I both reported it downtown. Her actions were clearly illegal, not to mention immoral. Yet nothing was done.

"This woman's hostility toward Negroes is incredible. I've seen her discipline Negro children by threatening to put them in the street and have the assistant principal run over them back and forth with his car. She has no more business as an educator than I have as a nuclear physicist. She is a dangerous person. Yet since the EMH incident she has been promoted to a larger Negro elementary school—one of the largest in the city—which means more money.

"With a system like this, I can only feel things are going to get worse before they get better."

What happens in the Chicago system to the teacher who does understand her children, who can reach across the gap and touch some hidden nerve to awaken a torpid child, who five hours a day can lift her students from the quicksand of utter poverty and blot out the distractions of the asphalt jungle? A lithe young white woman, who until recently taught sixth grade in a hard-core Negro ghetto school, has one answer. With time and effort, she says, she managed to overcome her students' indifference, home environment, discipline problems and racial suspicion. But in the end, she was herself overcome by an adversary she had not anticipated—the school system that was paying her to teach:

"This is kind of emotional, but teaching in this type of area was my entire life. I lived and breathed and ate it for seven years. My goal was to produce graduating classes that could compete in society, and I think I was beginning to do just that, despite these youngsters' backgrounds.

"That year [the year she resigned] we had for the first time produced a middle-class class in a low-income area. In my sixth-grade class, all children scored at least 7.0—that's seventh grade—in mathematics, and only five children scored beneath 6.7—sixth grade, seventh month—in reading. This had never happened in District —— before in a low-income Negro school. Twenty-two boys from that class are now at [a highly ranked technical school in the city]. There are two children on $1,500 scholarships at [an exclusive private school], and nine children are on religious scholarships in all-white areas.

"This successful program took four years to build. It was centered pretty much around an early morning tutoring program and a close-knit, three-teacher team-teaching program. There was never enough faculty stability at the first-, second- and third-grade levels to get team-matching going there. We three represented fourth, fifth, and sixth grades. One teacher was Negro, the other two of us white. We'd meet on our lunch hours and go over the errors we had made and try to improve each other and coordinate our teaching. For instance, the other two couldn't grasp modern math, so I'd stand at the blackboard and explain to them what it means and how you do it.

"The early morning tutoring ran from 8:00 to 8:53 A.M. The motivation in this area to come to school early is low, naturally. Conditioning is against it. So I began the second day of school to build the motivation. I presented it as a volunteer thing: 'You may come early to be with your teacher'; 'We do exciting things in the morning before school begins,' and so on.

Within two weeks the entire class was coming early. They *wanted* to be there.

"We used the time to work on science projects, or speeches for the speech contests, or writing plays and operettas or checking answers with each other to find out where their own errors were—anything to stimulate them. Last year this early-morning tutoring produced first- and second-place science winners in district competition with more than twenty schools, plus second place in math and third in speech. And this is unique, because we competed against white schools. We had never swept the district like that before. Besides this, reading levels in my room skyrocketed. IQs increased markedly. The children listened to and enjoyed symphonies and operas.

"Also this program gave me a chance to become acquainted with my children because they talked freely then. To them it was different from school. And they were loyal to me. When a civil rights group called a school boycott, I held my children in the classroom 100 per cent. I was the only teacher in a Negro school in District —— who had no absenteeism. The children in my room never wanted recess, either. We worked right through.

"The principal who was there when I started this program approved of it. Then recently we got a new principal, a white woman. She never visited my class, but she had been there only a month when one of her assistants refused to let my children in the door one morning for the early session. The assistant said that from then on I'd have to have special permissions slips for them to get in, and that early session could be held only from 8:30 to 8:53 and only twice a week. That meant that by the time the children got upstairs and got going, they have about eighteen minutes to do something. I went to [the principal] and told her I couldn't accomplish anything in that time. I said, 'These children come directly to the room when they enter the school. They're serious. They want to learn. This is done in —— School up north, an all-white school. I see no reason why I cannot carry on the program here as I've been doing.'

"She got out the rule book and read me the rule that teachers are due in the school at 8:30 and the children are due at 9:00. She said that even allowing the children in the school at 8:30 was stretching the rule and furthermore that the district superintendent did not approve of the program. I told her how the children had benefited from this program, about the scholarships we had. She said, 'These children don't need to go out of their own neighborhood. They should go to their own neighborhood schools.'

"I could see our concepts didn't agree. Each year it tore me apart to train maybe twenty students in a class to do two hours of homework a night and be absolutely down-the-line good students, and then only be able to get scholarships for two or three and have to send the rest to the snakepit of —— Upper Grade Center, a horrendous pile of junk that 'serves' this neighborhood.

"She went on stressing that she had come from a low-income background in Chicago and that she had made a success of herself by attending neighborhood schools. I brought the discussion back to the tutoring and said, 'Miss ——, I am a good teacher, a dedicated teacher. I'll take the responsibility for these children in the building.' She interrupted, 'How do I know you're a good teacher? Do you have any awards?' I said, 'No, I don't. The children—what they do—is what I teach for. I never thought about a physical thing you put in your hand or put on the wall.' She said, 'Well, my walls from corner to corner are *filled.*'

"I began to cry then, which is ridiculous for a woman my age. I said, 'Miss ——, I've been here seven years. I'll take the responsibility. The children are loyal to me. They'll come directly to the room.' And she said—she has since denied it, but I swear she said—'Miss ——, Negroes don't have loyalty. As long as you teach, you remember your children are Negroes first and students second.'

"The shock was insurmountable. I could have slapped her face. But to cover the shock, I didn't say much of anything. I had essentially been a system teacher, and the thought of disobeying authority or hollering at authority was alien to me.

"She was still talking. She said, 'Miss ——, I spotted you from way off as a person who doesn't obey rules. You're not going to have any more time for the nonsense of children. If I call a meeting in the basement and you are the only one who has to attend and I tell you to attend, you'll attend. If you don't like it, you can always get out.'

"In this system, we sell bits and pieces of our integrity and dignity year after year. I had now been asked to sell it all. I called the district superintendent and told him what had happened. He said that he was not prepared to take any action against the principal. Over the weekend I suffered, but I made up my mind to go back. Then on Monday morning the children came as usual at five after 8:00. They were conditioned, you see. They wanted to be there. And they came upstairs—you know, just walked up as they usually do. I jumped up and said, 'How dare you come to my room when I told you not to be here from now on except Tuesdays and Thursdays at 8:30.'

"And right then I knew that she had me. She had me by fear. I wondered if perhaps there wasn't a principle involved more important even than my feelings of insult or of immediate duty to the children. In all my years at the school, I had spoken of high standards and integrity in teaching—to teachers, students, and parents. I had insisted that there can be no compromise with honest teaching, no fake programs, no doctored grades, no lying.

"That morning, right there at five after 8:00, I decided I must resign."

At a ghetto upper-grade center on the Near North Side, a social studies teacher has met much of the same resistance. A tall, immaculately groomed Negro, he says he has joined fellow teachers on numerous occasions during his eight years in the system to suggest improvements to the administration. More often than not their proposals have been ignored. Teachers, he believes, are giving up fighting but this does not mean peaceful days ahead. He recalls some of his experiences and explains why he feels Chicago rides on a collision course with tragedy:

"Things became so bad last year that thirty-one out of our thirty-nine teachers began meeting after school to try to work out answers to some of the problems. The principal never attended a meeting of the group, but we came up with some pretty good ideas.

"We suggested that lesson plan books be kept. This, of course, is a board of education rule, but it wasn't being done in our school and often teachers lose control when nothing is planned. The first time the lesson plan books were turned in, the principal observed them carefully. Then he started just flipping through them. Then nothing; he ignored them. I tested this by writing 'Kiss my ass' in my lesson plan book. It came back the same way.

"We suggested holding reward assembly programs as an incentive to improve discipline. We worked out a merit system for evaluating rooms, with the better rooms being chosen to go to the assemblies. This worked well at first, but gradually fizzled out because of indifference on the part of the administration. They tolerated the teachers' plans, but there was no real support.

"To put on a program in our school, you have to bend over backwards. A girl student wrote a play for Christmas, a damned good one. It was an ideal opportunity to give the kids a feeling of pride, something they really need and seldom get. But first her teacher had to sell the administration on the idea of putting it on by guaranteeing that there would be no problems resulting from it. Then the day of the play—there were two performances at which the kids applauded like mad—the principal didn't even show up. I wish I knew why. If I thought he was a bigot, I'd say so. It's just disinterest. These aren't people to him: they're just things in the classroom and you work with them as easily as possible. You make no demands, you give no encouragement.

"The kids aren't learning because they aren't being taught. A couple of new teachers were told by the principal the day they arrived, 'Don't expect to teach here. Just keep these kids in the room, keep the roof on the place.' I've been at —— for seven years. Not once has anyone observed in my classroom. Improving the level of instruction has never been an administrative concern. Teachers are hard to get, and the principal just wants to have the bodies there.

"Teachers who can't make it anywhere else gravitate to these schools. Negro teachers, of course, often don't have much choice. They are often limited in the kinds of schools to which they can go. I know of two cases in which Negro teachers were pressured out of white schools. In one, a Negro physical-education teacher in a middle class school felt constant hostility from the administration and the staff. From the kids, oh, there was a little hostility at first, a few pranks. But within the first marking period that all disappeared. But in the teachers' lunchroom the other teachers would leave when he sat down at the table. The administration remained cold, too, and there was no let-up in the harassment. At one point he wanted to hold a gym show under P.T.A. auspices. The P.T.A. president was willing, but the principal wouldn't allow it. After one year, the teacher transferred out.

"The whole Chicago placement system bears investigation. There is supposed to be an impartial assignment system—you go where there is a vacancy when you are first assigned. But in practice many new teachers who have come out of good colleges get some pretty good schools, while others who are not so worldly and those who are inadequate wind up here. I know that some good, dedicated teachers have asked specifically for inner-city schools because they feel the best assignment is where the greatest need is—and the personnel office has tried to discourage them. Right now only two-thirds of our faculty is certified. The rest are either subs or provisional teachers.

"It's a rare thing to find a qualified teacher in an EMH classroom here. They are supposed to be specially qualified people who have had training to work with these kids, and the classrooms are supposed to be kind of laboratories, geared to these kids' needs. Instead, they are little basement dungeons. The teachers here are high school teachers—one an English major and the other a history major—who happened to be placed in an elementary school. Recently, money provided by the state for EMH training was used by our school administration to buy stationery for the principal's office.

"There's nothing provided for the gifted kid. Once I tried to get math books a couple of years above grade level for some kids who were ahead of the class. The principal said he didn't have any money but when I persisted and finally got to the district superintendent I found out that $300 was available. The principal just didn't want to make the effort to go through channels for it.

"Our counselor is a white lady who lives in [an all-white suburb] and attends John Birch Society meetings which she thinks are wonderful because they're run so efficiently. Her only contact with Negroes is this school. She has a totally different background, of course, and she is probably as naïve as anyone I ever met. In conversations with me she makes comments such as, 'Oh, Mr. ——, a nice fellow like you could live anywhere he wants to.' She really believes this kind of thing. Now a person this naïve is not going to understand these kids and their problems. When she sees a situation, she judges it with her [all-white suburban] background, and she is incapable of doing much to help.

"Many of Chicago's school problems can be traced back to Superintendent Willis and his philosophy of running a problem-free school system. A principal can be up to his ears in difficulty but he tries to cover it up. He's not going to make a wave by asking for help or grappling openly with his problems when he knows this is not going to be received well at the top. Instead of the principal and the staff in a school like this facing the fact that they have certain handicaps and then getting down and really working with them, they merely say, 'It's a tough situation,' throw up their hands and then proceed as quietly as possible without attracting attention to their problems.

"The whole city needs to react to the level of education at all schools in the system. But there is no question that the situation is dramatically worse in the inner-city schools. There are exceptions, of course. At —— School, which has the same kind of housing-project neighborhood and the same kind of kids we have, there is a marvelous administration, good teachers and some fine remedial programs. About 98 per cent of their teachers are assigned, and the principal is so conscientious that teachers are trying desperately to get in there. They started a sound reading program in the first grade, including remedial work, and carried it through for eight years. Those kids graduated at reading level, one of the highest groups in this whole area. Our kids graduate at an average of two years behind their class level. That school is the exception, ours the rule. In neighborhoods like this, all kinds of neglect goes on because the administration feels it can go on. People in these areas are starting to realize that by and large they are being gypped.

"Unless somebody really begins to give some genuine consideration to some of the problems we've been discussing, and tries to come to some real, down-to-earth, practical solutions, you are going to have real chaos. We could have another Watts. Things are close to that now. And if the powers-that-be think they're not, they're just deluding themselves."

VIII

No Siesta Mañana: The Mexican-American in Los Angeles

———•———

Anthony Gary Dworkin

THERE IS NO DISCRIMINATION among teachers in Los Angeles; there is not one single case of differential treatment of Mexican children or differential curriculum (*Anglo member of Los Angeles Board of Education, 1963*).

The administration is against Mexicans, Cubans, poor people, etc. The administration would be a lot happier if they could get rid of all of the Mexicans (*Anglo employee in an East Los Angeles elementary school, 1965*).

The only way we can end the problems of discrimination in East Los Angeles schools is to make our wants known. The way to do that is to get a Mexican-American on the school board (*Mexican-American educator, 1964*).

It is very difficult for a member of a minority group to get elected to the school board. A Mexican must not only win the election in East LA, but also in the rest of the city. And you know quite well that the rest of the city will resist voting for a Mexican (*Anglo member of Los Angeles Board of Education, 1963*).

We love all of the Mexican children as if they were our own (*Anglo member of Los Angeles Police Commission, 1965*).

If you keep these Mexican kids active, you keep them out of mischief. Punishment keeps them in line, just like it does in the army. If you keep after these damn kids on the playground, then all will be fine in the classroom. These kids are born liars; you can never tell when they are telling the truth and you can't trust them. Consistency is very important here, there is only one way to do things around here (*Anglo teacher in East Los Angeles elementary school, 1966*).

The Mexican leaders and adults want us to be proud of our Mexican heritage. But if we are proud of our heritage, we must also be proud of our inadequate education, our slums, our poverty, our hyphenated citizenship, our poor health, and our unemployment. Some cultures have a heritage to be proud of. If I were Japanese and were asking my prospective father-in-law for his daughter's hand in marriage, he would ask me about my job. I would tell him that I was a dentist making $15,000 per year. And he would welcome me to the family. But as a Mexican all I have to tell my prospective father-in-law is that I work for Ford and make $1.45 per hour, and I am welcomed into the family with equal enthusiasm (*A Mexican-American college graduate who Anglicized his name, 1965*).

He [the Mexican-American] has a culture upon which he can fall back. . . . The actual fact is that the Mexican-American individual, the Spanish-speaking individual, would much rather stay within his own realms of his own neighborhood because he speaks Spanish, he is at home there, why should he want otherwise? (*Mexican-American educator, 1964*).

Mexican-Americans want to be different. They don't want to be American. They insist on speaking Spanish in school. Don't they think that American is good enough for them? If you ask me, it is too good for them! (*Anglo East Los Angeles teacher, 1966*).

If you show the prejudiced Anglos what an advanced culture the Mayans and Aztecs had and prove to them that the Mexican has a great cultural heritage, they will wish that they were Mexicans and respect us. In fact many will want to leave the North and move to Mexico to live (*Mexican-American businessman, 1963*).

A City Founded, A People Lost

The story of the Mexican-American[1] in Los Angeles is as old as the city itself. Many of the Mexican-Americans in Los Angeles today are the descendants of the city's earliest residents.

An understanding of the condition of the Mexican-American and of the city he built and lost must go back to a time when there were no freeways, or bustling crowds, or smog. Instead, all that existed were grasslands, desert, a few Spaniards, a few Christianized Indians, a few other Indians, a few missions spaced a day's horse ride apart, and a dusty trail called *El Camino Real* —The King's Highway.

[1] "Anglo," derived from the term Anglo-Saxon, refers to a person living in the United States of European, but not Spanish ancestry.

A Mexican-American is a person living in the United States who was born in Mexico, or whose ancestors came from Mexico, no matter how many years ago.

The Spanish had been in the West for two centuries and the Indians for two hundred more when forty-six adventurers of mixed Indian, Negro, and Spanish descent founded Los Angeles. The exact date of the founding is uncertain; however, the city fathers officially recognize it as September 4, 1781. It is said that the first building the Spaniards established was a jail to guarantee that the settlers would not escape from their new home. From out of wastelands a city was carved.

Los Angeles flourished through the nineteenth century. With the overthrow of Spanish rule, the independence of Mexico in 1810, and the subsequent secularization of the California missions in 1834, the countryside around the pueblo of Los Angeles became a vast spread of great ranchos.

All this came to an end when gold was discovered in California. General Winfield Scott's capture of Vera Cruz, Mexico, and the exploits of General John C. Frémont spelled defeat for the Mexicans in 1848. Within two years California was a state. The United States paid off its claims to Mexico and guaranteed that the grant deeds would be honored and the Mexican families could hold their great ranchos. But with the drought of 1862–1864, which killed the cattle, and with the heavy United States land taxes against the ranchos, the *gente de razón,* or the great families from the days of Spanish rule, lost their land. Enormous ranchos, like the 265,000-acre Los Alimitos, were sold for $152 in delinquent taxes.

During the land boom of the 1880s many Midwesterners moved into Los Angeles and bought land. The poverty-stricken Mexicans retreated into the ghetto of East Los Angeles, especially into an area known as the Flats.

With the overthrow of the Diaz regime in 1910 and the Mexican revolution that ensued, a new stream of Mexican immigrants flowed into the expanding city of Los Angeles. These were the landlords and the middle class, abandoning a Mexico that no longer welcomed them.

In the 1920s, with the political and economic unrest in Mexico, a third wave of Mexican nationals migrated to Los Angeles. Many Mexicans were employed in the fields by Anglo fruit growers.

When the Depression came in the 1930s, the Anglo discovered that the Mexicans had not gone back to Mexico between harvests, but had settled in the East Los Angeles ghetto to crowd the relief rolls. While the Anglo was intolerant of the idea that Mexican "nationals" were getting relief, he was even more incensed by the fact that in the depths of the Depression the Mexican laborers were attempting to unionize.

The state decided to deport the laborers. From California about two hundred thousand Mexican-American laborers, their wives, children, and pets were boarded on trains and sent back to Mexico. In some cases the children of the field hands were American citizens, born in the Los Angeles ghetto. However, because they could not speak English and could not show proof of citizenship, they were "repatriated."

Most of the Mexican-Americans in East Los Angeles were not deported. Throughout World War II, with the zoot-suit riots of 1943, and after the war, the migratory laborers continued to move into the cities; by 1960 the Mexican-American was 80 per cent urban.

In many respects the condition of the Mexican-American has improved. He no longer is required to sit in segregated movies, ride in separate sections of buses, and has been given the vote and a partial education. But the wounds inflicted for more than a century do not heal quickly. There is much bitterness in the ghetto.

———•———

The Mexican Ghetto Today: The Hard Data of Discrimination

There are more individuals of Mexican descent in Los Angeles than in any city in the world except Mexico City. Mexican-Americans comprise Los Angeles' second largest minority group, and represent 11.5 per cent of the city's 2.5 million residents.[2] Only the Negro, who makes up 14 per cent of the city's

---

[2] Statistical data on the city of Los Angeles are taken from Fair Employment Practice Commission report, "Los Angeles City Schools," October, 1964.

population, is larger in numbers. However, for the county of Los Angeles,[3] Mexican-Americans are the largest minority group. Of the county's 6 million residents, 9.6 per cent are Mexican-Americans, while 7.6 per cent are Negro. The Mexican population increases on the average by 2,250 new residents per month.

The reason Mexican-Americans outnumber the Negro population in the county but not in the city may be explained by three facts. First, much of the largest Mexican-American ghetto in Los Angeles is not in incorporated territory, but lies just east of the city's boundary. Second, the Negro population has been in the city a shorter length of time and migrated from the South to a concentrated ghetto in the south and central parts of the city; while the Mexican-American, because of his long tenure in Los Angeles, has become dispersed throughout the county as well as concentrated into several ghettos. In fact, most of the incorporated suburbs in the county have sizable Mexican-American populations. Third, because the Mexican-American is a Caucasian, the lighter-skinned members of the population have found it much easier to escape from the ghetto and assimilate in to the Anglo middle-class communities, attend Anglo schools, and share in the dominant culture.

Table 1 presents the social characteristics of the Anglo and Spanish surname[4] populations in Los Angeles County. As might be expected the Anglo's condition is considerably better than the

[3] Statistical information on the county of Los Angeles and for the Mexican-American ghetto are derived from the Research Department of the Welfare Planning Council, Los Angeles Region report, "Background for Planning," 1963.

[4] The United States Census does not adequately differentiate the Mexican-American population from other Spanish-speaking groups. The term "Spanish surname" is employed instead by the census. Hence, Mexican-Americans, Puerto Ricans, Cubans, and Central and South Americans comprise Los Angeles' population of 576,716 people with Spanish surnames. However, this does not present too much of a problem. Over 90 per cent of the Spanish-surname population of Los Angeles are Mexican-Americans, and so the data on Spanish surnames are fairly accurate for Mexican-Americans as well. If anything, the data present a more conservative estimate of the Mexican-American plight as the Cuban population, most of whom are escapees from Castro's regime and were former professionals in Cuba, are better educated, earn better incomes, and have better jobs. However, because the Spanish-surname population who are not of Mexican descent represent only a small fraction of the total category, the discrepancy between statistics on Mexican-Americans and on all Spanish surname groups is slight. If anything, the total number of Mexican-Americans with Spanish surnames is an underestimate of the total Mexican-American population because some Mexican women change their surname by marriage to Anglo men, and some Mexican men Anglicize their surnames.

Characteristics of the Anglo-white and Spanish-surname Populations: Los Angeles County, 1960 *

MARITAL STATUS	ANGLO-WHITE	SPANISH-SURNAME
Population 14 and over	3,617,761	361,877
Per cent Single	19.1	25.3
Per cent Married	67.1	65.6
Per cent Married but Separated	11.5	2.7
Per cent Widowed	8.6	5.3
Per cent Divorced	5.1	3.8
FAMILY INCOME		
All families	1,302,933	128,018
Per cent <$4,000	16.9	25.7
Per cent $4,000–5,999	17.5	27.8
Per cent $6,000–7,999	21.9	22.5
Per cent $8,000–9,999	16.5	12.2
Per cent ≥$10,000	27.3	11.7
Median Income	$7,433	$5,759
EDUCATION		
Population 25 and over	2,966,703	265,928
Per cent no school	1.0	7.0
Per cent 1–7 yrs.	9.1	30.0
Per cent 8–11 yrs.	33.3	37.0
Per cent 12 yrs. (high school)	30.3	17.5
Per cent 1–3 yrs. college	15.4	5.9
Per cent 4 or more yrs. college	10.8	3.0
Median school yrs. completed	12.2 yrs.	9.0 yrs.
EMPLOYMENT STATUS		
Male, 14 and over	1,728,419	179,181
Per cent in labor force	80.4	80.0
Per cent unemployed	5.1	7.6
Female, 14 and over	1,892,023	182,696
Per cent in labor force	37.5	34.4
All occupied units	1,692,567	146,230
Per cent owner occupied	56.6	47.0
Per cent deteriorated or dilapidated	6.8	19.8
Owner occupied units	958,583	68,686
Per cent value $10,000	8.0	21.7
Per cent value $10,000–19,999	61.7	66.8
Per cent $20,000 or more	30.3	11.5
Median value	$16,900	$13,100
Median gross rent	$85	$68

* Adapted from Table 10, *Background for Planning*, Research Department of the Welfare Planning Council, Los Angeles Region, Research Report No. 17, February 1964.

Mexican-American's. More Anglos are married; but fewer people of Spanish surname are widowed or divorced. The divorce rate among the Mexican-American is considerably higher, however, than the statistics or Catholicism would indicate. As one Mexican-American newspaperwoman noted:

> Today, as never before, women are going down to Mexico to get divorces from their husbands if they are not satisfied. Before, the woman would just endure, but now women are freer. They go to Mexico for a divorce and it never gets recorded by the State of California. Therefore, population figures could never tell you anything about the shifts.

The Anglo, however, has a higher income (a median of $7,433 for the Anglo and $5,759 for the Mexican-American); he is better educated (the Anglo has completed 12.2 years of school while the Mexican-American has completed only 9); the Anglo is less affected by unemployment (5.1 per cent of the Anglos are unemployed as compared to 7.6 per cent of the Mexicans). And finally, the Anglo lives in a better home; the Anglo's home is worth $16,900 while the Mexican's is worth $13,100; further, 19.8 per cent of the Mexican homes are dilapidated or deteriorated, while only 6.8 per cent of the Anglo homes are in such condition.

The present paper is based upon research in one of the ghettos in the county—East Los Angeles and Boyle Heights. Within this area reside 180,000 people, of whom 67 per cent are of Spanish surname. This ghetto represents the largest single concentration of Mexican-Americans, is a center of Poverty Program work, produces the most militant Mexican-Americans, and is an area in which social scientists have been studying for the past twenty years, thus providing an invaluable storehouse of data.

It was in this area that the 1943 "zoot-suit riots" raged. Here in East Los Angeles and Boyle Heights, situated on the east and traditionally the wrong side of the Los Angeles River and Southern Pacific Railroad tracks, is the infamous Flats. The Flats has been the home of gangs and the repository for successive waves of immigrants. From the 1880s to the post-World War II period the Flats has been occupied by newly immigrated Irish, Armenians, Molokans, Slavs, Jews, and finally Mexicans. Each group turned the Flats into an interstitial area plagued with

problems of crime, delinquency, tuberculosis, and human decay
—physical, psychological, and social.

In order to make this report more meaningful, at times we
shall not restrict our discussion simply to the ghetto itself. Instead, we shall discuss the ghetto in relation to the county as a
whole, the Anglo communities to which the successful Mexicans
migrate, and Watts, one part of the Negro ghetto.

There is a distinct path taken by the mobile Mexican family
as it flees the ghetto. The stages seem to be as follows: out of the
ghetto to El Sereno, then to Montebello and Monterey Park, and
then, often with the name change and complete Anglicization,
into eastern San Gabriel Valley and other Anglo areas. In terms
of social class, as judged by income, education, occupation, living conditions, delinquency rates, property values, etc., the class
shift is roughly from lower-lower to upper-lower to lower-
middle to upper-middle. As one sociologist who has worked
with East Los Angeles Mexicans for fifteen years notes:

> There is a mass exodus from East LA to El Sereno. While East
> LA is lower class, El Sereno is upper-lower and lower-middle
> class. Thus, as the Mexicans get more money they move out of
> the LA ghetto and into the El Sereno ghetto. Another reason
> for the movement to El Sereno is the fact that it has a power-
> ful Catholic church and parochial school. The pattern of mi-
> gration is into East LA, to El Sereno, and then finally into
> Montebello and Monterey Park and east.

Table 2 presents the 1960 statistics on population density
and ethnic concentration. It should be noted that there exists a
linear relationship between these characteristics and the progressive movement out of the ghetto into successively higher socioeconomic levels. That is, as one moves out of the Mexican
ghetto of East Los Angeles and Boyle Heights, population density and percentage of ethnicity decrease. In addition the ratio of
Mexican-Americans to Anglos decreases. Furthermore, while
Watts has approximately the same high population density as
the Mexican-American ghetto, it is more segregated. East Los
Angeles is 70.9 per cent and Boyle Heights is 78.5 per cent
ethnic, while Watts is 94.5 per cent ethnic. Further, Watts is
more homogeneously ethnic. Eighty-five per cent of Watts is of
the same race (Negro), while only 67 per cent of the Mexican
ghetto is of the same ethnic group (Spanish surname).

Table 2: *1960 Census, Population
Density, and Ethnic Distribution* *

AREA	1960 POPULATION	PERSONS PER SQ. MI.	PER CENT NEGRO	PER CENT OTHER	PER CENT SPANISH SURNAME	PER CENT ALL MI-NORITIES
East Los Angeles	105,464	12,379	<1.0	3.8	67.1	70.9
Boyle Heights	75,065	14,463	3.7	8.0	66.8	78.5
El Sereno	29,477	6,110	1.2	3.8	37.4	42.4
Montebello	32,097	4,312	<1.0	1.6	22.6	24.2
Monterey Park	37,821	5,352	<1.0	2.9	13.1	16.0
Watts (Comparison population)	72,203	13,818	85.7	<1.0	8.8	94.5
L. A. County	6,038,771	1,479	7.6	2.0	9.6	19.2

* Compiled from Tables 2 and 7 of *Background for Planning,* Research Department of the Welfare Planning Council, Los Angeles Region, Research Report No. 17, February 1964.

The traditional indices of social rank and socioeconomic status also demonstrate a linear relationship between the progressive steps taken out of the Mexican ghetto and increasingly favorable economic, educational, and occupational conditions. The median incomes for the ghetto and the three steps beyond are as follows: the ghetto of East Los Angeles and Boyle Heights, $5,437 and $5,053, respectively; El Sereno, $6,461; Montebello, $7,351; Monterey Park, $7,650. In comparison, the median income in Watts is $4,365, a figure even lower than in the Mexican ghetto.

The median school years completed for East Los Angeles and Boyle Heights are eight each; for El Sereno it is ten years; for Montebello it is eleven years; and for Monterey Park it is twelve years. The educational level in Watts is nine years, and thus is higher than in the Mexican ghetto. As will be discussed later, the difference between the ghetto and Watts may be attributed to an extreme difference in the value system of the Mexican ghetto and that of the school system.

Unemployment rates also demonstrate the linear relation and the fact that conditions in the Mexican ghetto are somewhat better (except for education) than in Watts, the Negro area. In East Los Angeles and Boyle Heights the unemployment rates are 6 and 6.6, respectively; while the values for El Sereno, Montebello, and Monterey Park are 3.7, 3.5, and 3.9, respectively. The apparent deviant case of Monterey Park is confounded by the higher percentage of college students in the area. This group enters the ranks of the unemployed during the summer but are "employed" during the school year. Unemployment in Watts is much higher than in the Mexican ghetto. In fact, it is 50 per cent greater, with a 9.4 per cent rate.

Lastly, we note that housing conditions and values improve as we move out of the ghetto into the three other areas. In East Los Angeles and Boyle Heights, respectively, 29 and 23.5 per cent of the homes are deteriorated or dilapidated, and median property values are $11,861 and $11,563, respectively. In El Sereno 17.8 per cent of the homes are deteriorated or dilapidated, and the median property value is $12,581. In Montebello only 4.5 per cent of the homes are deteriorated or dilapidated, while the median property value is $16,834. And in Monterey Park 3.2 per cent of the homes are deteriorated or dilapidated, and the median property value is $17,833. Fewer homes in Watts (22.6 per cent) are deteriorated or dilapidated than in the Mexican ghetto; however, property value ($10,208) is less than in the Mexican ghetto. All of these statistics indicate that the path taken by the Mexican-American as he leaves East Los Angeles and Boyle Heights is one of upward mobility, as measured by these traditional indices.

While no statistics are available on the actual number of Mexican-Americans who escape from the ghetto, we can be sure that the percentage is small. One index is the relatively low percentage of people with Spanish surnames found in the more Anglo areas. Even the phenomenon of passing and name changing is not sufficiently frequent to allow us to conclude that most Mexican-Americans escape the ghetto. Rather, we must conclude that the majority of Los Angeles' Mexican-American population is destined to remain in the ghetto where one may live and die without the need for English, without knowing that the world outside is any better, without leaving the "culture of poverty."

"But They're Just Different" [5]

The educational level of the Mexican-American in the ghetto is lower than in the more disadvantaged Negro ghetto of Watts, because the Mexican value system is so much more at odds with the school system than is that of the Negro. In this section we shall discuss the cultural factors which make the Mexican seem so strange to the Anglo teachers.

There is a sharp split between the Anglo's and Mexican's culture. The Anglo is secular, practical, objective, competitive, materialistic, and future-oriented. Traditionally the Mexican was not.[6] The new Mexican-Americans are changing, but a viable culture, reinforced by generations of ghetto life and discrimination, and centuries of life in Mexico does not die easily. A conglomeration of Spanish, Indian, and Roman Catholic in origin, the Mexican-American culture has served as a defense against the exploitation by the Anglo. One Mexican-American teacher, who feared that busing Mexican children from the ghetto to Anglo schools out of the ghetto would cause the children to lose their grasp of the Mexican culture, proclaimed:

[5] A frequently heard statement among Anglo teachers in the Mexican-American ghetto in Los Angeles. One teacher elaborated on the statement by pointing out that "the reason Mexican kids get into so much trouble is that they are born Mexican."

[6] Of the sociological models available to explain the differences between the Mexican and Anglo societies, the most frequently used among researchers in Mexican-Anglo relations is that of the Folk-Urban asymtotic dichotomy. Born in the nineteenth-century tradition of Tönnies, Maine, and Durkheim, the distinction was tested empirically by Redfield, with data from villages in Mexico. Redfield characterized the ideal-typical folk society as follows: "Such a society is small, isolated, nonliterate, and homogeneous, with a strong sense of group solidarity. The ways of living are conventionalized into that coherent system which we call 'a culture.' Behavior is traditional, spontaneous, uncritical, and personal; there is no legislation or habit of experiment and reflection for intellectual ends. Kinship, its relationships and institutions, are the type categories of experience, and the familial group is the unit of action. The sacred prevails over the secular; the economy is one of status rather than of market." (Robert Redfield, "The Folk Society," *American Journal of Sociology,* 52, 1947, p. 294.)

[The Mexican American] has a culture upon which he can fall back. . . . The actual fact is that the Mexican-American individual, the Spanish-speaking individual, would much rather stay within his own realms of his own neighborhood because he speaks Spanish, he is at home there, why should he want otherwise? [7]

Since there is time to touch upon only a few aspects of Mexican culture, our concern shall be with those aspects which are of maximal importance to the Mexican-American in Los Angeles with respect to his educational opportunities. As such, our discussion shall touch upon the mystical belief in *La Raza* (the race), the Mexican world view; the dominance of *machismo,* or the male-oriented society; the importance of one's parents and extended family; and the cohesion-producing effect of speaking only Spanish in a society whose language is English.

In his discussion of the *Mexican-Americans of South Texas,*[8] William Madsen stated that:

The Mexican-American thinks of himself as both a citizen of the United States and a member of *La Raza* (the Race). This term refers to all Latin-Americans who are united by cultural and spiritual bonds derived from God. The spiritual aspect is perhaps more important than the cultural. . . . The spirit of the Spanish-speaking people, however, is taken to be divine and infinite. As one Latin expressed it, "We are bound together by the common destiny of our souls."

In Mexico, the concept of *La Raza* carries the idea of a splendid and glorious destiny. Mexicans see their greatest national strength in the spiritual vigor of *La Raza.* In Texas, the history of discrimination and economic subordination has modified the concept of the ultimate destiny of *La Raza.* Many Spanish-speaking Texans would say that God had originally planned a glorious future for the Mexican-American, but it probably will never be attained. The failure of *La Raza,* he would continue, is due to the sins of individual Latins. Some believe that *La Raza* is held back by the sins of all Mexican-Americans. . . . Other Latins think that only the worst sinners are holding back *La Raza.* . . . I once asked a Latin if he thought the Anglos were in any way responsible for holding back the Mexican-Americans from their God-given destiny. "Of course not," he replied. "If we lived by God's commands

[7] From the transcript of "Human Relations—Yesterday, Today, and To-morrow," Part 1-B (Education), aired on KNBC/television, Channel 4, Los Angeles, Sunday, October 4, 1964, 11:15–11:55 P.M.
[8] New York: Holt, Rinehart and Winston, 1964.

we would be so strong that no one could block us. Of course, the Anglos take advantage of our weakness but it is we who make ourselves weak, not the Anglos."

Not all Mexican-Americans believe that *La Raza* has failed. The militant members of the Mexican-American middle class, most of whom have escaped from the Los Angeles ghetto Anglo neighborhoods, often speak with pride of their Mexican heritage. One Mexican-American businessman who is a member of that category maintained:

> If you show the prejudiced Anglos what an advanced culture the Mayans and Aztecs had and prove to them that the Mexican has a great cultural heritage, they will wish that they were Mexicans and respect us. In fact many will want to leave the North and move to Mexico to live.

He is so confident that the Anglo would prefer to live in Mexico once he learned about the culture and history of the land that he has begun to manufacture phonograph records which tell of the Mexican heritage and contain guitar renditions of popular Mexican songs. He sells these at cost to the Anglos who can afford the two dollars, and gives them free to Anglos who are in economic straits.

A second component of Mexican-American culture is *machismo,* the cult of masculinity. The Mexican family, like the Catholic Church, is patriarchal and authoritarian. There is a double standard in which the restrictions upon the male are significantly less. Education is for the man, sexual liberties are for the man, material comforts are for the man, and politics are for the man. The woman is subordinate. She must be faithful to her husband and her children. She is controlled by her parents until she marries; then she is dominated by her husband. In theory and in practice the woman's role in life is one of wife and mother—and nothing more.

The cult of masculinity is at odds with the egalitarian material relationship of the Anglo. Within the ghetto, which is isolated from the Anglo community, strains are less apparent. Still, *machismo* affects female participation and support of such Anglo-operated activities as the school and P.T.A. As the East Central Area Director of the Los Angeles Region Welfare Planning Council observed:

In the United States the two sexes are on a fairly equal basis. In the culture of Mexico the man is head of the household. The term *machismo* is oftentimes attributed to that trait in the Mexican male where he is the dominant figure in the family. When this characteristic exists, it is the man—the husband—who generally decides if the wife is to attend a P.T.A. meeting, or if she is to participate in a community or civic activity. Thus, because of his own indifference or aloofness, neither he, nor she, becomes actively involved in the community.[9]

When, however, the Mexican-American moves from the ghetto into areas more heavily populated by Anglos, the cultural factor of *machismo* becomes dysfunctional. Mexican-American women compare their relationship with their husbands to that of their Anglo neighbors, and marital unrest often results. As we noted previously, divorces are on the increase and *machismo* is declining. A Mexican-American social worker whose specialty is marriage counseling pointed out that:

> An American middle-class tradition is rough on Mexican husbands. The de-emphasis of *machismo* goes against the strong cultural traditions. Husbands feel the pressure and often leave their wives. For the women the situation is better. It is the first time that they are independent. But both conditions affect the parent-child relationship. Many Mexican kids came to this country when they were very young. They never learned to speak either proper Spanish or proper English. They can't communicate with their parents or their teachers, and vice versa. They feel alienated at home and thus turn to gang life. Only here can they find a peer group that understands them and their problems.

It is in the area of family relations that the dichotomy between the Anglo and Mexican value systems is most apparent, and where its effects upon Mexican educational opportunities are most devastating. The Anglo family is child-centered, while the Mexican family is family-centered. This presents problems with the schools. The social worker continued:

> The schools can't understand why a mother would keep her kid home to tend her brothers and sisters and her cousins while her mother takes her aunt to the hospital. The middle-class parent defines his child's education as the most important thing. But the Mexican parent says that it is the family welfare and family solidarity, including the extended family, that is most im-

[9] Martin Ortiz, "Mexican Americans in the Los Angeles Region," unpublished report, 1965.

portant. School is less important than family life, but the middle-class schoolteacher would not understand this.

Couple this with the belief that the woman's place is in the home and that *machismo* is of great importance, and one can understand why there are so few Mexican-Americans in public education. Out of the eight thousand teachers in the in-service training program in Los Angeles, only seventy-five are Mexican-Americans. Public school teaching is not a masculine occupation in the ghetto, and women are not encouraged to become professionals.

In addition, the school is a symbol of Anglo authority. It is the force which Mexicans see as trying to dissolve family ties. The school demands that the parents obey its wishes. If Juanita's mother wants to have her stay home from school and tend her twelve siblings, the school can seek an injunction against her. The school demands that the child forsake his familial obligations for the needs of the larger society—a demand that rubs against the values of the culture. This is one of the factors which contribute to the high dropout rate among Mexican-American youth. As one Anglo social scientist with an extensive knowledge of the Mexican-American commented:

> Actually you are not going to affect dropout rates as long as the school stands as a symbol of Anglo-Saxon superiority. The Mexican community doesn't trust the schools. The schools threaten to take away the patriarchal rule in the families. A father cannot decide the fate of his children, because the women teachers do so. There is a good deal of paternal pressure on the kids to drop out of school.

Unlike the Anglo-American family, which puts a premium only upon loyalty to the nuclear family, the Mexican family ties extend to all relatives and even close friends. In a report to a group of public school teachers one sociologist noted:

> [In the Mexican-American community] there is the extended family, not just parents, grandparents, children, uncles, aunts, cousins, but also other formal ties with close friends. You may be asked to officiate at the baptism of a child of your friend. I guess the closest role Anglos have to it is a godparent. Of course this is a great honor. It means that you will be a foster parent, *Padrino* or *Madrina* to the child and *compadre* or *comadre* to its parents. It means that the two families are very closely tied. The *compadre* is technically responsible for the

religious instruction and for the vocational or professional training of the child. If there is any kind of trouble, he is considered to be a substitute parent. We do not have this relationship in the Anglo family system. I recall talking about a certain judge with a man who is prominent in the Los Angeles Mexican-American community. He said proudly, "I am *compadre* to him." That means he is a godfather to his children and has a formal relationship to the father. These are extensive family ties where everybody is close to everybody else.[10]

There is little question that the symbols which maintain a culture are best communicated through language, both written and spoken. Buttressing the culture of the ghetto is the Spanish language. The predominant number of members of the older generation of Mexican-Americans speak no English. Nearly 20 per cent of the entire population of the ghetto are functionally illiterate.[11] Among the school-age generation many are barely literate and barely fluent in either English or Spanish. In some sections of the ghetto it is not necessary to be able to speak English. A Mexican-American newspaperwoman observed:

> Did you know that many Mexicans live and die in the East LA ghetto without ever learning English or even leaving the ghetto? Many have never even seen downtown Los Angeles, which is about five miles away. They don't realize that the rest of the world is not a run-down dilapidated slum. I think that if they realized that things were better in other areas, they might get even more militant and would demand their rights. What is keeping the Mexican from overcoming his problems partly is the fact that he doesn't know that things are any different anywhere else.

Because many Mexicans speak little or no English, they have little opportunity to interact with the dominant society. Instead, they seek the security of the ghetto.

Anglos ask why the Mexican-American insists on speaking Spanish. One Anglo teacher observed:

> Mexican-Americans want to be different. They don't want to be American. They insist on speaking Spanish in school. Don't

10 Paul M. Sheldon, "Mexican Americans and the Public Schools: Some Contrasts in Culture and Social Class," in the report of the Conference on Understanding and Teaching Mexican-American Children and Youth, California State Department of Education, 1964, p. 8.

11 This, of course, does not mean that all members of this segment cannot read or communicate. Rather, it means that they cannot read English; however, an unknown percentage of this segment can read neither English, nor Spanish.

they think that American is good enough for them? If you ask me, it's too good for them!

This is not the issue; rather there is security in speaking Spanish. Ruth Tuck once observed that because Spanish is often the language spoken in the Mexican-American home, lapsing into this language often makes the Mexican-American feel more at ease. Besides, many idioms and turns of the tongue lose their meaning and significance when translated into English.[12]

In addition, there is considerable pressure within the community among the older generation to retain the Spanish language. As Madsen points out:

> From the Anglo viewpoint, Spanish is the primary symbol of "foreignness" of the Mexican-American. For the Latin, Spanish is the primary symbol of loyalty to *La Raza*. The Mexican-American who speaks English in a gathering of conservative Latins is mocked and regarded as a traitor to *La Raza*. Among members of the lower class such linguistic disloyalty is forgiven only when a man is drunk.[13]

Furthermore, Spanish allows the culture to flourish. Spanish permits the Mexican-American to maintain cultural pluralism and ties with his family in Mexico. There is reluctance to learn English, the language of the Anglo conquerors, the language of the Yankees who took Mexican land and forced the Mexican into the ghetto, stripping him of everything but his culture—his defense mechanism. As Sheldon notes:

> . . . Among a large part of the Spanish-speaking community English has always been labelled the language of authority spoken by the cop on the beat. English is spoken by the sheriff's deputies. English is spoken by the social worker who controls the mother's allotment. English is spoken by the Anglo teacher. . . . There is a carry-over of the Mexican image of the teacher. The *maestro* is much more a disciplinarian and authority figure than American figures. He is also a government figure in Mexican culture. Especially among new arrivals from Mexico, the teacher is held in awe, an attitude which, in a nation of almost universal literacy, is difficult to understand.[14]

We may thus conclude that the explanation for the difference between the educational level of the Negro and the Mexi-

---

12 *Not with the Fist* (New York: Harcourt, Brace, 1946).
13 William Madsen, *The Mexican-Americans of South Texas*, p. 106.
14 Sheldon, *op. cit.*, p. 7.

can-American can in part be accounted for by the fact that (1) because of the cult of masculinity, *machismo,* the father of the household determines whether or not his children will go to school, and girls are not encouraged to attend classes; (2) the school, being child-oriented, demands that the child forsake his family at times in order to attend classes, while the Mexican family is family-centered, and insists that the child not go to school if there are too many chores at home to do; and (3) that English, which has been the only language spoken in schools, is the language of the Anglo, the language of the person who conquered the Mexican, attempting to rob him of his culture.

The problems of ghetto life and the dichotomized world in which the Mexican-American lives do not affect the older generation as severely as they do the youth. The Mexican who came to the United States with his family may encounter discrimination in terms of socioeconomic variables, but he has his Spanish-speaking community and Mexican folk culture in the ghetto to fall back upon. He can find shelter in the ghetto. The youth, however, find themselves in a situation unique to children of immigrants in a pluralistic ghetto. In school they are taught to abide by the Anglo child-centered individualistic value system; at home they are reminded of their Mexican heritage and the emphasis on family loyalty. To satisfy the demands of one group is to reject the other. This is the plight of the marginal man. He is marginal to both societies, having full citizenship in neither. There are few cultural symbols available to him with which he can identify. There are few rewards offered for taking either stance. If he sides with the school, he loses his parents' support, but the Anglo community will not accept him, and so he is out of work and without a reference group and culture upon which to rely. If he sides with his parents, he must reject the schools and live his life in the slum—granted, with a culture—but a culture of the slums, and a culture of poverty.

The culture of poverty and the failure of the schools to realize the importance of the family unit in the Mexican culture has taken a great toll among the Mexican-Americans. The Mexican-American has "hyphenated citizenship." He is neither a Mexican nor an American. As a Mexican-American social worker pointed out:

The biggest source of strain is not with the school or the police. It is with the culture of poverty. Mexican-American kids are marginal men—marginal to their parents' generation and marginal to the Anglos. The Mexican kids can't speak English and they can't speak Spanish. They lack identity. Everything is defined for them in such a way that they cannot belong to either group. They are not wanted or accepted by the Anglos, and they are not wanted by their parents. The Mexican kid is in search of himself. He feels lost. Only in the gang participation does he find a group that understands him and sympathizes with his problems. It is only through gang activity and peer group activity that he can find himself.

But not all Mexican-American kids find themselves in gang activity. Sometimes the marginality is too much to overcome. One eighteen-year-old East Los Angeles girl wrote:

You can't really win. If you want to be a Mexican you are going to be secluded from the dominant society and you don't have a chance. If you want to be an American you are not going to get any help at home. After a while you get the feeling it isn't worth it. Then you take whatever you can get and have fun—there's nothing else to do.

Despite what she said, she did choose a course of action. One month after writing this she committed suicide.

Aside from taking his life, the Mexican has recourse to changing his name to escape the marginality, but even this doesn't work. A social worker told me of the following case:

I had one case of a Mexican-American about twenty-three who had tried to beat the stigma of being a Mexican and tried to assimilate into the Anglo world by changing his name. He ceased calling himself José Vasquez and became Robert Martindale. But he is still short, dark, and can't speak English very well. Changing his name didn't help. He still can't find work, and now neither the Anglos nor the Mexicans will talk to him.

The social worker suggested a plan of correcting the cultural poverty aspect of the culture of poverty:

One cultural disadvantage of the culture of poverty is the fact that there are few sources of intellectual stimulation in the Mexican community. There are no legitimate theaters, no music halls where classical music is played; there are only a couple of Mexican movie houses. The only contact with the classics from Mexico are through these two movie houses. One of the Poverty Program projects in northern California is bringing Mexican literature to the people so that they can be proud of their heritage. There is a need to teach the kids about Mexican art and history. The Japanese community provides classes for their children to teach them Japanese and to educate them about their heritage. This gives them a sense of identity. There ought to be a similar program for the Mexican kids, so that they can learn something about their heritage.

———— • ————

Widening the Gap

In a handbook soon to be released to the teachers and principals of the Los Angeles City School System's East District (the area serving the Mexican-American ghetto), it is pointed out that:

> Throughout the five Southwestern states, the educational level of the Spanish-surname population increased about one grade from 1950 to 1960, bringing it, in California, from an average of grade 8.3 to 9.1, a higher figure than that of any other Southwestern state. Meanwhile, however, the educational level of the total population also increased; in California, from 11.2 to 12.1, again the highest in the Southwest. It is evident that, while the Spanish-surname populations's average schooling level has gone up, the proportionate gap between it and the total population remains the same.[15]

Twenty years ago there were comparatively few Mexican-American children going to school, but this is no longer true. Over 80 per cent of the Mexican-American population are urbanites. Their children attend schools, segregated because of segregated housing, and are taught by Anglo, Japanese-American, and Negro teachers. Many Mexican-Americans are convinced that their teachers, like the rest of the non-Mexican community, do not understand them, and are still influenced by the old idea: "Why should José go to school? He is going to pick fruit anyway." [16]

[15] E. Farley Hunter, Paul M. Sheldon, and Duke Saunders, "Mexican Americans and the Public Schools," Chap. 1, pp. 14–15, 1966 (unpublished material).

[16] McWilliams, *op. cit.*

De facto segregation and its effects

According to a recent report by the California State Fair Employment Practices Commission (FEPC),[17] pupils in the school in the East Elementary District are over 50 per cent Mexican-American, 12 per cent Mexican Indian, 16 per cent Japanese-American, 3 per cent Negro, and 10 per cent Anglo. These figures are, of course, for the East District as a whole, rather than for the East Los Angeles and Boyle Heights Mexican ghetto, which is within the district's boundaries. In the ghetto itself the percentage of Mexican-American pupils is higher and the schools are more segregated. Furthermore, as Japanese-American families and Negro families become prosperous and move out, East Los Angeles and Boyle Heights may become more of a Spanish-speaking ghetto.

In one elementary school, which is typical of most in the ghetto, there has been an increasing pattern of *de facto* segregation over the past four years. In 1962 I sampled this school of a thousand pupils and found it to be comprised of 73 per cent Mexican-American, 19 per cent Japanese, and 8 per cent Anglo children; there were no Negro pupils at that time. In 1966, 95 per cent of the children were Mexican-Americans, while only 1 per cent were Japanese-American, and 3 per cent were Anglos; there were also a few Negro pupils. The total enrollment has remained constant over the four years. Similarly, the two major high schools that serve the ghetto are now 80 per cent Mexican-American and 20 per cent Japanese-American.

Despite the fact that segregated schools for the Mexican-American have been illegal and unconstitutional in California since 1945, the schools in East Los Angeles are still *de facto* segregated. The Supreme Court case which overturned the practice of providing separate schools for Anglo and Mexican children was the Méndez case, in Orange County (the county to the south of Los Angeles). McWilliams writes of the case:

> Gonzalo Méndez, a citizen of the United States, had been a resident of the town of Westminster, in Orange County, California, for twenty-five years. Of immigrant background, he had

[17] Fair Employment Practices Commission, State of California, "Los Angeles City Schools," October 1964.

come to be a moderately prosperous asparagus grower. There were two schools in Westminster: a handsomely equipped school with green lawns and shrubs for the Anglo-Americans; and a Mexican school whose meager equipment matches the inelegancé of its surroundings. . . . Concluding that this practice [of segregating Mexican schoolchildren] had gone on long enough, Méndez filed suit in a federal court on March 2, 1945, on behalf of some five thousand Mexican residents of the district, against the school officials of Orange County.

Oddly enough, this issue had never been squarely raised before in California. . . . Wiithout formal sanction, the practice of segregating Mexican children in the schools came about largely through default of any determined resistance on the part of the Mexican-Americans. Once established, of course, the segregated schools were defended and rationalized.

In some cases, segregation was acomplished by a fancy gerrymandering of school districts; but the more common practice was to use the arbitrary linguistic device of assigning all children with Spanish names to a separate school. Occasionally the school authorities would examine the appearance of youngsters so as to prevent the offspring of a Mexican mother whose married name might be O'Shaughnessey from slipping into the wrong school. While the practice varied from district to district, the general scheme was to segregate Mexicans from the first through the sixth, and in some cases through the twelfth grade.

In the trial of the Méndez case, the school authorities at first contended that Mexicans were a distinct and therefore an "inferior" race; but confronted by the testimony of some worldfamous anthropologists, they soon abandoned this position. The superintendent of schools then testified that Mexican children were "dirty"; that they had lice and impetigo; that their hands, face, neck, and ears were often unwashed . . . ; and that, generally speaking, they were "inferior" to other students in point of personal hygiene.[18]

Judge Paul J. McCormick, after hearing the contentions of the Mexican community and the school board, ruled on March 21, 1945, that segregation of the school was in violation of the "equal protection" clause of the Fourteenth Amendment. In so ruling, the Judge had anticipated the 1954 United States Supreme Court decision.

Three years later in Texas the Méndez decision was again supported by the 1948 Delgado ruling that segregation of Mexican children was unconstitutional in the eyes of the United States Supreme Court. The court ruled that separate classes could be

[18] Carey McWilliams, *op. cit.*, pp. 280–282.

permitted up through the first grade if, by means of scientific and objective evaluation, the children were found not to be able to understand English.

Mexican children are no longer required to attend separate schools because of their ethnicity; they are, however, frequently segregated within a single school from their Japanese and Anglo peers. Their segregation is legal, and within the provisions of the Delgado ruling. Most Mexican children in the ghetto speak no English when they enter kindergarten. Hence, they tend to score lower on the culture-bound intelligence tests, and tend to remain somewhat behind the Anglo children in reading ability. (They have first to learn to speak simple English before learning to read.) As a result, they are placed in special remedial reading, enrichment, and exceptional (retarded) children's classes, and there they remain.

Children are assigned to the retarded classes in the first or second grade and continue in those classes throughout their educational careers, even where their ability may be potentially that of the Anglo child in the regular class. In fact, a recent testing of some Mexican children, all of whom dropped out of school because of lack of stimulation in these classes, indicated that on a more culture-free measure, such as manual dexterity, they scored above the national average. The test used was part of the classification test administered by the Youth Opportunity Board, a training and employment project of the Poverty Program. The test itself was the General Aptitude Testing Battery (GATB), and the manual dexterity aspect involved the placing of small pegs into holes as rapidly as possible. The statistician on the YOB-YTEP project related the data to me and noted:

> On the index of manual dexterity 71 per cent of the 1,058 kids were above the national average. This is significantly greater than a chance relationship in which one would expect only 50 per cent above and consequently 50 per cent below. We can either assume that Mexicans are biologically superior or else that there is some socializing agency which exists in their peer group or community which makes them score so high. I would tend to believe the latter. The implications of this are fantastic: if it is not an artifact of the instrument, and there is much evidence to demonstrate that it is not, then this quasi-random sample of Mexicans, when given a somewhat culture-free intelligence test based upon the index of manual arts, which is the

primary source of training these youth receive, demonstrates intelligence significantly higher than that of the general population. Yet because they are Mexicans and do not speak English adequately, [they] are defined by the schools as unteachable and are denied the opportunity to develop their talents to maximal capabilities. I suspect that the kids have average intelligence, but that a manual dexterity skill is the only one available for them to learn and so, given average intelligence and proper training, they can perform at a superior rate. I suspect that if they were given skills in other areas such as language and math, they would record IQ scores quite comparable to the Anglo population. [Perhaps even higher, given higher motivation to leave the ghetto.] Evidently, then, manual dexterity is a functional alternative for reading and math skills for these kids.

The board of education denies the reliance upon intelligence tests and other objective measures to determine which classes the children will attend. One school board member held that:

Schools do not depend too much upon group IQ tests; rather, they depend upon observations of classroom behavior and upon judgments of the teachers.

Despite this claim there is much evidence, frequently from principals of elementary schools, which indicates that the placement of the children is determined almost entirely on the basis of the culture-bound tests:

At one of the elementary schools in the ghetto, the children are divided into two categories: those in Special Training classes have IQ scores between 50 and 75, and those in regular classes from grades kindergarten to sixth. The Special Training classes are further divided into four groups. The first is the Pre-Compulsory Special Training classes, consisting of low-IQ children under eight years of age. [This type of class gets its name from the fact that a child cannot be required to attend school until he is eight years old.] The second, third, and fourth groups are the Primary Compulsory, Middle Compulsory, and Upper Compulsory Special Training classes, respectively. The regular classes are broken up into two varieties: Medium to Low classes for slow and moderate achievers, and Fast classes for rapid achievers. The low and moderate achievers [with IQ scores above 75] are placed in the same class for the purpose of preventing the teachers from getting too depressed by having to teach all extremely slow learners.

The selection of children for the Special Training classes is made at the end of each semester. At this time the teachers meet in a conference and pool their lists of low achievers. These lists are matched with the lists of the children's IQ scores. The principal of the school stated that where a discrepancy existed between the teacher's rating and the intelligence test results, the test results are accepted as more accurate and dependable. Children are tested during their first- and second-grade years. The results of these tests determine the type of class and education they will subsequently receive. Once a child has been placed in a Special Training class, it is difficult for him to get out, even if the second intelligence testing indicates that he does not belong in the class. The reverse, however, is not the case. It is easy for a child to be taken out of a regular class and placed in the Special Training class. Nearly all of the children in the Special Training classes are Mexican-Americans. [A higher percentage than the percentage of Mexican-Americans in the school.]

Because of a facility with the English language and a cultural emphasis upon education, the Anglo and Japanese-American children are usually placed in the regular classes, while the Mexican-Americans are placed in the Special Training classes. Most remain in their respective classes throughout their elementary school experience. Thus, there is not only *de facto* segregation in the Los Angeles schools, but there is also segregation within each school in the Mexican ghetto.

It must be recognized that many of the Mexican-American children who are placed in the Special Training classes belong there because of mental retardation. However, due to the culturally biased testing situation, many Mexican-American pupils may not belong in the Special Training classes, but rather in a short-term enrichment program aimed at compensating for the child's deficient home environment. Children wrongly placed in classes for the retarded may have their curiosity and potential stifled.

There is some evidence to indicate that little is done for the Mexican-American pupil with high intelligence once he is out of elementary school. One Mexican-American mother related that although her son was an A student in his junior high school and had a 155 IQ (determined by independent testing by a private psychologist), he was not put in the accelerated classes at his school. The boy's counselor told the mother that there were too few classrooms available to accommodate all of the gifted children. She complained, "There were three hundred children in my son's junior high school last year, and only one classroom for advanced students. In the Anglo schools such as —— Junior High School, there were three such classrooms, for a school with the same size enrollment."

In most cities where there is *de facto* segregation the school board meets the demands of minority groups by attempting a busing plan. The Los Angeles board of education employed such a plan as early as 1951, but not to eliminate *de facto* segregation. Rather, it was an attempt to alleviate the burden on some of the schools which were on half-day sessions by transferring pupils from overcrowded schools to less crowded ones.

In the spring of 1964 the board again attempted busing. This time, however, it was to satisfy the demands of Negro leaders who charged that the schools in the Negro area were segregated. The plan failed. Only about 150 children participated in the busing. The educational chairman of the United Civil Rights Committee, a Negro, explained the failure in the following manner:

> If I had been a parent who had received a notice from school simply on a piece of paper from the hand of my child on Thursday, and I had to make a decision for my child to be bused across town to another school by the following Monday, I am certain that it would have been difficult for me to have answered the question, so I think that this is a first deterrent to parents in saying yes; they didn't know the school the children were going to, there was only one school day in which to contact the principals who had not been fully briefed; and there was no way.[19]

There have been no attempts to bus Mexican-American students to Anglo schools to eliminate *de facto* segregation. Most Mexican-American educators concur that such a plan would fail even with adequate school-parent communication. The Mexican-American is generally not in favor of busing. This is not because

[19] From the transcript of "Human Relations—Yesterday, Today, and Tomorrow," Part 1-B (Education).

the Mexican-American does not favor integration. Rather, it is because he fears that if he puts his children into predominantly Anglo schools, his children will lose their Mexican cultural ties which provide emotional support and cohesion within the ghetto.

Mexican-Americans want their children also to learn about the Anglo way of life, but not at the expense of the Mexican-American heritage and a knowledge of the Spanish language. This, however, creates a difficult problem. It is the dilemma of difference, the conundrum of cultural pluralism. If the Mexican-American wishes to retain his cultural ties to Mexico, many Anglos, including some teachers, will offer resistance. Some school administrators are unwilling to support demands by Mexican-Americans for enriched educational programs which will compensate for the child's academic deficiencies and at the same time give instruction on the contributions of Mexico to American society to make the child feel proud of his ancestry. These administrators feel that this will encourage the child not to want to "become an American." One teacher complained, "These Mexicans want to have their cake and eat it, too. They want to be Mexicans and they want to be accepted as members of our society, too." Much of the prejudice and discrimination centers around this issue.

Prejudice in the schools

There is considerable evidence that some Anglo administrators and teachers in the Mexican-American ghetto resent the community's attempts at cultural pluralism. Primarily through a misunderstanding of the Mexican culture and Mexican intentions, hostile attitudes, represented by statements like that of the previously quoted Anglo teacher, pervade the schools in the ghetto. The principal of one of the major high schools in the area begins his orientation session for each new group of teachers with the following statement:

> There are two or three cultures here. The kids run from the disciplined Japanese to the unconcerned Mexican race. If there are any doubts in your mind, you had better think it over before signing on to this school. Teaching at —— High School is an asset. If you have been successful here, you can

teach anywhere. You don't get things put on a silver platter here for you. This is not a gravy school. There are few top kids in this place. You have to be a super teacher to get anything out of Mexicans. If you fail at —— High School, it doesn't mean that you were not a good teacher. You could be a good teacher in a "white school."

Such a statement has four possible effects upon the neophyte teacher. First, it may ease his possible "culture shock," that is, in all probability the teacher may never have done any practice teaching in a school where a large number of the students do not have a facility in English, are not readily familiar with Anglo culture, and have been classified as delinquent by the police. Second, it may challenge some teachers to attempt to produce results in the children. Third, however, it also shifts the blame for failure onto the students; if a mediocre teacher fails, he may rationalize it as not his fault. Fourth and finally, in preparing the teacher for the worst, the statement may all but guarantee failure. Teachers expecting failure may not apply themselves to the job, and therefore fail at teaching. In short, what occurs is the "self-fulfilling prophecy."

I asked one employee of an elementary school in East Los Angeles what the school's policy was toward its predominantly Mexican-American student body. She replied bluntly:

> The administration is against Mexicans, Cubans, poor people, etc. The administration would be a lot happier if they could get rid of all the Mexicans.

I asked her who the administration was, and she stated: "The principal, the people in the school office, the district office people, and many of the teachers." She then related that the school often "washes their hands of the kids if they get into any trouble. For example, one little Mexican boy, about seven, was caught by his teacher sniffing glue. The boy was turned over to the police, and neither the teacher nor the administration ever bothered to call the boy's parents. They didn't bother because they believe that Mexican parents really don't care about their children."

The language barrier

One of the most frequently mentioned complaints by both the schools and the Mexican-American community concerns the issue of the use of Spanish in schools. As we noted previously, Spanish is the language of *La Raza,* and is the binding factor in the community. Thus, the Mexican-American activists demand that Spanish be permitted and taught in the schools, especially since it is the native and sometimes the only tongue of the entering children. In the past the schools have ignored the requests. However, even though there has recently been some token acceptance of the Spanish heritage in East Los Angeles schools, there is still resistance. As one Mexican-American educator observed:

> If it is true that the schools reflect the norms and values of the community, then perhaps it is equally true that its prejudices are also reflected, through acts of commission as well as omission. Few school systems can, or do, gear their curricula to the needs of this segment of the population. Few know, empirically, what the needs are. It is easier and safer to prohibit the speaking of Spanish on the school ground and in the school [the need being to learn English] than to take the imaginative step of teaching both English and Spanish to both Anglos and Spanish-speaking beginning in the elementary school. As a consequence, the "educated" Spanish-speaking person who has survived the school system is likely also to be one who has been stripped of his native language, or at best speaks and writes it imperfectly. To the enlightened, this situation is such a waste of human resources; to others, including some school teachers, the burden of proof is on the shoulders of the minority: "If you want to be American, speak American!" [21]

In most schools in the ghetto the faculty does not speak Spanish, and the children when they enter elementary school do not speak English. I asked one teacher what this meant. Her reply was:

[21] Julian Samora, "The Education of the Spanish-Speaking in the Southwest: An Analysis of the 1960 Census Materials." A mimeographed copy of a paper delivered at the Mexican-American workshop, Careers for Youth of the Mexican-American Community, Phoenix, Arizona, January 18, 1963.

. . . for the first two years the teacher looks at the child and the child looks back. They don't speak to one another because neither understands the other's language.

In some schools the Anglo teachers do communicate via translators to the Mexican children who speak no English. A principal said that some of the teachers in her school use the bilingual Mexican kids to help them with their teaching. She observed:

. . . the bilingual students translate the lessons from the teacher to their Spanish-speaking classmates. The teachers tell the bilingual kids and then they in turn translate the lectures.

There are few Anglo teachers who speak Spanish and few Mexican teachers in the school system. Of the eight thousand in-service training teachers in Los Angeles today only seventy-five are Mexican-American.[22]

The schools have met the demand by Mexican-American community leaders for more Spanish-speaking teachers, especially for the primary grades, with a token gesture. In one elementary school, for example, a teacher with a knowledge of Spanish comes once a week to talk to the children. In one of the high schools only five of the hundred and twenty faculty members speak Spanish. While most Mexican-American students in high school do speak English, many of them have only a minimal grasp of the language—a factor which contributes to the high dropout rate.

The Anglo teachers frequently do not realize that many high school students in the ghetto do not understand English well enough to achieve any satisfactory level of academic success. One teacher in an East Los Angeles high school demonstrated the lack of awareness of the Mexican's problem when he maintained that:

Most of the Mexican kids really do speak English well, but they use their Mexican heritage as an excuse to get out of doing homework. They just pretend that they don't understand English.

[22] Statistics taken from the Castro Report of the Council of Mexican-American Educators, 1965.

Besides the actual linguistic handicap, many members of the Mexican-American community have also protested that the text books are culturally biased against Mexican-American children. Books used in the predominantly lower-class Mexican schools do not portray a life-style with which the children can identify. The traditional Dick and Jane reader, which portrays an upper-middle-class Anglo family, is foreign to the children, and hence the reading material is not readily comprehensible. Mexican-American leaders have protested, but to no avail. One community representative in the Mexican ghetto pointed out:

> Another example of poor handling of Mexicans is the revision of the elementary school reader. They have changed the Dick and Jane book. They are Negroes and their father is portrayed as a laborer rather than as a businessman. Also, they have a next-door neighbor who is a Chinese girl. However, there are no Mexicans in the book. Once again the Mexican has been left out. The Council on Mexican-American Affairs has protested to the state, but nothing has been done. I guess one reason why they don't write more about Mexicans is that there is really very little information available about the Mexican. Thus, few textbooks have anything other than that the Mexican is a grape picker. That's the popular stereotype which is common in the press. When the State of California did publish a pamphlet on Mexicans entitled *Californians of Spanish Surnames,* published by the FEPC, it came out about two years after all the literature on Negroes came out.

Some teachers in the schools also acknowledge the problem, but the question of textbooks is an administrative decision farther along the chain of command than the teacher's authority. A high school math teacher notes:

> The textual material is not the best for the culture of the kids. They are some of the best books you can get; but just because they are some of the best books does not mean that they are best for a particular culture. The books don't communicate with the student. They are foreign to his experience and his culture.

Teacher hiring

In a 1963 conference on Mexican-American education, a member of the board of education stated:

> A major problem of the Mexican-American lies in the fact that there is a great lack of adequate recruitment by the Mexican-American community of Mexican-American teachers. There should be more encouragement of Mexican-Americans by Mexican-Americans to become teachers.

That year the Fair Employment Practices Commission (FEPC) noted that:

> In November, 1963, only 2.2 per cent of teachers were Mexican-American while pupils of that ethnic group represented more than 16 per cent of school enrollment.
> . . . The disparity between the proportion of Negro teachers and Negro pupils was far less severe with Negro teachers amounting to 13.3 per cent of all teachers, and Negro pupils 18.1 per cent of total enrollment.[23]

In one elementary school surveyed in 1962 there were five Mexican-American teachers, nine Negro teachers, seven Japanese-American teachers, and ten Anglo teachers. Such ethnic ratios prompted certain activists in the Mexican-American community as well as members of the board of education to attempt Mexican-American teacher recruitment programs. An indication of the success of the endeavor may be seen in the 1966 restudy of that school. There are ten Anglo teachers, ten Japanese teachers, twelve Negro teachers, and no Mexican-American teachers. This elementary school, which has a total enrollment of one thousand children, is 92 per cent Mexican-American and is representative of the elementary schools in the ghetto.

The reasons there are so few Mexican-Americans in education are complex, and probably not attributable to blatant discrimination in hiring practices by the board of education. If anything, the board of education will sometimes waive certification requirements to hire Mexican teachers. One educator noted that:

[23] California Fair Employment Practices Commission, *op. cit.*

. . . the few Mexicans who do go into teaching are usually those who can't make it elsewhere. The board of education often scrapes the bottom of the barrel to get teachers, and sometimes is even willing to accept a Mexican-American with normally unacceptable grades in college for a credential.

While the board of education frequently attempts to attract Mexican teachers, some administrators in the high schools attempt to prove to the board that attracting Mexican teachers would solve no problems. One teacher related the following example:

To prove to the Mexican community that even if you got a lot of Mexican teachers in the school you would still have great discipline problems with the Mexican kids, they gave the four Mexican teachers in our school the most difficult kids to teach. The principal proved that the teacher with the best knowledge of Spanish had the most discipline problems.

By so manipulating the situation, the principal could not avoid verifying his foregone conclusion.

In general, however, Mexican-Americans with a college education are scarce and in great demand, especially since the advent of the Poverty Program. Teaching salaries do not compare favorably with government and industrial wages. One newspaperwoman put it like this:

You know, it's becoming profitable and favorable to become a Mexican. At least if you're a Mexican with a college degree and can speak Spanish. There are very high federal salaries for such persons. I was offered a job for $17,000 per year, but most Mexicans don't qualify since only a few per cent get more than a high school education. Those with a college degree used to go into teaching, but school salaries don't compare with what you can get elsewhere.

Another and traditionally important reason why there are so few Mexican teachers relates back to our discussion of *machismo*. Public school teaching is viewed by Mexicans as an effeminate profession. Consequently, very few men entertain the idea of becoming teachers. Furthermore, Mexican girls are not encouraged either to stay in school or to seek a career. A woman's place, according to most Mexican males, is in the home, satisfying the wants of her husband and tending her children. In many cases a Mexican girl who seeks to become a public school teacher alienates herself from her family.

Because the school has remained a symbol of Anglo authority and a place where Mexican-Americans have suffered failures, the college graduate of the East Los Angeles ghetto is hesitant about entering public school teaching. As a result the teachers in the ghetto schools are primarily Anglo and Negro. If it appears that the Mexican-American is hostile toward the Anglo, his anger is even greater toward the Negro. Many Mexican parents have said:

> I can tolerate my kid having a Negro teacher in first grade, but when he has another Negro teacher in second grade and in third grade, it just burns the hell out of me.

In an editorial from a now defunct East Los Angeles newspaper, *The Eagles,* an organ of the vocal Anglicized Mexican-American population, appeared the following example of Mexican hostility toward Negroes:

> The Negro in California finds himself in the unique position of being a minority who is in the minority and who, furthermore, cannot claim to be the only or worst victim of discrimination. . . .
> Many a Mexican-American still remembers when he had to go to a separate section in the movies; when there were schools for "Mexicans" and schools for "whites"; when municipal swimming pools were out of bounds for Mexicans; when lynchings took place; when a Mexican had to step down the curb when a policeman walked toward him; when restrictive deeds, excluding Mexican-Americans from the purchase of land or house, were in effect.
> It must be realized, then, that the Mexican-American paved the way for the Negro and that, if for no other reason, the Negro leadership should be extremely careful not to step on Mexican-American toes. . . .
> If the Rumford Act is repealed by a comparatively narrow margin and the Mexican-American precincts vote heavily against the Act, perhaps then a second, hard look will be taken by the Negro leadership, for it will become evident that the Negro cannot win without the help of the Mexican-American.[24]

24 *The Eagles,* Vol. I, No. 10, July 3, 1964, pp. 2–3.

By election time "YES ON PROPOSITION 14" stickers became a common sight on walls, fences, and telephone posts in the ghetto. A "yes" vote meant the repeal of the Rumford Act and the end to a fair housing law in California. The Mexican ghetto voted overwhelmingly in favor of the proposition as did the Anglo community. The Rumford Act was dead and so was equal opportunity housing law in California. Such is the hostility of the Mexican-American toward the Negro. Rather than help the Negro cause, the Mexican is willing to destroy his own hopes for integrated housing.

If there is a paucity of Mexican-American teachers, there is an even greater shortage of Mexican-Americans in higher administrative positions. An FEPC report indicated that for the whole Los Angeles School System, "ninety-four per cent of all principals and vice principals are members of the majority group."

In 1962 an Anglo-American principal of one elementary school pointed out to me that:

> While it is not official administrative policy, positions as principal and vice-principal are generally not open to Mexican-Americans, regardless of their seniority or academic degrees.

There are no Mexican-Americans on the board of education. Educators in the Mexican-American community have frequently stated that equal educational opportunities cannot be guaranteed until Mexican-Americans are placed on the school board. However, as one board of education member observed:

> It is very difficult for a member of a minority group to get elected to the school board. A Mexican must not only win the election in East LA, but also in the rest of the city. And you know quite well that the rest of the city will resist voting for a Mexican.

Assignment of teachers

As in most other issues involving the possibility of discrimination, the school administrators and the Mexican-American community are at odds on the question of whether or not an excessively large percentage of Mexican-American teachers are being placed in predominantly Mexican schools. According to one educator affiliated with the administration and guidance and counseling program:

> Teachers are placed everywhere. There is no evidence that a predominant number of Mexican-American teachers are placed in the East Los Angeles schools.

One teacher concurred by maintaining that:

> Teachers are assigned to schools in a more or less random fashion according to the needs of the schools.

The FEPC, however, disagrees with the claims by these administrators. It acknowledged that the concentration of Mexican-American teachers in Mexican-American schools is not as extensive as the concentration of Negro teachers in Negro schools. "Still," it claimed, "more than 42 per cent of all Mexican-American teachers were in the East District, where more than 50 per cent of Mexican-American pupils were enrolled." [25] They went on to say that the heavy concentration of minority teachers in minority schools may have resulted from

> . . . a tendency in the past to send minority teachers to those areas and schools which had a large minority pupil population. Some principals, given a choice, have been reluctant to hire minority teachers, particularly if the minority pupil population was small or if the principal felt he might encounter the slightest negative community reaction . . . [and a] reluctance by minority teachers to seek or accept appointment in areas very far from their places of residence. This reflects the present pattern of housing segregation, which makes it virtually impossible for minority-group persons to secure housing in certain areas. Individuals understandably do not wish to travel long distances to and from work.[26]

Many Mexican-Americans complain that the schools try to direct "bright" Mexican-American students into the teaching profession with the hope that they will return to the ghetto to teach "their people and uplift the community." This too is interpreted as discrimination. One Mexican-American who is a com-

[25] California Fair Employment Practices Commission, *op. cit.*
[26] *Ibid.*

munity representative for one of the Poverty Program projects held that:

> The schools do a lot to keep the Mexican where he is. Counselors in the high schools channel the bright Mexicans into social work and teaching jobs. They don't tell the kids about opportunities in the professions like medicine and law. The few Mexicans who are lawyers or doctors are overworked. Most of them are assigned many poverty or charity cases to handle and don't get enough money to really make much off of the profession. They are overworked and underpaid. The schools feel that bright Mexicans should work to help their community, so they are not encouraged to enter into business or industry on the executive level. Rather, they are told that the jobs they should go after are social work and teaching. Scholarships are not given to kids who are very poor. Thus, most Mexican kids never even get to go to college even though they may have the native ability. To get a scholarship, a kid has to make high grades. He must compete with Anglo kids who come from better schools, better homes, etc. The Mexican schools have a policy of teaching the kid to accept the *status quo*. The Mexican homes are overcrowded and not conducive to learning.

This apparent inconsistency in the Mexican-American position is an example of the dilemma between group and individual mobility. It is an issue of the rights of the individual versus those of the group. If you encourage Mexican students to become teachers and then send them back to the ghetto to teach, they may be able to uplift the whole community, but at the expense of other more lucrative opportunities for these teachers. If, however, you do not channel Mexican kids into teaching and have them help their community, they may have greater opportunities, but the community won't.

The Cost of Stereotypes

Frequently the Anglos in the East Los Angeles schools teach and counsel on the basis of old and incorrect stereotypes. Many of the stereotypes of the poorly educated Mexican are true, but he is uneducated because he has been held back, not because he is innately inferior. One Mexican-American social worker told me that:

> In the schools of East LA the counselors counsel on the basis of prejudice. The counselors say why inspire the kids to seek unrealistic aspirations. After all, the Mexican is good with his hands, so why give him anything intellectually stimulating. The counselors go on the assumptions fostered by the old stereotypes. They do so usually with good intentions, however. They hold to the Dewey principle. They see the job of the school as one which will allow the kid to adapt to his social situation. The school pushes for the *status quo*. If Mexicans traditionally do this kind of work, why try to change him? The school's job is to help the Mexican stay where he is and to learn to live in the slum. Thus, there is an intensive emphasis upon manual training, and a de-emphasis of intellectual topics.

Another Mexican-American, this time a counselor for one of the Poverty Program projects, corroborated the Mexican-American social worker's statement:

> The Mexican kids are told by their counselors to major in art. This I think is guided by the old stereotypes that the Mexican is an "artistic race." I don't think the teachers are maliciously doing this. But what I think is that they are guided by the old prejudices and old stereotypes. The schools say that Mexicans are not academically inclined, but that they are good at working with their hands. Thus, Mexicans are channelled out of academics.

An Anglo counselor in one of the high schools in the ghetto contended that the Mexican-Americans were wrong. He felt that their claims were "just defensive arguments." As he pointed out:

> Mexican leaders argue that the counselors are against them. It's just a defensive argument. In the math department of our school, for example, it is a policy that anyone can have a chance to take math classes even if he has had no math background. But just let him try to make it. We counselors try to discourage him from taking these classes so that he won't run into constant failure, but if he insists, we let him try. We have given nonverbal arithmetic skill tests and two-thirds of the Mexican tenth-graders tested at seventh or eighth grade. We can almost predict who won't make it. But just let him try.

After speaking with him, I left somewhat dissatisfied. It is an acceptable policy to discourage students from taking advanced math courses when their ability in the subject matter is far below acceptable levels. But one is left curious about exactly what he meant when he stated repeatedly, "but just let them try." How many able Mexican students have been discouraged from taking academic courses because the counselors acting on the old stereotypes felt that Mexicans ought not train for such professions? The following biography, told to me by the mother of the boy involved, has been corroborated by several other people, including an Anglo educator.

A case of school's treatment of kids that I can give you is one that involves my own boy, Bill. He's fourteen now. When Bill was little, I had him in what we call the co-op nursery, which is run by the mothers in the area. I could see that he was far advanced in comparison to the other children. I had taught him to read and given him lessons in arithmetic when he was four and one-half. No other kid in the nursery could read. When he was in grammar school, his IQ was taken and he scored 140 on the test, I later found out. When he went to Belvedere Junior High School, he was put in the same class with all of the other kids and he wasn't being challenged. I went to the school principal and to his counselors and asked that he be put into the academically enriched class. It is a special class where he gets material on the level ahead of his peer group. He got all As in the class and graduated from Belvedere on the honor roll. Now he is in high school and the counselors suggested to him that he take a manual arts program rather than a college prep. He went home complaining. Again I went to see his teachers, counselors, and principal. I got him switched to the science-math program for college prep. He got all As again. Last week he won a trophy on the debate squad at the city forensics tournament. Because he's a Mexican, the Anglos have been trying to keep him down. The problem is that there are many Mexican boys like my Bill, but if their parents don't know that they can complain to the school about the mistreating of their kids, then these kids will never get ahead. A mother has to fight for her boy. But most Mexican mothers don't know about the workings of the school system, or if they have no husband but many kids, do not have the time to visit the schools. I guess Bill is lucky because I have a college education and am familiar with school policies. Most parents would not have known enough to try to keep the school from pulling something. Parent education is vital for the Mexican community. The parents must learn about the opportunities available for changing things they don't like.

Her boy *is* fortunate that she has a college-education and has learned to challenge the school's authority. A great part of the difficulty in the Mexican ghetto is that too few parents realize that the schools will respond to critical questions by parents.

Given the fact that the intelligence tests are biased against the lower-class Mexican-American, that many counselors counsel on the basis of outmoded stereotypes, that all too often Mexican children are placed in Special Training classes solely on the basis of tests administered in the first and second grade and are left in these classes so that their achievement level remains several years behind that of Anglo students, too many potentially able students, like Bill Gonzales, of whom we just spoke, may never have the opportunities they deserve.

The reasons for the weakness of the counseling program and the errors made by counselors are many. The primary ones, however, center upon (1) the fact that there are too few counselors available in the schools of East Los Angeles; (2) the fact that most counselors in the ghetto are untrained for the specialized field of counseling; and (3) the fact that the Anglo counselors do not understand the Mexican-American's social and cultural conditions.

Considering the number of problems faced by the students in the ghetto, there are too few counselors. In most of the high schools in the Mexican-American ghetto there is only one counselor for every five hundred students. With such heavy pupil loads counselors are more prone to, and are often compelled to, assign students to vocational or college preparatory programs by fiat, rather than by considering the nature of the individual's case. With a limited opportunity to speak to their counselors individually, many otherwise qualified students may not be informed of the career and college opportunities open to them.

In addition, most counselors in the ghetto schools, and to a great extent throughout the entire Los Angeles city school system, are not particularly qualified to counsel. One social scientist, associated with the East Los Angeles schools for several years, observed that "there are really no counselors in the Mexican schools. There are only Anglo teachers who say they are interested in kids and so get promoted to counselor." A Mexican-American educator concurred:

> There are really no counselors *per se*. The people who get to be counselors are teachers who have been with the school long enough to get a promotion. The counseling job is just a way to increase a teacher's wages. It is a step up in the pay scale. However, most of the counselors have neither the specific training nor the understanding of the problems of Mexican-American children to handle the job. Many do not have the slightest bit of knowledge of psychological principles. This is because they are older Anglo teachers who went to teachers college long before educators even heard of psychology.

While he overstated his case when he contended that the counselors were that old, he was not incorrect when he contended that the counselors in the Mexican-American ghetto are not well prepared for their task. The apparent reason for the counseling lag in East Los Angeles, and in the rest of the city as well, stems from a point made by the professor of counseling at the local college: "Unlike the rest of Southern California, the Los Angeles board of education has defined a counselor as a nonprofessional. His main job is to do busywork—paper work—and not to counsel."

With such a board of education policy, there is little wonder that counselors in Los Angeles are so ill-prepared. When a person spends several years in training to receive a counseling degree from a university, he is unwilling to work for a school system that does not value his knowledge enough to consider him a professional or to allow him to engage in the work he was trained to do. The majority of the better-prepared counselors seldom seek careers in the Los Angeles city school system.

———•———

The Dropouts

Social strains rarely occur in isolation. Their effect is almost always additive. In the case of the educational problems of the Mexican-American, the combined effects of the culture of poverty, the language barrier, prejudice and discrimination by counselors and teachers, and the lack of communication between the school and the culture of the community have resulted in high dropout rates.

In a 1963 conference on Mexican-American education one member of the Los Angeles board of education proclaimed: "We, on the board of education, are bewildered by the fact that so many Mexican-American youngsters drop out of school. Twenty per cent of the Mexican-American youth drop out before the eighth grade, and three out of every four are gone by the time of high school graduation."

The schools have had many conferences on what ought to be done about the dropout problem, but the rates have not changed over the past three years. One educator noted:

> The school board says that the dropout rates have declined, but they really haven't. If anything, they have remained more or less constant. Perhaps they have even increased.

The board of education based its claims of success upon the results of an attempt by the schools to encourage students who actually were not seriously considering dropping out of school to continue toward their diploma. By emphasizing programs aimed at only the students who, because of economic reasons, felt that they might at some time be forced to drop out of school, the board's success rates have been unduly inflated. The vast majority of the potential and actual dropouts are never affected. In this group is found the marginal man who is not able to identify with either his parents' culture or the culture of the schools and the Anglo. One Mexican-American prominent in the community called these youths the "hard-core dropouts." He comments: "The dropout rates for the hard core have not changed in the past twenty years."

"Who are the 'hard core'?" I asked him.

> They are often, but not always, the gang members. They don't drop out because of economics alone, but because they give up. You can't tell them too easily except by how they talk. They reject their families and the schools. They are the Mexicans who have been defeated in terms of middle-class values. They are really the proud ones—the last of the proud Mexicans. They have been hurt since the time they were born. They won't conform, but just carry a chip on their shoulder. They are sick

of taking rough treatment from the Anglos. They won't take any more. They refuse to learn to read or speak English. They have built up defense mechanisms to protect them from further harm. The Anglo has punished them so long that they can't take any more pain. They have no hope. When you talk to them, you get the idea that it is too late. The Anglo has hit them so often and hurt them so badly that they can only withdraw. They ask me why they should work hard in school when they will not be able to use their education anyway. The Anglo won't let them.

The "hard core" represents only one of three types of dropouts. He is usually referred to as the "voluntary dropout." Besides this category there are the "economic dropout" and the "*de facto* dropout." The economic dropout is the student who is forced to leave school because of his family's financial position; he must drop out to help support his younger siblings. The economic dropout is the easiest to aid; after-school jobs and other financial assistance can help him to stay in school until graduation. The *de facto* dropout presents a greater problem; he is the pupil who leaves one school presumably to transfer to another, but somehow never enters another school. There is a substantial segment of the Mexican-American school-age population who falls into this category. This is in part due to the high population turnover in the ghetto.

The schools have been directing their efforts toward helping the economic dropout, because his problems are less complex and because corrective action may be more easily taken. Little has been done to help the voluntary dropout, and even less, because of the difficulty of locating him, to help the *de facto* dropout.

Recently the board of education has attempted to minimize the dropout problem. As one member of the board commented:

> The dropout problem is not as serious as the statistics say. Many children return to night school to get their high school diplomas. Forty-two per cent of all diplomas granted in Los Angeles come through night school.

The students who attend night school to acquire a high school diploma are rarely the voluntary dropouts or the *de facto* dropouts who have been disillusioned by the school system. Rather, they are the economic dropouts, who never wanted to give up their education. The vast majority of the voluntary dropouts and the *de facto* dropouts never return to school. These two categories comprise the majority of all of the dropouts in the Mexican ghetto.

The board of education has also contended that the blame for the dropout rates does not rest with the schools, but rather with the community's insistence that school is not for girls. They have argued that relatively few Mexican-American boys drop out of school. A board member put it this way:

> Most of the dropouts are girls. This is due to the fact that many Mexican-American fathers feel that a girl does not need more than an eighth-grade education. They feel that after that she belongs home, helping her mother and tending her brothers and sisters.

A study conducted by Occidental College in Los Angeles in 1959, however, found that there was no significant difference between the number of girls and the number of boys who dropped out of school. The main reason given by the girls was marriage, and the boys' was to find a job. Again, the board of education was incorrect. In addition, the Occidental study found that:

> As an aggregate, the Mexican-American students tended to drop out in disproportionate numbers. . . .
> Mexican-American students had the highest dropout rate at the school whose student body was predominantly Mexican-American. . . .
> Analysis of scores on standardized tests of capacity, such as the Otis, showed that students who dropped out had received lower scores. . . .
> Students who received low academic marks tended to drop out or to transfer. . . .
> The incidence of dropping out and of transferring was highest in the tenth grade. . . .
> Three-quarters of the students who dropped out were at least seventeen years of age, and were at least one year behind the appropriate grade for their age. . . .
> The grades given to Mexican-American students in citizenship subjects such as "work habits" and "cooperation" were consistently lower than those given to non-Mexicans, even for students who graduated.[27]

[27] Paul M. Sheldon, "Mexican-Americans in Urban Public Schools: An Exploration of the Drop-Out Problem," *California Journal of Educational Research*, Vol. XII, No. 1, January 1961, pp. 21–26.

The dropout problem is a symbol of the educational problems of the Mexican-American in the ghetto. The solution to the
dropout problem will come only after a mutual understanding
between the schools and the Mexican-American community is
established. As one educator stated, "Until you get the teachers
to accept the Mexican kids and the Mexican community to accept the schools, no amount of money will help. As long as the
administration defines the Mexican as a problem and the schools
as only custodial, nothing will ever be accomplished."

In Search of a Solution

We have pointed to some of the social strains existing in
the school and community which have contributed to present
deficiencies in Mexican-American education. These strains and,
consequently, potential corrective measures fall into three general categories: the school, the family, and the community.

The School

It is important that the schools change the image they present to the community. One way to accomplish this is to acquire
more Mexican-American teachers, counselors, and administrators. To accomplish this, a more effective recruitment program
must be implemented in which economic incentives are offered
to those who enter public school teaching. Too many college
graduates of Mexican-American descent are lured away from
the schools by industry because the schools are unable to compete. The presence of Mexican-American teachers, especially
male teachers, may produce the necessary snowball effect to
counteract the assumption, fostered by *machismo,* that teaching
is a feminine thing to do. There are too few Mexican men in
teaching to provide sufficient numbers of role models for the
children.

In addition, in-service training programs might be offered

to the Anglo teachers presently in the schools to familiarize them with the principles of race and ethnic relations, the nature of Mexican-American culture, and the problems of the Mexican community. Spanish could be required for certification of teachers in the Los Angeles city school system who will be teaching in the Mexican ghetto. This requirement would do much to enable the school to assume a function other than as a custodial institution.

There should be more counselors in the high schools. It is advisable to require that counselors have a university degree in counseling. Counseling should not be a means of increasing the wages of teachers who have seniority but no other qualifications.

The board of education has argued that the education given to the Mexican-American is the same as is given to the rest of the children in the school system. However, as one Mexican-American educator observed:

> Equal educational opportunities do not mean "same" educational opportunities. They must be better; they must go beyond in order to bring the Mexican-American child's standards up to those of the Anglo.

One such method of uplifting the educational level of the Mexican-American is through a system called "Compensatory Education," a program approved by the California state legislature. One Mexican-American educator described such a program as follows:

> Compensatory education is a program directed to aid those whose educational level is low. It is a program designed to help him to fulfill his potentialities. Compensatory education includes: (1) developing individual psychological evaluation of the students through tests designed, administered, and interpreted by bilingual individuals; (2) breaking up the classes into small groups, thus providing for more individualistic instruction; (3) special training in arithmetic, English, and social studies beyond that now taught. These subjects must be enriched since the teachers should not expect the children to have the understanding of the assumptions often expected of Anglo children; (4) broadening of cultural horizons of the children by introducing them to art, music, etc., through frequent field trips to concerts, museums, art exhibits; (5) teaching the children about their Mexican heritage and teaching the

children about the contributions Mexico made to the West, so that the children are not ashamed to be Mexican-American; (6) encourage the learning of proper Spanish and teach English as a second language; (7) provide counseling in the home to both the child and his parents so that the importance of the family unit is emphasized by the schools; (8) teach the Mexican kids that they are different, not inferior or superior to the Anglo; and (9) begin the teaching experience of the Mexican child prior to kindergarten.

Another Mexican-American educator reported that on the basis of the preliminary information gathered on an enrichment program, in which pre-kindergarten Mexican-American children were taught English, by the time these children had entered second grade they were able to compete effectively with the Anglo children in the class.

Unless the Mexican-American child receives special training in the primary grades, the gap between his English reading and comprehension level and that of the Anglo will continue to widen until he finds that he is unable to compete in school and hence drops out. At present the most advanced regular pupils in the elementary schools in East Los Angeles are expected only to have a fourth-grade reading level when they enter junior high school (seventh grade). Many even enter high school with no more than a fifth-grade reading level and a sixth-grade comprehension of arithmetic. Given such a deficit, there is little question why the Mexican-American fails in high school, becomes disillusioned, and drops out.

In the present system, even if a Mexican-American child is proficient at "reading" books in school, there is no guarantee that he understands what he is doing. A Mexican-American social worker noted:

The problem in the dropout situation is that the Mexican never breaks into the Anglo culture. He is told that he must learn English. His [reading material] is in English and he is taught in English, but he often learns without understanding. He can read the words, but he was never taught what the words mean. It was generally assumed by the schools that the kids knew the meaning of the spoken English words and only needed to associate the written letter with the spoken words, but the Mexican kids don't have the fundamental understanding of the spoken sounds. Words in English are not symbols to them.

The social worker went on to propose a plan to teach the children to understand English:

> What is needed is a transitional system. . . . The children who speak no English and do not understand English should first be taught the material in Spanish, with special classes in English, sort of as a foreign language. Then after a while, the child should be transited over to English, with perhaps Spanish as a foreign language. The child will be trained to be facile in both languages. He will be able to communicate and carry on his affairs in correct English. Such a program would lessen the shock of suddenly being thrust into an English-speaking world when you know little or no English.

Culture-free indices of intelligence should be used to determine whether or not the children are educable and the types of class into which they should be placed. Until such tests are perfected, more emphasis should be placed upon the teacher's judgment than upon a single test result.

The textbooks used might also be oriented to the Mexican-American population. It is difficult for a Mexican child who lives in the slumlike ghetto to identify with *Dick and Jane* and other books depicting Anglo upper-middle-class children and family life.

The Family

The schools could encourage parent participation in the school activities. Mother's club or P.T.A. meetings should be scheduled in the evening rather than the afternoon, so that working Mexican parents can attend. Some incentive is needed to get the parents interested initially.

Incentives would be helpful to get parents to bring their children to the pre-kindergarten English programs, as well as to encourage them to allow their children to remain in school. If schools provided free meals to the children in the pre-kindergarten and elementary school classes, several problems would be solved. The free meals would be an incentive to attract the pre-kindergarten children, and since these children would be out of the house, there would be no need to pull the older girls out of school to tend their brothers and sisters. The mother will have more free time; the children will have an education and meals.

The Community

The schools should open their doors to the community. They might do this by providing meeting places for Mexican-American action agencies. Furthermore, the school might provide for more adult education programs and encourage residents to take vocational skills classes. By training the adults for better jobs, the community's socioeconomic level could be raised.

There is much waste in a slum. Several Mexican-Americans have suggested that the schools teach the children to take pride in their community. The schools could be a springboard for community-improvement activities. Adult evening classes as well as high school programs in consumer economics could be offered to lessen some of the economic strains of the slum community.

Finally, as the hold of the older generation upon the youth diminishes, there is an increasing need for sex education in the schools. The illegitimacy rate in the ghetto is several times higher than in the Anglo areas. Four attempts to remedy the situation are being financed by the Poverty Program.

The first of the programs is Project Incentive, which takes Mexican-American children and gives them extensive counseling on career opportunities, holds discussions on Mexican culture, takes the children on field trips outside of the East Los Angeles ghetto to museums, plays, concerts, and art exhibits, takes the children to camp in the summer, and attempts to raise their horizons. The program is much like New York City's Higher Horizons.

A second program is the Student Achievement Center (SAC), which operates in the schools. A high school teacher described the program as follows:

> We try to get the children with potential. Most of the students in the program are not in college preparatory programs. They are bright kids, however, as determined by their IQ scores, but they have not been getting good grades. We have 125 kids in the program. After the counselors find the group of kids, they are put into small classes of 12 to 14 students each. They are given intensive, individualistic instruction, and much individual and group counseling.

A third program is the School Opportunity Center (SOC), also operated within the school system. This project, sponsored by the 1964 Economic Opportunity Act, provides a before- and after-school tutorial program for the students. The faculty is made accessible to the students. Any student can participate. The better students are hired by the program to be tutorial aides for the teachers.

The fourth is an employment program called the Economic and Youth Opportunities Agency (EYOA), which provides jobs for the potential economic dropout. The school hires a student to do such part-time jobs as gardening or secretarial services.

There are three basic problems with the projects as seen by the Mexican-American community. First, because only a few students can be helped by the projects due to their small budgets, those who have easily remedied problems tend to be selected. The so-called hard core dropout is less likely to be helped. Second, the projects are handled through the schools, which are so highly bureaucratized that, as one Mexican-American teacher pointed out, "they have so much red tape they spend most of their time undoing what they have just done." Finally, there is a problem in trying to communicate with the children. One Mexican-American student put it this way:

> The Mexican has learned to accept the blame for everything. He has been conditioned to believe everything he is told by an authority figure, whether it is true or not. He is told that the cops are never wrong. He believes that he can't fight city hall. If you tell a person that he is stupid for a long enough time and that he is no good for a long enough time, he will believe it. The Mexican kids believe that no matter what happens they are responsible. The Anglo is never wrong. The police beat up the Mexican because he deserves being beaten up. That's what the kids have been conditioned to believe. This is why they have such a great deal of trouble getting the Poverty Program to work. Kids have been taught that they always are wrong and that the authority figures are always right when they say that the Mexican is no good. They are told that the Mexican is dirty, sloppy, lazy, and uneducable. Now the Poverty Program promises the Mexican that he can fight city hall— that he can make it. The kids don't believe the Program. This is why the Program is having trouble.

Epilogue: *Mañana* Is Today

Appearing in the ghetto for the first time is a new kind of Mexican. There are more young men who are staying in school than ever before. This new Mexican is not content to live in poverty. A Mexican-American newspaper reporter hinted at this change when he said, "The ghetto is somehow different. Two years ago if you stepped on a Mexican's foot he would apologize for being in your way. Now if you did that, he would ask you why you stepped on his foot and demand that you apologize. Mexicans are not afraid to protest any more. The community is changing."

The community *is* changing. The community has rallied an impressive grass-roots support of the Delano Farm Worker's Association, the group of Mexican-American agricultural laborers who have gone on strike in protest of less than minimum wages and substandard housing conditions provided by the Anglo growers of Delano, California. Nearly every automobile in the Mexican ghetto bears the bumper sticker *"Viva la Huelga!"* ("Long live the labor strike!"), and for several months the ghetto families have refused to buy fruit from the Anglo merchants who own markets in the ghetto.

The resistance is having an effect. The Anglo is vulnerable in his pocketbook, and that is where the Mexican-American is directing his challenge against a century and a quarter of discrimination in California. Because of the economic sanctions applied, many of the Anglo merchants have begun offering Mexican-American students part-time after-school jobs. This has helped several to stay in school.

The walls of prejudice are difficult to scale, but the first foothold has been made. The Mexican-American is still confined to the ghetto by cultural, linguistic, economic, and educational barriers, but tomorrow he will be free. *No siesta mañana* —no sleep tomorrow.

IX

Summary and Conclusions

Raymond W. Mack

School Desegregation: Case Studies of Conflict and Change

We have looked in nine American communities at American citizens, Negro and white, grappling with their most trying domestic social issue. These nine little educational ethnographies gain value and utility viewed as complements of the nationwide sample survey statistics reported in James S. Coleman *et al., Equality of Educational Opportunity* (Washington: U. S. Government Printing Office, 1966). Coleman and his associates studied district superintendents, principals, teachers, and third-, sixth-, ninth-, and twelfth-grade pupils in 4,000 schools, as well as first-graders in about 2,000 schools—in all, more than half a million students and 60,000 teachers. The basic findings are not surprising: staff, facilities, and services are distributed unequally, and whites, on the average, get more and better of each than Negroes.

There are, of course, interesting exceptions. Because some Southern states made a desperate attempt to beat the 1954 Supreme Court decision by providing truly equal separate facilities, the average Negro in the South attends school in a newer building than does the average white. Even so, nationwide, the average Negro attends a school with inferior facilities and programs. The migration pattern for American Negroes is from the rural South to the urban North, and in the urban North, Negro pupils, as compared with white ones, have fewer library books, laboratories, auditoriums, cafeterias, gymnasiums, and playing fields. Teachers of Negroes score lower on tests of verbal ability, have lower morale, and are more likely to request transfers out of their schools. Negro students go to older, larger, more crowded schools, less likely to offer accelerated programs for rapid learners or opportunties for advanced placement or college credit.

Table 1: Years Behind Grade Level In Achievement Scores of Negro Students in the Metropolitan District At Sixth, Ninth and Twelfth Grades

TEST	SIXTH GRADE	NINTH GRADE	TWELFTH GRADE
Years Behind in Verbal Ability	1.6	2.4	3.3
Years Behind in Reading Comprehension	1.8	2.6	2.9
Years Behind in Mathematics	2.0	2.8	5.2

Some Negro students do overcome such environments, but their achievements are swamped statistically by the cumulative retardation of the majority. Achievement tests show that the average sixth-grade Northern Negro has fallen more than one and a half years behind the average white in reading comprehension. By grade nine, he is more than two and a half years behind, and at grade twelve, he is nearly three years behind. (See Table 1.)

These differences in achievement are much greater than the gap in staff and facilities. The discrepancy between Negro and white schools is clear, but it is not all that great. Indeed, the differences between Negro and white schools are significantly less than the variation between Northern and Southern schools, or the gap between rural and urban ones. Coleman asserts that:

> School to school variations in achievement, from whatever source (community differences, variations in the average home background of the student body, or variations in school factors), are much smaller than individual variations within the school, at all grade levels, for all racial and ethnic groups. . . . Over 70 per cent of the variation in achievement . . . is variation within the same student body. Our schools have great uniformity insofar as their effect on the learning of pupils is concerned. . . . Variations in school quality are not highly related to variations in achievement of pupils.

What, then, accounts for the disparity in performance? Certainly not motivation, for as can be seen in Table 2, Negro pupils equal or excel whites in eagerness to stay in school, to be one of the best students, and to continue beyond high school. But they do not parallel their white counterparts in planning for and moving toward college. Why not?

The data in Table 3 suggest an answer: they do not believe that success is possible for them in a discriminatory environment. As the Coleman report says:

> For children from disadvantaged groups, achievement . . . appears closely related to what they believe about their environment: whether they believe the environment will respond to reasonable efforts, or whether they believe it is instead merely random or immovable.

With the information from the nationwide sample survey providing a context for our own analysis, our case studies of these nine communities suggest five general trends in educational desegregation:

(1) Small towns and medium-sized cities, North and South, are desegregating their schools, at least to a token extent.

Table 2: Distribution by Race of Some Responses of Metropolitan Northeast Twelfth-graders to Questions Concerning Education

	12TH-GRADE PERCENTAGE DISTRIBUTION	
Question and Response	*White*	*Negro*
If something happened and you had to stop school, how would you feel? *"Would do almost anything to stay."*	47	47
How good a student do you want to be? *"One of the best students."*	36	48
About how many days did you stay away from school last year just because you did not want to come? *"None."*	61	68
How far do you want to go in school? *All responses for beyond high school.*	86	86
Do you plan to go to college next year? *"Definitely yes."*	46	31
Have you ever read a college catalog? *"Yes."*	73	59
Have you ever written to or talked to a college official about going to college? *"Yes."*	46	32
What type of job do you think you will have when you finish your education? *"Professional or technical."*	53	39

(2) Huge metropolitan areas, North and South, are reseg-regating their schools; the trend is toward more rather than less segregated educational facilities.

(3) Negro parents have defined equal educational oppor-tunities as the route to the achievement of a better life for their children; Negroes equate desegregated education with improved education, and see both as providing access to the American dream of economic prosperity coupled with respect for one's personal worth.

(4) Social organization is a critical variable for under-standing the amount of desegregation in a community; protest pays.

(5) Americans are asking their children to bear the brunt of the difficult social process of desegregation.

(1) Small Town and Middle-Sized City Desegregation

There is no difficulty in keeping the process of desegrega-tion gradual, because local school boards reflect a power struc-ture which is never radical and often reluctant. California is the largest and in many ways one of the most progressive states in

Table 3: Responses by Race of Northeast Metropolitan Students to Questions Concerning Feeling of Control Over Environment

Per cent Who Agree That:	White	Negro
"Good luck is more important than hard work for success."	4	9
"Every time I try to get ahead, something or somebody stops me."	13	21
"People like me don't have much of a chance to be successful in life."	5	12

the country. Yet Riverside, California, is one of the three com-munities in the state which has instituted a systematic plan of in-tegrating its public school system.

The primary reason Riverside integrated its schools is that someone set fire to the Lowell Elementary School. True enough, the school board voted unanimously to integrate the schools because, in their own terms, they had come to believe "that it was the right thing to do." The important point of this analysis, however, is that they were led to come to that conclusion only after a threat of violence hung over the city. They did not come to that conclusion independently, or if they did, they would certainly not have acted upon it without the fire as a catalyst.

Without Title VI of the Civil Rights Act of 1964 there would have been no desegregation at all in Mississippi during 1965. If one looks closely at the law, existing desegregation falls short of both its spirit and its letter. River City has gone slightly farther and somewhat more smoothly than Bayou County.

If one compares the requirements with reality, the gap is wide. Literal interpretation of the law calls for the desegregation of five specific grades. The document demands faculty integration, as well as the integration of any activities, facilities, or services provided or sponsored by a school system. River City as well as Bayou County are wanting on all counts. Desegregation was typically extended to only four grades, and the four were often chosen to discourage Negro attendance by concentrating on the high school level, where the dropout rate has taken its toll and where the Negroes who remain have a great deal to lose in transferring. Nor has there been real faculty integration. It is true that River City has held integrated faculty meetings and has begun to plan ahead for integrated staffs; it is also true that Bayou County has non-college-educated white shop teachers who serve both Negro and white high schools. But all of this is meager compliance indeed. Finally, neither River City nor Bayou County has witnessed extensive integration of activities. There has been no provision for Negroes in varsity athletics; Negroes are discouraged from participating equally in glee clubs or drama groups; the most common pattern is simply to drop the spring prom and reschedule it as a private white party without formal school sponsorship.

The Office of Education relaxed some of its standards for 1965–1966, and River City did meet the adjusted requirements sufficiently to gain full federal funds. Moreover, the Office of Education was obliged to continue funds in Bayou County although desegregation occurred on an even lesser scale. Bayou County was desegregated by federal court order and did not submit a plan. The Office of Education has felt obliged to accept compliance with the federal courts as satisfactory, even though the court requirements often fall short of its own.

The power structure of the Savannah community, in which traditionally the Negro has had from very slight to no representation, has responded to the demand for integration in a piecemeal fashion. The Savannah school board waited until events rendered immobility no longer possible. These events took the form of agitation by representatives of the Negro community, and crystallized in the form of a lawsuit brought against the Savannah school board by the NAACP. In addition there was the economic boycott of local white merchants who traditionally gave their consent and assistance to those elements within the community desiring maintenance of the status quo.

On the surface at least, integration has come to Newark. Reactions vary from favor to horror, but in general the community seems to accept the fact of Negro advances with equanimity. There are still loopholes: the silent nature of the whole change and refusal of officials to take open stands result in considerable uncertainty as to what expectations actually are. Some teachers complained that they were not certain about what they "were supposed to do about Negroes." Restaurant owners, real estate officials, etc., still find ways to discriminate. It certainly cannot be argued that equality exists in fact, but *official* barriers to Negro advancement have been removed. Only doubt and uncertainty among public officials appear to stand in the way of further progress.

The future of Newark's integration looks generally favorable. As the state legislature adjusts to its recent reapportionment, and as urban in-migration continues, the anti-integration interests in town are almost certain to lose influence. There is some question as to how long it will take officials to assess these changes accurately, but no doubt they will react to evolving publics. The school board is reported to have reflected changes already, and the city council is said to be facing increasing criticism from "liberal" elements in town. The university appears to be changing its stance cautiously, as it initiates programs to attract Negro students.

Newark's school system, its polity, and the University of Delaware all tend to react to issues perceived by them to be publicly sensitive by removing the decision-making process from public view. The result of this is twofold: externally, it creates suspicion and hostility on the part of the publics involved; internally, it produces an almost anomic situation, lacking in open, firm guidelines for policy on issues such as race. The organizations appear to exaggerate or distort the intensity of public opinion on matters of integration, removing themselves even further from open public debate. The "self-fulfilling prophecy" clearly operates in Newark. One might legitimately ask how any useful consensus on racial issues is achieved under the present conditions. The situation is mediated by the small size of the community itself, its small Negro minority, and perhaps most important of all, changing public reactions to racial integration. There is negative reaction to integration in the community, quite strong in some quarters, but it no longer appears to reside with power.

In Hempstead, too, desegregation is grudging. The school board does not tend to initiate independently any progressive, action-oriented policies. Past performances suggest that the board yields only when it appears necessary for the passage of budgets and bond issues.

In Kalamazoo, desegregation is ground out tortuously between the millstones of responsibility and gradualism. Even the liberal social-action-oriented community organizations tend to discourage support for spontaneous grass-roots attempts to address the problems effectively because their very existence suggests that something is already being done. These organizations serve as means for the community leaders to control the situation since they acknowledge the legitimacy of conventional middle-class processes of social change. And they are all incapable of making any consequential alteration in the situation because, if nothing else, they lack the intellectual radicalism to see the problem as a complex, many-sided one. They all persistently view the problem in the narrow paternalistic perspective which defines the issue as "The Negro Problem."

Desegregation occurs as an accommodation of conflicting views of what is most desirable, and in this sense Kalamazoo is typical of all of the small and middle-sized cities, Northern and Southern. Gradual change is taking place in Kalamazoo race relations—too much change and too rapidly to suit some citizens, too little change and too slowly to satisfy others. In the time since this book was written, evidence has mounted in support of our first conclusion. In White Plains, N.Y., Evanston, Illinois, Teaneck, N.J., and other small towns and medium-sized cities, the trend is clearly toward desegregation.

(2) Metropolitan Resegregation

We have seen grudging desegregation in Riverside and tokenism in the Delta. We have seen small and middle-sized cities gradually desegregating. Savannah, Kalamazoo, Newark are all less segregated today than they were a few years ago.

But we have also seen that the big cities, the metropolitan areas, seem to tend toward resegregation rather than desegregation. The Mexican-Americans in East Los Angeles have become more ghettoized during the very period when Newark, Savannah, and even Mississippi are beginning to desegregate.

In addition to the communities described in this book, our project included a study of Atlanta, which is losing its Southern-style, legally segregated schools and learning Northern, residential segregation ways. After five years of deliberate speed and despite Negro lawsuits and the urgings, warnings and guidelines of the Health, Education and Welfare Department wielding federal school money, there were by 1966 only some 4,000 Negro children studying with whites in a city school population of 120,-000 which is 55 per cent Negro. And in the modern city tides of middle-class whites flowing to surrounding suburbs and poor colored people moving to town, Atlanta schools are rapidly resegregating, with what appears to be the brisk assistance of the school board. In at least a half dozen schools neighborhood white children exercising "free choice" walk past Negro schools on the way to white schools farther from home.

Atlanta, operating under its latest court order pushing school desegregation with "free choice" of all children for any schools which have room for them, is as yet unaffected by new guidelines of the Health, Education and Welfare Department which demand integration by neighborhood and other considerations to bring most systems in the South out of tokenism.

In the 1963–1964 school year in Chicago 87.8 per cent of Negro pupils attended schools which were all or predominantly Negro; in 1964–1965, the percentage had risen to 89.2. During the same time period Negro pupils attending all or predominantly Negro high schools increased from 63.8 to 68 per cent. It is true that in Mississippi only .59 per cent of Negro pupils attend desegregated schools, but in metropolitan areas the trend seems toward segregation rather than desegregation.

(3) The Social Definition of Desegregated Education as the Route to Success

Men behave on the basis of what they believe to be true. It is interesting to note that biologists know that there are no pure races, but this will not explain the behavior of a racist. To understand the horror a man may feel about "race mixing," you do not need to know biology; you need to know what that man believes.

Social facts are multiple facts. Unlike the three- (or four-) dimensional objects of physical space-time continua, social objects do not lend themselves to simple demonstrations of truth or falsity. This is not only a matter of a lack of refined measurement in social science, as is popularly supposed; it is inherent in the nature of society itself. That is, one's perception and definition of a social object depends, in part, upon his social relationship to that object. For example, a school principal can define a student as a "troublemaker," "hoodlum," or whatever; the student's father may see him as a "good boy," "gentleman," etc., and *both* may be correct. The social scientist's problem is not to determine who is correct, but rather to point out the social-structural characteristics underlying those different interpretations of fact.

There are, of course, some statements of sociological relevance which do lend themselves to objective measurement. However, the debunking of popular myth does not explain how people come to hold the sets of social reality they act upon.

All human beings belong to a single species. The races of man which today inhabit the earth probably developed through a combination of mutations (some of which permitted survival more easily in one environment than in another), long periods of relative isolation which facilitated inbreeding, and a selection resulting from various cultural standards of what were and were not desirable physical traits. The major groups of races formed through mutation, isolation, adaptation, and selection have not remained unchanged, because the peoples have not remained absolutely unchanged, because the peoples have not remained absolutely isolated. Since the earliest period of human history, individuals, armies, traders, and whole tribes have migrated and intermarried with other physical types, thus breaking up the distinctive hereditary patterns.

As a result there are no pure races within the human species. It is therefore impossible to devise a system of classification on the basis of inherited physical traits. African Bushmen-Hottentots, for example, may have "Mongoloid" eyes. Australian aborigines may have "Negroid" skin and "Caucasoid" hair. Some Polynesians have white skin and some dark-brown skin; most have wavy hair, but there are many with straight or kinky hair. Some have broad and short faces, others long and narrow features. Since there is no such thing as a pure race among human beings, one obviously cannot set up a classification scheme for pure races and expect the data to correspond to the theory.

But this does not mean that race is unimportant, or that it has no consequences. Race in the biologist's sense has no biologically caused consequences, but what men *believe* about race has social consequences. In other words, most of men's discussions about race are discussions of their beliefs, not of biological fact. Most of men's actions about race are based on what they have been taught to believe about it, not on what scientists know about it. Race is usually not a biological concept. It is a social concept.

Two social beliefs widely held among Americans are (1) that every American can and should improve himself, that by striving one can get ahead, and (2) that more and better education is one of the surest routes to success. The scramble among the wealthiest and best-educated Americans to get their children into what they believe to be the best colleges provides ample evidence of the esteem in which both these beliefs are held.

To these dicta American Negroes have added a third principle, which they endorse with equal fervor: integrated education is quality education.

"Integration Is No Longer the Main Goal," announces a recent headline in the *New York Times*. The story quotes Roy Innis, Associate National Director of CORE: "People today talk about control of their community schools. Integration is counter to the mood of the black people."

American schools have taught white history for more than three centuries; that such discrimination is standard in American society is not at issue here. The question is whether most Negro Americans want to replace white discrimination with black segregation, or whether they still have some hope for the integration of American society.

Just when social scientists are tackling the problem of ethnocentrism and the chauvinistic tunnel vision of too many textbooks, we hear demands that black students should be taught black economics and black history by black teachers in black neighborhood schools.

For those of us old enough to remember the impact on science of such Stalinist-era concepts as "Soviet genetics" versus "bourgeois genetics," it is disquieting to see national or racial categories hooked as modifiers to scholarly subjects. But it is probably more disquieting because integration has been a liberal article of faith for both white and black Americans. Most Americans now alive have grown up with the assumption that citizens opposed to desegregation are anti-Negro. Now we find black militant spokesmen addressing us from diverse platforms —the Public Broadcast Laboratory, the New Left Politics convention, *Esquire* magazine—with insistent pleas that black Americans must build their own separate political and economic base on black pride and within the black community.

Do most American Negroes agree? The question is whether black militant *spokesmen* are *leaders*. We have had extensive experience in the United States with white extremist spokesmen such as Lincoln Rockwell, but most Americans have not mistaken white extremists for white leaders.

H. Rap Brown has demonstrated his leadership ability in at least one arena where success is critical for an aspiring public figure: he is able to lead TV newsmen. Whether he has a comparable ability to lead Negro Americans is another question.

It is in the nature of urbanism and the organization of the mass media that the opinions of articulate militant Negroes in New York may get more coverage and be more widely disseminated than the feelings of most Negro Americans. How do Negro Americans (not "spokesmen," but most Negro Americans) feel about desegregation of American institutions as opposed to the new separatism?

Duster has described the automobile workers study, in which Chinoy wanted to know if these men still held on to the American Dream that success and moving up in the social and economic levels of society comes from hard work, perseverance, and thrift. He wanted to know if Americans in such working-class occupations as factory piecework retained the hope that they would succeed in these terms.

He found that very young adults still talked about their own eventual social movement, but that by the time factory workers reach their late thirties, they are more or less resigned to their continued existence in that social, economic, and occupational status. Interestingly, however, they have not abandoned the American Dream in a larger sense. These men transfer their own hopes for success onto their children, and firmly believe that the American class system is open to those who work hard and take advantage of the opportunities. The automobile workers felt strongly that their children could realize a better life, and invested themselves completely in this possibility. In a very similar fashion many American Negroes cling to the American Dream. Like the auto workers, elderly or middle-aged Negroes are often resigned to their own stagnant position, but cherish the idea that someday their children will make a great success in their stead. The pathway that they see is education.

In 1960 over half of the adult Negroes in the Delta had less than five years of education (compared with less than 15 per cent of the whites), and less than 5 per cent of the Negroes had completed high school (compared to 45 per cent of the whites). Not only do many older Negroes have little to lose, but they have little hope of gaining anything in the future. Here is still another vicious circle in which poor schooling contributes to low occupational skills, which means high unemployment and, in turn, a need to pull one's children out of school to support the family in whatever fashion possible. The problem is perpetuated across generations. But the civil rights movement offers a ray of hope in a dismal climate:

> I didn't get a good education. That's why I have to work with my back. If I had known then what I know now, I would have stayed in school and worked hard at that. Now my child has

got to understand that education and schooling is the way. You can't get anything in this world from the white man until you get enough education to outsmart him.

It is not hard to understand why this parent can become involved directly in issues of public education. It is the one arena where there is immediate and direct contact with the possibilities of achievement, and if Negro parents believe that their children are not being given the best opportunity for a good education, they can become aroused to action as in no other sphere of community life. The context for a battle is set, therefore. As has been suggested, the whites on their side say that educational standards are primary, and many equate high educational standards with the absence of Negroes. In that Negroes assume that white city administrators will give preferential treatment to white schools, they equate high educational standards with integration into these schools.

(4) *The Effectiveness of Social Organization in Achieving Desegregation*

The pattern of urban growth which we so often refer to as new is, in several sociological essentials, the same pattern of urban growth which we have always had in this country. The oldest, least desirable housing has customarily been located in or near the centers of American cities; the newest, most desirable housing has been located beyond the city limits. We speak with wonder of man's newest social invention, the suburb. The new thing about having desirable housing away from the center of the city is that unrealistic political boundaries in metropolitan areas are separating the wealthier, better-educated citizens from control of their central city.

The fact that an increasing proportion of middle-class housing falls outside the city limits in most metropolitan areas has an obvious corollary: an ever increasing proportion of the people inside the city limits are members of minority populations.

From the sociologist's point of view, the bulk of the traits which most people cite as typical of a minority are actually characteristics of people in lower socioeconomic statuses. This is precisely why people are so frequently forced to defend their stereotypes by consigning some specific case to the category of "an exception to the rule." When someone who is convinced that Negroes do not take care of their property is driven west on Emerson Street in Evanston, Illinois, he has to concede that these Negroes are exceptions to the rule. When he tours West Madison Street in Chicago, he is forced to the conclusion that the whites there live like Negroes—but not like the Negroes in Evanston. A much simpler way to interpret these data is to note that lower-class people do not take as good care of their property as middle-class people.

Many class distinctions of this variety are bound to become more obvious as the social distance between dominant and minority categories decreases, and as people become less accustomed to viewing one another through race-colored glasses. Not the least of these is the strong tendency of public schools in metropolitan areas to be segregated—not necessarily by race, but virtually always by social class.

A great deal of sociological research indicates that social distance declines with increased socioeconomic status. The higher a person's occupational prestige, or the higher his income, or the more formal education he has, the less likely he is to be an ardent segregationist, or to condone violence as a weapon in dominant-minority relations. Social distance is least where both Negro and white have high socioeconomic status; social distance is greatest where both Negro and white have low socioeconomic status.

Given the constantly increasing educational attainment of our population, both Negro and white, our steadily rising level of living, and the fact that the cities are drawing as in-migrants the better-educated members of the Negro minority, it seems reasonable to predict a decrease in social distance between the races in the coming decades. Most of the rationalizations justifying our treatment of the Negro as a minority are descriptions of lower-class behavior: poverty, disease, ignorance, irresponsibility, poor property upkeep, and so on. Most American Negroes must, at the present time, be objectively rated as occupying a low socioeconomic status. As more and more of them achieve the education, income, and behavioral prerequisites of middle-class "respectability," they will not automatically escape from their minority position, but the beliefs which justify keeping them at a castelike distance will be greatly weakened.

All that we know of the sociology of revolution indicates that—contrary to the popular fiction that people rise up against their masters when they are too downtrodden to bear further oppression—a group is most amenable to revolution when its status has been improving. Galley slaves do not revolt; they have neither the opportunity nor the strength. The French bourgeoisie overthrew the social structure, not because they were a crushed and miserable minority, but because they had gained so many concessions and were doing so well that it seemed to them that their world might be an even better place if they took it over and ran it. The Thirteen Colonies which united to throw off the yoke of English oppression in the 1770s were probably the best and most generously governed colonies in the world at that time. The Russian serf lived for centuries under conditions of political and economic subjugation almost impossible for us to imagine, and was too busy just staying alive to question the justice of his lot, much less to initiate any effective protest against it. But a series of political and economic reforms in the late nineteenth and early twentieth centuries vastly improved his status and culminated in the bloodiest revolution of this century.

Three conditions are necessary for intergroup conflict: the groups must be (1) in contact with each other, (2) in competition with each other, and (3) visible to each other. All three of these conditions will obtain in Negro-white relations in the United States in the coming years. The very conditions that define city life—crowding and rapid movement, for example—will throw the groups into a closer and more frequent contact than was customary when the Negro was a rural dweller. Every improvement within the status of the Negro throws him into more direct competition with the white. Visibility, contact, competition—all are intensified in the urban environment.

Add to these the uncertain definition of the situation, the ambiguity of role expectations that is a concomitant of urban life and of rapid social change, and you have an almost ideal situation for engendering conflict.

Conflict promotes the formation of groups. American Negroes used to be a social category, after the fashion of males or people in the labor force aged nineteen through forty-four. Interested citizens who were not sociologists used to ask, thirty years ago, "What do American Negroes want?" Thirty years ago the question was relatively meaningless, because American Negroes were a social category, not a group. However, Negroes were taught the rules of competition within the American social structure, and within the past generation, had our society abided by the rules, many of them would have won. But they found that American society refused to play by its own rules. We refused to pay off rewards to winners in the mobility sweepstakes if they were Negro. Moreover, we meted out punishments to non-losers simply for being Negro, and, worst of all, punished rather than rewarded insistent competitors. Contrary to what one might believe from reading many current editorials, it was whites, not Negroes, who initiated conflict, violating economic and political rules for boycotts and sit-ins, and in the process were transformed from a social category into a group. Nowadays the pollsters can get meaningful answers to questions about what American Negroes want, because a social category has been transmuted into a social group—by conflict.

Conflict not only promotes the formation of groups; it also defines and maintains group boundaries and contributes to social cohesion. The contribution to solidarity made by an attack from outside is a phenomenon easily observed, whether among small brothers or in the improvement in the status of the American Negro during World War II.

In each of these nine communities it is obvious that change has been implemented as a result of citizens' organizing and protesting. From Riverside to Savannah to Kalamazoo desegregation has proceeded haltingly, grudgingly, and in response to organized demands. The changes which have occurred have come about as the result of overt acts such as picketing and filing of complaints, by members of the Negro community and their white allies. Until these pressures were brought, most whites had gone on for years believing that "our" Negroes were well treated and had no major complaints. The uproar arising from Negro demands illustrates how complacent the white community has been.

(5) A Children's Crusade

Racial segregation in schools is an institutional complex. The establishment and maintenance of a system of segregated educational facilities depends upon segregation not only of pupils, but of teachers, administrators, politicians, worshipers, and the residential segregation of white parents from Negro parents. Segregated education depends upon and feeds upon segregated churches, segregated businesses, segregated recreational facilities, and segregated neighborhoods. Segregated education, in turn, reinforces segregation in churches, barber shops, parks, banks, and city halls.

In America we have deemed desegregation too difficult a social process to be dealt with by realtors, bankers, clergymen, and community leaders. We have assigned the task to children.

Children have been sent from the deprived minority background of segregated schools to cope with the process of desegregation in an environment often too hostile to be conducive to education. We know that the performance of children in minority schools is behind that of those in segregated white schools. One important explanation for this is the pattern of expectation which the teacher builds up around the Negro child vs. that of the white middle-class child. The teacher comes to expect more from the latter, and thereby evokes a response by communicating this expectation. As a direct counterpart there is often a feeling of resignation in the minority school teacher which also gets communicated. True, the working-class home does not provide the kind of background which middle-class teachers find "tractable." This is not to be ignored, but it is hardly the kind of thing that can be dealt with as part of public policy in a multi-class democracy.

We have placed the burden upon our children through voluntary transfer plans in Chicago and freedom-of-choice procedures in Atlanta and in Mississippi. This means that desegregation will occur at a slow pace because of the fears and anxieties of Negro students. It also means that the shift from freedom-of-choice to geographical attendance areas will occur on local initiative instead of at the behest of the federal government itself. Federal regulations have the advantage of being imposed and possibly enforced from outside. Local decisions are much more vulnerable to local pressures and are much more likely to provoke recriminations.

Middle-class people pay little of the price of social change, for desegregation is more likely to occur in lower-class residential areas. It is no surprise that River City Negroes do not live among the middle- or upper-class whites, but rather among the lower-class "rednecks." Negroes in Chicago and Mexican-Americans in Los Angeles, too, are more likely to live near poor whites than near middle-class whites. These are precisely the whites who are least pleased to have their children attend school with Negroes, let alone attend formerly all-Negro schools with a high proportion of Negroes remaining. But these are also the people who cannot afford to move out of the area. Even now, these are people who cannot afford to take advantage of the current freedom-of-choice to send their children to white schools in the middle-class suburbs. More like the Negroes than high-status whites, they cannot afford the transportation. All of this means, then, that under a geographical system in a town like River City, the Negroes will be integrated not with whites at random but with lower-class whites, those most likely to provoke and carry through incidents. The further consequence is that the Negroes may find futile their hope of greatly improved educational quality. Quality differentials may merely begin to occur along class lines rather than caste distinctions, even as they do in Northern cities.

At the very moment when responsible Negro and white Americans are trying valiantly to cope with it, there is pressure for more and more rapid change.

Inequalities remain, and while they remain there will be continuing agitation for change. When the NORC asked a national sample of Americans, "Do you think most Negroes in the United States are being treated fairly or unfairly?" one-third of the whites and two-thirds of the Negroes answered, "Unfairly." Together these people constitute a sizable group of dissatisfied citizens.

They are dissatisfied because equality of opportunity is basic to the American ethic of self-realization and achievement, and the American Negro is denied equality of opportunity.

American children are assured that the Supreme Court rulings are the law of the land, but these nine communities are a picture of segregated education in America fourteen years after the court ruled that separate facilities are inherently unequal.

What does the Negro American want? To answer that question, one need only strike out the word "Negro." He wants what other Americans want: a home, a car, good clothes, economic security, a friendly community. Above all, as an American citizen, he wants a fair chance to compete for a share in the American way of life—a chance dependent upon equal educational opportunity.

At the moment black extremists who preach separatism and resegregation probably do not speak for most Americans. But they will be speaking for an increasing number of black Americans unless our society makes integration an attainable route to equality.

If middle-class Americans, white and black, unite in an honest, vigorous effort to make equality of opportunity a reality in American society, we may, in James Baldwin's words, "achieve America." If we allow race to remain—not to become, but to remain—an invariably relevant reference group in our social structure, then I think that social scientists must sadly predict that the holocaust is nearly upon us, for we shall have abdicated the role of agent of change, and abandoned the American revolution to racial extremists, black and white.

Index

About the Authors

RAYMOND W. MACK is Professor and Chairman of the Department of Sociology at Northwestern University, where he has taught since 1953. A specialist in stratification and race relations, he is the author of *Race, Class, and Power,* and co-author of *Patterns of Minority Relations* and of *Social Mobility: Thirty Years of Research and Theory.* He has conducted research in the Caribbean under the auspices of the Ford Foundation and in England and Spain as Faculty Research Fellow to the Social Science Research Council.

TROY DUSTER, co-author of *Patterns of Minority Relations,* is presently a lecturer at the University of California's Center for Research and Development in Higher Education at Berkeley.

MICHAEL AIKEN is a Visiting Associate Professor at Columbia University and has taught at the University of Wisconsin.

N. J. DEMERATH III, has been Associate Professor of Sociology at the University of Wisconsin since 1962 and has published a book and several articles.

RUTH P. SIMMS has been a social worker in Savannah, done research in Ghana, and is presently Assistant Professor of Sociology at Iowa State University.

HERBERT R. BARRINGER is Professor of Sociology at the University of Hawaii and is engaged in research at the Social Science Research Institute there. He recently returned from a year in Korea on a Fulbright grant.

ROSALIND J. DWORKIN has taught in the Department of Sociology at Northwestern University in Evanston, Illinois.

JOHN PEASE, co-author of *Attrition of Graduate Students at the Ph.D. Level in the Traditional Arts and Sciences,* is Assistant Professor of Sociology at the University of Maryland.

BONNIE REMSBERG is a Chicago TV personality and the author of several magazine articles.

CHARLES REMSBERG is a free-lance writer on sociological problems who is a Special Consultant to the United States Office of Economic Opportunity.

ANTHONY G. DWORKIN is Assistant Professor of Sociology at the University of Missouri in Columbia, Missouri.